The Terrorism Reader

Praise for previous editions:
'A comprehensive, nuanced survey of international terrorism . . . the Reader has both a better sense of the complexity of terrorism as an international phenomenon and . . . the distinctiveness of the historical and political conditions.' Athan Theoharis, *Marquette University*

'One of the book's strengths is its ability to see beyond particular conflicts to analogies across the world, including chapters on Libya, Sri Lanka, Algeria and Italy.' *The Australian Jewish News*

The Terrorism Reader is an intriguing introduction to a notorious and disturbing international phenomenon. The book draws together material from a variety of experts and clearly explains their opinions on terrorism, allowing understanding, conjecture and debate.

David J. Whittaker explores all aspects of terrorism, from its definition, psychological and sociological effects, and legal and ethical issues to counter-terrorism. In a particularly original way, this Reader illustrates the growth and variety of terrorism with a series of case studies from four continents including:

- the Taliban and the al-Qaeda terror network, and America's war against terrorism
- ETA and Spain
- the Revolutionary Armed Forces of Colombia
- the Liberation Tigers in Sri Lanka
- the IRA and UFF in Northern Ireland
- the Shining Path in Peru.

This new edition includes fully updated chapters on Palestine and Israel, the London 7/7 bombings and a new chapter on Jihad, as well as a focus on issues of contemporary concern such as state terrorism, terrorist withdrawal and deradicalisation, and human rights.

David J. Whittaker was formerly Senior Lecturer in International Relations at the University of Teesside. His many books include *Terrorists and Terrorism in the Contemporary World* (2004) and *Refugees and Asylum Seekers* (2005), both published by Routledge.

Routledge Readers in History

The Decolonization Reader
Edited by James Le Sueur

The Enlightenment: A Sourcebook
and Reader
Edited by Olga Gomez, Francesca
Greensides and Paul Hyland

The European Women's History
Reader
Edited by Christine Collette and
Fiona Montgomery

The Fascism Reader
Edited by Aristotle A. Kallis

The Feminist History Reader
Edited by Sue Morgan

The Global History of Childhood
Reader
Edited by Heidi Morrison

The Global History Reader
Edited by Bruce Mazlish and Akira
Iriye

The History and Narrative Reader
Edited by Geoffrey Roberts

The History of Sexuality in Europe
Reader
Edited by Anna Clark

The History On Film Reader
Edited by Marnie Hughes-Warrington

The Irish Women's History Reader
Edited by Alan Hayes and Diane
Urquhart

The Modern Historiography Reader
Edited by Adam Budd

The Nature of History Reader
Edited by Keith Jenkins and Alun
Munslow

The New Imperial Histories Reader
Edited by Stephen Howe

The Oral History Reader
Edited by Robert Perks and Alistair
Thomson

The Postmodern History Reader
Edited by Keith Jenkins

The Postmodernism Reader:
Foundational Texts
Edited by Michael Drolet

Renaissance Thought: A Reader
Edited by Robert Black

The Slavery Reader
Edited by Gad Heuman and James
Walvin

The Twentieth Century Russia Reader
Edited by Alistair Kocho-Williams

The Victorian Studies Reader
Edited by Kelly Boyd and Rohan
McWilliam

The Witchcraft Reader
Edited by Darren Oldridge

The World War Two Reader
Edited by Gordon Martel

The
Terrorism
Reader –
Fourth Edition

Edited by

David J. Whittaker

Routledge
Taylor & Francis Group

LONDON AND NEW YORK

First edition published 2001

This edition published 2012
by Routledge
2 Park Square, Milton Park, Abingdon, Oxon OX14 4RN

Simultaneously published in the USA and Canada
by Routledge
711 Third Avenue, New York, NY10017

Routledge is an imprint of the Taylor & Francis Group, an informa business

British Library Cataloguing in Publication Data
A catalogue record for this book is available from the British Library

Library of Congress Cataloging in Publication Data
The terrorism reader/edited by David J. Whittaker. – 4th ed.
    p. cm. – (Routledge readers in history)
    Includes bibliographical references and index.
    1. Terrorism.   I. Whittaker, David J., 1925–.
    HV6431.T488 2012
    363.325 – dc23   2011045629

ISBN13: 978–0–415–68731–7 (hbk)
ISBN13: 978–0–415–68732–4 (pbk)

Typeset in Bell Gothic and Perpetua by
Florence Production Ltd, Stoodleigh, Devon

Printed and bound in Great Britain by the MPG Books Group

Contents

Preface   vii

Acknowledgements   x

PART ONE
Characteristics of terrorism   **1**

1   Definition of terrorism   3

2   Motivation for terrorism   14

3   Terrorism's worldwide occurrence   28

PART TWO
Sixteen terrorism case studies   **45**

4   Jihad: mission and campaigning   47

5   United States: Ground Zero   60

6   Britain: London as target   69

7   Israel   79

8   Libya   88

9   Lebanon I   106

10   Lebanon II   124

11   Sri Lanka   133

12   Spain   150

13   Northern Ireland   165

14   Algeria   187

15   Peru   201

16   Colombia   216

17   Germany   234

18   Italy   253

19   South Africa   271

20   Sixteen terrorism case studies: conclusion   288

PART THREE
Prevention and control of terrorism   **293**

21   Terrorism: some ethical issues   295

22   Terrorism and the law   306

23   Counter-terrorism: programmes and strategies   324

     Notes   346
     Guide to further reading   360
     Index   365

Preface

THIS READER, NOW APPEARING IN ITS fourth edition, does so at a time of seismic change in that region where terrorists acting *externally* have long menaced much of the world. The first months of 2011 saw dramatically terror *internalised* as state after state in Mediterranean Arab lands turned wrathfully upon protesting crowds of their own people. One after another states Tunisia, Egypt, Libya, Bahrain, Syria, Yemen, Morocco, Lebanon, Oman encountered an Arab Awakening and met it with repressive force. Riot police, rifle fusillades, tear gas, even helicopter gunships were used in places in a toe-to-toe revolutionary struggle. State terrorism, that old-fashioned, crude, unthinking response to popular agitation, is now having to cope with an Internet generation networking complaints and demands across region and world.

Vilified by most people though justified by those resorting to extremist violence, terrorist outrages claim prominence in the media. Their incidence has more than doubled in the past 40 years. Every day brings reports of devastating incidents all over the Middle East, in Sri Lanka, in South-East Asia and in Latin America. Nobody can forget the killing of around 3,000 people in New York and close to Washington on 11 September 2001. While most countries have experienced some form of conspiratorial violence, often tragic and indiscriminate, today ten of them bear the brunt of three out of four incidents. Terrorism has become one of the most pressing political problems during the last half-century. Its many-sidedness, inexpensive lethality and unpredictability make prevention and control difficult, costly and undependable. There has never been such a wide degree of interest, conjecture and discussion. Unhelpfully, too much of the discussion is not case-specific, as it needs to be, although the terrorism manifestations run the gamut, perhaps bewilderingly, of apparent mindlessness, firm faith and rational calculation. Terrorists may be villains, ruthless criminals, heroes or admired trailblazers and some have made the transition from hunted insurgent to state president.

Guidelines for the exploration of a multiple political riddle its origins, its significant contrasts, and the possibilities of dealing with it effectively are offered in this Reader. As a survey it is not one of those volumes, loaded with theory and full of facts and figures, that crowd library shelves. Rather, it is a 'taster', deliberately designed to introduce students, teachers, researchers and the general public to a topic notoriously complicated to discuss. As a reader, it is offered as an edited selection of the views of a number of well-known authorities on political terrorism, together with the editor's interleaving comment. Given the diversity of opinion among the contributors, it is hoped that this Reader will stimulate plenty of speculation and debate, particularly where this text may be updated using Internet key words.

There are three parts to this book. Part One presents a definition, deals with motivation (with an added section on suicide terrorism) and global incidence, and presents a typology. A list of contemporary groups will be found there. Part Two illustrates the growth and variety of terrorism with a series of 16 contrasted case studies from four continents. Largely 'updated' and rewritten, these give special attention of al-Qaida and the Taliban. Lebanon is given an extensive study in the light of the Israeli strike of summer 2006 and of the controversy surrounding the relevance of Hizbullah terrorists to that. A concluding chapter summarising these case studies raises a number of questions deserving further enquiry and debate. Part Three looks comprehensively at the topic of counter-terrorism and separates ethical issues and legal provision, bearing in mind their increasingly questionable interrelationship. Control strategies being employed by governments are also surveyed at this point. This book concludes with Notes, giving, among other things, the origins of the extracts quoted in this Reader together with suggestions for further reading and specifies places where more information may be sought.

Above all this fourth edition aims to emphasise that there are terrorism changes in the air and on the ground: changes in concepts, techniques, locations, incidence, scale and organisation. Readers will have been aware of the extraordinary and historic political change sweeping Arab states during the first six months of 2011. Discussion of this circumstance will be found in Chapter 3. Encouragingly, here and there, as the case studies reveal, there are budding growth points in transition from mayhem to stability, peace and some reconciliation. Even so, the question at the beginning and end of this Reader is the one put by lawyers Rosalyn Higgins and Helena Kennedy: 'Before we can deal with terrorism in law we need to ask what it really is.' Definition is the heart of the matter and it grows ever more problematic as the case studies show.

This survey of terrorism originated as a gleam in the publishing eye of Routledge. Its completion would have been impossible without the ready willingness of authors and publishers to have work cited and quoted. Cogency and easy-to-read clarification have been my aims and sometimes extracts have had to be 'filleted'. I apologise for any resulting offence; it was never deliberate.

I am grateful, also, to many people for their unstinting helpfulness and patience. In particular, I should like to thank the following: Professor James Connolly, Sindy Goldberg (South Africa House), Walter Kirwan (Secretary-General, Forum for Peace and Reconciliation, Dublin), Simon Partridge, Marianne Whittaker (indefatigable reader of manuscripts), the Sri Lanka High Commission in London, Adrian Norton (for technical assistance), and library staffs in the universities of Durham,

Newcastle, Bradford, Teesside and St Andrews. Special thanks must go to diplomatic staff at the Embassy of Brazil, London Colonel de Almeida Filho and Ana Caroni-Brito for suggesting and arranging translation of this Reader into Portuguese in response to interested demand from Brazil. At Routledge I am indebted to the kindness especially of Eve Setch and, earlier, of Professor Eric Evans, Alex Ballantyne, Heather McCallum, Victoria Peters, Liz O'Donnell and Gillian Oliver. This edition would not have been possible without the meticulous collaboration of the co-editor, my youngest daughter, Ms Helena Vadher.

David J. Whittaker
North Yorkshire

Acknowledgements

The editor and publishers wish to thank the following for their permission to reproduce copyright material:

Charles Townshend, 'The culture of paramilitarism in Ireland', pp. 330–1, 324, 317, 336–7, 339–40. From *Terrorism in Context*, edited by Martha Crenshaw. Copyright © 1995 by The Pennsylvania State University Press. Reprinted with permission of the author and publisher.

Goldie Shabad and F. J. L. Ramo, 'Political violence in a democratic state: Basque terrorism in Spain', pp. 411–13, 415–17, 418–19, 422, 423, 427–8, 436, 444–5, 441–3, 465, 466–9. From *Terrorism in Context*, edited by Martha Crenshaw. Copyright © 1995 by The Pennsylvania State University Press. Reprinted with permission of the author and publisher.

David Scott Palmer, 'The revolutionary terrorism of Peru's Shining Path', pp. 251–3, 254–5, 257, 260–1, 262–3, 265–6, 267–8, 270, 270–8, 285, 280, 301–2, 305. From *Terrorism in Context*, edited by Martha Crenshaw. Copyright © 1995 by The Pennsylvania State University Press. Reprinted with permission of the author and publisher.

P. H. Merkl, 'West German left-wing terrorism', pp. 176–8, 202–5. From *Terrorism in Context*, edited by Martha Crenshaw. Copyright © 1995 by The Pennsylvania State University Press. Reprinted with permission of the publisher.

Donatella Della Porta, 'Left wing terrorism in Italy', pp. 156–9. From *Terrorism in Context*, edited by Martha Crenshaw. Copyright © 1995 by The Pennsylvania State University Press. Reprinted with permission of the author and publisher.

Material from www.terrorism.com, February 2003. Reproduced with permission of the Terrorism Research Center, Inc., Arlington, VA.

Walter, Reich (ed.). (New foreword by Walter Laqueur.) *Origins of Terrorism: Psychologies, Ideologies, Theologies, States of Mind*, pp. 25–8, 31–3, 35–6, 38, 54–5, 58, 132–3, 136–7, 156–7, 163–76, 190. Copyright © 1998 Woodrow Wilson International Center for Scholars. Reprinted with permission of Johns Hopkins University Press.

Walter Laqueur, *The New Terrorism* (Oxford University Press, 1999), pp. 22–30, 31–6, 45–6, 100–1, 168–72, 191–6, 230–1, 256–7, 259–60. By permission of Oxford University Press, Inc.

Bruce Hoffman, *Inside Terrorism* (Victor Gollancz, 1998, a division of The Orion Publishing Group), pp. 191–2, 196–7, 211–12. Reprinted with permission of Columbia University Press.

Elizabeth Picard, 'The Lebanese Shi'a and political violence in Lebanon'; Bruce Kapferer, 'Remythologizing discourse: state and insurrectionary violence in Sri Lanka'; Paul Arthur, 'Reading violence'; Michel Wieviorka, 'ETA and Basque political violence'; David E. Apter, 'Political violence in analytical perspective'; and David Moss, 'Politics, violence, writing: the rituals of armed struggle in Italy', from David E. Apter (ed.), *The Legitimization of Violence* (Palgrave Macmillan, 1996). Reproduced with permission of Palgrave Macmillan.

P. Edward Haley, 'Qaddafi and the United States since 1969', from *Qaddafi and the United States Since 1969*. Copyright © 1984 by Praeger Special Studies, New York. Reproduced with permission of Greenwood Publishing Group, Inc., Westport, CT.

Magnus Ranstorp, *Hiz'ballah in Lebanon: The Politics of the Western Hostage Crisis* (Macmillan, 1997). Reproduced with permission of Palgrave Macmillan.

Christopher Thomas, 'British Tamils fund war in Sri Lanka', *The Times*, 23 October 1997. By permission of NI Syndication Ltd.

David Whittaker, *Conflict and Reconciliation in the Contemporary World* (Routledge, 1999). Reproduced with permission of Taylor & Francis.

Cyrus Ernesto Zirakzadeh, *A Rebellious People: Basques, Protests, and Politics*. Copyright © 1991 by University of Nevada Press. Reproduced with permission of the University of Nevada Press.

Martin Stone, *The Establishment of Algeria* (London: Hurst and Co., 1997), pp. 1–3, 37, 42, 177–8, 180–1, 185–6, 189–96. Reproduced with permission of Hurst Publishers Ltd.

Cynthia McClintock, 'Why peasants rebel', *World Politics*, 37:1 (1984), pp. 81–2. Copyright © The Johns Hopkins University Press. Reprinted with permission of The Johns Hopkins University Press.

C. R. Izaguirre, 'Shining Path in the twenty-first century: actors in search of a new script', *NACLA Report on the Americas*, vol. XXX, no. 1, July/August 1996, pp. 37–8, 38. Reproduced with permission of North American Congress on Latin America, www.nacla.org.

Jenny Pearce, *Columbia: Inside the Labyrinth* (Latin American Bureau, 1990), pp. 4–5, 64–5, 69, 76–9, 52–4, 55–6, 56–7, 61–2, 165–6, 167–8 (quoting from *L'Humanité*, 3 June 1966), 168–9, 171–2, 173, 207, 231, 278–9, 284 (quoting from W. R. Tobon, *Analisis Politica*, no. 5, 1988), 286–7, 287. Reproduced with permission of the Latin American Bureau, www.latinamericabureau.org/.

Jose Trevino, 'Spain's internal security: the Basque autonomous police', from Y. Alexander and K. A. Myers, *Terrorism in Europe* (Croom Helm, 1982). Reproduced with permission of Taylor & Francis.

Schura Cook, 'Germany: from protest to terrorism', from Y. Alexander and K. A. Myers, *Terrorism in Europe* (Croom Helm, 1982). Reproduced with permission of Taylor & Francis.

David Whittaker, *United Nations in Action* (University of California Press, 1995). Reproduced with permission of Taylor & Francis.

Nelson Mandela, *Long Walk to Freedom* (Abacus, 1994), pp. 132, 135, 146–7, 181–2, 277, 320–1, 321–4, 325–6, 336–8, 434. By permission of Little, Brown Book Company Limited.

Brian Jenkins, 'Defense against terrorism', from *Political Science Quarterly*, vol. 101, no. 5, 1986, pp. 779–81. Reprinted with permission.

David Schiff, in Rosalyn Higgins and Maurice Flory, *Terrorism and International Law* (Routledge, 1997). Reproduced with permission of Taylor & Francis.

M. R. L. Smith, 'Holding fire', in Alan O'Day, *Terrorism's Laboratory* (Ashgate, 1995), p. 23. Reprinted with permission of the publisher.

Grant Wardlaw, *Political Theory, Tactics and Counter Measures* (Cambridge University Press, 1982). Reproduced with permission.

Boaz Ganor, 'Countering state sponsored terrorism', 28 April 1998, International Policy Institute for Counter-terrorism, Herzliya, Israel, www.ict.org.il/inter/org.cfm (accessed 9 December 1999), pp. 1–2. Reproduced with kind permission of the author.

David Whittaker, *Terrorism: Understanding the Global Threat* (Pearson, 2002), pp. 99–101, 101–2, 103–4. Reproduced with permission of the publisher.

Amal Saad-Ghorayeb, *Hizbu'llah: Politics and Religion* (Pluto Press, 2002), pp. 98–9, 132, 145–7, 160. Reproduced with permission of Pluto Books Ltd.

Yossef Bodansky, *Bin Laden: The Man Who Declared War on America*. Copyright © 1999 by Yossef Bodansky. Used with permission of Prima Publishing, a division of Random House, Inc.

David Whittaker, *Terrorists and Terrorism in the Contemporary World* (Routledge, 2004), pp. 39–42. Reproduced with permission of Taylor & Francis.

United Nations, *UN Chronicle*, no. 3, 1996, p. 31. Reproduced with permission of United Nations Publications.

Paul Williams, *Al-Qaeda: Brotherhood of Terror* (Alpha, Pearson Education, 2002), pp. 76, 76–77, 79–80. Reproduced with kind permission of the author.

Richard Kearney, *Postnationalist Ireland* (Routledge, 1997). Reproduced with permission of Taylor & Francis.

H. P. Habib, *Politics and Government of Revolutionary Libya* (Le Cercle du Livre de France, 1975), pp. 13–15, 121, 122, 124, 127, 151. Reproduced with kind permission of the author.

David Blundy and Andrew Lycett, *Quaddafi and the Libyan Revolution*. Copyright © 1986 by David Blundy and Andrew Lycett. Reproduced with permission of Little, Brown and Co. and Weidenfeld & Nicolson, a division of The Orion Publishing Group.

Manoj Joshi, 'On the razor's edge: the liberation Tigers of Tamil Elam', *Studies in Conflict and Terrorism*, vol. 19, nos. 19–42, pp. 21, 25–6, 27. Reproduced with kind permission of Taylor & Francis, www.tandf.co.uk/journals.

A. A. Khalil, 'Ideology and practice of Hizballah in Lebanon: Islamization of Leninist organization and principles', *Middle Eastern Studies*, vol. 27, no. 3, 1991, pp. 390–9. Reproduced with kind permission of Taylor & Francis, www.tandf.co.uk/journals.

Reprinted from Paul Oquist, *Violence, Conflict and Politics in Colombia* (London: New York Academic Press), copyright 1980, pp. 1–6, 133, 134–5 (quoting Antonio Garcia, 1971), 135, 138, 139, 143–4, 145–6, 147, 150, 153. With permission from Elsevier.

Geoffrey Pridham, 'Terrorism and the state in West Germany during the 1970s: a threat to stability or a case of political over-reaction?', in Juliet Lodge (ed.) *Terrorism: A Challenge to the State* (Martin Robertson, 1981) pp. 18, 16–17, 20–2, 22–5, 27–8, 28–9, 41, 44, 52. Reproduced with kind permission of the author.

Paul Furlong, 'Political terrorism in Italy: responses, reaction and immobilism', in Juliet Lodge (ed.) *Terrorism: A Challenge to the State* (Martin Robertson, 1981), pp. 61–2, 63, 69–71, 74–8, 80, 85–6, 88–9. Reproduced with kind permission of the author.

Joanne Wright, *Terrorist Propaganda: The Red Army Faction and the Provisional IRA 1968–1986* (Palgrave Macmillan, 1991). Reproduced with permission of Palgrave Macmillan.

Jillian Becker, *Hitler's Children* (Pickwick, 1989), pp. ix–x, 250 (quoting Norman, 1970, *The Pursuit of the Millennium*). Reproduced with kind permission of the author.

Richard Gibson, *African Liberation Movements: Contemporary Struggle against White Minority Rule* (Oxford University Press for Institute of Race Relations, 1972), pp. 38, 64, 92. Reproduced with kind permission of the Institute of Race Relations, 2–6 Leeke Street, London, WC1X 9HS.

A. de Braganca and I. M. Wallerstein, *The African Liberation Reader*, vol. 2 (Zed Press, 1982), pp. 33, 43. Reproduced with permission of the publisher.

Walter Laqueur, *No End to War: Terrorism in the Twenty-first century* (Continuum, 2004), pp. 71, 79, 92, 209–10. Copyright © 2003 by Walter Laqueur. Reproduced with kind permission of the author and the Continuum Publishing Group.

Bruce Hoffman, *Inside Terrorism*, pp. 1–3, 16–17, 20–3, 26, 28, 35–8, 40–1, 131–3, 267–8, 269, 271–2, 295. Copyright © 2006 Columbia University Press. Reprinted with permission of the publisher.

David Whittaker, *Terrorism: Understanding the Global Threat* (Pearson, 2006), pp. 26–7, 34–5, 35–7, 37–8, 53–4, 181, 193–4, 197, 221. Reproduced with permission of the publisher.

Declan Walsh, 'Generals think again in Taliban onslaught', *The Guardian*, 3 July 2006. Copyright © 2006 Guardian News and Media Limited.

Ken Booth and Tim Dunne, *Worlds in Collision* (Palgrave Macmillan, 2002). Reproduced with permission of Palgrave Macmillan.

Daniel Sobelman, *New Rules of the Game: Israel and Hizbollah after the Withdrawal from Lebanon*, Memorandum No. 69, January 2004 (Jaffee Center for Strategic Studies, 2004), pp. 48–9, 84, 85–6, 89, 102, 103, from www.tau.ac.il/jcss/memoranda/memo69. Reproduced with permission.

Report of the Official Account of the Bombings in London on 7th July 2005 (The Stationery Office, 11 May 2006), pp. 26–7. Reproduced under the terms of the Click-Use Licence C2006010948.

Intelligence and Security Committee (ISC) Report into the London Terrorist Attacks on 7 July 2005 (The Stationery Office, May 2006), p. 4. Reproduced under the terms of the Click-Use Licence C2006010948.

Government Response to the Intelligence and Security Committee's Report into the London Terrorist Attacks on 7 July 2005 (The Stationery Office, May 2006), pp. 2–4, 7, 11. Reproduced under the terms of the Click-Use Licence C2006010948.

From Crispin Black, *7–7: What Went Wrong?* (Gibson Square, 2005, 978–1–903933–71–8), pp. 8, 38. Reproduced with permission of the publisher.

Haig Katchadourian, *The Morality of Terrorism* (Peter Lang, 1998), pp. 40, 129, 9. Reproduced with permission of the publisher.

Jonathan Moreno (ed.) *In the Wake of Terror: Medicine and Morality in a Time of Crisis* (Cambridge, Mass.: MIT Press). Copyright © MIT Press. Reproduced with permission of the publisher.

The Guardian, 5 November 2005. Staff, 'Protecting the Magna Carta'. Copyright © 2005 Guardian News and Media Limited.

C. Walker, 'Anti–terrorism laws for the future', *New Law Journal*, vol. 146, 1996, pp. 586–8.

Kiron Reid, 'Prevention of Terrorism (Additional Powers) Act 1996', *Web Journal of Current Legal Issues* (Blackstone Press, 1996), p. 12. Reproduced with kind permission of the author.

Foreign and Commonwealth Office, *Counter Terrorist Legislation and Practice: A Survey of Selected Countries*, London Research Paper (Foreign and Commonwealth Office, 2005) (also on www.fco.gov.uk), paras 124–5, note 12, paras 39, 97, 110. Reproduced under the terms of the Click-Use Licence C2006010948.

Helena Kennedy, *Just Law* (Chatto & Windus, 2005). Reprinted with permission of The Random House Group.

J. M. Brachman, *Global Jihadism Theory and Practice* (Routledge, 2009). Reproduced with permission of Taylor & Francis Ltd.

B. Hoffman, 'Rethinking Terrorism and Counter Terrorism since September 11', *Studies in Conflict and Terrorism* 25:303–16. Reproduced by kind permission of Taylor & Francis Ltd, *http://www.tandf.co.uk/journals*.

D. Whittaker, *Counter Terrorism and Human Rights* (Pearson, 2009), pp. 71–6. Reproduced with permission of the publisher.

P. Heyman, *Terrorism, Freedman and Security* (MIT Press, 2003). Reproduced with permission of the publisher.

J. Strawson, *Law After Ground Zero* (Glasshouse Press/Routledge Cavendish, 2002). Reproduced with permission of Taylor and Francis Ltd.

P. Wilkinson, Editorial in *Terrorism and Political Violence*, 13:4, p.x. Reproduced by kind permission of Taylor & Francis Ltd, *http://www.tandf.co.uk/journals*.

J. Gunning, *Hamas in Politics* (Hurst, 2009). Reproduced with permission of the publisher.

J. Horgan, *The Psychology of Terrorism* (Routledge, 2006). Reproduced with permission of Taylor & Francis Ltd.

P. Wilkinson, *Terrorism Versus Democracy: The Liberal State Response* (Routledge, 2007). Reproduced with permission of Taylor and Francis Ltd.

While every effort has been made to trace and acknowledge ownership of copyright material used in this volume, the publishers will be glad to make suitable arrangements with any copyright holders whom it has not been possible to contact.

Definition of terrorism

THIS CHAPTER ADDRESSES THE QUESTION: what is terrorism and how may it be defined? It presents a selection of straightforward definitions that should help understanding and discussion. This is followed by a brief editorial resumé and by excerpts from two acknowledged authorities in the clarification of issues. The selection defines terrorism as follows.

- The unlawful use of force or violence against persons or property to intimidate or coerce a government, the civilian population, or any segment thereof, in furtherance of political or social objectives (FBI).
- The calculated use of violence or the threat of violence to inculcate fear, intended to coerce or intimidate governments or societies as to the pursuit of goals that are generally political, religious or ideological (US Department of Defense).
- Premeditated, politically motivated violence perpetuated against noncombatant targets by subnational groups or clandestine agents, usually intended to influence an audience (US State Department).
- The use or threat, for the purpose of advancing a political, religious or ideological cause, of action which involves serious violence against any person or property (United Kingdom Government).
- Contributes the illegitimate use of force to achieve a political objective when innocent people are targeted (Walter Laqueur).
- A strategy of violence designed to promote desired outcomes by instilling fear in the public at large (Walter Reich).
- The use or threatened use of force designed to bring about political change (Brian Jenkins).

- The deliberate, systematic murder, maiming, and menacing of the innocent to inspire fear in order to gain political ends [. . .] Terrorism [. . .] is intrinsically evil, necessarily evil, and wholly evil (Paul Johnson).
- [International terrorism is] the threat or use of violence for political purposes when (1) such action is intended to influence the attitude and behavior of a target group wider than its immediate victim, and (2) its ramifications transcend national boundaries (Peter Sederberg).[1]

In this list of definitions the common ground is evident but there are differences of emphasis. The first four 'official' definitions reflect institutional positions. The FBI, for instance, stresses coercion and unlawfulness, and offences against property, in furtherance of social as well as political objectives. The US State Department lays stress on premeditation. The potential political motivation of 'subnational groups' is noted. There is no reference to spontaneous violence or to the psychological significance of threatened action. More comprehensively the US Department of Defense gives equal prominence to actual or threatened violence, cites a wider range of objectives, and includes as possible targets not only governments but also whole societies.

The United Kingdom's definition is to be found in a bill laid before Parliament in December 1999. There is controversy that this definition is too wide and that it may lead to the Government restricting or even denying the legitimate rights of a wide range of protest groups.

Reich, a psychiatrist, emphasises the intimidatory strategy that instils widespread fear and a sense of personal vulnerability in the civilian population. Sederberg focuses on the use of deliberate intimidation instancing the effects of this on attitudes and behaviour. Johnson's definition is judgemental, a highly charged voicing of disapproval. Lack of objectivity here throws little light on the nature of terrorism.

DEFINITION WITHIN A CONTEXT

Bald words in a printed definition do not advance understanding very far. Questions spring to mind. By what criteria should terrorists be considered to carry out unlawful or illegitimate acts? How rational are they who advocate and plan the use of force to achieve political objectives? Is the calculated spreading of fear anything other than barbarous and inhumane? How far can intimidation and coercion establish and secure desirable outcomes? Is it possible to appraise terrorist motivation dispassionately and without bias?

Questions such as these are touched upon in Part One of this book and they have received much attention from political scientists. It is generally agreed that it is important to examine the context within which terrorism and terrorists operate, that is to say, the historical, social, economic, ethnic and even psychological factors that have some influence on thought, behaviour and action. Moreover, these factors change. Two writers, Bruce Hoffman (2006) and Martha Crenshaw (1995), have looked closely at the contexts in which definition becomes more adequate.

WHY IS TERRORISM SO DIFFICULT TO DEFINE?

Hoffman's understanding of terrorism is that it is inherently political and that it is a calculated process. He describes shifts in the meaning of the term and changes, in the way that terrorist organisations regard themselves and in their modes of behaviour, whether it is domestic or international violence. Used pejoratively, the term terrorism is often confused with guerrilla warfare or ordinary criminality. In Hoffman's view intellectual fervour and a degree of altruism may be added to those characteristics that distinguish the terrorist:

What is terrorism? Few words have so insidiously worked their way into our everyday vocabulary. Like 'Internet' – another grossly over-used term that has similarly become an indispensable part of the argot of the early twenty-first century – most people have a vague idea or impression of what terrorism is, but lack a more precise, concrete and truly explanatory definition of the word. This imprecision has been abetted partly by the modern media, whose efforts to communicate an often complex and convoluted message in the briefest amount of airtime or print space possible have led to the promiscuous labelling of a range of violent acts as 'terrorism'. Pick up a newspaper or turn on the television and – even within the same broadcast or on the same page – one can find such disparate acts as the bombing of a building, the assassination of a head of state, the massacre of civilians by a military unit, the poisoning of produce on supermarket shelves or the deliberate contamination of over-the-counter medication in a chemists, all described as incidents of terrorism. Indeed, virtually any especially abhorrent act of violence perceived as directed against society – whether it involves the activities of anti-government dissidents or governments themselves, organized-crime syndicates, common criminals, rioting mobs, people engaged in militant protest, individual psychotics or lone extortionists – is often labelled 'terrorism'. [. . .]

Terrorism, in the most widely accepted contemporary usage of the term, is fundamentally and inherently political. It is also ineluctably about power: the pursuit of power, the acquisition of power, and the use of power to achieve political change. Terrorism is thus violence – or, equally important, the threat of violence – used and directed in pursuit of, or in service of, a political aim. With this vital point clearly illuminated, one can appreciate the significance of the additional definition of 'terrorist' provided by the *OED*: 'Any one who attempts to further his views by a system of coercive intimidation'. This definition underscores clearly the other fundamental characteristic of terrorism: that it is a planned, calculated and indeed systematic act.

Given this relatively straightforward elucidation, why, then, is terrorism so difficult to define? The most compelling reason perhaps is because the meaning of the term has changed so frequently over the past two hundred years.[2]

Following the Second World War, in another swing of the pendulum of meaning, 'terrorism' regained the revolutionary connotations with which it is most commonly associated today. At that time, the term was used primarily in reference to the violent revolts then being prosecuted by the various indigenous nationalist/anti-colonialist groups that emerged in Asia, Africa and the Middle East during the late 1940s and

1950s to oppose continued European rule. Countries as diverse as Israel, Kenya, Cyprus and Algeria, for example, owe their independence at least in part to nationalist political movements that employed terrorism against colonial powers. It was also during this period that the 'politically correct' appellation of 'freedom fighters' came into fashion as a result of the political legitimacy that the international community (whose sympathy and support was actively courted by many of these movements) accorded to struggles for national liberation and self-determination [. . .] Many newly independent Third World countries and communist bloc states in particular adopted this vernacular, arguing that anyone or any movement that fought against 'colonial' oppression and/or Western domination should not be described as 'terrorists', but were properly deemed to be 'freedom fighters'. This position was perhaps most famously explained by the Palestine Liberation Organization (PLO) chairman, Yasir Arafat, when he addressed the United Nations General Assembly in November 1974. 'The difference between the revolutionary and the terrorist', Arafat stated, 'lies in the reason for which each fights. For whoever stands by a just cause and fights for the freedom and liberation of his land from the invaders, the settlers and the colonialists, cannot possibly be called terrorist.'

During the late 1960s and 1970s, terrorism continued to be viewed within a revolutionary context. However, this usage now expanded to include nationalist and ethnic separatist groups outside a colonial or neo-colonial framework as well as radical, entirely ideologically motivated organizations. Disenfranchised or exiled nationalist minorities – such as the PLO, the Quebecois separatist group FLQ (Front de Liberation du Quebec), the Basque ETA (Euskadita Askatasuna, or Freedom for the Basque Homeland) and even a hitherto unknown South Moluccan irredentist group seeking independence from Indonesia – adopted terrorism as a means to draw attention to themselves and their respective causes, in many instances with the specific aim, like their anti-colonial predecessors, of attracting international sympathy and support. [. . .]

Although the revolutionary cum ethno-nationalist/separatist and ideological exemplars continue to shape our most basic understanding of the term, it was not long before 'terrorism' was being used to denote broader, less distinct phenomena. In the early 1980s, for example, terrorism came to be regarded as a calculated means to destabilize the West as part of a vast global conspiracy [. . .] By the middle of the decade, however, a series of suicide bombings directed mostly against American diplomatic and military targets in the Middle East was focusing attention on the rising threat of state-sponsored terrorism. Consequently, this phenomenon – whereby various renegade foreign governments such as the regimes in Iran, Iraq, Libya and Syria became actively involved in sponsoring or commissioning terrorist acts – replaced communist conspiracy theories as the main context within which terrorism was viewed. Terrorism thus became associated with a type of covert or surrogate warfare whereby weaker states could confront larger, more powerful rivals without the risk of retribution.[3] [. . .]

Not surprisingly, as the meaning and usage of the word have changed over time to accommodate the political vernacular and discourse of each successive era, terrorism has proved increasingly elusive in the face of attempts to construct one consistent definition. At one time, the terrorists themselves were far more cooperative in this endeavour than they are today. The early practitioners didn't mince their words or hide behind the semantic camouflage of more anodyne labels such as 'freedom fighter' or 'urban guerrilla'. The nineteenth-century anarchists, for example, unabashedly proclaimed themselves to be terrorists and frankly proclaimed their tactics to be terrorism. [. . .]

Terrorist organisations almost without exception now regularly select names for themselves that consciously eschew the word 'terrorism' in any of its forms. Instead these groups actively seek to evoke images of:

- freedom and liberation (e.g., the National Liberation Front, the Popular Front for the Liberation of Palestine, Freedom for the Basque Homeland);
- armies or other military organisational structures (e.g., the National Military Organisation, the Popular Liberation Army, the Fifth Battalion of the Liberation Army);
- actual self-defence movements (e.g., the Afrikaner Resistance Movement, the Shankhill Defence Association, the Organisation for the Defence of the Free People, the Jewish Defense Organization);
- righteous vengeance (the Organisation for the Oppressed on Earth, the Justice Commandos of the Armenian Genocide, the Palestinian Revenge Organisation);

— or else deliberately choose names that are decidedly neutral and therefore bereft of all but the most innocuous suggestions or associations (e.g., the Shining Path, Front Line, al-Dawa (The Call), Alfaro Lives — Damn It!, Kach (Thus), al-Gamat al-Islamiya (The Islamic Organisation), the Lantero Youth Movement. [. . .]

Cast perpetually on the defensive and forced to take up arms to protect themselves and their real or imagined constituents only, terrorists perceive themselves as reluctant warriors driven by desperation — and lacking any viable alternative — to violence against a repressive state, a predatory rival ethnic or nationalist group, or an unresponsive international order. This perceived characteristic of self-denial also distinguishes the terrorist from other types of political extremists as well as from people similarly involved in illegal, violent avocations. A communist or a revolutionary, for example, would likely readily accept and admit that he is in fact a communist or a revolutionary. Indeed, many would doubtless take particular pride in claiming either of those appellations for themselves. Similarly, even a person engaged in illegal, wholly disreputable, or entirely selfish violent activities, such as robbing banks or carrying out contract killings, would probably admit to being a bank robber or a murderer for hire. The terrorist, by contrast, will *never* acknowledge that he is a terrorist and moreover will go to great lengths to evade and obscure any such inference or connection. [. . .]

On one point, at least, everyone agrees: 'Terrorism' is a pejorative term. It is a word with intrinsically negative connotations that is generally applied to one's enemies and opponents, or to those with whom one disagrees and would otherwise prefer to ignore. 'What is called terrorism,' Brian Jenkins has written, 'thus seems to depend on one's point of view. Use of the term implies a moral judgement; and if one party can successfully attach the label *terrorist* to its opponent, then it has indirectly persuaded others to adopt its moral viewpoint.' Hence the decision to call someone or label some organisation 'terrorist' becomes almost unavoidably subjective, depending largely on whether one sympathises with or opposes the person/group/cause concerned. If one identifies with the victim of the violence, for example, then the act is terrorism. If, however, one identifies with the perpetrator, the violent act is regarded in a more sympathetic, if not positive (or, at the worst, an ambivalent) light; and it is not terrorism.[4] [. . .]

Terrorists, as we have seen, deliberately cloak themselves in the terminology of military jargon. They consciously portray themselves as bona fide (freedom) fighters, if not soldiers, who – though they wear no identifying uniform or insignia – are entitled to treatment as prisoners of war (POWs) if captured and therefore should not be prosecuted as common criminals in ordinary courts of law. Terrorists further argue that, because of their numerical inferiority, far more limited firepower, and paucity of resources compared with an established nation-state's massive defence and national security apparatus, they have no choice but to operate clandestinely, emerging from the shadows to carry out dramatic (in other words, bloody and destructive) acts of hit-and-run violence in order to attract attention to, and ensure publicity for, themselves and their cause. The bomb in the rubbish bin, in their view, is merely a circumstantially imposed 'poor man's air force': the only means with which the terrorist can challenge – and get the attention of – the more powerful state. [. . .]

International terrorism disdains any concept of delimited areas of combat or demarcated battlefields, much less respect of neutral territory. Accordingly, terrorists have repeatedly taken their often parochial struggles to other, sometimes geographically distant, third-party countries and there deliberately enmeshed people completely unconnected with the terrorists' cause or grievances in violent incidents designed to generate attention and publicity.[5] [. . .]

Terrorism is often confused or equated with, or treated as synonymous with, guerrilla warfare and insurgency. This is not entirely surprising, since guerrillas and insurgents often employ the same tactics (assassination, kidnapping, hit-and-run attack, bombings of public gathering-places, hostage-taking, etc.) for the same purposes (to intimidate or coerce, thereby affecting behaviour through the arousal of fear) as terrorists. In addition, terrorists as well as guerrillas and insurgents wear neither uniform nor identifying insignia and thus are often indistinguishable from noncombatants. However, despite the inclination to lump terrorists, guerrillas and insurgents into the same catch-all category of 'irregulars', there are nonetheless fundamental differences among the three. 'Guerrilla', for example, in its most widely accepted usage, is taken to refer to a numerically larger group of armed individuals, who operate as a military unit, attack enemy military forces, and seize and hold territory (even if only ephemerally during daylight hours), while also exercising some form of sovereignty or control over a defined geographical area and its population. 'Insurgents' share these same characteristics; however, their strategy and operations transcend hit-and-run attacks to embrace what in the past has variously been called 'revolutionary guerrilla warfare', 'modern revolutionary warfare', or 'people's war' but is today commonly termed 'insurgency'. Thus, in addition to the irregular military tactics that characterize guerrilla operations, insurgencies typically involve coordinated informational (e.g., propaganda) and psychological warfare efforts designed to mobilize popular support in a struggle against an established national government, imperialist power, or foreign occupying force. Terrorists, however, do not function in the open as armed units, generally do not attempt to seize or hold territory, deliberately avoid engaging enemy military forces in combat, are constrained both numerically and logistically from undertaking concerted mass political mobilization efforts, and exercise no direct control or governance over a populace at either the local or the national level. [. . .]

It is also useful to distinguish terrorists from ordinary criminals. Like terrorists, criminals use violence as a means to attain a specific end. However, while the violent act itself may be similar – kidnapping, shooting, and arson, for example – the purpose or motivation clearly is different. Whether the criminal employs violence as a means to obtain money, to acquire material goods, or to kill or injure a specific victim for pay, he is acting primarily for selfish, personal motivations (usually material gain). Moreover, unlike terrorism, the ordinary criminal's violent act is not designed or intended to have consequences or create psychological repercussions beyond the act itself [. . .] the fundamental aim of the terrorist's violence is ultimately to change 'the system' – about which the ordinary criminal, of course, couldn't care less. [. . .]

Finally, the point should be emphasized that, unlike the ordinary criminal or the lunatic assassin, the terrorist is not pursuing purely egocentric goals; he is not driven by the wish to line his own pocket or satisfy some personal need or grievance. The terrorist is fundamentally an *altruist*: he believes that he is serving a 'good' cause designed to achieve a greater good for a wider constituency – whether real or imagined – which the terrorist and his organization purport to represent. The criminal, by comparison, serves no cause at all, just his own personal aggrandizement and material satiation. Indeed, a 'terrorist without a cause (at least in his own mind)', Konrad Kellen has argued, 'is not a terrorist'. Yet the possession or identification of a cause is not a sufficient criterion for labelling someone a terrorist. In this key respect, the difference between terrorists and political extremists is clear. Many people, of course, harbour all sorts of radical and extreme beliefs and opinions, and many of them belong to radical or even illegal or proscribed political organizations. However, if they do not use violence in the pursuance of their beliefs, they cannot be considered terrorists. The terrorist is fundamentally a *violent intellectual*, prepared to use and, indeed, committed to using force in the attainment of his goals. [. . .]

By distinguishing terrorists from other types of criminals and irregular fighters, and terrorism from other forms of crime and irregular warfare, we come to appreciate that terrorism is:

- ineluctably political in aims and motives;
- violent – or, equally important, threatens violence;
- designed to have far-reaching psychological repercussions beyond the immediate victim or target;
- conducted either by an organization with an identifiable chain of command or conspiratorial cell structure (whose members wear no uniform or identifying insignia) or by individuals or a small collection of individuals directly influenced,

motivated, or inspired by the ideological aims or example of some existent terrorist movement and/or its leaders; and
• perpetrated by a subnational group or nonstate entity.

We may therefore now attempt to define terrorism as the deliberate creation and exploitation of fear through violence or the threat of violence in the pursuit of political change. All terrorist acts involve violence or the threat of violence. Terrorism is specifically designed to have far-reaching psychological effects beyond the immediate victim(s) or object of the terrorist attack. It is meant to instil fear within, and thereby intimidate, a wider 'target audience' that might include a rival ethnic or religious group, an entire country, a national government or political party, or public opinion in general. Terrorism is designed to create power where there is none or to consolidate power where there is very little. Through the publicity generated by their violence, terrorists seek to obtain the leverage, influence and power they otherwise lack to effect political change on either a local or an international scale.[6]

THE SEARCH FOR OBJECTIVITY

In the light of the 200 or so extant definitions of terrorism and also the arguments about appropriateness, it is not useful to add to the catalogue. An alternative is to indicate to readers some of the more useful guides to definition.

In regard to understanding what terrorism is or is not, Martha Crenshaw (1995) writes of the search for objectivity in addressing the concept and the contexts in which this takes place. For her, terrorism is highly symbolic and perceptual: it is difficult to be neutral in the task of definition when perceptions are so often affected by the language of politics. Labelling activity as terrorist and detailing policies for dealing with it must frequently include moral judgement. Many concepts and the changes in them will form part of the belief system of political actors and their constituents.

For the analyst in search of definition, the main task will be to prise apart the bonding of ideological and symbolic criteria and, in so doing, to avoid the appearance of taking sides. For Crenshaw, labels are shorthand, combining descriptive and symbolic elements without unfortunately avoiding ambiguity, even contradiction.

Shorthand risks shaping 'meaning' towards preferred objectives – zealous affirmation by revolutionaries or authoritarian repression. The shorthand label reads as prescriptive and brevity may pitch definition in adversarial terms. Crenshaw has a warning for those defining in this fashion. Depicting the terrorist as fanatic and irrational is likely to foreclose any possibilities of negotiation and compromise.

Clearly, concepts of terrorism bear upon the extent to which governments proceed to sketch out their interests and it is often these interests that determine reliance on labels or their abandonment when judged politically inconvenient. Stunted definition never helped governments or public to appreciate the full extent of cause célèbre in the case of the PLO, the IRA or the Tamil Tigers. All too often, for Crenshaw, labels fail to help governments to distinguish clearly between violent and non-violent dissent. One instance that she has in mind is that of Argentina in the 1970s, when the army saw the radicalism of the Montoneros, originally student radicalism, as virulent social disease and, accordingly, an entire society had to be cleansed – through indiscriminate state terrorism.

A concluding assertion from Crenshaw is often met in the literature. Terrorism persists, she says, and is persistent in projecting images, building myths and communicating messages. In a very real sense, historical circumstances are likely to be transcended or skewed. Future generations only too easily find ample motivational material there, even though some will react to terrorist methods with revulsion or reluctant approval as, say, happened in Northern Ireland, Peru and Colombia.

More recent writers also acknowledge the impossibility of neutral definitions of terrorism, given its splayed-out communication of message and myth. David C. Rapoport and Paul Wilkinson (2005) stress the action-intensity and multiple-focus of terrorist activity, where the combined use and threat of violence is furtively planned and commonly carried out without warning:

[It] is directed against one set of targets (the direct victims) in order to coerce compliance from a second set of targets (targets of demand) and to intimidate or impress a wider audience (target of terror or target of attention).[7]

Understanding the meaning of terrorist acts in these contexts will then be clothed in a differing guise among the targeted and the selectors of targets.

In Wilkinson (2006) there is a hint of impatience with the time spent on the minutiae of definition and the delay in reaching consensus, for example, via a United Nations General Assembly definition. He goes on:

However, governmental and inter-governmental conferences on problems of terrorism no longer waste days in definitional issues: they have made genuine progress in improving cooperation against terrorism.[8]

For Wilkinson, and doubtless numerous others, action-in-response must go further than reflectively standing back from a label. For him there are crucial differences, in regard to what terrorists do, that put meaning also into responsive action.

One distinction that is worth adding to our typology is that between potentially *corrigible* terrorism – where there is a real possibility of finding a political/diplomatic pathway out of the conflict by addressing its underlying causes, thus very probably reducing, if not ending, the terrorist violence spawned by the conflict – and *incorrigible* terrorism. In the latter case, the movement/group has such absolutist and maximalist aims and poses such a major threat to the lives and well-being of civilian communities that the only recourse is to use all possible measures to suppress the group before it can wreak more mayhem.[9]

The notion that terrorism is something one 'does' as opposed to something one 'is' features in the persuasive arguments of the Irish forensic psychologist, John Horgan

(2005), of Tore Bjorgo in Norway (2005), and of Alex P. Schmid, seminal author of many books on terrorism.[10] In Horgan's words:

Schmid proposes that a narrower definition may help us more than that of a broader one open to interpretation by many. He recommends that we should seek to always define terrorism in terms of the methods used, allowing no room for rhetoric as a measure of legitimacy. By defining terrorism as the 'peacetime equivalent of war crimes', Schmid offers a potential exit from this problem of deciding the righteousness of acts of violence.[11]

Even so, such a measure of definition will not necessarily guarantee neutrality, either in preliminary approach or in subsequent decisions.

Considering the idea of terrorism in action-mode, Horgan goes on to develop in some detail what he terms 'a possible process model of terrorism'. This device:

may begin to move the debate away from complex and essentially sterile discussions about definition of terrorism as some sort of abstract event to identifiable behaviours and their antecedents, expected consequences and outcomes that are associated with terrorism.[12]

The analytical process-model Horgan builds up in detail:

this approach represents a very different approach in traditional analyses of the terrorist in that there is an explicit effort made to consider involvement in terrorism as a process comprising discrete phases to '*becoming*' a terrorist, '*being*' a terrorist (or what might be considered as both (a) remaining involved and (b) engaging in terrorist offences) and '*disengaging*' from terrorism [my italics].[13]

Horgan is keen to stress to readers that he is not 'pathologising terrorist activity for its own sake'. His process-model, he believes, is an aid to identifying issues relating to 'how' people become involved in violent terrorist activities as well as throwing some light upon 'why' they become involved. A further direction in enquiry, and a most difficult one to explore, again, in process terms, is the transition from engagement to 'disengagement' from terrorist association and activity. Why do they join? Why and when do they leave? A point is made, none too explicitly, that methodical scrutiny, Horgan-style, has much to offer those who strive for neutrality.

All in all, many of these arguments found in recent work point up the more tentative suggestions of Hoffman and Crenshaw that have to do with valid and rounded definitions of terrorism. Judging from much of the recent research and conference discussion, analysts seeking to define terrorism are spending a good deal of time considering what might be described as its root causes. Bjorgo has edited an invaluable collection of papers to do with the isolation and detailing of what are held to be causal factors. If definition is hinged on what is presumed initiated-action-and-response, then we had better be careful, Bjorgo warns, in our approach:

The notion of 'addressing the root causes of terrorism' may become a dead end if by 'root' we mean the distant and general issues such as poverty, globalisation and modernisation that are far removed from the actual acts of terrorism and extremely difficult to change. The approach is far more promising if we focus on the more immediate causes and circumstances that motivate and facilitate specific campaigns and acts of terrorism. Future research and efforts should move in this direction.[14]

Does our speculation about the root causes of terrorism diminish the problems of searching for objectivity in definition? It seems most unlikely.

Motivation for terrorism

A USEFUL INTRODUCTION to a study of terrorist motives is that of
Martha Crenshaw (1995), who explores settings in which violence is likely to
occur. Her standpoint, which may not be acceptable universally, is that terrorism is
an expression of logical choice and political strategy. Terrorists appraising the
parameters of a situation display a collective rationality. Crenshaw's argument, in
the first place, isolates a number of preconditions that set the stage for terrorism
and then, as so-termed permissive factors, stimulate and direct motivation, providing
opportunities for violent action. Finally, it is thought, precipitating events as catalysts
may trigger violence, then seen as the only feasible option.

CONTEXTUAL FACTORS

Urban living, in its crowdedness and complexity, accentuates, for Crenshaw, volatility,
vulnerability, discontent and often deprivation − factors that frequently lead to
growing dissatisfaction, an ingrained sense of grievance, feelings of victimisation,
maybe heightened by historical dissident tradition, all of which may engender resort
to violence. An urban context, too, creates opportunities for lashing-out strategies
for many possible targets may be sought, a sophisticated network of transport and
communication eases access, anonymity is not too difficult, and publicity can be
offered a wide audience. A lack of opportunity for constructive and peaceful political
participation may be compensated for, in the blackest of terms, by the chance of
individual and group notoriety and a spectacular demonstration of intent and
destructive capability.

Important for Crenshaw is when the direct causes of terrorism affect an elite
rather than the mass of a population. Violence now is the recourse of a disaffected

minority, young and often well educated, who may act, as it were, on behalf of a majority whose interest and approval are not guaranteed. With this point in mind, Crenshaw speculates that terrorism is most likely when elite dissatisfaction encounters mass passivity that does not seem sufficiently provoked. Elite frustration may even go as far as suicidal violence. In Northern Ireland, in Spain, and among Palestinians, the element of sacrifice has been a minority weapon, bringing in its train authoritarian repression. Against that terrorist retaliation sees the gun and the bomb as tactics to 'talk up the cause'. In Crenshaw's words, 'For the terrorist, the end may now justify the means.'

PSYCHO-DYNAMIC SCRUTINY

More modern writers take up the Crenshaw listing of enabling contexts, to look further into those factors that predispose individuals to follow the path of violence and particularly to maintain their disposition. Bjorgo, in an edited work, gives a detailed perspective of contexts and factors of significance in initial recruitment and eventual sustaining of motivation.[1] He and several of his contributors emphasise that preconditions alone are not sufficient to lead to outbreaks of terrorism; precipitants are more likely to trigger occasional violent commitment and to consolidate it. Elsewhere, it is the psychological approach of Horgan that is well worth study, given his justification of it as something going beyond the risk of superficial determinism. For him, as usual, scrutiny of motivation deserves psychological tools. We need to prise open the individual oyster to look inside. So we must frame our questions:

- 'Why do people want to become involved in a group that engages in terrorist violence?'
- 'How do people become involved?'
- 'What roles or tasks do they fulfil as a member?'
- 'How and why does the individual both "assimilate" the shared values and norms of the group and how and why [does] he then "accommodate" to engagement qualities not previously considered or expected prior to membership [. . .]?'
- 'How and why do the members commit specific acts of violence [. . .]?'[2]

However, asking questions we believe germane to the direction of enquiry may lead us up wrong paths. Horgan is quick to point to the snags in conjectural method:

> Answering questions about why people may wish to become involved in terrorism then may have little bearing on the answers that explain what they do (or are allowed to do, as we shall see) as terrorists, or how they actually become and remain involved in specific terrorist operations [. . .] Notions of causality are unhelpful and imply a sense of predictive value that belies the complexity of terrorism as well as the strategic factors underpinning decisions to adopt terrorism [. . .].[3]

Altogether, Horgan's method of enquiry may not be all that far from Crenshaw's assertion that most terrorist behaviour is rational in character. Yet, there is a warning of a critical nature, namely, '[. . .] the issues that each of these individual questions address may (a) not be necessarily related to each other, and (b) answering one may not necessarily reflect upon another [. . .].'[4]

Indeed, Horgan's logical caution is probably necessary for us all. Certainly, preconditions alone are never sufficient to lead to an outbreak of terrorism. The thrust of argument with Horgan (and well worth our careful reading) is to legitimise his particular style of analysis but, more generally, there is a careful emphasis on a number of points that almost certainly will gain wide currency:

> [. . .] identifying issues relating to 'how' people become involved [in terrorism] may be more valuable than attempting to arrive at answers 'why' people become involved. Essentially, then, we need to shift our expectations about arriving at a simple, and probably naïve, answer about terrorist motivation [. . .].[5]

> [. . .] a sense of gradual socialization into terrorism appears to be a common theme, with an initial sense of involvement seemingly characterized by gradual increases in commitment. Combined with this, group factors are centrally important in attempting to identify supportive qualities of initial engagement.[6]

What does the individual becoming a terrorist get out of it? In some senses this must represent some sort of motivational dividend. Horgan, Hoffman, Laqueur, Schmid and Jongman have all given attention to this.[7] Horgan puts the matter quite succinctly:

> [. . .] there are frequently overlooked and misinterpreted positive features of increased engagement for the individual terrorist, and these include the rapid acquisition of some sort of skill or skills, an increased sense of empowerment, purpose and self-importance, an increased sense of control, which appears to reflect the common effects of ideological control and auto-propaganda [. . .] a tangible sense of acceptance within the group, and in combination with this, the acquisition of real status within the broader community [. . .].[8]

For the researcher with a dynamic approach, there is a key question to do with individual motives. Addressing it calls for a real flair for intellectual adventure. It is this: 'why is "a sense of openness to engagement" found more readily in some people than in others?'

TYPES OF TERRORIST MOTIVATION: RATIONAL, PSYCHOLOGICAL AND CULTURAL

There have been many studies of the motivation presumed to underlie terrorist acts. Most studies assume that political violence follows a calculated rationale to which a collective subscribes at least for a time. Not all commentators would go as far as Crenshaw to term a line of action with its priorities, its planning and its execution as a logical process. Those attempting to analyse terrorist thinking as a prelude to decisive action have had to consider factors that inspire both a group as a whole and the individual within it. An example of such analysis is to be found in a 1998 essay from the US Army's Command and General Staff College printed by the Terrorism Research Center in the United States. There is a concise and clear outline of goal-centred terrorism with a recognition that the common objectives of 'old-school' terrorism have given way to modern variegated motives, targeting and techniques. Consequently, counter-terrorism by way of prediction and combat has become very much more difficult. The essay goes on to deal with motivation classified into three categories – rational, psychological and cultural – stating that terrorist action may be shaped by combinations of these:

Terrorism may be motivated by political, religious, or ideological objectives. In a sense, terrorist goals are always political, as extremists driven by religious or ideological beliefs usually seek political power to compel society to conform to their views. The objectives of terrorism distinguish it from other violent acts aimed at personal gain, such as criminal violence. However, the definition permits including violence by organized crime when it seeks to influence government policy. Some drug cartels and other international criminal organizations engage in political action when their activities influence governmental functioning. The essence of terrorism is the intent to induce fear in someone other than its victims to make a government or other audience change its political behavior.

Terrorism is common practice in insurgencies, but insurgents are not necessarily terrorists if they comply with the rules of war and do not engage in those forms of violence identified as terrorist acts. While the legal distinction is clear, it rarely inhibits terrorists who convince themselves that their actions are justified by a higher law. Their single-minded dedication to a goal, however poorly it may be articulated, renders legal sanctions relatively ineffective. In contrast, war is subject to rules of international law. Terrorists recognize no rules. No person, place, or object of value is immune from terrorist attack. There are no innocents.

This situation did not always prevail. Throughout history, extremists have practiced terrorism to generate fear and compel a change in behavior. Frequently, terrorism was incidental to other forms of violence, such as war or insurgency. Before the nineteenth century, terrorists usually granted certain categories of people immunity from attack. Like other warriors, terrorists recognized innocents – people not involved in conflict. Terrorists usually excluded women, children, and the elderly from target lists. For example, in late nineteenth-century Russia, radicals planning the assassination of Tsar Alexander II aborted several planned attacks because they risked harming innocent people. Old-school terrorism was direct; it intended to produce a political effect through the injury or death of the victim.

The development of bureaucratic states led to a profound change in terrorism. Modern governments have a continuity that older, personalistic governments did not. Terrorists found that the death of a single individual, even a monarch, did not necessarily produce the policy changes they sought. Terrorists reacted by turning to an indirect method of attack. By the early twentieth century, terrorists began to attack people previously considered innocents to generate political pressure. These indirect attacks create a public atmosphere of anxiety and undermine confidence in government. Their unpredictability and apparent randomness make it virtually impossible for governments to protect all potential victims. The public demands protection that the state cannot give. Frustrated and fearful, the people then demand that the government make concessions to stop the attacks.

Modern terrorism offers its practitioners many advantages. First, by not recognizing innocents, terrorists have an infinite number of targets. They select their target and determine when, where, and how to attack. The range of choices gives terrorists a high probability of success with minimum risk. If the attack goes wrong or fails to produce the intended results, the terrorists can deny responsibility.

Ironically, as democratic governments become more common it may be easier for terrorists to operate. The terrorist bombings of the New York City World Trade Center and the Oklahoma City Federal Building prove how easy it is for terrorists to operate in a free and democratic society. Authoritarian governments whose populace may have a better reason to revolt may also be less constrained by requirements for due process and impartial justice when combatting terrorists.

As commanders and staffs address terrorism, they must consider several relevant characteristics. First is that anyone can be a victim. (Some terrorists may still operate under cultural restraints, such as a desire to avoid harming women, but the planner cannot count on that. Essentially, there are no innocents.) Second, attacks that may appear to be senseless and random are not. To the perpetrators, their attacks make perfect sense. Acts such as bombing public places of assembly and shooting into crowded restaurants heighten public anxiety. This is the terrorists' immediate objective. Third, the terrorist needs to publicize his attack. If no one knows about it, it will not produce fear. The need for publicity often drives target selection; the greater the symbolic value of the target, the more publicity the attack brings to the terrorists and the more fear it generates. Finally, a leader planning for combatting terrorism must understand that he cannot protect every possible target all the time. He must also understand that terrorists will likely shift from more protected targets to less protected ones. This is the key to defensive measures.

The terrorists

Terrorists are inspired by many different motives. Students of terrorism classify them into three categories: rational, psychological, and cultural. A terrorist may be shaped by combinations of these.

Rational motivation

The rational terrorist thinks through his goals and options, making a cost–benefit analysis. He seeks to determine whether there are less costly and more effective ways to achieve his objective than terrorism. To assess the risk, he weighs the target's defensive capabilities against his own capabilities to attack. He measures his group's capabilities to sustain the effort. The essential question is whether terrorism will work for the desired purpose, given societal conditions at the time. The terrorist's rational analysis is similar to that of a military commander or a business entrepreneur considering available courses of action.

Groups considering terrorism as an option ask a crucial question: can terrorism induce enough anxiety to attain its goals without causing a backlash that will destroy the cause and perhaps the terrorists themselves? To misjudge the answer is to risk disaster. Recent history offers examples of several groups that had apparently good prospects for success which paid the price of misjudging reaction to terrorism. In the early 1970s, the Tupamaros in Uruguay and the ERP (People's Revolutionary Army) and Montoneros in Argentina misjudged a hostile popular reaction to terrorism. They pushed the societies beyond their threshold of tolerance and were destroyed as a result.

Psychological motivation

Psychological motivation for terrorism derives from the terrorist's personal dissatisfaction with his life and accomplishments. He finds his *raison d'être* in dedicated terrorist action. Although no clear psychopathy is found among terrorists, there is a nearly universal element in them that can be described as the 'true believer'. Terrorists do not even consider that they may be wrong and that others' views may have some merit. Terrorists tend to project their own antisocial motivations onto others, creating a polarized 'we versus they' outlook. They attribute only evil motives to anyone outside their own group. This enables the terrorists to dehumanize their victims and removes any sense of ambiguity from their minds. The resulting clarity of purpose appeals to those who crave violence to relieve their constant anger. The other common characteristic of the psychologically motivated terrorist is the pronounced need to belong to a group. With some terrorists, group acceptance is a stronger motivator than the stated political objectives of the organization. Such individuals define their social status by group acceptance.

Terrorist groups with strong internal motivations find it necessary to justify the group's existence continuously. A terrorist group must terrorize. As a minimum, it must commit violent acts to maintain group self-esteem and legitimacy. Thus, terrorists sometimes carry out attacks that are objectively nonproductive or even counterproductive to their announced goal.

Another result of psychological motivation is the intensity of group dynamics among terrorists. They tend to demand unanimity and be intolerant of dissent. With the enemy clearly identified and unequivocally evil, pressure to escalate the frequency and intensity of operations is ever present. The need to belong to the group discourages resignations, and the fear of compromise disallows their acceptance. Compromise is rejected, and terrorist groups lean towards maximalist positions. Having placed themselves beyond the pale, forever unacceptable to ordinary society, they cannot accept compromise. They consider negotiation dishonorable, if not treasonous. This may explain why terrorist groups are prone to fracturing and why the splinters are frequently more violent than their parent group.

The psychodynamics also make the announced group goal nearly impossible to achieve. A group that achieves its stated purpose is no longer needed; thus, success threatens the psychological well-being of its members. When a terrorist group approaches its stated goal, it is inclined to redefine it. The group may reject the achievement as false or inadequate or the result of the duplicity of 'them'. Nicaragua's Recontras, The Basque ETA (Euskadi Ta Askatasuna, 'Basque Fatherland and Liberty'), and many Palestinian radical groups apparently suffer from fear of success. One effective psychological defense against success is to define goals so broadly that they are impossible to achieve. Even if the world proclaims the success of a political movement, the terrorists can deny it and fight on.

Cultural motivation

Cultures shape values and motivate people to actions that seem unreasonable to foreign observers. Americans are reluctant to appreciate the intense effect of culture on behavior. We accept the myth that rational behavior guides all human actions. Even though irrational behavior occurs in our own tradition, we seek to explain it by other means. We reject as unbelievable such things as vendettas, martyrdom, and self-destructive group behavior when we observe them in others. We view with disbelief such things as the dissolution of a viable state for the sake of ethnic purity when the resulting ministates are economically anemic.

The treatment of life in general and individual life in particular is a cultural characteristic that has a tremendous impact on terrorism. In societies in which people identify themselves in terms of group membership (family, clan, tribe), there may be a willingness to self-sacrifice seldom seen elsewhere [. . .] At times, terrorists seem to be eager to give their lives for their organization and cause. The lives of 'others', being wholly evil in the terrorists' value system, can be destroyed with little or no remorse.

Other factors include the manner in which aggression is channeled and the concepts of social organization. For example, the ambient level of violence is shaped by the political structure and its provisions for power transfer. Some political systems have no effective nonviolent means for the succession to power. A culture may have a high tolerance for nonpolitical violence, such as banditry or ethnic 'turf' battles, and remain relatively free of political violence. The United States, for example, is one of the most violent societies in the world. Yet, political violence remains an aberration. By contrast, France and Germany, with low tolerance for violent crime, have a history of political violence.

A major cultural determinate of terrorism is the perception of 'outsiders' and anticipation of a threat to ethnic group survival. Fear of cultural extermination leads to violence which, to someone who does not experience it, seems irrational. All human beings are sensitive to threats to the values by which they identify themselves. These include language, religion, group membership, and homeland or native territory. The possibility of losing any of these can trigger defensive, even xenophobic, reactions.

Religion may be the most volatile of cultural identifiers because it encompasses values deeply held. A threat to one's religion puts not only the present at risk but also one's cultural past and the future. Many religions, including Christianity and

Islam, are so confident they are right that they have used force to obtain converts. Terrorism in the name of religion can be especially violent. Like all terrorists, those who are religiously motivated view their acts with moral certainty and even divine sanctions. What would otherwise be extraordinary acts of desperation become a religious duty in the mind of the religiously motivated terrorist. This helps explain the high level of commitment and willingness to risk death among religious extremist groups.[9]

TERRORIST BEHAVIOUR

Psychodynamic theories of terrorist motivation and behaviour have been outlined recently by Jerrold M. Post (1998), a psychiatrist and political scientist working in Washington DC. Under the rubric, 'Terrorist psycho-logic: terrorist behaviour as a product of psychological forces', Post argues that individuals are drawn to terrorism by means of a special 'logic' that is used to justify their violence. Frequently, terrorist rhetoric strikes us as absolutist; terrorist personalities reveal aggressiveness, a degree of flawed self-concept, a tendency to blame and scapegoat others, and a proneness to failure. Post, having suggested these traits, warns against their generalisation. Individuals feeling 'significant' for the first time readily succumb to leader dominance and group pressure. In conclusion, Post sees a terrorist group's 'success' in achieving a cause as a threat to the goal of survival:

[. . .] *Political terrorists are driven to commit acts of violence as a consequence of psychological forces*, and [. . .] their special psycho-logic is constructed to rationalize *acts they are psychologically compelled to commit*. Thus the principal argument of this essay is that *individuals are drawn to the path of terrorism in order to commit acts of violence*, and their special logic, which is grounded in their psychology and reflected in their rhetoric, becomes the justification for their violent acts.

Considering the diversity of causes to which terrorists are committed, the uniformity of their rhetoric is striking. Polarizing and absolutist, it is a rhetoric of 'us versus them'. It is a rhetoric without nuance, without shades of grey. 'They', the establishment, are the source of all evil, in vivid contrast to 'us', the freedom fighters, consumed by righteous rage. And if 'they' are the source of our problems, it follows ineluctably, in the special psycho-logic of the terrorist, that 'they' must be destroyed. It is the only just and moral thing to do. Once the basic premises are accepted, the logical reasoning is flawless. Shall we then conclude, because their reasoning is so logical, that terrorists are psychologically well balanced and that terrorist campaigns are the product of a rationally derived strategic choice? [. . .]

If we dismiss the notion of a terror network with a central staff providing propaganda guidance, what accounts for the uniformity of the terrorists' polarizing absolutist rhetoric? The author's own comparative research on the psychology of terrorists does not reveal major psychopathology, and is in substantial agreement with the finding of Crenshaw that 'the outstanding common characteristic of terrorists is their normality'. Her studies of the National Liberation Front (FLN) in Algeria in the 1950s found the members to be basically normal. Nor did Heskin find members of the Irish Republican Army (IRA) to be emotionally disturbed. In a review of the social psychology of terrorist groups, McCauley and Segal conclude that 'the best documented generalization is negative; terrorists do not show any striking psychopathology'.

Nor does a comparative study reveal a particular psychological type, a particular personality constellation, a uniform terrorist mind. But although diverse personalities are attracted to the path of terrorism, an examination of memoirs, court records, and rare interviews suggests that people with particular personality traits and tendencies are drawn disproportionately to terrorist careers.

What are these traits, these personality characteristics? Several authors have characterized terrorists as action-oriented, aggressive people who are stimulus-hungry and seek excitement. Particularly striking is the reliance placed on the psycho-logical mechanisms of 'externalization' and 'splitting', psychological mechanisms found in individuals with narcissistic and borderline personality disturbances. It is not my intent to suggest that all terrorists suffer from borderline or narcissistic personality disorders or that the psychological mechanisms of externalization and splitting are used by every terrorist. It is my distinct impression, however, that these mechanisms are found with extremely high frequency in the population of terrorists, and contribute significantly to the uniformity of terrorists' rhetorical style and their special psycho-logic.

In this regard, it is particularly important to understand the mechanism of 'splitting'. This is believed to be characteristic of people whose personality development is shaped by a particular type of psychological damage during childhood which produces what clinicians have characterized as narcissistic wounds. This leads to the development of what Kohut has termed 'the injured self'.

Individuals with a damaged self-concept have never fully integrated the good and bad parts of the self. These aspects of the self are 'split' into the 'me' and the 'not me'. An individual with this personality constellation idealizes his grandiose self and *splits out* and *projects* onto others all the hated and devalued weakness within. Individuals who place high reliance on the mechanisms of splitting and externalization look outward for the source of difficulties. They need an outside enemy to blame. This is a dominant mechanism of the destructive charismatic, such as Hitler, who projects the devalued part of himself onto the interpersonal environment and then attacks and scapegoats the enemy without. Unable to face his own inadequacies, the individual with this personality style needs a target to blame and attack for his own inner weakness and inadequacies. Such people find the polarizing absolutist rhetoric of terrorism extremely attractive. The statement, 'It's not us – it's them; they are the cause of our problems', provides a psychologically satisfying explanation for what has gone wrong in their lives.

In summary, most terrorists do not demonstrate serious psychopathology. Although there is no single personality type, it appears that people who are aggressive and action-oriented, and who place greater-than-normal reliance on the psychological mechanisms of externalization and splitting, are disproportionately represented among terrorists. Data indicate that many terrorists have not been successful in their personal, educational, and vocational lives. [. . .]

Although not all the people who find their way into a terrorist group share the characteristics just described to the degree that many in the group do, the group takes on a particular coloration. For many, belonging to the terrorist group may be the first time they truly belonged, the first time they felt truly significant, the first time they felt that what they did counted. As Bion has persuasively demonstrated, when individuals function in a group setting, their individual judgment and behavior are strongly influenced by the powerful forces of group dynamics. This is true of psychologically healthy people, including successful business executives and educators. Bion's constructs are particularly useful in understanding the group dynamics of terrorist behavior.

In every group, according to Bion, there are two opposing forces – what Bion calls 'the *work group*' and 'the *basic assumption group*'. The work group is that aspect of the group that acts in a goal-directed manner to accomplish its stated purposes. But as anyone who has ever worked on a committee or task force will ruefully testify, the occasions when a group proceeds to work in a fully cooperative manner to accomplish its goals in a conflict-free manner are rare indeed. Rather, groups, in their functioning, often sabotage their stated goals. They act, to use Bion's words, as if they are operating under 'basic assumptions', in what Bion calls the basic assumption group. He has identified three such psychological symptoms: the '*fight-flight*' group, the '*dependency*' group, and the '*pairing*' group:

1   The *fight-flight* group defines itself in relation to the outside world, which both threatens and justifies its existence. It acts as if the only way it can preserve itself is by fighting against or fleeing from the perceived enemy.
2   The *dependency* group turns to an omnipotent leader for direction. Members who fall into this state subordinate their own independent judgement to that of the leader and act as if they do not have minds of their own.
3   The *pairing* group acts as if the group will bring forth a messiah who will rescue them and create a better world.

If these states characterize the healthiest of groups, it should hardly be surprising that, when the group contains a disproportionate number of members who have fragmented psychosocial identities as well as a strong need to strike out against the cause of their failure, there should be an especially strong tendency to fall into these psychological postures, with extremely powerful group forces emerging. In my judgment, the terrorist group is the apotheosis of the 'basic assumption' group, and regularly manifests all three 'basic assumption' states.

Given the intensity of the need to belong, the strength of the affiliative needs, and, for many members, the as-yet incomplete sense of individual identity, terrorists have a tendency to submerge their own identities into the group, so that a kind of 'group mind' emerges. The group cohesion that emerges is magnified by the external danger, which tends to reduce internal divisiveness in unity against the outside enemy. 'The group was born under the pressure of pursuit' according to members of the Red Army Faction, and group solidarity was 'compelled exclusively by the illegal situation, fashioned into a common destiny'. Another Red Army Faction member went so far as to consider this pressure 'the sole link holding the group together'.

Doubts concerning the legitimacy of the goals and actions of the group are intolerable to such a group. The person who questions a group decision risks the wrath of the group and possible expulsion. [. . .]

In attempting to clarify whether acts of political violence are chosen as a wilful strategy or are products of psychological forces, it is of central importance to evaluate the goal of the act of violence. The rationalist school, as explicated by Crenshaw in the previous chapter, would aver that in an unequal political struggle, acts of political terrorism become an equalizer. These acts of political violence call forceful attention to the group's legitimate grievances and are designed to have an impact on a much wider audience than the immediate target of the violence. (Schmid has observed that it is very important to differentiate between the target of the violence and the target of influence; what distinguishes terrorism from other forms of political violence is the differentiation of the target of violence, that is, the innocent victim or non-combatant, from the target of influence, that is, the broader public or élite decision makers.) But implicit in this line of reasoning is an assumption that the political violence is instrumental, a tactic to achieve the group's political goals, to help it achieve its cause.

The position argued in this essay – that political violence is driven by psychological forces – follows a different line of reasoning. It does not view political violence as instrumental, but as the end itself. *The cause is not the cause.* The cause, as codified in the group's ideology, according to this line of reasoning, becomes the rationale for acts the terrorists are driven to commit. Indeed, the central argument of this position is that *individuals become terrorists in order to join terrorist groups and commit acts of terrorism.*

That is surely an extreme statement, but since we are discussing political extremism, perhaps that excess can be forgiven.

Consider a youth seeking an external target to attack. Before joining the group, he was alone, not particularly successful. Now he is engaged in a life-and-death struggle with the establishment, his picture on the 'most wanted' posters. He sees his leaders as internationally prominent media personalities. Within certain circles, he is lionized as a hero. He travels first class, and his family is provided for should his acts of heroism lead to his death as a martyr to the cause. Heady stuff that; surely this is the good life, a role and position not easily relinquished.

Now if authenticity is defined as 'revolutionary heroism', then this definition has important implications for the outcomes of debates and personal rivalries within the group. A leader who advocates prudence and moderation is likely to lose his position quickly to a bolder person committed to the continuation of the struggle. Indeed, on the basis of his observations of underground resistance groups during World War II, Zawodny has concluded that the primary determinant of underground group decision making is not the external reality but the psychological climate within the group. He has described the unbearable tension that builds when a resistance group is compelled to go underground. For these action-oriented people, forced inaction is extremely successful. What, after all, are freedom fighters if they do not fight? *A terrorist group needs to commit acts of terrorism in order to justify its existence.* The wise leader, sensing the building tension, will plan an action so that the group's members can reaffirm their identity and discharge their aggressive energy. Better to have the group attack the outside enemy, no matter how high the risk, than turn on itself – and him.

For any group or organization, the highest priority is survival. This is especially true for the terrorist group. *To succeed in achieving its espoused cause would threaten the goal of survival.* This fact suggests a position of cybernetic balance for the group. It must be successful enough in its terrorist acts and rhetoric of legitimation to attract members and perpetuate itself, but it must not be so successful that it will succeed itself out of business.

Post's rather deterministic line of argument ends with a grim declaration. 'Terrorists whose only sense of significance comes from being terrorists cannot be forced to give up terrorism, for to do so would be to lose their very reason for being.'[10]

THE SUICIDE BOMBER

Lastly, and also deterministic in a sense, is the technique of the suicide bomber. Its ubiquitous occurrence is evident in 24 countries; its underlying motivation is most difficult to comprehend. What possible purpose, for instance, can be served by the young Israeli woman lawyer who straps explosives to her breast in order to wreck a Jerusalem street café? In this case, the attack fails and later in prison interviews she does not make a case that is either logical or credible, save that she will use 'shrapnel to pierce the hearts of the Israeli enemy'.

Much is being discussed and written about the suicide cult. Two well-known authorities, Walter Laqueur (2004) and Bruce Hoffman (2006) have recently devoted an entire chapter, full of detail, to the subject. Laqueur introduces his discussion very straightforwardly:

Suicide bombing, one of the most prominent features of contemporary terrorism, has been one of the most difficult to understand for those living in what is commonly known as the post heroic age. It has led some to believe that those willing to sacrifice their own life must be supreme idealists and the cause for which they are willing to make this greatest of all sacrifices must be a just and noble one. At the same time, it is frequently maintained that suicide attack is something new in history and specifically Muslim. (At one time, in the 1980s, it was believed to be specifically Shi'ite.) However, such missions have occurred over a long time in many countries and cultures. In fact, a review of the history of terrorism over the ages up to the 1960s shows that in the great majority of cases all terrorism was suicide terrorism. The number of attackers who got away with terrorism was very small. From what we know about their mind-set it appears that they did not expect to escape, and in many instances they did not even try. An attempt to understand the suicide bombers ought to take into account a great variety of circumstances and motives and should not focus on one specific group and religion, even if that group happens to figure very prominently at the present time.[11]

Laqueur continues:

Common to suicide bombers is the belief that they were warriors in a just struggle in the best tradition of their religion (or nation), that their group was cruelly oppressed, and that their sacrifice was not just desirable but imperative. Common also was the belief that the collective (the religion, the sect, the nation, the race) was infinitely more important than the individual [. . .] Common also was the belief not only that their memory would live on for ever but that in choosing death they were opting for eternal life in one form or another [. . .].[12]

As for religious suicide:

The motivation of the religious suicide terrorists is in many ways easier to explain than the secular. The radical Muslim has been promised various rewards such as life in Paradise, his family will be taken care of, he knows he will not really be dead but continue another and much richer existence in the future. Support for the families of martyrs is an important consideration, as is the religious obligation to repay one's debts prior to the suicide mission – hence the financial help (amounting to about twenty-five thousand dollars) given to the families of suicide bombers by Iran and Iraq, as well as other Arab countries and Muslim foundations. [. . .]
    The secular suicide terrorist cannot have such expectations. But the difference between religious and secular motivation could be less wide than often assumed, for the underlying motives might be quite similar. There is the feeling of doing one's duty (religious, patriotic, or a mixture of the two) and of hate of the enemy, the infidel, the occupant. The readiness to sacrifice one's life is generated through a process of indoctrination – in orthodox religious schools or computational circles. Religious or ideological indoctrination needs some rootedness [sic] in an objective situation; the age and the hate of the enemy have to be perceived as obvious. But in some cases the personality of the leader is sufficient to play the decisive role in committing acts that otherwise are incomprehensible such as the collective suicide of groups of sectarians.[13]

Hoffman, meanwhile, has thoughts about the ubiquity of the cult of suicide and about what he believes may be its tactical advantages:

As of 2005, more than 350 suicide attacks had taken place in at least twenty-four countries – including the United Kingdom, Israel, Sri Lanka, Russia, Lebanon, Turkey, Italy, Indonesia, Pakistan, Colombia, Argentina, Kenya, Tanzania, Croatia, Morocco, Singapore, the Philippines, Saudi Arabia, Kuwait, and Iraq. By comparison, at the dawn of the modern era of religious terrorism some twenty years ago, this was a phenomenon confined exclusively to two countries, Lebanon and Kuwait. Toward the end of the 1980s, however, suicide terrorism began to spread beyond the Middle East: first to Sri Lanka but then, as the 1990s unfolded, to India, Argentina, Israel, Saudi Arabia, Kenya and Tanzania.

The suicide mode has undoubted advantages:

Suicide tactics are devastatingly effective, lethally efficient, have a greater likelihood of success, and are relatively inexpensive and generally easier to execute than other attack modes. The terrorist decision to employ this tactic therefore is neither irrational nor desperate, as is sometimes portrayed: rather, it is an entirely rational and calculated choice, consciously embraced as a deliberate instrument of warfare.

Moreover, it is different from other terrorist techniques:

[. . .] because the perpetrator's own death is an essential requirement for the attack's success. The suicide terrorist is the ultimate 'smart bomb', a human access. The suicide terrorist thus has the ability to effect last-minute changes in his or her attack plan, on the basis of ease or difficulty of approach, the paucity or density of people in or around the target, and whether or not security personnel are present or other countermeasures are visible.

Public attention and media coverage are guaranteed:

[. . .] an especially powerful psychological weapon. With the exception perhaps of only weapons of mass destruction (WMD) terrorism, no other terrorist tactic arguably induces the same fear and paralysis in the terrorist's target audience [. . .] thus deliberately conceived by its practitioners to have far-reaching and profound psychological effects and repercussions well beyond the immediate victims or object of the attack.[14]

It may be recalled that Jerrold Post had argued that individuals are drawn to terrorism by means of a special 'logic' that is used to justify their violence. An issue calling for debate is the 'logic' that justifies a terrorist's motivation for suicide. Laqueur and Hoffman have certainly put forward a number of useful points.

Prominent in Hoffman's view of the cult is his belief that there are causal factors beyond the individual terrorist's sense of motivation. Organisations such as Hamas and Hizbullah and the Tamil Tigers 'employ' volunteers from a steady team of recruits for whom the prime motives are part political, part religious and part needing to be one-of-the-crowd. In the strangest of respects volunteers feel driven (and are driven by others) to impress their friends, and strike fear into the hearts of their enemies. In this way they will be catapulted to the forefront of their respective national struggles and earn society's veneration and the promise of Paradise.

Seen from the outside we can appreciate that, politically, suicide bombing is, to use Hoffman's term, something of an 'instrumental decision'. That notion, though, does not altogether help us to understand the individual heart-and-mind motivation of the one who sets out to wreak carnage.

Terrorism's worldwide occurrence

THIS READER, now appearing in its fourth edition, does so at a time of seismic change in that region where terrorists acting *externally* have long menaced much of the world. The first six months of 2011 saw terror dramatically *internalised* as state after state in Mediterranean Arab lands turned wrathfully upon protesting crowds of their own people.

One after another – Tunisia, Egypt, Libya, Bahrain, Syria, Yemen, Morocco, Lebanon, Oman – states' leaders encountered an Arab Awakening and met it with repressive force. Riot police, rifle fusilades, tear gas, even helicopter gunships were used in places in a toe-to-toe revolutionary struggle. State terrorism, that old-fashioned, crude, unthinking response to popular agitation, is also now having to cope with an Internet generation networking complaints and demands across region and world.

This chapter addresses the question: what form does terrorism take and where is it mostly to be found? First, excerpts from a recent overview of terrorism since 1945 are presented. A number of the groups referred to there are described in detail in the 16 case studies in Part Two of this book. Second, the excerpts are followed by a note on terrorist organisation. In the third place, there is an outline typology of terrorism, which, despite its being a rather bare framework, may offer scope for discussion and comparison. Finally, there is a list of the main contemporary terrorist groups with a note about state-sponsored terrorism.

OVERVIEW OF TERRORISM SINCE 1945

Using a historical approach, Walter Laqueur (1999), an authoritative and prolific writer on terrorism, has surveyed terrorist activity after the Second World War in broad detail. The following text contains excerpts from Laqueur:

With the end of the Second World War, the terrorist action shifted from Europe to the Middle East and Asia. There was no neo-Nazi or neo-fascist terrorism in the years after 1945, as many had feared; with the defeat of the Axis powers, the fanatical enthusiasm had vanished. In Eastern Europe and the Balkans, including those areas in which terrorism had been endemic, the presence of the Red Army and, later on, the heavy hand of the local secret police were sufficient to act as a deterrent.

But in the colonies and other dependencies in North Africa and the Middle East, violent campaigns were launched by nationalist groups striving for independence. Terrorist acts had, of course, taken place before in the East, for example, prime ministers had been assassinated in Iraq and Egypt. But with the weakening of the colonial powers, violence gained a new, powerful momentum.

Terrorism in Palestine, spearheaded by Irgun, had first appeared on the eve of the Second World War, but then Irgun called an armistice and some of its members joined the British forces. However, even before the war ended, the group renewed its attacks against the mandated power. A smaller, even more radical offshoot, the Stern Gang (Fighters for the Freedom of Israel), had attacked ceaselessly, and their leader was hunted down and shot by the British police in Tel Aviv in 1942. The politics of the Stern Gang were more than a little confused; in the early phase of the war they had looked for cooperation from the Italians and even the Germans, and later on they were attracted to Soviet communism. Their anti-imperialist manifestos often read as if they had been composed in Moscow. But their left-wing motivation was not deeply rooted. Both Irgun and the Stern Gang dissolved after the state of Israel came into being [. . .] The leader of Irgun, Menachem Begin, and one of the leaders of the Stern Gang, Yitzhak Shamir, in later years became prime ministers of Israel. These are just two examples of the many cases of guerrilla or terrorist leaders having a second, political career after their fighting days were over.

The Algerian war for independence began in 1954 in the mountainous regions of the country, was carried to the cities, and lasted for seven years. The terrorist part of the campaign was not too successful – the French smashed the rebel FLN cadres in the capital and the campaign did not go well in the countryside. But the rebels had the great advantage of having sanctuaries in the neighbouring countries. Twenty thousand of their fighters were assembled outside the reach of the French, who gradually lost the stomach for making the effort needed to keep the renitent country under its control.

As in Israel, the terrorist campaigns were followed by decades of peace, but eventually radical elements again asserted themselves. This led to the second Algerian war in the 1990s and, in Israel, the murder of Prime Minister Rabin in 1995.

Generally speaking, Middle Eastern politics remained violent, marked by the assassination of a great many leaders – among them King Abdullah of Jordan in 1951 and Anwar Sadat of Egypt in 1981 – and a variety of Syrian, Lebanese, and Iranian government ministers. After the emergence of radical Muslim elements, terrorism became even more rampant. Political assassinations, needless to say, occurred in many other parts of Asia and Africa. The murder of Gandhi in 1948, and in later years of Indira Gandhi and Rajiv, her son who succeeded her as prime minister, are particularly striking examples. But it was above all in the Muslim countries of North Africa and the Middle East that systematic and sustained terrorism prevailed in the 1950s, even before anti-Israeli terrorism became a major and well-publicized feature of world politics in the 1960s.

Latin American terrorism

In Latin America, there was a recurrence of terrorism in the late 1960s that was not nationalist–separatist in character but drew its inspiration from the extreme left. The Tupamaros of Uruguay were the prototype of this new terrorism. They emerged in a country that for years had been the most progressive in Latin America, and even in the 1960s was among the more liberal. The Tupamaros, who stood for radical political and social change, attracted some of the best and most idealistic from the younger generation, and they engaged in bank robberies and kidnappings but not in indiscriminate murder. Initially their activities were quite successful, proving that a civilian government could be easily disrupted. The Tupamaros attracted a great deal of attention in the world media, but in the final analysis the only result of their operations was the destruction of freedom in a country that almost alone in Latin America had an unbroken democratic tradition, however imperfect. The campaign of the Tupamaros caused the rise of a military dictatorship and destroyed the democratic system, and, at the same time, brought about the destruction of their own movement. By the 1970s, the remaining Tupamaros were in exile bemoaning the evil doings of an oppressive regime they themselves had helped to bring to power.

Terrorism in Argentina began a few years after the outbreak in Uruguay. It was on a far more massive scale, and both the terrorist operations and the backlash were more indiscriminate and bloody. In contrast to their Uruguayan comrades, Argentinian terrorists consisted of two groups: the Montoneros (basically Peronist in orientation and social composition) and the smaller but better-equipped and organised ERP (more doctrinally left-wing in character, consisting mainly of students). The Montoneros, who had the whole Peronist left wing as a base of recruitment, began their campaign with the killing of ex-President Aramburu in May 1970. Initially, a considerable number of foreigners (or locals representing foreign economic interests) were among the victims, but gradually the terrorism turned against the army, the police, politicians, and moderate union leaders. There were also a great many unintended victims who died because they happened to be where bombs exploded.

Argentina is perhaps the only recorded example of urban guerrilla activity – that is, where terrorists came close to establishing liberated zones in urban areas. But the terrorists over-reached precisely because they engaged in large-scale operations that made it easier for the army to combat them. Once the army received a free hand to retaliate, no mercy was shown. Four thousand members of the Montoneros and the ERP were detained, thousands more were arrested, and many were tortured or disappeared without a trace, including many innocent people. Thus, a terrible price was paid for the ill-conceived terrorist campaign. True, within a decade military dictatorship in Argentina, as in Uruguay, gave way to a civilian government that gradually became more democratic, but the experience of these countries did show that even weak and ineffective governments were capable of defending themselves when terrorists had no hope of gaining the support of significant sections of the population.

Left-wing terrorism in Germany and Italy

A new wave of terrorism of left-wing inspiration appeared in Europe in the late 1960s, partly in the wake of the student revolt of 1968. The German 'Red Army' (the Baader Meinhof group) was active for about seven years, and it was succeeded by the movements 'June 2nd' and the 'Red Cells'. According to Red Army ideology, this group was the vanguard of the exploited and oppressed Third World, terrorism being the only feasible strategy of weak revolutionary movements. But the Third World they invoked was a figment of their imagination, and if it had existed, it would not have wanted any part of these three dozen young men and women who called themselves an 'army', and who lived in a world of infantile dreams.

Over the years the Red Army attacked several banks, burned a department store or two, and killed a number of bankers, industrialists, and judges. But none of the victims was very prominent, nor could they have been regarded as major enemies, of either Baader Meinhof, of the revolutionary movement, or of the Third World. Their names seem to have been picked out of a telephone directory.

Initially, the Red Army had hundreds of supporters, some of whom were willing to give active help. But gradually they lost sympathy, as it became obvious that the terrorists were living in a fantasy world and that their ill-conceived actions had no political impact whatsoever, except perhaps to tarnish the image of the left.

If Baader Meinhof had originally been deeply if unrealistically motivated by ideology, the second and third generation of German left-wing terrorists did not tend towards reflection. They engaged in terrorism because their predecessors had done so. If they had a specific political orientation, they were unwilling or unable to express it. A few terrorist acts took place during the 1980s and early 1990s, but by and large these groups had become irrelevant, and even the media, which originally had devoted inordinate attention to their activities, lost interest.

Italian left-wing terrorism was conducted on a considerably wider scale; it was spearheaded by the Brigate Rosse, which came into being in 1970. The inspiration in Italy came less from the New Left, which had never been very strong in that country, and more from radical groups within the Communist Youth League and, to some extent, from the student groups of the left wing of the Christian Democrats, which had undergone a rapid process of radicalization. As the Red Brigades saw it, Italy was not a democratic country but a bourgeois dictatorship; the language of arms was the only language understood by the ruling class. The Communist Party, these young radicals believed, was a reformist party that had lost its belief in revolution and radical fervour. The movement was also helped by a general feeling of discontent with the lack of progress on the domestic front; the social structures had been frozen since the end of the war, and one party had been in power throughout the period. As in Germany, the membership was predominantly middle class. [. . .]

The Red Brigades engaged in some 14,000 terrorist attacks within their first ten years. While some parts of Italy were relatively free of terrorism, Rome and the industrial regions of the north were strongly affected. The legal system was almost paralysed, since jurors were afraid to fulfill their duty; not all judges were prepared to be heroes, and the police were by and large unprepared to deal with this unprecedented challenge. Nevertheless, the Red Brigades alienated many of their erstwhile well-wishers as the result of their attacks on journalists and union officials, and above all their murder of Aldo Moro, who had been the most leftist of all the Christian Democrat prime ministers. Far from bringing about a weakening of the state apparatus, the abduction and murder of Aldo Moro caused a closing of ranks of all the democratic parties, including, for once, the Communists.

Gradually, the Italian police and the courts began showing greater sophistication in dealing with the terrorists. By 1982, some 1,400 leftist terrorists were in prison and more than a few of them, the so-called *pentiti*, had recanted. This led to splits in the ranks of the terrorists who had not been arrested. By 1984, only one member of the high command of the Brigades had not been apprehended, and the movement had ceased to exist.

America and Japan

The upsurge in terrorism of the 1960s was not limited to Europe. It manifested itself in various ways in the United States and Japan. In America, it appeared on the radical fringe of the New Left in groups like the Weathermen. In a largely unconnected development, terrorism found adherents among black militants, above all the Black Panthers. The motives that induced young blacks to join the terrorist scene were quite different from those that made middle-class white students join the Weathermen. The students knew nothing about the problems of the ghetto and about unemployment. They were motivated by a crisis of identity, suburban boredom, and the desire for excitement and action. For them, more often than not terrorism was the cure for personal problems. All this was immersed in intellectual confusion that espoused the idea that almost anything was permitted and denounced the absence of values. But the things the white radicals were saying about the wickedness of American culture were *a fortiori* true of the radicals themselves.

Contemporary Japanese terrorism, which was limited principally to the Japanese Red Army, reflected native traditions as well as Western influences. Many of the ideological disputations of Japanese terrorists were imported from the West, but they also invoked the spirit of the samurai. Japanese terrorists hijacked a Japanese aircraft, committed murders, including several of their own comrades, and perpetrated a few acts of sabotage, most notably of a Shell refinery in Singapore and of the French embassy in the Hague. They were also instrumental in the massacre at Lod Airport in Israel, and they collaborated with Carlos, the famous multinational terrorist, as well as the Palestinians, and ultimately found asylum in Lebanon. This being the whole extent of their terrorist activities, the Japanese Red Army was much less dangerous than the Japanese sectarian terrorists of the 1990s, who had a true base inside Japan, which the Red Army never had.[1]

The Palestinians

Palestinian terrorism grew out of the Palestinian resistance movement against Israel. There had been attacks against Israeli settlements since the state came into being, mainly small raids across the border, but it was only after the war of 1967 and the occupation of the West Bank that a major terrorist campaign began.

Eventually the PLO, which was both a political organization and something akin to a guerrilla movement, also opted for terrorism through Black September and other ad hoc groups. The Palestinians engaged in a variety of horrific operations, such as the killing of Israeli athletes at the Munich Olympic Games in 1972 and the blowing up of several jumbo jets at Dawson Field in Jordan in September 1970. But these major operations usually backfired: for example, the Dawson Field incident threatened the existence of Jordan, whereupon Black September was suppressed by the Jordanian army. The Israelis retaliated with counterterror inside Israel and abroad, and the hijacking of planes, which at one time had been a main strategy, was given up.

Palestinian terrorism [. . .] although not a success per se, had a great advantage over most other terrorist movements – namely, the support extended by many Arab countries, which created considerable political difficulty for Israel. Eventually this pressure exerted by the Arab states through the major powers, combined with the Intifada (which was mass rather than individual violence), brought about concessions from Israel. Israel was also hurt by the enormous publicity given even to very minor terrorist events in Israel as compared with the much more destructive terrorism in Sri Lanka and Algeria, for example. The reason was obvious: the media were concentrated in Jerusalem rather than Sri Lanka or Algeria.

Terrorism old and new: IRA and ETA

A new age of terrorism is dawning, but the old terrorism is far from dead, even though it has declined markedly in Europe. An example is provided by the situation in Northern Ireland [. . .] Terrorism in Ireland developed in 1968–69 following Catholic and Protestant demonstrations and has not ceased since. The last phase of the Troubles in Northern Ireland began in 1969. The early years of the Troubles (1972–76) were by far the bloodiest. Thereafter the annual number of victims declined to about a third of what it had been in the early years.

But the IRA could have conducted many more widescale and frequent attacks, given the financial support they received and the arms supply at their disposal. What kept their activities down to relatively low levels? The IRA leadership seems to have realized early on that their campaign against the British would be long, and that if it became too formidable a danger, especially on the British mainland, they would not only turn public opinion against themselves but also invite much sharper and more effective counterblows. Nor could they hope to substantially strengthen their position in their own community; in parliamentary elections they hardly ever scored more than 15 per cent of the vote.

Their strategy from the late 1970s on seems to have been to wear out the British, perhaps to await a time when Britain would be in so weak a position that it would have to make concessions it had been reluctant to consider in the past. The aims of the Republicans were, after all, limited in scope compared with those of Palestinian groups such as Hamas. They wanted not the total destruction of their enemy but merely a united Ireland.

Hence the political negotiations that began in 1993 [. . .] After many setbacks, these talks led to agreement in 1998.

Whether the peace will last cannot be predicted with certainty. But as of this writing in 1999, terrorism in Ireland has come to an end after long negotiations and the intervention of the American president, Bill Clinton, and the British prime minister, Tony Blair.

The parallels between the IRA and the Basque ETA are striking in many respects: both are motivated by enormous enthusiasm, even though the groups constitute only a minority within their own community. Basque opposition against what is perceived as oppression by the Madrid centralists goes back to the nineteenth century and possibly even further.

The ETA has achieved considerable political concessions, but this success has not been remotely sufficient to satisfy the nationalists. The aim of the extremists remains an independent Basque state.

The high tide of ETA terrorism came in 1978–80, certainly as far as the number of victims is concerned.

ETA's prospects seem dim [. . .] Nevertheless, ETA still has the support of a fanatical minority in their own region. Eventually, a political solution might be found; this will undoubtedly lead to a split, as in the case of the IRA, since the ultranationalists cannot possibly achieve all they want.

In the Basque region, as in Northern Ireland, a culture of violence has developed over the years that tends to perpetuate itself. It is, in all probability, a generational question. As one generation of professional terrorists ages and by necessity opts out of the armed struggle, a new one may or may not emerge. Or it may appear after an interruption of a few decades, as has happened in Irish history time and again.[2]

TERRORISM: CHANGES

The survey of 1999 by Laqueur now needs updating. An important point to make, though, at the outset is something that Laqueur and others have stressed, namely, that terrorism – violence in political activism – has changed and is changing all the time. Hoffman, a fellow authority, traces changes especially over the last 20 years:

Although the revolutionary cum ethno-nationalist/separatist and ideological exemplars continue to shape our most basic understanding of the term, it was not long before 'terrorism' was being used to denote broader, less distinct phenomena. In the early 1980s, for example, terrorism came to be regarded as a calculated means to destabilise the West as part of a vast global conspiracy [. . .] By the middle of the decade, however, a series of suicide bombings directed mostly against American diplomatic and military targets was focussing attention on the rising threat of state-sponsored terrorism. Consequently, the phenomenon – whereby various foreign governments such as the regimes in Iran, Iraq, Libya and Syria became actively involved in sponsoring or commissioning terrorist acts – replaced communist conspiracy theories as the main context within which terrorism was viewed. Terrorism thus became associated with a type of covert or surrogate warfare whereby weaker states could confront larger, more powerful rivals without the risk of retribution. In the early 1990s the meaning and usage of the term 'terrorism' were further blurred by the emergence of two new buzzwords, 'narco-terrorism' and the so-called gray area phenomenon. [. . .]

Those who drew attention to this 'gray area phenomenon' were concerned less with grand conspiracies than with highlighting the increasingly fluid and variable nature of sub national conflict in the post-cold war era. Accordingly, in the 1990s 'terrorism' began to be subsumed by some analysts within the 'gray area phenomenon'. Thus, the latter term began to be used to denote 'threats to the stability of nation states by non-state actors and non-governmental processes and organizations' to describe violence affecting 'immense regions or urban areas where control has shifted from legitimate governments to new half-political, half-criminal powers'; or simply to group together in one category the range of conflicts across the world that no longer conformed to traditionally accepted notions of war as fighting between the armed forces of two or more established states, but instead involved irregular forces as one or more of the combatants. Terrorism had shifted its meaning again from an individual phenomenon of sub national violence to one of several elements, or part of a wide pattern, of nonstate conflict.[3]

The changes, Hoffman believes, are quite radical:

Meanwhile, the face of terrorism is changing in other ways. New adversaries, new motivations, and new rationales have emerged over the past decade to challenge at least some of the conventional wisdom on both terrorists and terrorism. In the past terrorist groups were recognizable mostly as collections of individuals with a well-defined command and control apparatus, who had been previously trained (in however rudimentary a fashion) in the techniques and tactics of terrorism, were engaged in conspiracy as a full-time avocation, lived underground while constantly planning and plotting terrorist attacks, and at times were under the direct control, or operated at the express behest, of a foreign government (as, for example, in the case of Libya's sponsorship of IRA operations claimed in the names of the Anti-Imperialist International Brigades) [. . .] These organizations engaged in highly selective and mostly discriminate acts of violence. They targeted for bombing various 'symbolic' targets representing the source of their hostility [. . .] in order to attract attention to themselves and their causes.[4]

The conventional wisdom held that terrorists were interested not in killing but in publicity. Violence was employed less as a means of wreaking death and destruction than as a way to appeal to and attract supporters, focus attention on the terrorists and their causes, or attain tangible political aims or concessions [. . .] Terrorists, it was thus argued, believed that only if their violence was calculated or regulated would they be able to obtain the popular support or international recognition they craved or achieve the political ends that they desired.[5]

Not only changes in techniques are taking place. More importantly, for terrorists and for those 'outside' there are modifications, it appears, where decisions and commands are the result of a 'linear' (or 'spaghetti') arrangement of participants, isolated sometimes, rather than what was formerly a hierarchical, cell-like structure. Again, it is Hoffman's analysis:

The absence of any existing, publicly identified command authority is especially significant in that it may remove any inhibitions on the terrorists' desire to inflict widespread, indiscriminate casualties. These individual networks may be less sophisticated or less technically competent but they could have greater freedom and independence in tactical decisions than traditional terrorist cells, given the absence of a central command structure or physical headquarters otherwise available to victim states to target in retaliation. Accordingly, this particular trend in terrorism potentially represents a very different and possibly more lethal threat than that posed by more familiar, traditional terrorist adversaries. Further, the anonymity intrinsic to this type of operation coupled with the lack of a discernible organizational structure with a distinguishable command chain behind the attackers is deliberately designed to prevent easy identification and to facilitate the perpetrators' escape and evasion. Finally many terrorist movements today are also seen to have less easily defined aims or identified objectives. Some are motivated by unswerving hostility toward the West in general and the United States in particular or a desire for revenge and retaliation that is frequently fuelled by religious imperatives and justifications rather than abstract political ideologies. Thus, in contrast to the intelligible demands of the more familiar, predominantly secular terrorist groups of the past who mostly claimed credit for and explained their violent acts, some of the most heinous and lethal attacks perpetrated by terrorists over the previous two decades – primarily those directed against innocent civilians specifically and therefore designed to inflict the maximum casualties possible – have gone unclaimed. By maintaining their anonymity, terrorists may believe that they are able to capitalize further on the fear and alarm intrinsically generated by their violence [. . .].[6]

Organisational changes bear directly upon the style and location of terrorist activity one would expect. Walter Laqueur (2004) has no doubt that this is important both for those who contemplate carrying out terrorist activity and certainly for those responsible for countering such activity:

The smaller the group, the more difficult it is to trace and penetrate, the more far-fetched and strange its motivation and ideology is likely to be. Very small groups of people do not aim at conducting propaganda, building up political mass movements, and seizing power, they aim at destruction in the hope that out of the ruins of what they have destroyed a better world will emerge or at least one more in line with their ideology. Furthermore, society has become far more vulnerable than it has ever been in the past as the result of urbanisation and technological progress. Not only have the arms become far more lethal, the targets have become so much softer.

Lastly, prospects have greatly increased for the use of terrorism as substitute warfare precisely because old-fashioned, conventional warfare has become much more risky and expensive; there is the temptation to inflict harm on an enemy through the use of substitutes. Such practices are based on the hope that state-sponsored terrorism will be difficult to prove conclusively. These assumptions are almost certainly mistaken, but the temptation will still be great and miscalculations may lead precisely to what the initiators wanted to avoid – regular warfare, possibly with the use of weapons of mass destruction.

The world is passing at present through a transitional period as far as the weapons of terrorism are concerned, the damage that is caused, and also its basic strategies. The form of terrorism present at the present time is religious or nationalist in inspiration, or a mixture of the two, and the weapons used are usually improved versions of conventional weapons, more effective explosives, missiles and so on. Suicide terrorism has made terrorism both more indiscriminate and more deadly. But at the same time the search has been under way for non-conventional weapons which might kill not thousands but possibly hundreds of thousands. And while there is every reason to believe that jihad and similar doctrines will persist for a long time to come, there are on the political horizon a great many other potential sources of terrorist motivation. At the same time the danger of escalation has greatly increased, terrorist provocation turning into a full-scale war.[7]

Changes in approach, in style and in organisational arrangements must surely be taken into account when trying to predict or calculate the extent of occurrence of terrorism.

TERRORISM: LOCATION

Locational descriptions of terrorist activity are legion. The 16 case studies in this Reader will give some idea of the width of spread, and of the diversity of approach and technique. There are 'hot spots' readily in flame, there are places where tension and turbulence may at any time engender explosion, and there are zones of relative calm where violence is either under control temporarily or perhaps where negotiations are taking place. As pointed out above, it seems useless to generalise.

Nor is it helpful to place hope in prediction. Middle Eastern states are clearly volatile in nature and susceptible to the ingenuity and malevolence of al-Qaida. Of late, there is evidence that terrorists-in-training are finding remote villages in the Balkans as safe places for equipping and operational planning. Much of Latin America is suffering narco-terrorism, where the mafia drug barons are literally 'calling the shots'. So many countries in that region – Bolivia, Venezuela, Uruguay, Brazil, Argentina, Chile, Peru – have had to cope with a transition from rural guerrilla warfare to 'urban terror', notoriously difficult to control where people struggle for existence.

Currently, there is something of a transition to ordered calm in Spain and Northern Ireland. Otherwise, apart from the levelled hostility to government of the Tamil Tigers in Sri Lanka there are those countries where peaceful progress can never be assured, often on account of the liberationist, separatist preferences of those whom governments regard as deviationists ready to make trouble.

Canada, Turkey, Uzbekistan, Kazakhstan, Chechnya, the Philippines, Indonesia, Croatia, Puerto Rico, Kashmir, Somalia and South Yemen all have violence as the end product of disaffiliation by strident minorities. At times an incident or two may provide a detonator, where public meetings may launch 'a people's war', or may accompany actual turmoil with such a slogan as 'kill one to scare a thousand' (originally Kurdish and heard loudly in Ankara). Clearly, behind terrorists in the making are the sympathisers. They range from journalists to ex-soldiers, ousted politicians, land-less peasants, town dwellers confined in squalor, rival ethnic minorities and religious fanatics. Their allegiance may be that of the crowd justifying damage and disorder. They are not likely to be invisible. More shadowy influences on a violent outcome lurk in the shadows. They are the fundraisers and the fund providers. They are particularly influential on the Tamil separatism in Sri Lanka and above all in endow-ing the strength of Islamic 'togetherness' (which, of course, does not necessarily result in violence). Terrorist funding is something David Whittaker (2007) considers:

Added to the groundswell of public sympathy for standing firm against injustice and disbelief, there is also a readiness to meet financial costs. Both in the Muslim world and among Muslim communities in the West there is massive fundraising by political, social, educational and charitable groups and projects. Institutions and individuals in such countries as Saudi Arabia, Pakistan, Iran, Kuwait, Bahrain, Sudan are able to donate immense sums to what they innocently regard as support of their religion and their culture. Most of them, particularly those living in communities in non-Arab land, would be horrified if this money were seen to be siphoned off to a front organisation to fund, however, indirectly, violent political activity or terrorism. It is more likely (according to United States State Department investigators) that certain terrorist networks find ways of hiding behind the legitimate activities of charities and then divert or launder some of the proceeds. Some financial support of terrorism does come from the production and handling of narcotics, above all in Afghanistan and Pakistan, otherwise, there is not a large amount of corruption or crime.[8]

Finally, we return to the issue of change as being a prime factor in any measurement of the incidence and scale of terrorism. Martha Crenshaw (1995) has this very much in mind:

The causes and effects of terrorism are comprehensible only in terms of political conflicts in specific historical time period. There are commonalities among instances of terrorism, but each case is unique. Terrorism remains unpredictable in part because its multiple contexts are dynamic. Governments and challengers respond differently to similar circumstances. Original conditions change as a result of terror-ism. Even the meaning of the term changes as politics and society change [. . .].[9]

TERRORIST ORGANISATION

Earlier chapters have shown that for the most part terrorist activity is the work of organised groups, some simple, perhaps of a fleeting nature, others more complex and long-lasting. The Terrorist Research Center in the United States published, in December 1998, a note about the main points of terrorist organisation:

Organizational details are situation-specific. There are, however, a few general organizational principles. Because terrorists must operate in a hostile environment, security is their primary concern. Security is best served by a cellular structure in which members do not know and cannot identify more than a few of their colleagues in the event of capture or defection. Defection is rare in most groups; defectors or even dissenters are frequently killed or maimed. Yet, terrorists are not immune to human weaknesses. Unless they are united by a charismatic leader, terrorists are affected by group dynamics that produce both problems and opportunities for security forces. Opportunities arise because internal dissension causes security leaks; problems arise because operational patterns may change as different factions prevail.

Terrorist groups that are not supported by a government usually create a support structure of sympathizers and people who have been coerced into helping them. The support structure may comprise active and passive members. It furnishes the active terrorists with logistic support, intelligence, dissemination of propaganda, recruiting, and money.

Terrorist recruitment and training are, predictably, security-sensitive. Among groups that are not ethnic-based, the usual sources of recruits are high school and college students who show commitment to the cause. Ethnically based terrorist groups recruit new members personally known to them, people whose backgrounds are known and who often have family ties to the organization. Intelligence penetration of organizations recruited in this way is extremely difficult.

Terrorist training varies considerably. Those with military experience or who have received prolonged training at sophisticated facilities are the equals of most state security forces. At the other end of the spectrum are 'throw away' operatives who get little more than inspirational talks before being activated. Typical training includes instruction in the use of small arms and explosives along with intelligence collection and indoctrination in the group's cause.

Contemporary terrorist actions include the traditional assassinations, bombings, arson, hostage-taking, hijacking, kidnapping, seizure and occupation of a building, attacks on a facility, sabotage, and perpetration of hoaxes. New categories of operations include ecological terrorism and the still largely potential 'high-tech' terrorism using nuclear, biological, and chemical (NBC) weapons and materials. Target selection considerations are equally diverse but include the target's value in terms of its contribution to group goals, its accessibility given group capabilities, and the purpose of the attack, such as to gain attention, collect resources, eliminate a threat, or demonstrate a capability. All these factors are reflected in the group's organization and training.[10]

CONTEMPORARY TERRORIST GROUPS

It is not easy to compile a list of terrorist groups that are active today. The tally worldwide is never a static one. There are high-profile organisations with dynamic leaders and enterprising and consistent strategies. Many of these have been 'in business' for many years and the counter-terrorist institutions know them well. There are small organisations with shifts in management, numbers, motives and political action. Their goals and intentions may be difficult to discern. This list is derived from the International Policy Institute for Counter-terrorism, Herzliya, Israel. Published in October 2006, it is far from comprehensive, but it does show contemporary terrorism as both diverse and far-flung and is a useful accompaniment to the discussion in Chapter 3 earlier. This list gives organisational names and national affiliation or locales.

Organisation	*National affiliation (or locale)*
Abu Sayyaf Group	Philippines
Al-Gama'a al-Islamiyya	Egypt
Al-Qaeda	Afghanistan
Al-Takfir W'al Hijra	unknown
Ansar Al-Islam	Iraq
Armata Corsa	France
Armed Islamic Group	Algeria
Aum Shinrikyo	Japan
Basque Homeland and Freedom	Spain
Chukaku-Ha	Japan
Democratic Front for the Liberation of Palestine	Palestine
Fatah – Revolutionary Council	Lebanon
Fatah Tanzim	Palestine
Force 17	Palestine
Great East Islamic Raiders Front (IBDA-C)	Turkey
Hamas	Palestine
Harakat ul-Mujahedin	Pakistan
Hizballah	Lebanon
Hizb-ul Mujehideen	Pakistan
Irish Republican Army	Northern Ireland
Jamaat ul-Fuqra	Pakistan
Japanese Red Army	Japan
Jihad Group	Egypt
Kach and Kahane Chai	Israel
Kurdistan Workers' Party	Turkey
Lashkar-e-Toiba	Pakistan
Lautaro Youth Movement	Chile
Liberation Tigers of Tamil Eelam	Sri Lanka
Loyalist Volunteer Force	Northern Ireland
Manuel Rodriquez Patriotic Front	Chile
Martyrs of al-Aqsa	Palestine
Moranzanist Patriotic Front	Honduras
Moro Islamic Liberation Front	Philippines
Mujahedin-e Khalq Organization (MEK)	Iran
National Liberation Army Colombia	Colombia
National Liberation Front of Corsica	France

(cont. on p. 42)

USA

Since 11 September at 'war' with terrorism. Rigorous legislation, increased defence spending, despatch of military units overseas. Thousands of illegal immigrants rounded up, detained, deported.

UK

The government's Anti-terrorism, Crime and Security Acts allow internment without trial. Suspends obligations under the European Convention on Human Rights. No other European country has taken such a drastic step.

Israeli/Palestinian territories

Could the events of 11 September provide the brutal shock to dislodge all sides from their cycle of violence? Now that hope fades.

Arab world

All Arab states formally condemned the 11 September attacks though most criticised the ensuing Afghanistan war.

Russia

A fundamental shift in foreign policy moves Russia closer to the US with far-reaching implications for the West.

China

US-China relations much improved now that Washington has a new enemy.

North Korea

Included in Bush's 'axis of evil' despite their condemning terrorism. Accused of preparing mass-destruction weapons. North-south peace process now set back.

Afghanistan

Fierce war against Taliban since 2001. Coalition force.

South-East Asia

Several governments using war on terror as excuse to crack down on internal dissenters, e.g. US 'hit squads' active against Philippine rebels.

India/Pakistan

India moves against own 'terrorists' in Kashmir and introduces draconian anti-terrorist laws. Pakistan rewarded with US aid for endorsing US Afghan bombing. India demands end to covert support of Islamic militants.

Iraq/Iran

Iraq named in 'axis of evil' and so in firing line. Iran opposed both bin Laden and Taliban but lumping with Iraq and North Korea probably strengthened position of hardliners opposing rapprochement with the West.

Europe

US exclusion of NATO from the Afghan war reinforces existing anxiety about US unilateralism; threats against Iraq intensify those fears.

South and Central America

Increased political instability since 11 September – Argentina's riots, civil unrest in Venezuela, worsened civil war in Colombia.

Key

al-Qaida arrests

Latin America, Dubai, Russia, Kenya, Canada, Somalia, Spain, Belgium, France, India, Pakistan, Philippines, Singapore, US, Egypt, Iran, UK, Malaysia, Italy, The Netherlands, Germany, Turkey, Afghanistan

Conflict related to 11 September

Sudan, Kashmir, Philippines, Indonesia, Yemen

Bush's 'Axis of evil' countries

Iran, Iraq, North Korea

Nestor Paz Zamora Commission (CNPZ)	Bolivia
New People's Army	Philippines
Palestine Liberation Front	Iraq
Palestinian Islamic Jihad	Palestine
Party of Democratic Kampuchea	Cambodia
Popular Front for the Liberation of Palestine	Palestine
Popular Front for the Liberation of Palestine – General Command	Palestine
Popular Struggle Front	Syria
Qa'idat Al-Jihad Fi Bilad Al-Rafidain	Iraq
Qibla and People Against Gangsterism and Drugs	South Africa
Real IRA	Northern Ireland
Red Army Faction	Germany
Red Brigades	Italy
Revolutionary Armed Forces of Colombia	Colombia
Revolutionary Organization 17 November	Greece
Revolutionary People's Liberation Party/Front	Turkey
Revolutionary People's Struggle	Greece
Sendero Luminoso	Peru
Sipah-e-Sahaba Pakistan	Pakistan
Tupac Amaru Revolutionary Movement	Peru
United Self-Defense Forces of Colombia	Colombia

STATE-SPONSORED TERRORISM

This note is also from the same Israeli institute and was published in December 1999.

For many years, terrorism was perceived as a contest between two sides: on the one hand, a group of people or an organization, and on the other, a sovereign state. However, during the course of the second half of the twentieth century, various countries began to use terrorist organizations to promote state interests in the international domain. In some cases, states have established 'puppet' terrorist organizations, whose purpose is to act on behalf of the sponsoring state, to further the interests of the state, and to represent its positions in domestic or regional fronts. In other cases, states sponsor existing organizations, on the basis of mutual interests.

The patron state provides its beneficiary terrorist organization with political support, financial assistance, and the sponsorship necessary to maintain and expand its struggle. The patron uses the beneficiary to perpetrate acts of terrorism as a means of spreading the former's ideology throughout the world, or in some cases, the patron ultimately expects the beneficiary to gain control of the state in which it resides or impart its ideology to broad sections of the general public.

State-sponsored terrorism can achieve strategic ends where the use of conventional armed forces is not practical or effective. The high costs of modern warfare, and concern about nonconventional escalation, as well as the danger of defeat and the unwillingness to appear as the aggressor, have turned terrorism into an efficient, convenient, and generally discrete weapon for attaining state interests in the international realm.[11]

States generally acknowledged to be sponsors of international terrorist activity are Iran, Iraq, Lebanon, Sudan and Syria.

POSTSCRIPT

In late May 2007 there occurred in regard to state-sponsored terrorism a most interesting and innovatory development. The International Criminal Court Chief Prosecutor formally accused Libya's leader Muammar Gaddafi, his son and his brother-in-law of crimes against humanity and called for the arrest of these three. Their state-sponsored terrorism had orchestrated a campaign of mass murder against Libyan pro-democracy protestors. The brother-in-law, Abdullah Senussi, was a Libyan intelligence chief, an 'executioner' who masterminded mass arrests and torture, and was almost certainly in league with the terrorists who had carried out incidents in Britain and France. The ICC has no police force to carry out arrest warrants by way of enforcement. It would be for Libya to hand over the accused to the ICC for trial. That is not a very certain prospect. As Arab countries are in the thick of a popular, pro-democracy Awakening met by concerted repression many now are asking: 'Are not rulers in, say, Syria and Bahrain and Yemen, similarly indictable for terrorising their own people?'

PART TWO

Sixteen terrorism case studies

E ACH OF THE FOLLOWING case studies is titled under the name of the host country. There is a final chapter by way of conclusion.

Jihad: mission and campaigning

'JIHAD: MISSION AND CAMPAIGNING' is the first of 16 case studies in this Reader. It represents a pattern of violence and desperation that the whole world has been talking about since the autumn of 2001. As the smoke cleared away from the ruins of New York's World Trade Center in September 2001, government investigation identified with increasing confidence three elements having some responsibility for that outrage and for a chain of terrorist atrocities directed mainly at the United States. The three were a terrorist enterprise – al-Qaida (al-Qaeda), the al-Qaida leader Osama bin Laden and a fundamentalist regime known as the Taliban in Afghanistan. The coming together of these three has raised the profile of international terrorism. Politicians and the media are employing a scenario starkly put into such terms as a 'universalist jihad', 'a global conspiracy' and 'This Means War', and these are held to justify a forceful response from a grand coalition.

JIHAD AND JIHADISM

Broad brush discussion in the media almost every day borrows the Muslim term *jihad,* and talks of it and its consequence adopting the term *jihadism*. Commonly, jihad is used to denote personal and collective striving of some Islamic followers to prosecute a holy war against the Infidel. Religious logic justifies a fateful, relentless struggle where violence (victims call it terrorism) is inescapable. Generally, jihadist zeal is considered theologically derived where some degree of nationalist fervour is combined in an outward drive part-offensive, part-defensive. Understood, it seems, is an individual and brotherly duty to fight and defend in God's cause and as such it may all too easily turn into a global mission.

Breadth in discussion invariably neglects significant specifics and leads to misinterpretation. It is best to refer to expert scholars. Jarret M. Brachman in her *Global Jihadism Theory and Practice* (2009) clarifies things most usefully:[1]

Jihadismis a clumsy and controversial term. It refers to the peripheral current of extremist Islamic thought whose adherents demand the use of violence in order to oust non-Islamic influence from traditionally Muslim lands en route to establishing true Islamic governance in accordance with *Sharia,* or God's law. The expression's most significant limitation is that it contains the work *Jihad,* which is an important religious concept in Islam. For much of the Islamic world, *Jihad* simply refers to the internal spiritual campaign that one wages with oneself. Although not one of the five key Pillars of Islam it is considered by most Muslims to be a critical element of living a pious life. It can also refer to the act of physically waging warfare, most commonly in defence of Islam.[2]

The word *Jihadism,* on the other hand, is a modern neologism. It is not native to Islamic history and, therefore, its use has little religious significance to Muslims. Those who employ the term do so out of convenience because, despite its inherent problems, the word communicates a vital point, namely, that al-Qaeda and groups like it are distinguished from other Muslims by their singular focus on the violent side of the Jihad concept. In recent years the Jihadism label has been validated as the least bad option across the Arabic speaking world, appearing throughout Arab television and print media. It has also grown in appeal across the world's counter-terrorism community, if only because it is a quick, albeit problematic way to refer to Sunni Muslims who use violence in order to pursue their universalistic political agendas.[3]

Brachman helps answer questions which are unsettling among those facing jihadist violence in the shape of terrorism:

Now the question is: how can the Jihadist movement continue to conduct massive terrorist attacks worldwide in the midst of a global war against it and in an era when billions of dollars are being poured into homeland security, intelligence and law enforcement efforts that are meant to defend against such atrocities? There are three interrelated reasons for the Jihadist movement? endurance in the face of what seems overwhelming pressure to defeat them: first, the Jihadist message provides a universal rallying call that resonates locally but applies globally; second, Jihadists are continuously empowering one another with the new skills and knowledge that they need to counter the security efforts that are being launched against them; and third, America's invasion and subsequent destabilisation of Iraq have provided an proving-ground for the perfection of insurgency and terrorist operations.[4]

Global Jihadism is global in almost every sense. It inspires a sense of mission among the mujahedeen, holy warriors of Islam, inciting them in compliance with God's order to go out and conduct an unrelenting struggle that may even end in suicide (that is, martyrdom). Their campaigning readiness is authorised in an edict, the fatwa. Behind the frontliners will be the authorisation and support of a radical intellegentia elaborating ideology rhetoric, using wide-spanning radio and television channels, Internet websites and videos. This movement uses computer sophistry, packaged terrorism manuals and instruction kits, regional training schools recruit and go on to consolidate skills in man-and-situation management and explosives expertness. Jihadism operates under the cover of safe-houses in Afghanistan, Pakistan, Iraq, India and the Arabian Peninsular and, most clandestinely in the United States, Canada, the United Kingdom and here and there in mainland Europe.

In sum, Jihadism in the contemporary world is held to be the mercurial challenge of a politico-religious mission carrying out a campaign absolutely violent in action. Pre-eminent is the unholy alliance of al-Qaeda, Osama bin Laden and the Taliban.

THE UNHOLY ALLIANCE – AL-QAIDA

The story of al-Qaida is long and complex. Something of its beginnings and later development is described by Paul L. Williams (2002), a former consultant on international terrorism to the Federal Bureau of Investigation:

In 1979, the year Soviet troops invaded Afghanistan, Abdullah Azzam, a Palestinian member of the (Muslim) Brotherhood, established a recruiting office called Maktah al-Khidamat (the Office of Services) to recruit young Muslims for the Afghan front. This office, in time, would be transformed into the terrorist group known as Al Qaeda [sic] (the Base).

One of the young recruits was a Saudi millionaire, Osama bin Laden, a Wahabist. Bin Laden was enthusiastic about the war effort and agreed to fund the establishment of branches of the Office of Services throughout the world, Europe and the United States included.[5] [. . .]

Azzam travelled throughout the Middle East, the United Kingdom, and the United States to raise money and recruits for the Afghan cause, while bin Laden provided financial support, handled military matters, and brought to Afghanistan from around the world experts in guerrilla warfare, sabotage, and covert operations.

Within a year thousands of volunteers were training in bin Laden's boot camp in Peshawar. Most (more than 5,000) came from bin Laden's native Saudi Arabia. Others came from Algeria (3,000), Egypt (2,000) and thousands more from other Muslim countries such as Yemen, Pakistan and Sudan. A major function of the Office of Services was to prevent outbursts of violence between the Sunni and the Shi'a volunteers and to keep the focus of the recruits on the jihad and the teachings of the Koran.[6] [. . .]

In 1988, a year before the Soviet withdrawal from Afghanistan, bin Laden and the Egyptian terrorists formed Al Qaeda. They began to move ahead with their plans. They funnelled huge sums into creating an infrastructure of what was to serve as the base for their *jihad* against the apostate Muslim governments, Israel and the United States. They represented a small band of believers, but they had the potential to accomplish their mission. They had received training in sophisticated weapons. They had an arsenal of high-tech weapons, including Stinger anti-aircraft missiles. They had financial resources through bin Laden's personal fortune, contributions to charitable organizations, and the lucrative drug trade in Afghanistan, with laboratories to refine heroin. The ruling Taliban, enforcers of the most extreme and repressive form of fundamentalist Islam, became Al Qaeda's private militia. Al Qaeda became, in effect, the shadow government of a sovereign state. The madrasahs turned out students steeped in the teachings of Islam and hatred of the West. The training camps transformed those chosen to fight the jihad into skilled and disciplined terrorists.

An office that had been used to support the Afghan war effort had become a highly financed and structured terrorist organisation.[7]

A detailed discussion of al-Qaida and of its relationship with the United States is provided by David Whittaker (2002):

Although Afghans had received substantial United States military aid and money from Saudi Arabia, bin Laden and his battle-hardened associates soon concluded that they must fight on all fronts, against Communism, capitalist countries such as the United States, their former backer, corrupt Arab regimes, and expansionist Israel. It was a potent, demonic mixture of an ultra-narrow religious creed, twisted politics, and a well-armed adventurous band. Highly-trained Afghan Veterans began to show up wherever there was an Islamic struggle in Bosnia, Kosovo, Chechnya, Algeria, Somalia, and Sudan.

United States intervention in the Gulf War of 1991–2 put them into the front rank of bin Laden's enmity. They had sent 20,000 of their infidel troops to sacred cities in Saudi Arabia. American dollars had seduced Arab monarchs. It was vital to defend Islam against a 'Christian' crusade (even though the American advance was a rather materialist one). It was a Muslim duty to do away with those who sinned against the Muslim world and this would give Islamic religion and teaching extra power. It was necessary to take the battle right across to America.

On 12 October 1996 bin Laden declared a *jihad* against the United States and two years later put his name to a *fatwa*, a decree, to all Muslims to kill 'Americans and their civilian and military allies to be carried out in which ever country they are'. It was in an interview with TIME magazine in 1999 that he made no secret of intensifying a wish to obtain non-conventional weapons. 'Acquiring weapons for the defense of Muslims is a religious duty. And if I seek to acquire these weapons, I am carrying out a duty. It would be a sin for Muslims not to try to possess the weapons that would prevent the infidels from inflicting harm on Muslims'. [. . .]

With al-Qaida, of course, there could be no compromise. Agents of the CIA now and then despatched snatch squads to extricate bin Laden from his supposed cave bunker in the Hindu Kush mountains. President Clinton, in 1996, signed an Anti-Terrorism Act authorising the freezing of terrorist assets. Every possible United States device was used to search for and punish al-Qaida, for an attack on United States soldiers in Somalia in October 1993 which killed 18, in 1998 for their bombing of two United States embassies in Kenya and Tanzania when 224 people died, and, once more, for an attack on the US warship, USS Cole in Aden when 17 of the crew perished. The despatch towards Kabul of seventy Cruise missiles and a five million dollar reward for bin Laden's head did not achieve anything other than provoke bin Laden to issue another *fatwa* placing upon all Muslims the duty of killing all Americans and their allies. Round-the-clock surveillance of Afghanistan was able to locate al-Qaida terrorist training camps for war veterans and fundamentalist converts, as well as arms stores and communication centres. Ultimatums went from Washington to the mullahs in Kabul warning them that they would be held responsible for aggression against American citizens by terrorists in Afghanistan. These had little effect. Polite replies were despatched westwards saying that, of course, Islamic hospitality would never permit its 'guests' to be extradited.[8]

THE 'TAKING-OUT' OF TERRORISTS

When an aggrieved United States, in 2001, went to war against international terror-ism and against the Taliban as hosts of terrorists, the debate raged internationally, according to Whittaker. On all sides, questions were asked (and not always authoritatively answered):

Was a general battle strike, hopefully pinpointing the whereabouts of just one group of terrorists, the most effective way of countering an estimated fifty to sixty terrorist organisations, diverse in nature and motivation and locale? It was true that al-Qaida personnel were supposed to be at the core of many of these groups but the contexts in which they operated were so different. Was bombing the religious Taliban the best approach to 'taking out' the terrorists they harboured? In sponsoring a coalition, military and political, against a Muslim country (Afghanistan), was President George Bush calling for a contest with Islam in general? Many Muslim states like Iran, Saudi Arabia, and Egypt, were unhappy about this believing that the people of the 'umman', the Islamic world community, should stand by Afghanistan, attacked in the name of a move against terrorism. There were Muslims in Indonesia, the Philippines, and Malaysia who had to put up with sporadic terrorist activity at home and who now began to fear the prospect of United States counter-action fanning out into South East Asia as well as the Middle East.[9]

After the horrendous strike against Manhattan and a consequent pounding of Afghanistan by the United States Air Force, al-Qaida and its satellites are thought to be still potent in perhaps 50 or so countries. The possibilities of further, well-planned terrorist action cannot be ruled out. The danger, also, is long term, for the attacks against New York and the embassies in East Africa are reckoned to have been four to five years in preparation. The problem is discussed by Whittaker:

Bin Laden's al-Qaida remains a formidable world menace very much because it has tapped into the emotive springs of fundamental religious belief and linked them with other things that are fundamental in a different sense, that is, political imperatives that are coloured by hunger for power and hunger for food. A 'believing community' can easily become an unrestrained and violent force, not necessarily in general, but it may condone violence to achieve basic objectives. Al-Qaida is a well-organised and highly secretive terrorist network. Bin Laden's executive circle, the Shura, includes a dozen aides and representatives of the network in other lands, all experienced in mounting a jihad. There are a number of committees, for instance, a military one in charge of training, arms procurement, and terrorist strategies, a financial one whose resources are reputedly awash with vast proceeds from heroin and opium dealing, and a media one which has impressive technology and media competence. All these functionaries take an oath of allegiance. It has been suggested that al-Qaida is not a hierarchical structure but a loose, rambling one, a 'spaghetti' type of organisation. Whatever its nature there is no doubt about its effectiveness. Apart from the military vanguard, al-Qaida draws strength from a web of commercial undertakings in various parts of the Middle East. There are companies trading in import-export, currency, chemicals, and explosives. Roads and bridges and housing schemes are constructed by al-Qaida engineers. There are swathes of al-Qaida land, again in several countries, growing sesame, corn, peanuts, and narcotic crops. This brand of international terrorism has a very substantial and commercial foundation.[10]

In the view of Paul Wilkinson (2001) Al-Qaida and its leader, bin Laden, mark a new form of terrorist movement that is a more dangerous form of sub-state terrorism than we have seen before:

It is a genuinely transnational organisation with multinational membership with the finances and support networks that, as far as we can understand, are independent of states. Undoubtedly there are many dormant cells, preparative cells, and sleepers still undiscovered and it is important to remember whatever happens on the military front in Afghanistan, that that network still remains to be discovered and eradicated.[11]

THE UNHOLY ALLIANCE – OSAMA BIN LADEN

It is interesting to look at the persona of Osama bin Laden in some detail. Here is somebody universally demonised as arch-instigator of violent atrocities planned and executed as a deliberate threat to American interests. Nothing perhaps is entirely straightforward in understanding bin Laden's origins, career and likely future activities. He has been known to Western intelligence sources for some years but only since 2000 has he emerged as a figure, vilified in the media and in public discussion around the world.

   Yossef Bodansky (2001), director of the United States Congress Task Force on Terrorism and Unconventional Warfare, has compiled a comprehensive study of bin Laden, not only as 'The Man Who Declared War on America' but as 'part of a dynamic, political intrigue, involving the heads of state of many countries'. Bin Laden, his ideological militancy forged during the Afghan war against the Soviet Union, has an appeal that resonates throughout the Muslim world and one that helps recruit terrorists worldwide. The origins of this global hate-figure and the makings of a terrorist are surveyed by Bodansky:

Now in his mid-fifties, a university graduate with computer skills, Osama bin Laden lives with his four wives and some fifteen children in a small cave in eastern

Afghanistan. They have no running water and only a rudimentary heating system against the extreme cold of winter. Bin Laden is always on guard against assassins, commando raids and air strikes. Had he followed the path chosen for him by his father, bin Laden could have been a respected building contractor in Saudi Arabia and a billionaire in his own right. Instead he freely elected to abandon the life of affluence and commit himself to waging a *jihad* under extremely hard conditions.

Osama bin Laden is not the only Islamist who has abandoned a good career and comfortable lifestyle in order to wage a *jihad*. Dr Ayman al-Zawahiri – bin Laden's right-hand man – now in his late forties, could have been one of Egypt's leading pediatricians but gave up a promising career and affluence to fight the Egyptian government. He then refused political asylum in Western Europe (with a generous stipend) and ended up living in eastern Afghanistan not far from bin Laden.

Although bin Laden and Zawahiri are the most notorious Islamist terrorists, there are hundreds like them. These dedicated commanders in turn lead thousands of terrorists in a relentless and uncompromising holy war against the United States and the West as a whole. The bombings of the US embassies in Kenya and Tanzania in 1998 were the latest but by far not the last shots in this rapidly escalating war of terrorism. What makes these individuals – the leaders and symbols of the new Islamist upsurge – commit themselves to this kind of war?

The rise of the new radical Islamist elite is a recent phenomenon in the developing world. These leaders, from the affluent and privileged segment of society, are highly educated and relatively Westernized. They are not the underprivileged, impoverished, and embittered isolates who usually constitute the pool that breeds terrorists and radicals. These Islamist terrorist leaders are different from the typical European middle-class revolutionaries and terrorists – from the anarchists of the nineteenth century to the Communist revolutionaries of the twentieth century – because the Islamists have become popular leaders of the underprivileged masses, while the European terrorists remained isolated from a generally hostile population. Only Ernesto 'Che' Guevara – the Argentinian doctor turned revolutionary fighter of the early 1960s – came close to being the kind of populist leader these Islamists use.

To understand these Islamist leaders – particularly Osama bin Laden – one needs to understand their break with the past, their motivation, the fire in their veins, and the depth of their hatred of the United States and what it stands for.[12]

Bodansky sees these leaders as the product of the tumultuous 1970s and 1980s. Key events in the Middle East have engendered their volatile radicalism – the oil boom of the 1970s, the revolutionary triumph in Iran, and the cause of defending Islam occasioned by the Soviet assault on Afghanistan. Bin Laden's origins and early education were conventional at the outset:

Osama bin Muhammed bin Laden was born in the city of Riyadh, Saudi Arabia, probably in 1957. At the time, his father Muhammed bin Laden was a small-time builder and contractor who had arrived from Yemen in search of employment. Osama was one of numerous siblings – his father had more than fifty children from several wives. Muhammed bin Laden was conscientious about education and advancement in life and tried to provide his children with proper schooling. [. . .]

The oil boom of the 1970s changed Muhammed bin Laden's fortunes [. . .] During the 1970s, the bin Laden company was involved in the construction of roads, buildings, mosques, airports, and the entire infrastructure of many of the Arab countries of the Persian Gulf.[13]

Osama was destined to follow in his father's footsteps as an executive of a now very prosperous large construction enterprise. He went to Jedda to high school and on to management and economics studies at the university there. For Bodansky, Jedda was a strong formative influence:

In Jedda, Osama bin Laden was constantly exposed to the often contradictory trends influencing Saudi society at the time [. . .] The wealth and worldly character of Jedda also transformed it into a shelter for Islamist intellectuals persecuted throughout the Muslim world [. . .] the best experts and preachers were sheltered in the universities and mosques [. . .] They addressed the growing doubts of the Saudi youth. Their message to the confused was simple and unequivocal – only an absolute and unconditional return to the fold of conservative Islamism could protect the Muslim world from the inherent dangers and sins of the West.[14]

Clearly, bin Laden was no ordinary youth. Fired by both religious orthodoxy and the shaping of political radicalism, he was ready to move against those who would challenge the Muslim world. His opportunity, according to Bodansky, came in the last days of 1979, when Red Army divisions were launched against Afghanistan to buttress a puppet government, a regime that the Kremlin saw as Communist and secular:

Within a few days after the Soviet invasion bin Laden, who was genuinely and selflessly committed to the cause of all-Islamic solidarity, went to Pakistan to assist the Afghan mujahideen. On arrival bin Laden was appalled by the chaos in Pakistan and the lack of Arab unity and devoted himself to political and organisational work, establishing a recruitment drive that over the next few years would funnel thousands of Arab fighters from the Gulf States to the Afghan resistance.[15] [. . .]

By the mid-1980s bin Laden saw that his real calling lay on the jihad battlefield, where he gained a reputation as a courageous and resourceful commander [. . .] Throughout the 1980s Osama bin Laden maintained close relations with the Saudi ruling elite and particularly Saudi intelligence [. . .] In 1989 Osama bin Laden returned to Saudi Arabia a hero.[16]

BUILDING A TERRORIST GROUP

Then, in August 1990, Iraq invaded Kuwait. Saudi Arabia gave Washington and its allies logistical support, allowing them permanent bases in Riyadh and other places. Bin Laden was outraged at this heretical threat to the sacred heart of Islam. Nevertheless, the soldier returned to Sudan to resume his business career and, in

Bodansky's opinion, to build financial resources and Muslim collaboration in the furtherance of Islamic defence:

By the mid-1990s, relying on family connections, and benefactors from his days in Afghanistan, Osama bin Laden completed the organisation of a comprehensive and in essence detection-proof financial system in support of the high-quality terrorist networks his closest friend, Ayman al-Zawahiri, was organising in Europe [. . .] Meanwhile Osama bin Laden organised yet another, completely separate, financial system to push funds to Islamist terrorists, particularly those operating in the West under quasi-legal status.[17]

Somalia was collapsing in internecine violence in 1992–3 and Washington, in conjunction with the United Nations, felt bound to intervene. Somalian insurgents were aided by bin Laden's trained fighters from Ethiopia, Eritrea, Kenya and Uganda. US–UN forces were compelled to give ground to the ferocity of guerrilla campaigning. The West withdrew in 1994, chastened certainly, but now quite sure that their foes represented the cutting edge of what they soon christened Terrorism Incorporated. Control was centred on the Saudi-born leader. Bodansky reckons that bin Laden was now established as Public Enemy Number One and as the lynchpin of international terrorism:

For Osama bin Laden and his comrades in arms, the next year or so would be a crucial time of reorganizing and building up their forces. The Islamists, who had emerged on the world scene as a major anti-American and anti-Westernization force, now had to regroup and prepare for the next round of confrontation. At the top of the list, they needed to lay the foundations for a worldwide infrastructure.[18] [. . .]

Bodansky and others have tracked something of the tremendous spread of bin Laden's terrorist network, where al-Qaida is the core and spearhead. Training centres, activist squads, financial centres and data-dissemination systems have been located in most parts of the Balkans, the Middle East, Cyprus, Chechnya, Pakistan, India, the Philippines, Latin America, and even Germany, Canada, California and London. Outside intelligence has confirmed explicit terrorist strategies, to create an 'environment of terror' and to launch a 'series of spectacular operations'. The world has seen a chain of horrific incidents in recent years – the attempted assassination of Egypt's President Mubarak in June 1995, and the bombings of a United States Army training centre in Riyadh, Saudi Arabia, and of the Egyptian embassy in Islamabad six months later. Careful reconnaissance and meticulous planning enabled bin Laden's al-Qaida to demolish US embassies in Nairobi and Dar es-Salaam with heavy loss of life in 1998. Bin Laden's so-called Declaration of War in 1996 had targeted the United States and Britain and only prompt intelligence then foiled major attacks.

The case against al-Qaida and Osama bin Laden has lengthened and broadened since the massive attack on New York and Washington in September 2001. It was in October 2001 that the United States and British governments published what were styled dossiers of evidence. Some of the detail is tantalisingly circumstantial but there is enough there to pin responsibility upon perpetrators commissioned by bin Laden. Briefly, the identities and methods used by the aircraft hijackers on this occasion have been firmly established. Two things are quite certain. First, there remains a potential threat of terrorist attacks on Western cities and installations and, of course, their specificity cannot be predicted. Second, the essence of the threat from al-Qaida and bin Laden is that it is not time-bound – together these important components of an unholy alliance will outlast the demise of the master-terrorist.

Particularly in the United States and in Europe, al-Qaida is the reputed shadow behind more terrorist outrages. Among security agencies in Europe, the malevolence of the group is currently seen as visible in three respects. First, there is the influenced radicalisation, mainly, of young Muslims, and the potential threat therein. Second, and going rather further, there are the 'sleeper cells' of already committed terrorists who may be of a domestic variety rather than foreign imports. Third, and a relatively new term, there is the 'blowback' of incoming seasoned terrorist veterans moving westwards out of the training grounds in the Middle East. In this multiplicity it seems obvious that al-Qaida is more of a movement than an organisation and its reach and arsenal of techniques are unquestionably vast. Equally difficult to quantify is its size and the identity of a corps of 'operators'. Given, though, the lack of 'specifics', it appears virtually certain that this is a movement at the moment unquenchable and in the broadest sense responsible for incidents as far afield as India, Indonesia, Saudi Arabia, Turkey, Spain's Madrid, Egypt and Qatar. Whatever the target (most often with an American element), the 'jihadists' pin their commitment on an obligatory attack against 'infidel enemies'.

With al-Qaida in mind, Bruce Hoffman (2006) considers the 'seismic effect of terrorist violence on the United States and the entire world'. He believes that:

Bin Laden is in fact one of the few people alive who can claim to have fundamentally changed the course of history [. . .] Even Bin Laden's death is unlikely to collapse the movement he created [. . .] Although much of what Bin Laden says is a mixture of bravado and braggadocio, in the past when we have failed to take him at his word, it has often been to our detriment.

A realistic view of this, Hoffman says, should put us on our guard:

The tragic loss of innocent life in any attack linked to al Qaeda is calculated by its masterminds to rekindle worldwide the same profound fears and anxieties that the attacks on 9/11 ignited. Al Qaeda's stature and reception in parts of the world today is a product of the extraordinary success achieved and attention generated by the attacks that day [. . .].

Countering terrorism is akin to taking a series of time-lapse photographs. The image captured on film today is not the same as the image yesterday, nor will it be the same tomorrow [. . .] Winning the war on terrorism will take decades, not years, to accomplish. If we are to succeed, our efforts must be as tireless, innovative, and dynamic as those of our opponents.[19]

THE UNHOLY ALLIANCE – THE TALIBAN

In 1994 a group of Sunni Muslims, the Taliban, took over from a weak government in Kabul, capital of Afghanistan. Whittaker has described the nature of this well-mobilised clique:

We have here a certain and rather intriguing link between religion and terrorism. It is worth examining in some detail. Taliban was headed by a number of mullahs, leaders of prayer with ministerial responsibilities. They emerged around 1992, after the retreat of Soviet forces coming to the rescue of a Communist administration had plunged Afghanistan into civil war. The mullah-ministers from the Taliban centre in Kabul stated that Taliban had a 'rescuing religion' whose function was to rid Islam of poisonous Western influences. Afghans were to be purified by these all-knowing fundamentalists. There would be no doubts, no debate, no wide scholarship, no gambling, no music, and nothing much for women denied any education and sunk in total inequality and subservience. A Ministry of Vice and Virtue was to keep morals on the straightest of paths and the Religious Police would deal with any dissidents. In this bizarre setting the Taliban regime kept control through exercising violence, although they could not in themselves be termed terrorist. There was every incentive for a ruthless international terrorist gang to feel welcome there.[20]

The story of both al-Qaida and the Taliban appears without conclusion, with the difference that, if the former is more a global movement, the Taliban is a ferocious battle where present containment techniques and the future are often in serious doubt among military and civilian opinion. Early optimism about the outcome of a successful campaign has been thoroughly discounted. Nor do too many outside nations show eagerness to join the fray, despite a very considerable pouring of arms and men into Afghanistan.

The years 2004–6 threw up issues that need dramatic and inventive resolution. In May 2006, hard-pressed American and British expeditionary forces were to be joined by a more substantial NATO contribution. The defeating of Taliban terrorism lacerating Afghanistan was to be the task of a 'beefed-up' International Security Assistance Force (ISAF), a body originally put in place in January 2002. Contingents from Canada, Germany, Italy, the Netherlands and Romania were to be fielded, but only as a rather desperate response to frequent requests from Brussels. Over against the general assumption that NATO's conventional role was in 'holding' a crisis situation, in peacekeeping and peace-building and in reconstruction and preliminary development schemes, here 25 nations were being asked to put 'more credibility, more visibility, more clout' into a devastating parcel of South-East Asia overrun by violent fanatics. To do this would involve fierce toe-to-toe fighting, not the usual style of engagement. Heading an official appeal was the point that it was not counter-terrorist numbers that mattered: NATO must pull together to meet everybody's challenge.

By June 2006 the moves to oust the Taliban were enumerated. Operation Mountain Thrust would push into four provinces with a force of 11,000 – 3,300 from Britain, 2,300 from the United States, 2,200 from Canada, and 3,500 Afghans.

This, the most ambitious strike since 2001, was to meet the Taliban in the open and to flush them out from an underground network. After a month or so, NATO, with as many deployed as possible, would take over the Thrust campaign. There is a growing imperative, now, to deploy troops of the order of 20,000.

Already, several unsettling questions are agitating the military. Basically, how far do we defuse the Taliban's fervour and capability by resorting to heavy gunfire and air strafing? Does this 'crushing of insurgency', as the remit puts it, not inflame a new generation of anti-foreign fighters? Then there is the nature of enemy contact. So many localised 'firefights' are with invisible opponents rather than the out-in-the-open tactics that are rehearsed at Staff College. Already, in the first six months of 2006 NATO fatalities totalled 36. US deaths since 2001 amount to 233. How appropriate is a battalion-strength response to agile terrorists? Most problematic is the existence of a 930-mile border with a Pakistan now thought to offer sanctuary to battle-weary Taliban as well as recruits and fresh weaponry. Nearby, in Baluchistan, 200,000 Afghan refugees cannot be relied upon for being sanitised from the Taliban, who move, it has been said, 'like a dark whisper, ruling the night'. For the army there is evidently a lack of clear backup from the Afghan Government of President Hamid Karzai in Kabul, appointed in 2004, who sits isolated behind razor wire facing a population easily accessible to the rebels. As for the Taliban, a Western diplomat's view from Kabul is quoted in July 2006 in *The Guardian*:

It is a convenient brand name for a very complex situation. This is about narcotics, corruption, tribal tensions, warlordism, illegal armed groups, Arabs, Iranians, Chechens – and all of these factions are interrelated. You never know who you are dealing with. You probably have some guys working for good and bad at the same time.[21]

A further factor in Afghanistan's mind-boggling complexity, and one impossible for general or minister to handle, is the spread of a multi-media onslaught, a 'virtual war' orchestrated by al-Qaida. Market stalls readily display videos and DVDs supplied by al-Qaida. Small radio stations close to Pakistan beam a strong message to passers-by. The US State Department is estimating that there are possibly 5,000 internet sites throughout the world carrying Taliban agendas.

How will the heavy hands of armed men cope with the super-problem of Afghanistan – its reliance on opium crops and narcotics dealing? Strong-arm, perhaps terror tactics are almost inevitably the recourse of farmers prohibited from living off their land and middle men denied any sort of profiteering. This is a country that produces 90 per cent of the world's heroin. Helmand Province, the most conflict-wracked of all, has bumper harvests that essentially underpin the local economy and the survival of countless family wage-earners. Is it likely that this dependence (and the funding of terror) will be satisfactorily reduced by crop-spraying planes, by armed sorties, or by Western officials carrying briefcases full of 'redevelopment projects'?

How will the conventional assignment of force-to-beat-terror cope with the undoubted salience of politico-religious adherence among violent and less-violent Afghans? Much is being written about Islamic religion and its influential impulses. The debate, of course, must go beyond readily categorising Muslim worshippers as intolerantly fundamental in attitude and belief. One thoughtful statement is that of Ken Booth and Tim Dunne (2002). They have the Taliban in mind:

Part of the religious message these groups are putting across is that they represent a kind of purified, uncompromising Islam which can quite readily be characterized as primitive and atavistic insofar as it is intended to re-establish contact with the faith of the Prophet and the original community of Believers.[22]

Certainly, in its religious tenets, as was pointed out earlier in this chapter, the Taliban is ultra-fundamental. Skewed into this orthodoxy, however, are the political constants of anti-Americanism and this makes for a virulent, unyielding approach. The firmest believer is morally strong and physically strong with a duty to defend what they regard as inescapably 'right'. Terror might be said to 'rule'.

Somehow, in facing up to al-Qaida and the Taliban, will not a 'search and destroy mission' need to be replaced with a 'hearts and minds' approach? Will this involve 'turning' terrorists by talking with them? For the moment this is an Unmentionable Idea, though it has been done in numerous other places at various times. More troops will never 'finish the job'. Do we, then, pull out, as some have suggested? Is there a 'Vietnam syndrome' looming? Afghanistan requires us, urgently, to debate possibilities.

POSTSCRIPT

The debate about involvement in Afghanistan was sharpened dramatically on Sunday 1 May 2011. That day, four helicopters carrying a small United States task force landed in the Pakistani garrison town, Abbottabad. They broke into a large three-storey house neighbouring the Pakistani Military Academy, evidently carefully briefed as to what they would do. It was Osama bin Laden they encountered. They shot him and one or two associates dead, took him away and buried him at sea. (There is, in fact, a good deal of controversy as to the international legality of what looks like an unindicted lynch-style killing.)

The demise of the arch-terrorist after so many years of malevolence raises a number of large political issues beyond the scope of this Reader. Particularly as a *Guardian* headline put it: with Bin Laden dead, the story of why we're in Afghanistan is falling apart. Is it likely now that this incident will lead to a shortened war? The token troop wind-down of US and NATO soldiers may now be enhanced as a significant prelude to wholesale withdrawal. Washington and London are expected to have important discussions about the consequences of such a step. There are considerable risks here in that, as more than one commentator has put it, we may have destroyed the body but not the cause. Bin Laden, as everyone knows, was a keen recruiter of terrorists who now have an appetite for wreaking revenge. It is possible, however, that with the mass of documents and tapes recovered from the Bin Laden mansion we may have data about names and incident proposals so avoiding another 9/11 apocalypse. Yet, it is almost certainly true that the end of one man will not result in the end of much that he believed in and practised.

United States
Ground Zero

ANTECEDENTS

THE UNITED STATES IS NO stranger to terrorist outrage though it was relatively small scale and infrequent. Much of it originated with three main groups – ethnic and émigré separatists; radical organisations on the political left; racist, right-wing partisans – all tending to be powered by their own aims and grievances rather than reaction to US domestic politics save that American participation in foreign wars like Vietnam, Iraq and Afghanistan has tended to bring in the bomb and the bullet.[1]

Black militant cults like the Black Panthers and Nation of Islam fervently earnest about civil rights and racial equality carried out random attacks against those responsible for municipal power in New York, New Orleans and San Francisco. Ethnocultural identity qualms and a sense of frustration and dispossession among Islamic, Asian, South Pacific, Cuban and Slav minorities has occasionally flared into violence in the larger cities of eastern and western USA notably in Chicago. Such conflict situations have been difficult to contain and resolve. Left-leaning activists, whether branded as 'Communist' or 'anti-American', have resorted to terror tactics that demonstrate social and economic antipathies and despair at not being treated with understanding and tolerance. Proclaiming right-wing beliefs has also culminated in atrocity down the years. Among these adherents are anti-Semites, the Jewish Defence League, militant Christian fundamentalists and racial extremists. Car bombing, fire-raising, sharpshooting, hit squads, kidnapping have been extremes following wire tapping, telephone hacking and domestic intervention, offences which Federal surveillance regards as indictable.

THE DAY OF RECKONING: 9/11

If US citizens are grimly aware of terrorist attacks over a century or so then what happened on 11 September 2001 must have transfixed them in horror and incredulity. Nothing had ever remotely approached this scale of human loss and devastation. Known realistically and symbolically as 'the day of Ground Zero', a line-out of events that day is unspeakably chilling.

- Four passenger aircraft flying on US domestic routes were hijacked by 19 terrorists.
- Two of the planes were crashed deliberately at 400 mph into the North and South Towers of the New York World Trade Center. Everybody on board was killed, as well as many occupants of the buildings which collapsed subsequently causing extensive locality damage. Fires, fed by 10,000 tons of aviation fuel, were to burn for days.
- A third airliner was directed into the western face of the Pentagon building in Arlington, Virginia, close to Washington.
- The fourth aircraft went down into a field near Shanksville, Pennsylvania, en route to Washington or the White House or the Capitol. Frantically, flight crew and a number of passengers had battled to retake control but failed in the attempt.
- There were no survivors from any flight. On the ground and mainly in New York there were 2,752 fatalities with 6,000 injured. The Pentagon incident claimed 184 lives. Of the total, 60 policemen and 343 firemen perished. No hijacker survived.
- Large-scale rescue and clearance attempts were mounted over nine days. It took almost 10 months to search the Ground Zero site minutely. Recovery and reconstruction operations were reckoned to last until 2011.
- The FBI (Federal Bureau of Investigation) was able to establish quickly the identities of the 19 hijackers. Four of them had passed out as pilots from a Minnesota flight training school. Fifteen were from Saudi Arabia, one from Egypt, one from Lebanon, two from the United Arab Emirates. From the Egyptian leader's luggage there was seized information as to personal backgrounds, motivation and incident planning. Strangely, all of them had passed easily enough through security checkpoints.
- Prime blame for 9/11 was by Security fastened on 19 followers of al-Qaeda and Osama bin Laden. Something like three years must have gone into scheming for the attacks. There was apparently plenty of motivation like sanctions imposed against Iraq, the Gulf War and its political reverberations, and US support for Israel.
- Immediately following the mayhem all non-emergency civil flights were grounded. International flight entry to US airspace was closed.
- President George Bush ordered a 'Global War on Terror'. The aims were to bring initiators of Ground Zero to justice if at all possible. Economic and military sanctions were to be levied at any state suspected of harbouring terrorists.

- The NATO Council declared that the US attack was a possible forerunner of attacks on other NATO member states and as such met the stipulations under Article 5 of the NATO Charter. Washington urgently contacted other states internationally to establish coalition agreement on terrorist search, identification and handling.[2]

COUNTER-TERRORISM SCHEME FOLLOWING 9/11

The US Government and Congress acted swiftly to meet 'a grave emergency'. Brought forward was a Category One Plan to ensure administrative continuity and provide for safe evacuation of the President, his staff, and designated executive personnel. Surveillance and protection provision were expedited under hastily drafted legislation, notably the USA Patriot Act to authorise critical law enforcement under detection-and-arrest procedures. Overall implementation of the legislation would be the remit of a National Security Agency.

Improved intelligence gathering, accumulation, analysis and consequent action were to be the focus of Government monitoring and the coordinated measures already in the hands of the FBI and the Central Intelligence Agency (CIA). Additional resources and staff were the crux to progress. Nothing must impede direct access to the President and his front-line advisory team. Detention centres were to be set up for the holding of so-termed 'illegal enemy combatants' under special conditions and length of tenure. 'Suspect and hold' was the authorising maxim.[3]

President Bush put his whole weight into endorsing the investigative purpose of a National Commission on Terrorist Attacks on the USA. Formed eventually in early 2002 and known eventually as 'the 9/11 Commission', the Commission team would compile a detailed set of findings about what had or had not happened. They would go for straight facts avoiding the cataclysmic hyperbole of many public statements from Capitol Hill. They were given a maximum period of two years in which to work. Periodically, what they were doing would be accountable to public sessions.

COUNTER-TERRORISM FOLLOWING 9/11: DEBATE

In the wake of 'the day that changed America', the day that 'reminded us of Pearl Harbour', there had been heavy distress, loud disbelieving, confusion and procrastination. Informed comment and discussion were slower to emerge but when they did the 'harder-edge' of counter-terrorist provision was subjected to keen liberal scrutiny. For instance, the USA Patriot Act had been put before Congress as an enabling act for generally conventional counter-terrorism measures. Soon, though, there was public disquiet, especially in legal and academic circles, that the Act was being used much too widely. What could justify the Act's rounding up of harmless vagrants and their incarceration in cells already holding youth charged with intimidating behaviour in the street? There was, too, a good deal of anxiety that the overall drive to secure intelligence data might lead to the United States becoming an 'intelligent-state' and one insensitive to the basic survival of rights and freedoms.[4]

A marked feature of the counter-terrorism debate was what might be thought of as 'patriotic (red-blooded) patriotism', the 'unwavering resoluteness' that Defense Secretary Donald Rumsfeld prescribed. Too much 'soft liberalism' in countering terrorists was deplored and it was Rumsfeld who had wanted US Special Forces to root out supposed terrorist leaders for assassination. Public apprehension and resolve is understandable given the trauma of 9/11 and the flood of press 'revelations' and speculation. Would the next bombs be 'dirty' radioactive devices? Was widespread poisoning of water resources and crop lands likely? Why were anti-bacteriological squads in protective gear out inspecting city buildings?

The President and Defense Department were minded to accelerate 'shock and awe' restraining action in Iraq and Afghanistan, places where intending terrorists reportedly were recruited, trained and briefed. Such a compulsive overrode those who complained of the imprecision of US-directed air strikes on crowded towns. As the White House saw it, the Forces of Evil confronting the Forces for Good were to be vanquished with 'no holds barred'.

The sooner the 9/11 Commission cleared the fog of speculation the better. Was there any suspicion before 9/11 that the United States might be the victim of suicidal attack? Very possibly agencies such as the FBI and CIA, both monitoring round the clock worldwide, could have tapped into a variety of dependable intelligence sources. There was an imperative need to know whether disbelief and complacency had clouded vision.

As to disbelief and complacency, there is every sign that US intelligence analysis was not acute enough even to understand al-Qaeda's anti-US 'grand strategy' publicised in the group's own utterances and intercepted e-mails. Bin Laden's ideological stance and rhetoric were well-known to the FBI but they were never acted upon thoroughly enough.[5]

THE 9/11 COMMISSION REPORT: FINDINGS

The 9/11 attacks were 'a shock but they should not have come as a surprise'. Islamist extremists had frequently warned the United States about likely attack yet vigilant security failed to act decisively. By 2001 Osama bin Laden, terrorist-in-chief, had built up an impressive organisation with executive field staff, trained personnel, an effective communications network, appreciable finance, sophisticated intelligence banks, ease of transporting men and materials which were all big enough to face up to terrorising the USA itself. The CIA, with an eye on these developments, could do little other than break up some identified cells in the US as part of their 'millennium alert'. In early 2001 there was even a watch-and-follow of known al-Qaeda people, trained intensively in Hamburg and now living openly in California and Arizona. There was not enough definite evidence to arrest and detain them. By early 2001 US intelligence agencies had netted a string of warnings that al-Qaeda was planning 'something very, very, very big'. Director of Central Intelligence, George Tenet, believed now that 'the system was blinking red'. As one of his aides put it, 'No analytic work foresaw the lightning that could connect the thundercloud to the ground.' (Press reports spoke of the great unhappiness this admission caused in one of the public sessions.)

The Report admits candidly to security lapses despite Red Alert. How was it hijacked planes received clearance to take off? Interceptor aircraft were scrambled without clear instructions about where to go and what to look for. A shoot down authorisation to NORAD Air Defense (the North American Aerospace Defense Command) took 28 minutes to be activated. Emergency response to the incident at Ground Zero was necessarily improvised to deal with something unimaginable yet some problems of control and communication ought to have been foreseen by better pre-incident training. Apart from a number of inadequacies there was everything to commend 'the incredible bravery and presence of mind of the heroic "emergency responders" of New York's police, fire and ambulance departments'. In the White House and in Administration departments 'the most important failure was one of imagination'. Indeed, 'we do not believe leaders understood the gravity of the threat'. Consequently, there were failures of policy, capabilities, direction, management. Clearly, 'America's homeland defenders faced outward'. Analytical structures in the FBI and the Defense Department were weakly built.[6]

THE 9/11 COMMISSION REPORT: RECOMMENDATIONS

Finally and conclusively the Report outlined in detail things that now needed implementation to make America safer. Two questions were posed: what to do?; and how to do it? Recommendations were in very plain language.

What to do

- A global plan was needed 'to dismantle' the al-Qaeda network of 'perverse Islamism'.
- Terrorist groups where located must be attacked and their sanctuaries 'rooted out'.
- Develop comprehensive coalition strategies with other states to devise coordinated policies of detection, arrest, detention in agreement with legal processes.
- Priority to be given to furnishing a first-rate security system with improved standards and methods of screening, identification, intervention, detention and with guidelines that will always integrate safeguards for essential rights and liberties.
- Base heightened Federal funding for emergency preparedness on estimates of risks and vulnerabilities. New York and Washington to head the list. Priority in resource allocation to go as far as possible to an incident command system.

How to do it

Unity of effort means 'one fight, one team' in five areas, as outlined below.

*   Integrate strategic intelligence via a National Counterterrorism Center.
*   Appoint a National Intelligence Director to unify intelligence centres and agencies and that will report directly to the President.
*   Accumulating and analysing security intelligence must replace 'need to know' with 'need to share'. Mainframe system is to become a decentralised network.
*   Congress must enter into much improved security oversight and regular review. They are to ensure that if the Administration changes (viz. at election time) security systems are reported, cleared and confirmed.
*   A specialised, integrated national security workforce – FBI, Defense Department, Department of National Security – must be established with a clear, agreed delineation of roles, missions and authority.

Such a mammoth presentation of findings and recommendations inevitable raised a storm of controversy. There was disquiet about the Commission's independence from the White House and the corridors of Congress. Why was the Commission so meanly funded and granted such a relatively short time-line? Was it being set up to screen and hide facts and reputations? Was some evidence from intelligence agencies carefully edited and selectively presented? And was some of this evidence obtained through 'enhanced interrogation' methods? More needed to be known about the slow-footedness of alert systems and control. Could it have been that in some respects a blind eye was complacently turned upon those reported pre-incident attack warnings? Report critics included survivors and their families, medical staff, engineers and architects, military men, aviation experts, lawyers, welfare personnel, ready to applaud truth-telling and contempt for whitewash.

THE GLOBAL WAR ON TERROR: DOUBTS, RESERVATIONS

War as a response to terrorism, and war globally expressed, was the thrust of a Presidential directive of 2001. It deserves a little more scrutiny to conclude this chapter. The overarching purpose and some of the apparent consequences of this command received sustaining examination by Philip Heymann two years later. Heymann, a Harvard Law Professor, considers the implications of the dictum rather more pragmatically than legally. His book, subtitled *Winning Without War*, is a rich compilation of ideas, prime material for debate.[7] To begin with there is the recognition that conventional war requires an all-out harnessing of resources and a national set of agreed goals and priorities. There must be a conscious, massive commitment of fighting power. The extraordinary powers of a wartime, grand executive, master control in its fullest sense inevitably lead to some erosion of rights and freedoms. The enemy is 'out there', recognisable, challengeable. That is actual, realistic war, something the United States had chosen to embark upon in the 1940s against totalitarian regimes.

Terrorists and terrorism represent for Heymann's way of thinking a very different challenge in the contemporary world. The enemy 'out there' is comparatively disembodied. Confrontations are hard to predict and generally short-lasting. Encounters for the most part are intangible and the by-product of alien attitudes, prejudices and hostility varying in tone, time and place. What happened at Ground Zero was nothing that could be calculated operationally as a set of targeted tasks and intercalated risks such as the military analyse 'prioritise' and prepare for. There is in spasmodic terrorist activity no semblance of what President Eisenhower termed 'the totality of war'. So for Heymann and many critics since 2001 the concept of 'war on terror' is a clumsy, misleading and unhelpful concept to apply to rebellious outrage. Understandably, facing the debris and death of 9/11, there was a public call for leaving it to the military to put in hand a massive retributive response as in state versus state conflict. Heymann acknowledges that when security coalitions activate counter-terrorist programmes they are taking part in what might be thought of as 'metaphorical war'. War on terror in its basic heavy-footed mode 'will not do'. 'Winning without war' must counter terrorism thoughtfully, patiently, with the aid of first-class listening devices, and comprehensive intelligence gathering and data-banking. There will be less hand-to-hand encounter and some tentative engagement with mind-sets as in talking with the Taliban. (Interestingly, among those prepared to consider 'talking out some of the terror' is more than one US Army general.)

Counter-terrorism as Heymann sees it is:

a rich set of alternatives for dealing with any particular type of terrorism at any specific time and place to be adequately assessed against an adequately rich set of goals.[8]

A number of the other options will require judgement as to their appropriateness and realisability, and they have to be governed by compliance with the law – domestic and international.

The law and the countering of terrorism is, of course, a matter much discussed in all countries. In Britain, using international perspectives, John Strawson, School of Law, University of East London, heads a research group whose publication *Law After Ground Zero* asks penetrating questions about terrorism (particularly as it had struck the United States some twelve months earlier). At one point they ask:

Were the attacks discrete events – an outrageous crime - or a sudden – war like action – understandable on their own terms, or were they evidence of something new in history, even a marker of a new historical period? How could they be located in master narratives so that they can be understood as exceptions to the norm? Was terrorism an exception to the social structure we inhabit or is it so embedded that it becomes a symptom of normalcy?[9]

Are we, then, sufferers from terrorism and, indeed, are terrorists themselves caught between the master narratives of 'crime' and 'war'? Do those wishing to define the events of 11 September 2001 (and terrorist incidents elsewhere) as 'crimes' do so 'partly to structure the response', it is asked? Legal parameters then demand investigation, identification, the tracking of suspects, the tabling of admissible evidence, court routine and, if guilty, statutory punishment. Does this legal way of working, however, place discernable limits upon the power of the state to do something prompt, right and proper? Limiting our power to do something hyper forceful by way of counter-action? Could this have any bearing on the United States denying the universal jurisdiction of the International Criminal Court in 2002? Was not preference for the narrative of 'war' quite clear in the smoking ruins of New York's Twin Towers?

Strawson et al write of the inevitable consequences of choosing one narrative – that of a 'war' threat at perpetrators:

In the context of domestic politics, the quick response of the Bush Administration to September 11 represented a virtual coup d'etat in government. The Bush Administration seized the opportunity posed by the outpouring of patriotic fervour in the wake of September 11 to consolidate and expand executive powers and to override the nation's tradition of civil liberties with draconian legislation . . . In the context of international politics, America's war on terrorism initiated a bandwagon which states in the global community with restive minority or broader problems climbed aboard to legitimate their efforts to settle their own political scores.[10]

The use of the 'war narrative' in these circumstances is perhaps not surprising. Yet Strawson suggests that the narratives themselves are concepts to be handled with care. In regard to mopping up after 9/11:

The task was, first, to understand the effects of the attack and take measures to alleviate them, and, second, to identify the perpetrators, track them down, and punish them.[11]

Dealing with the perpetrators was more difficult and perplexing: were they criminals or were they agents of war?

Immediate reactions used both terms, almost interchangeably, but although they seemed instinctively to fit and enable the events to be satisfactorily related to achieve a unified response, they were themselves undergoing considerable revision. The concepts of crime and war may themselves no longer hold coherence.[12]

Were the lawyers outpaced in the United States? Clearly in the aftermath of 9/11 the risks and dividend of a less-than-legal approach to counter-terrorism were questionable. There may well be time and space now for a shaping of newer contours of firmer military-political-legal collaboration that have less to do with warlike response and more to do with some judgement as to the terrorist working out ambitions politically rather than violently.

Paul Wilkinson, of the Centre for the Study of Terrorism and Political Violence, University of St Andrews, doubtless with the recent 9/11 incident in mind, sees definition and redefinition in straightforward terms:

However, I believe it would be very dangerous to assume that there is a quick fix military or political solution to every manifestation of the complex phenomenon of modern terrorism . . . There is no universally applicable counter-terrorism policy . . . what is needed is a custom-built, multi-pronged approach geared to the type of terrorism threat confronted.[13]

Britain: London as target

THIS IS A CHAPTER WITH a difference, in that it outlines a major terrorist incident that occurred in London on 7 July 2005 – subsequently known as '7/7'; a catastrophe that ultimately yielded a great deal of information about terrorist motives and methods. In the most painful of ways lessons have been learned. Readers will understand that, following an incident of this magnitude, many of the conclusions publicly drawn in official reports remain hypothetical and tentative. In fact, counter-terrorist investigations arising from London's attack are still being vigorously pursued by a large number of specialists.

THE FOUR ATTACKS

David Whittaker (2007) has given the following account (slightly amended here):

In common with 9/11 and the bombing of Madrid (11 March 2004), this was coordinated terrorism. London's transport system was hit as the morning rush hour drew to a close. Three bombs went off in Underground trains just outside Liverpool Street and Edgware Road stations and on a packed train moving between Kings Cross and Russell Square. An hour later, a bomb tore off the upper deck of a London Transport bus in Tavistock Square, killing thirteen of the passengers (the later toll was fourteen killed and 110 injured).

The bombings led to severe day-long disruption of transport and movement in the capital. Passengers had first been told that a 'power surge' was closing down the Underground system: only gradually did it become clear that the chaos was due to a criminal act of vast extent. Rescue and medical services worked unceasingly and heroically, bandaging bleeding, blackened passengers and retrieving the dead. The first casualty reports gave 53 (eventually 56) people as being killed and more than 700 injured of whom half were admitted to a hospital bed. Somehow 200,000 people were evacuated from the Underground system within the first hour to what were hoped to be safer areas. A fact causing much pain and confusion was the impossibility of establishing who might be missing and who might have escaped. Mobile phones were out of action and grievous confusion was a result.

Inevitably, the question on all lips was: who could have done this thing? It did not take too long for police and security services to work out the logistics. This was partly because close circuit cameras at Kings Cross station at the peak hour of 8.30 am had afforded close scrutiny of people's movements just before the blasts. Particularly useful was the discovery of personal clothing and documents left near the bomb scenes which identified the bombers, all of whom resorted to suicide. This was surely an astounding piece of luck for those searching for evidence. Piece by piece the jigsaw could be assembled.[1]

Three young men left Leeds. They hired a car and drove to Luton. There they met a fourth man also using a hired car. The four abandoned their vehicles, loaded rucksacks from the car with high-grade explosives and together took a Thameslink train from Luton to Kings Cross, London, where they moved out in different directions to sites scheduled for destruction.

Much detail about the 7/7 incidents may be gleaned from the *Report of the Official Account of the Bombings in London on 7 July 2005*, published 11 May 2006. At about 8.50 am on 7 July (according to closed-circuit television and forensic evidence), one of the bombers, Shehzad Tanwear, entered the second carriage of a Circle Line underground train, put his rucksack on the floor and, as the train pulled away from the platform, detonated his bomb. There was smoke, flames and a great explosion. Eight passengers died, including Tanwear, and 171 were injured. About the same time, at Edgware Road station, an explosion tore through a train. Again, the bomber, Mohammed Sidique Khan, died, taking seven with him and injuring 163. A heavily crowded train on the Piccadilly Line was the next target. The explosion claimed the lives of 27, including Jermaine Lindsay, the bomber, and injured over 340. It was an hour later that Hasib Hussain boarded a number 30 bus travelling eastwards from Marble Arch. Following closures on the Underground, the bus was packed with people. Hussain and 14 others did not survive the bus being blown apart. The 110 people who had to be hospitalised included passengers and passers-by.[2]

WHO WERE THE BOMBERS?

The Report of 11 May 2006 describes them in detail. Whittaker has a briefer account (slightly amended here):

Like the 9/11 attack, the bombers themselves did not survive. Much, however, became known about them and their movements as 200 police scanned several thousand phototapes. They were neatly dressed men in their twenties, unexceptionable in a crowd. Two from Beeston, in Leeds, were university graduates, one of them teaching in a Leeds primary school. These were from close-knit Pakistani shopkeeper families who all attended the local mosque. Of the sports science graduate, Shehzad Tanwear, his mother said: 'He was proud to be British. He had everything to live for [. . .] It wasn't him [. . .] It must have been forces behind him.' (This seems a percipient view in the light of defining terrorism.) As for Hasib Hussain, he was seen as a fanatic – but about cricket when Pakistan played a Test Match at nearby Headingley. Then there was a Jamaican, Jermaine Lindsay, a 'plodding sort of fellow', looking around at nineteen for a reasonable job. The fourth in this quartet was Mohammed Sidique Khan, keen gymnast, book reader, teaching children with special needs in a local primary school. Graduating with a 2:2 in Business Studies he seems, already in his thirties, to have been mentor and role model, with enough charisma, perhaps, to indoctrinate others.

Who had 'infected' these young men, if this is an appropriate term? Who began to brief them? Were there 'others', more desperate ones, out there? In what ways might they have 'radicalised' those who became conspirators? Had they learned about bomb making from the Internet and then gone on as recruits to the 'bomb factory' discovered later in south-west Leeds? As far as could be made out subsequently, there was no link with al-Qaida. There is still some speculation as to the motives of others, those who surely indoctrinated the four to be their nefarious agents. Why 7 July? It is true that London had recently been chosen to be the venue for the Olympic Games. At Gleneagles in Scotland, eight world leaders were in consort at an important summit meeting. The connections-in-terror are not obvious except that it might be possible for those so minded to make a chaotic impression upon England, the partner-in-war of the United States. Apart from speculation of this sort, there remained the powerful thought that further terror attacks somewhere in Britain could not be ruled out and, if new terrorists were to strike as anonymously as the London four, from an unusual background, what were the chances of preventing another attack?[3]

AFTERMATH: ENQUIRY AND REPORT

The immediate aftermath of the bomb blasts was a period of intense activity as a massive police operation coordinated with intelligence and government agencies sought to deal with the catastrophic consequences of what had occurred. The Cabinet Office Briefing Room A (COBRA), the national crisis control centre, was activated. Within a week, the recovery of personal effects and DNA evidence had identified the bombers.

There appeared to be a new element in what has been referred to as 'home-grown' terrorism. This is the unpredictability of attacks by unremarkable people, that is those who would be unlikely suspects. They are reared in Britain and are not the 'foreign extremists' so prominent in the press. In the case of 7/7, the Beeston four would have been regarded locally as well-behaved 'Leeds lads' from supportive families, integrated and respected in a multicultural community. Generally, these young men had done well at school, attended the mosque regularly, and had prospects of settled careers. Were they then so alienated as to pose a problem to anyone else?

Preliminary conclusions about the quartet are set out in the Report of 11 May.

(a)   this case demonstrates the real difficulty for law enforcement agencies and local communities in identifying potential terrorists. All 4 [sic] were open about their strict religious observance but there was little outward sign that this had spilled over into potentially violent extremism [. . .]

(b)   there is little in their backgrounds which mark them out as particularly vulnerable to radicalisation, with the possible exception of Lindsay. Khan, Tanwear and Hussain were apparently well integrated into British society. Lindsay appears to have had more instability at various points in his life but not exceptionally so

(c)   in the absence of evidence of other methods, the process of indoctrinating these men appears principally to have been through personal contact and group bonding [. . .] their indoctrination appears to have taken place away from places with known links to extremism [. . .]

(d)   it remains unclear whether others in the UK were involved in radicalising or inciting the group, or in helping them to plan and execute it [. . .]

(e)   the planning was deceptively simple. The operation did not cost much and was financed by methods that would arouse little suspicion [. . .]

(f)   the group showed good security awareness and planning discipline. They employed methods which seems [sic] to have been effective in disguising what they were doing from others [. . .].[4]

Something that adds fuel to speculation and conclusion at this later date was the instance of a failed bombing attempt in London on 21 July, two weeks later. This account is that of Whittaker:

It was another Thursday. Mimicry, possibly, of the earlier 'success'? There were four attempted bombings, with three Underground stations and a bus as targets, yet again. It was the detonators going off in plastic food container packages that alerted the police and led, once more, to an organised evacuation of bystanders. There were no injuries. Very likely these bombers were less technically competent individuals. Certainly, a fifth would-be bomber had dumped his device and this proved to be a less than sophisticated model. Again, close circuit photo images of young men with rucksacks helped in the tracing and arrest of four suspects within a week. They were all Middle Eastern in origin and were all convicted of explosives handling.

Unhappily, the next day in July brought grief and much controversy. A Brazilian electrician, Jean Charles de Menezes, was fatally shot by a Metropolitan Police squad. His bulky clothing and perhaps his tool bag were thought to betray the would-be bomber. In accordance with Scotland Yard's 'Operation Kratos', and a shoot-to-kill requirement, no police questions were asked. Following what appeared to be a highly unfortunate occurrence, there have been many enquiries, in Parliament and in the media, as to the nature of surveillance, the possibilities of interrogation, the extent of police communication, and the advisability of an 'overkill' strategy. The police, who may yet be blamed for rashness and incoherence, have replied that you cannot take any chances with an apparent terrorist about to act. One supposes that that rejoinder would have been well understood by those responsible for security in New

York and Madrid, although there, too, a number of security measures have met criticism where they appear to endanger certain human rights.[5]

The narrative so far owes much to the Report of 11 May, which set out to summarise the facts of the 7/7 happenings and to pose questions about the four bombers. Two other reports were to follow: a report to parliament from the government's Intelligence and Security Committee (ISC), published in May 2006, and, also in the same month, the so-termed Government Response to the ISC findings. The first report from the ISC lays down aims and structure:

The Report examines intelligence and security matters relevant to the July 7 terrorist attacks and focuses in particular upon:

• Whether any intelligence which may have helped prevent the attacks was missed or overlooked;
• Why the threat level to the UK was lowered prior to the attacks and what impact this has had; and
• What lessons were learned on the back of the attacks and how these are being applied, in particular:

   – what reassessments of the threat have been made; and
   – what is being done to increase coverage of the threat.[6]

There is a great deal of detail in the ISC Report and consideration especially of what might be improved. Clearly, lessons had been learned. The shape of the Government Response to this detail is a most useful set of conclusions and recommendations. A number of the more significant assertions may be quoted briefly:

Terrorists make great efforts to ensure that intelligence about their intentions is difficult to obtain and analyse. Intelligence is generally fragmentary, of varying reliability and difficult to interpret. Complex and challenging investigative judgements have to be made on the basis of often incomplete data. There is always a difficult balance to strike between those known to be a current threat and working to discover other possible threats.

In regard to threat levels:

The Government agrees that greater transparency about the threat level and alert state system itself, and a managed process for communicating it to the public, will enhance its effectiveness and increase public confidence and vigilance.[7]

The ISC Report had 'flagged up' (so they say) the possibility of suicide attacks in Britain in this statement:

We remain concerned that across the whole of the counter-terrorism community the development of the home-grown threat and the radicalisation of British citizens were not fully understood or applied to strategic thinking. A common and better level of understanding of these things among all those closely involved in identifying and countering the threat against the UK, whether that be the Security Service, or the police, or other parts of Government, is critical in order to be able to counter the threat effectively and prevent attacks.[8]

The government noted the committee's concern and agreed with the importance it placed on improving understanding of the radicalisation process.

A further point underlined in the ISC Report was the importance of collaboration internationally, since terrorist activity was a global occurrence. In the longer term, at the heart of future efforts must be success in 'countering the spread of the terrorist message in the UK and overseas'. The Government Response took up this point and, using the term 'empowering', sought to launch an educational and promotional programme directed at the Muslim world within Britain and in other countries aimed at radicalisation. Something on these lines was envisaged:

an FCO (Foreign and Commonwealth Office) foreign policy awareness and outreach programme, involving:

— discussion fora in the UK to explain foreign policy and debate issues around extremism, with the participation of Ministers;
— visits by British Muslim delegations to Muslim countries to encourage debate on Islam and communicate positive realities of British Muslims;
— work on educational reform in Muslim countries, including in Pakistan and Bangladesh; and
— diplomatic activity with key international partners and international organisations to reach agreement on the nature and dangers of radicalisation and frame common approaches to address it.[9]

WHAT WENT WRONG?

Since 7/7 there has been a flood of comment and some criticism. Generally, this has sounded responsible both in intent and styling. Most critics will have been aware that a fair amount of information about the attack, some of which is in the hands of the government is both confidential to security authority and also sub judice. One interesting compilation is that of Crispin Black (2005). Black, an ex-army officer, is at present an independent intelligence analyst, having served the Downing Street Cabinet Office as a security adviser from 1999 to 2002.[10]

Both Black and the ISC Report have in mind the unhelpful division of operation and report that is the consequence, in Britain, of two tenuously associated security agencies, namely MI5 and MI6. Domestic and 'foreign' remits should not be diverging. For Black, 'home equals MI5, abroad equals MI6'. Judging from the ISC Report, Whitehall now believes, 'that the July attacks have acted as a catalyst for change within the intelligence and security agencies'. Black certainly believes the unichannel procedures put in hand by France and the United States make for more effective measures.

Were there intelligence failures? Misinterpretation? Faulty choice of alternative scenarios? Too much complacency? Political pressures distracting judgement? Black is careful in speculation, but there is the inference that in some ways there was not so much 'failure' as perhaps a lack of resoluteness in deciding on priorities. Reading the official report's conclusions and recommendations, there is the implication that things were confidently being handled, but why did the Joint Analysis Centre (JTAC) on 2 June lower the national status of alert from 'severe general' to 'substantial', adding in explanation that, 'at present there is not a group with both current intent and capability to attack the United Kingdom'? Black is uneasy about this decision. However, the official reports (not unexpectedly) restate the validity of the status reduction and Black goes on to quote the words of the then Home Secretary, Charles Clarke, to the House of Commons Home Affairs Committee on 13 September 2005:

While the alert state is heavily influenced by the threat level, it is JTAC (MI5's Joint Terrorism Centre) which sets the threat level independently, and is not responsible for deciding on what mitigating action should be employed. Hence the reduction in threat level was not directly connected to the alert state and was for local planners to determine. There was therefore no significant diminution to specific protective measures.[11]

Black finds it almost impossible to defend Clarke's assurance, nor is it likely that he would give much credence to the Government Response in their report, namely: 'The reduction (in threat level) is unlikely to have altered the alertness of responders (including the emergency services) or to have affected the chances of preventing the 7 July attacks.'[12]

Black notably doubts assertions such as these and wonders, further, who decided to siphon off a large number of London police to deal with any threat to the Gleneagles summit meeting. That would perhaps be an 'improbable' threat. Did any complacent 'groupthink', he wonders, blunt the edge of analytical and operational readiness? We shall never know. Black could possibly have given rather more acknowledgement to the preparedness of the ISC Report writers to show a degree of candour in their statements. They admit that all was not perfect before, during and after the 7/7 affair:

It could be argued (but it would be largely with hindsight) that better appreciation of the speed and scale with which the threat against the UK could develop might have led the Services to achieve a step change in capacity earlier despite the risks involved in rapid expansion. The story of what was known about the 7 July group prior to July indicates that if more resources had been in place sooner the chances of preventing the July attacks could have increased. Greater coverage in Pakistan, or more resources generally in the UK, might have alerted the Agencies to the intention of the 7 July group.[13]

Another pointer to a possible 'step change' is visible in another Government Response recommendation:

The Government agrees that a clearer delineation of threat level, including within it a more formal recognition of the limitations of our knowledge of terrorists' intentions at any one time, will significantly assist in the subsequent consideration of whether a change in the alert state, and therefore the security stance, is required.[14]

Once more, Black might have commended in a word or two the apparent readiness of government to think afresh its 'security stance'. Nevertheless, and usefully, he is quick to stress two points bearing crucially on 'stance' and in general on our counter-terrorist work. First, there is a 'new strategic reality', he says, which:

is not that Al-Qaeda's operational reach extends into the heart of the west but that it does not have to. The message from the men in hiding on the Pakistan/Afghanistan border or possibly somewhere on the Horn of Africa is not 'we can attack you' but rather 'we can persuade your own people to attack you'.[15]

And so there is a need to reorder the counter-attacking system, Black affirms:

The system does need fixing, but my real targets have turned out to be ideas, mind-sets and ways of looking at things, which appear to permeate not only our intelligence and security apparatus but also our national life. And which make it easier for terrorists to exist unhindered in our midst and more difficult for the police and security services to do their job. These ideas may in part be imposed from above, but generally are so dangerous not because anyone has to subscribe to them but because many people do – naturally.

Simply put, we have a bad and confused attitude to terrorism. If we do not make immediate efforts to level the playing field on which terrorists have to operate – the next bomb plots will be as easy to carry out as the last.[16]

Plain speaking. An aid to further reflection – and advance?

POSTSCRIPT

Almost certainly we have not heard the last of 7/7. In 2010 and 2011, five to six years after the incident, there is a good deal of debate centred on the progress in London's Royal Courts of Justice of coroner's inquests on the victims.

Within the courtroom and across the press and the Internet reportage and questioning raise the issue of how far the four bombers were known in Security circles. Were they even regarded as 'clean skins'? Or were they escaping continued scrutiny of their adherence and expressed beliefs? Could an MI5 watch have been inconsistent, complacent, perhaps confused (as Crispin Black had wondered)? Court and public were unlikely to know much unless 'top secret' records were to be made open at least to the coroner or to an independent enquiry panel. In many ways outside the coroner's court there appears to be a 'trial by media'. Relatives of the 7/7 dead and injured are calling continually for a legitimate 'truth and justice' process.

Another issue prompts earnest discussion in the House of Commons and in socio-political circles. Despite the provisions of Whitehall's printed Government Response of 2006 and its echo by ministers is it not possible that the Muslim community is alienated by neo-conservative counter-terrorism measures? The Home Office 'Preventing Extremism Together' task force, for instance, might be regarded as a faint-hearted attempt at dialogue and dispelling of West–East myth.

Terrorism, indeed, has many roots and many aspects and the tackling of it is multivariate.

At last on 6 May 2011 the Coroner's Report was made public. Almost six years since the London bombings the Coroner, Lady Justice Hallett, had most ably conducted a six-month hearing helped by 500 witnesses and 16 legal teams. An Appeal Court judge when acting as coroner works without a jury and is limited not to forensic and expansive statement but merely to a brief, factual verdict. In this instance, the terse ruling was that the 52 victims had been 'unlawfully killed'. An accompanying reassurance was that every one of the victims would have died 'whatever time the emergency services reached them', and regardless of the miscalculations and mistakes that occurred in coping with such a catastrophic event. There would be no separate inquest into the fatalities of the four bombers.

A number of recommendations were listed. Emergency services should integrate with each other to a greater degree to enable prompt response. There was clear room for inter-agency staff training, improved unit capabilities, and for more adequate funding. Assessment methods, liaison, communication procedures all needed simplifying and streamlining. Even so, dealing with the 7/7 attacks had seen emergency teams and the involved public displaying extraordinary bravery, initiative and determination. More implicit than explicit in the Coroner's findings is the point that the intelligence services, especially MI5, did not discharge their essential tasks with clearer accountability and robust persistence. Their investigations already focusing on at least two of the bombers should have been more consistent and analytical before the attack.

How far were the four bombers already known about in Security circles? Were they even regarded as 'clean skins'? Or were they somehow escaping continued scrutiny of their adherence to extremist motivation? Could an MI5 watch been wavering, complacent, perhaps confused (as Crispin Black had wondered)? In many ways outside the coroner's court there appears to have been a 'trial by media'. Relatives of the 7/7 dead and injured call for a legitimate 'truth and justice' investigative process but a further enquiry is unlikely to be set up. The government's Intelligence and Security Committee has not, it seems, earned much in the way of approval of its ways of working and of its readiness to report openly and constructively.

Another issue prompts earnest discussion in the House of Commons and in socio-political circles. Despite the provisions of Whitehall's Government Response Report of 11 May 2006 and its echo by ministers is it not possible that the Muslim community is alienated by neo-conservative counter-terrorism measures? The Home Office 'Preventing Extremism Together' task force, for instance, might be regarded as a faint-hearted attempt at dialogue and dispelling of West–East myth.

Has the 7/7 terror pushed us into thinking through and probably drastically reordering policies and methods of counter-terrorism? Before a similar incident reoccurs?

Israel

ISRAEL HAS BEEN TROUBLED and torn by violence for more than 50 years. The violence is a consequence of the frustrated activism of two Arab political groups – Fatah and Hamas – and of the retributive counter-action of the Israeli government, mainly of their Israeli Defence Force (IDF) seeking to restore order. All too often international comment in the media and much political opinion has dismissed Fatah and Hamas as irresponsible 'terrorists'. However, each group sees itself as a government-in-exile. They own to the degree of credibility which would justify seats in the Knesset, Israel's parliament. Their leaders are pragmatic, visionary and well-educated. These parties have written constitutions incorporating carefully defined political aims. Structurally, they depend upon committees, councils and conferences. And, yes, they depend upon having seasoned, well-trained military wings.

It is very much the purpose of this Reader to propose that we do not dismiss groups such as these without a fair amount of close examination of motives and methods. Otherwise, we are using labels simplistically and that is unhelpful to any resolution of conflict. Certainly, a prelude to consideration must be to look rather carefully at the context in which contest takes place.

CONTEXT AND CONTEST

At least one encyclopaedia has it that Israel is 'a historical-geographical expression rather than a political entity'. In the eyes of many it is a land ravaged by terrorism endemic over very many years. Geographically, Israel is a mix of limestone rock, full desert and partial scrub, expanses of fertile corn-land and orchard, the lush pastures of the River Jordan basin – all these make for a territory variegated in landscape and climate. Historically, and long a bridge between Asia and Africa, the area has invited peaceful travelling and settlement yet also been a battleground between the rivals of empires and the ambitions of caliphates. It must have been this mix of attractive and forbidding territory once styled 'Palestine' that led Field Marshal Allenby, the hero of the British Mandate in the 1920s to declare that the Holy Land was a 'damned unholy land'. In most respects it remains so.

Historically, too, the terms Israel and Palestine have a particular significance. Generally, known as Palestine the Palestinian territories comprise the West Bank and the Gaza Strip. They are the homelands of the Palestinian Arabs, between the Mediterranean Sea and the River Jordan. The United Nations and international legal bodies often refer to them as the 'Occupied Palestinian Territories' referring to the capture and occupation of these lands by Israel in 1967. Portions of the Territories have been governed by varying degrees by the so-termed Palestinian Authority.

The ancient realm of Palestine was entrusted to Britain as a mandatory power by the League of Nations in 1920. It was always likely to be a place of dogged contest between neighbouring Arab states and Jewish Zionism, the product of a mature Hebrew culture amplified after the First World War by large-scale Jewish immigration and financial investment. What was a politico-economic principle of 'absorptive capacity' as a limiting factor on numbers was trampled underfoot by Jews fleeing from Nazi Germany in the 1930s and in their many thousands seeking the asylum of a Jewish homeland. Arab antagonism flared bitterly into violence and sabotage exacerbated by the UN proclamation of the State of Israel in May 1948. Palestine, as an integral part of the new state, had exchanged its historical-geographical expression for that of an internationally recognised 'political entity'. Inevitably tension and trouble were to flare and the Arab dominions became a running sore in the eyes of many Israelis and their government. Generally, those living in a newly endowed state can look to a prospect of peace, order, amity on all sides. That was not to be in the Israel of the 1940s, nor has it been for more than five decades since then. One can hardly imagine a scenario less civilised, less progressive, less reassuring for settler or immigrant.

Terror struck the land after 1948 as a Jewish defence band, Haganah, fought off Palestinians and Jordanians cutting off roads between Jerusalem, the capital and Tel Aviv. Vanquished Arabs took it out on Jewish settlers by burning their houses. Other Arab terror groups — mercenaries from Egypt, Syria, Lebanon, Iraq — spasmodically gained, lost and regained a foothold in towns and villages systematically destroying orchards, farms and water resources. By 1957/58 Israel and Egypt were so engaged in fighting that UN forces had to intervene. Yet again, in 1967, there was a wholesale state of war between Israel and Egypt, the so-called Six Day War.

One of the saddest consequences of conflict in Israel has been the flight or expulsion of a large number of Arabs from their homes there. Numbering something like 700,000 they have escaped to the West Bank or the Gaza Strip to shelter at first in makeshift camps funded by the UN. The homes of these refugees have been appropriated by a great flood of Jewish immigrants from Eastern Europe and North Africa.[1] Again, the Arab has felt provoked and in this instance displaced by Jewish people and a build-up of their Zionist national elitism. For Arab zealots on the other side restitution had to use the planted bomb or the bullet.

After 15 years or so of sectarian conflict within the ironically named 'Promised Land' the masterminds of Jewish and Arab worlds felt they must recruit battalions of political power and armed readiness. In 1964 Palestinian Arabs put together, as freedom fighters, a nascent government, the Palestinian Liberation Organization (PLO). Their goals were an independent Palestinian state in territory under Israel control and the established right of Palestinian refugees to return to Israel. For them activism would be strategically conceived and tactically controlled both by their spokesman in Israel's parliament, the Knesset, and, if necessary, by hit-and-run guerrilla raids in the field. This bifocal style of Arab pressure led to problems at the UN and elsewhere when more than 100 states recognised the PLO as the official voice of the Palestinians. Could they support the existence of a terrorist wing housed in 'safebases' in Gaza and the West Bank?

On the ground retaliatory initiatives by a beleaguered Jewry resulted in splintering among the Palestinians, outgunned but not lacking fervour. Two groups emerged – Fatah and Hamas – both of them in various ways ready to justify violence and terror tactics as an inescapable response to the harrowing of their kinsfolk. Was not their terrorism moral and legitimate in the face of the state terrorism of Jerusalem? It is worth taking a close look, if only in outline, at these two groups absolutely feared by Jews and condemned by much international opinion.[2]

FATAH

This movement was founded in 1959 as a vehicle expressing Palestinian nationalist ideology in which Palestinian Arabs would be liberated through their own purposive action. One of the originators was Yasser Arafat, a well-schooled, thoughtful and charismatic young man. Fatah was to have sustained involvement in a revolutionary struggle where the main aim, stated in Article 12 of the Fatah constitution is 'complete liberation of Palestinian territories and the eradication of Zionist economic, political, military and cultural existence'. This pugnacious declaration was sure to win widespread support. Zealots, lightly armed, and in the front rank, began night-time sabotage of Israel's government installations, sniping at IDF guards and maintenance personnel. Arafat and his planning team at headquarters were reported to be unhappy at such actions seen as wildfire terrorism. Rather, the constitution's brave words merited larger, synchronised action. For this weaponry must be procured from supporters in, say, Syria, Egypt, Iran. Other states, like Jordan, must be persuaded to acknowledge Fatah's serious intentions and its politico-military drive.[3]

Throughout the early and mid-1960s there was a state of attrition as Fatah irregulars met IDF units proficient with heavy weaponry, armoured vehicles, aerial reconnaissance and strafing. Israel saw Fatah commando squads as attacking the Israeli state proper rather than as a movement with community independence as its proclaimed goal. The aim of 'eradication' hardly squared with any declared intention to enter a political engagement rather than a military one.

It was in late March 1968 that Fatah together with Jordanian army support joined battle with the IDF and forced them to withdraw. What seemed decisive victory for the Palestinians was soured by Jordanian reluctance to do much to risk Israeli displeasure. Fatah decided to look further afield for military supplies and they secured some help with munitions from Russia, and a number of east European communist regimes and Lebanon. Looking to the possibility of enlisting allies for their field work Fatah set up a training scheme in the late 1980s for militants from other Arab states. Associated with this was intensive grooming of Fatah guerrilla fighters, spearheaded by the Black September group who would wreak devastation on Israeli outlying settlements, transport and communications.

Fatah's unity and its mastery in the political arena were to be dissipated after the year 2000. Arafat, much disillusioned, retired to Tunis and died in 2004. Different factions within the movement split apart: those younger ones who accompanied a political approach with shooting from the hip; and the 'old guard' forlornly making overtures now and then to those Israelis in the Knesset they felt able to talk to. That Fatah in 2011 is no longer regarded as terrorist by any state rather points to its effete nature underlined by a firm electoral defeat in the Occupied Territories in 2006. Some of the younger Fatah loyalists, adept in explosives use and always ready to cap terrorism with suicide, have now formed a Martyrs Brigade and gone in with Hamas. They are certainly devoted to the notion of 'eradicating' everything Israeli, and can easily draw upon a steady stream of keen recruits.

The note of division and uncertainty was put into fresh light in March 2011. On 15 March a crowd of many thousands (it was said) demonstrated widely in the Palestinian towns calling for political unity between Fatah in the West Bank and Hamas in Gaza. According to BBC reports the protesters wanting an end to rivalry and deadlock had seen the impact of 'people power' in Tunisia, Egypt, Libya and Bahrain, and they wanted 'a piece of the action'. Pacifically, one hopes.

HAMAS

'Hamas, eh?' 'Hamas, today?' Benjamin Netanyahu, Israel's Prime Minster, is not usually lost for words. On this occasion, however, in Tel Aviv, February 2011, a questioning television reporter found his interviewee somewhat taken by surprise. 'Hamas, these days?' Pause. 'Well, they're terrorists. Been so for 25 years. With impossible demands. But, um, they're terrorists with a difference . . . that's it.'

Netanyahu, Premier and veteran internationalist, was right. Hamas is significantly different from other activist groups. There are three elements here – the maintenance of a focused political agenda; a welfare-social services wing; and a well-trained, battle-hardened military wing. Overall, Hamas shares with its Arab neighbours a carefully observed, consistent Islamic fundamentalism. Given the extent and inter-relatedness of these elements to label Hamas as 'terrorist' without any qualification represents the narrowest of 'that's it' perspectives.[4]

HAMAS – THE POLITICAL AGENDA

Created in 1987 as the Islamic Resistance Movement, the Gaza Strip of Palestine was the natural locale for Hamas. The aims were numerous. Palestine was to be liberated from Israeli occupation. An independent Islamic state should be established where autonomy would be commensurate with that of Israel. Palestinian refugees from the Israeli–Palestinian conflict must hold the right of return to their native land. Israeli settler-occupation and investment in Palestinian territory should cease. East Jerusalem was to be the capital of the new nation.

Hamas maintains political continuity through a decision-making council, the Majlis al-Shura. Consultative day-to-day work is discharged through a Political Bureau and regional committees. The more detailed administrative procedures are handled by bodies working at a distance in the Syrian capital, Damascus. Hamas 'terrorists' have formed a constitutional Charter or Covenant dating from 1988 where the basic position on many issues is set down. Hamas, as the Palestinian Muslim Brotherhood, raises the banner of Jihad in the face of infidels and oppressors. Essentially, there is a clarion call for an Islamic state in Palestine and for the dissolution of Israel since Arab–Jewish reconciliation appears impossible. All too clearly a final solution will come about through either victory or martyrdom.

Despite the inimical postures of Hamas in print and public utterance there have been occasions when a two-state truce and eventual settlement has been tentatively suggested for the parties in conflict. US Presidents Jimmy Carter and Bill Clinton in 2006 and 2008 unsuccessfully tried to broker some sort to deal based on agreed territorial boundaries and a recognition of national rights. In the end Jewish and Arab hardliners rejected compromise believing that a military truce would only be used to prepare for further fighting rather than for pacification.

The Hamas Charter and much of the group's rhetorical flourish is regarded by most Israelis (and certainly by Netanyahu) as precluding any useful rationale. They see Hamas' arguments as all too obviously buttressed by weaponry. Israeli governments have judged it easier to get along with another Palestinian movement, Fatah. Its leader, Yasser Arafat, realised that a liberation struggle must provide for settled two-state contiguity. In 1990 Fatah arranged to set up the Palestinian Authority as a provisional instrument for this manoeuvre. Hamas was to go along with tacit recognition of Israeli–Palestinian co-existence while, as it were, relegating the rifle to the weapons store. In 2006 a landslide election sidelined the more peaceful Fatah and brought to majority power (and international disdain and suspicion) the more virulent Hamas.

HAMAS – SOCIAL WELFARE WING

These are the terrorists with a social conscience and with welfare training and provision. Palestinians in the Occupied Territories now benefit from an extensive welfare service which is funded, so it is estimated, by 90 per cent of the Hamas annual budget of some US$70 million. Elaborate social services are responsible for a comprehensive network of healthcare clinics, medical facilities and surgery in hospitals, soup kitchens, infant care and orphanages, centres for the elderly, mosques, sports clubs. Relief and health education programmes are a particular concern. Medical treatment generally is free or inexpensive. Islamic charities in association with Hamas have helped to build nurseries, kindergartens and libraries, and have done a great deal for physically and mentally disabled Palestinians. In addition, Hamas financing in the social and educational sector is supplemented (with careful safeguards) by UNRWA (United Nations Relief Works Agency) and UNICEF (United National Emergency Fund).

HAMAS – THE MILITARY WING

This is the sector which attracts most international notice, fear and opprobrium. Clearly seen are resolve, morale discipline and efficiency. Heading the wing are the al-Qassam Brigades, competently led and trained. Their mission is to set up a defensive screen to protect Palestinian people and land. They maintain an aggressive front against their Israeli oppressors. In some senses these moves might have a basic justification but unfortunately their weapons have been employed too often leading to appreciable loss of life and damage to property. Hamas, it has to be said, has resorted to barbarous terror methods widely and without much discrimination against perceived enemies, their settlements and their transport links. The bombs, the mortar, the rocket, the artillery piece, the shotgun have all caused havoc in Israel. Very definitely Hamas is classified as a terrorist organisation by European Union countries, the USA, Canada, Japan and Israel. A number of states including Russia, China, Norway, Switzerland and Turkey have not gone as far as that. Israel, as expected, has launched fierce retaliatory attacks. In December 2006 Israel invaded Gaza and spent several months there hoping to extinguish 'a hornet's nest'.

The Hamas front-line cadre has been trained in Iran and Syria especially in the handling of sophisticated, extra-sensitive explosive devices. If the need arises a fair number of stand-by reserve personnel can be put into the field. The al-Qassam Brigades are seen as elite, ideologically driven action men. Something that troubles Israel, observers elsewhere and also a number of committed stalwarts in Hamas, is the vicarious violence of 'others' not belonging to Hamas itself who on occasion are responsible for murderous incidents in Israeli towns and villages, buses and trains.

Terror shootings and bombings, the work of Hamas and with a seemingly unpredictable momentum have been interrupted now and then by feelers put out as to a possible cease fire between the contestants. Little success has been seen since each side appears quite distrustful of the other. The terrorism of Hamas and of its Fatah ally reached fever pitch in 1987 and again in 2000 when Palestinians organised an Intifada, a concerted uprising against Israel's rule in the Occupied Territories. Intifadas were marked not only by military engagement but also by prolonged calling for Israel's complete withdrawal from Palestinian territories captured and occupied since the Six Day War of 1967.

HAMAS IN REALITY

The toll of terror in Israel and Palestine strikes most observers as both horrendous and question begging. Given the Hamas record of violence over decades and, yet, the observable differences compared with other groups, how far is it possible to balance out the inherent contradictions? Jeroen Gunning in his *Hamas in Politics* (2009) has compiled a masterly, detailed study of the Hamas 'reality', capturing, he says:

a reality that renders as a travesty the politically motivated and reductionist view of the group as merely a 'terrorist movement'.

Gunning's analysis is strong and objective and his views will doubtless make many readers keen to go further with the argument. (There should be much to interest Netanyahu.)

The adversarial posture of Hamas in relation to Israel and in view of the terror toll presents for Gunning a series of key questions:

To what extent is Hamas' violence informed by religion, to what extent by other, political considerations? Does religious commitment make Hamas more intransigent and violent? How did changes in public opinion affect Hamas' behaviour? To what extent is Hamas' opposition to the peace process a function of inter-Palestinian rivalry, and a quest for domestic power? What role do elections, negotiations with Fatah or political inclusion play?

Objectivity is all-important for by focussing exclusively on violence we risk ignoring the impact of the movement's social and political embeddedness on its use of violence.

And our analysis needs to be wide-ranging:

To study Hamas' approach to violence as if it were simply a socially isolated resistance group with no domestic political ambitions and a static attitude towards violence would be to miss the tensions between Hamas' various goals, wings and constituencies and how these affect its approach to violence and the peace process.[5]

As for the violence, a stark background to our surmise and readiness to explore the total scenario are there signs that the usage of violence may sometimes wane? Gunning quotes the changes in constituency approval/disapproval that Crenshaw and others have noticed. A decrease in an organisation's wider popularity is 'backlash' and a lessening in its members' commitment to violent struggle is 'burn out'. Gaza, the land of Hamas, has experienced such turns in fortune.

How humane (in reality) is the Hamas cause? What is its considered view of human rights and justice for all? If the basic position as we see it (and very likely Gunning) is one focussing on tactics, strategic calculations and the maximisation of one's bargaining power then does this help to explain Hamas rejection now and then of peace proposals which affect at least a liberal stance? Could it be, as Gunning suggests, that Hamas has to have violence around since without it Palestinians have no leverage over Israel? A peace process not leading to a viable two-state finality is not worthwhile. They might as well carry on fighting. Their political influence is strengthened down the barrel of the gun and in the blast of the car-bomb.

Not only Gunning but a host of politicians and informed commentators have struggled with the contradictions and sought to reconcile the logic in diverse Palestinian scenarios. We get nowhere without multi-dimensional insights.

TERRORISM – THE HUMAN TOLL

Something of the consequences of the Israeli–Palestinian conflict may be gauged by a study of casualty figures. These can be obtained from various sources. They are, of course, only rough pointers to the costs of a conflict situation:

Fatalities[6]

1948–1997	Overall Israelis and Palestinians 13,000
1948–2009	Overall Israelis and Palestinians 14,500
2000–2006	Palestinian deaths 3,824; Israelis 1,011 (764 were minors)
1987–2007	Palestinian deaths 5,928; Israelis 1,443

Casualty demographic percentage: (estimates for the conflict overall)

	Combatants	Civilians	Children
Palestinians	41%	59%	20%
Israelis	31%	69%	12%

Casualties are the consequence of *direct* conflict viz military operations, artillery barrage, search-and-arrest operations, demonstrations. Security forces and civilians are included. Generally, Palestinian casualties are three of four times those of Israelis. This is partly because Palestinian attacks are more often intercepted and also on account of superior Israeli fire-control and quality of ordinance.

Weaponry: small arms, mortars, rockets, artillery (mobile and placement), mines, tanks, personnel carriers, bombs, helicopters. Reported use of white phosphorus missiles. Generally, firing systems, deployment control, ready availability give Israeli Defence Force the advantage. Israel has used United States arms suppliers; the Palestinians from Russia, Eastern Europe, China.

In regard to violence once more, there appeared in April 2011 the Goldstone Report where a British judge, Richard Goldstone, had led a UN factfinding mission commissioned by the UN Human Rights Council into the effects of conflict on human rights observance. Goldstone particularly found Israel guilty of wilful civilian killing in Gaza and this was intended to 'punish, humiliate and terrorise'. The publication of this assertion was vigorously opposed by Jerusalem and in fact Goldstone himself, on further enquiries of the Israeli Defence Force, withdrew the statement satisfied that this and other incidents, were the result of erroneous intelligence and not deliberate targeting of non-combatants.

CONCLUSION

The Israeli–Palestinian conflict generations old, is so larded with disputed interpretation that any conclusion risks being read as a set of rather open assertions. An interesting line of thought, arguable certainly, is to be found in Martha Crenshaw's *Terrorism in Context* (1995) where there is a full chapter on the conflict. Here a Crenshaw associate, Ian Lustick, compares so-termed 'other-directed terrorism' with 'solipsistic terrorism'.[7] That is to see terrorist violence as a matter for self-perception. Crudely put, each contestant asks 'what does violence do to the enemy and for them?' and 'what does violence do *to* us and *for* us?'. Put this way the purpose of violence against an enemy serves the psychological needs of the group on whose behalf the violence is undertaken. Violence is a necessary, useful 'therapeutic' device. It fills out self-esteem, leads to inspiring examples of Zionist and Arab prowess and heroism predisposing the majority against a posture of compromise. 'We fight, therefore we are!' (paraphrasing Descartes). Violence against them (the enemy) and on our behalf confers on us vitality, builds self-respect, for that is the only way forward. Our resolve, sense of righteousness, in addition to continued warring, heavy defence spending, costly casualties must convince them to accept political arrangements in which our demands are granted. So the brutal acts of terrorism in the strangest of ways may bring about coherence and confidence among violence-users. For Lustick 'it is fair to call such violence terrorism, but it is also communication'. Violence conveys messages for them and for us. If they are we listen and engage there may be a hope of peaceful accommodation.

POSTSCRIPT

The news in early May 2011 that the Palestinian rivals Fatah and Hamas were on the verge of reconciliation has taken most people by surprise. Is there a prospect of a unity government superseding the largely discredited PLO? Has Egypt, the broker behind the promise of accord, brought into being at last a mixing of the modestly-fashioned Fatah alongside the now restrained armed virulence of Hamas? Is the possibility of these two working together an inevitable consequence of agitation from the thousands now crowding streets in the Arab Spring? Could there ultimately be a prospect of a firm and lasting concordat that takes into account contextual features such as Arab nationalism and Zionist expansionism and finds some sort of settlement pathway?

The Egyptian initiative calls for presidential and legislative elections no later than early 2012. Israel blanches at the prospect of any participation by terrorism-prone Hamas. Is it not obvious, they fear, that Hamas, even in government, would want to maintain its terrorist brigades and its fortifications along the Gaza Strip? The prime need for Israel and for Washington is to demilitarise somehow moves to institutionalised reconciliation.

Libya

R EADERS WILL no doubt look at this case study with extra interest and perhaps some scepticism. This discussion of Libya and terrorism was composed in December 2010. Indeed, then, things had improved with Libya and its leader being widely applauded for their attempts at a peaceful, cooperative resolution of differences. Yet, some 10 weeks later, the autocratic head of state, Colonel Gaddafi, had initiated a regime of terror against these of his own people whose revolutionary ardour was surely in key with the ongoing Arab Awakening. Gaddafi now lost all credibility as a civilised statesman and faced the wrath of many nations at his barbarism. The UN Security Council on 18 March 2011 passed Resolution 1973 by a 2 to 1 majority authorising 'all necessary measures' to protect civilians in Libya. Foreign occupation forces would not be allowed to intervene. A ban on all aircraft flights in Libyan air space was enforced to help in civilian protection.

March and April 2011 saw NATO airstrikes seeking to rid Libyans of their terror ordeal. A number of UN member nations, led by Russia and China, termed these strikes a disproportional use of unmandated force. More general international discussion is worried about the appropriateness of humanity and weapons accuracy of airborne measures when protective facilities and moves towards eventual security and settlement are very clearly ground-based logistically and patience-demanding politically.

All too obviously most world opinion regards Gaddafi and his supporters as master-terrorists, reversing their pacific intentions of a year earlier. Libya's revolutionaries are militarily at a disadvantage and their continuous suffering is appalling.

Three months into the Libyan regime of state terrorism the situation on the ground remains unclear. Even when the terrorist-in-chief is removed what will be the shape of his devastated country? Apropos removal there was an assassination attempt on Gaddafi by NATO aircraft on 2 May 2011. It failed (though the same day a United Nations attack unit located and killed Osama bin Laden in Pakistan). Is this type of mission not incompatible with international law? If Libyans are able to work towards renunciation of violence how meaningful and lasting is it likely to be? And reconciliation? Who will help, inside or outside Libya, to bring that about and in what ways?

With all the foregoing in mind, the original case study presented mainly unaltered should provide a 'good read'.

For 30 years, certainly in the Western world, Libyans and their leader, Colonel Quaddafi (also known as Qaddafi, Khadafi), have been regarded as the pre-eminent exponents of state terrorism. Why, though, should any state and state leader deliberately adopt terrorist policies? To understand how this can come about and how the rest of the world responds to it, a number of issues deserve scrutiny. First is an outline of the geographical context. Second, how is the persona of Quaddafi best described? Third, since Libya is a revolutionary state, what ideals and policies energise political action and lead to violence? Fourth, what are the initiatives and the scale of state-sponsored violence as it has been directed at other countries? Fifth, what has been the shape of international response to sponsored terrorism? Why is it that Libya's relations with the United States, in particular, have deteriorated so markedly since the early 1980s? Finally, is it possible to see an end to the terrorism, which, at the end of the 1990s, has been much reduced in scale?

LIBYAN TERRORISM: AN OVERVIEW

A useful introduction to the Libyan scenario, before we give it a more detailed examination, is the overview of Walter Laqueur (1999):

In the 1970s and 1980s, Libya was one of the foremost sponsors of international terrorism. Its involvement was almost as pervasive as that of Iran, a much larger and more populous country. Libya's sponsorship of terrorism predates that of Iran, dating back almost to the coup in 1969 that brought Colonel Khadafi [Quaddafi] to power. Khadafi's ambition was to spearhead an Arab–Islamic revolution in which he saw himself not only as the chief ideologist (by virtue of his little 'Green Book') but also as chief strategist. Libya's income from the sale of oil provided the where-withal to finance a variety of terrorist activities, but in subsequent years it became apparent that the country was too small and backward to sustain any major political and military initiatives. Furthermore, Khadafi's erratic behaviour (to put the best possible gloss on it), his inordinate ambitions, and his rapidly changing alignments antagonized virtually everyone in the Arab world and isolated him from all but his most needy clients. Doubts were expressed concerning his mental state, not only in the West but also in the Arab and Third World capitals. Was he a madman in the clinical sense, or just highly emotional, unbalanced, and unpredictable? Khadafi even became an embarrassment to those closest to him in outlook.

Though Libya experienced strong economic growth in the early years of the Khadafi regime because of massive oil exports, its growth stalled after 1985 and eventually declined by 1995. Nevertheless, the Libyan regime was still able to spend considerable sums sponsoring terrorist activities abroad and on the construction of factories to produce poison gas and other chemical weapons. Support was given primarily to Arab terrorist groups, but also to a variety of Central and West African groups, and eventually to terrorists from Ireland to the Philippines. Among the recipients of Libyan help were the German RAF as well as the so-called Black September. According to unconfirmed reports, about eight thousand foreign terrorists, most of them Arabs, were trained each year in Libyan camps in the 1980s, and those select Palestinian groups favoured by Khadafi received an annual subsidy of $100 million. Among the most famous terrorists on the Libyan payroll was Carlos the Jackal, who had been enlisted by the Popular Front for the Liberation of Palestine.

However, the list of recipients of Libyan money changed quickly, sometimes overnight. While relations with Fatah and Arafat had been close at one time, they deteriorated later, and the PLO (and many thousands of Palestinian guest workers) were expelled from Libya as Khadafi shifted his support to the most extreme Palestinian factions, such as the one headed by Abu Nidal. Even Carlos, who had been of so much use to the Libyans, was ultimately refused entry to Libya.

Libyan-sponsored terrorism manifested itself in a variety of other activities, including attacks against Libyan political émigrés. In 1984, some twenty-five such attacks were counted in Europe and the Middle East, and the assassinations continued in later years, albeit on a reduced scale. In one famous instance, Khadafi personally gave orders to his agents in London to open fire on the British police in front of the Libyan legation, an action that annoyed even the Soviets. Khadafi, they felt, was giving international terrorism a bad name. Attacks were carried out by Libyan agents against American and European targets but also against moderate Arab countries. To give a few examples, mines were laid in the Red Sea near the entrance to the Suez Canal after plots to kill President Mubarak of Egypt failed. The bombing of the Berlin nightclub La Belle Discothèque in April 1986 killed three American soldiers, wounded eighty, and claimed some two hundred German civilian victims. Six years later a German court established that while the attack had been carried out by a Palestinian, two officials of the Libyan legation in East Berlin had provided the explosives and logistic support and cover, and that East German espionage services had also been indirectly involved. In Africa, Libyan agents tried to destabilize and overthrow the then moderate government of Sudan, as well as those of the Central African countries of Chad, the Central African Republic, and Zaire.

By 1985, Khadafi's prestige was high among the terrorists, even though they were aware that the Libyan dictator tended to promise more than he delivered. But he certainly seemed more willing to accept the risks of provoking major powers than any other country. The more extreme the group, the more likely it was to find help and, if need be, a refuge in Tripoli. At the same time Khadafi's active and seemingly successful opposition to Islamic fundamentalism made some of Libya's unfriendly neighbours hesitate to take drastic action against Khadafi. Those who did not admire him seemed to fear him, at least in the Arab world. Khadafi's successes made him lose whatever remnants of a sense of reality he still possessed. He overstepped the limits of what was internationally acceptable, and invited a reaction that led to a drastic decline in his standing and a reduction of Libyan-sponsored terrorist operations.

Following Libyan terrorist attacks in Vienna and Rome airports, the Belle Discothèque bombing in West Berlin, and an attempt to bring down a TWA plane over Greece, the United States launched an air strike called El Dorado Canyon in April 1986 against selected targets in Libya. El Dorado Canyon was a one-time strike, not all targets were hit, and the damage caused was not very great. Nevertheless, to the surprise of most of America's European allies, the attack had an immediate effect. The Libyans showed much greater caution afterward, whereas earlier they had boasted of not being afraid to tackle a superpower.

America's European allies assumed that the American attack would have the opposite effect. France and Spain banned the F-111 aircraft engaged in the operation from flying over their territory. However, their fears were misplaced. During 1986–9, there was a decline in terrorist operations all over the Arab world, not just on the part of Libya. The fear that once America lost patience and felt that its vital interests were involved it might react violently and indiscriminately on a massive scale had been planted. While this might not have frightened small extremist groups, it certainly frightened their sponsors.

It was clear that the effect of a limited operation such as El Dorado Canyon would wear off, and after a number of years the bombing of Pan Am flight 103 over Lockerbie, Scotland, and the French airliner UTA flight 722 over Chad took place. (Khadafi apparently wanted to humiliate the French for having ousted the Libyan armed units from Chad, which Tripoli thought part of its sphere of influence.) In both cases, no one claimed credit for the operations, and traces of Libyan involvement were well hidden. Indeed, it seems likely that in the case of the Lockerbie disaster Iran and Syria might also have been involved. However, only Libyan involvement could eventually be proven with reasonable certainty. The matter was taken to the United Nations, where the Security Council unanimously adopted resolution 731, according to which the Libyan government was requested to hand over two of their agents who had been indicted in the United States and in Britain for their part in the Lockerbie disaster. The Security Council resolution also stipulated that Libya accept responsibility for the downing of the French airliner, disclose all evidence, and pay appropriate compensation. The Libyans refused to do so and brought upon themselves a series of sanctions, including an aviation embargo, limitations on the Libyan diplomatic presence in foreign capitals, drastic reductions in oil sales, and other measures that did considerable harm to the Libyan economy and to Libya's international standing. It was a humiliation for Khadafi, and for once he had no response.

The Libyan refusal to comply had no immediate dramatic consequences inasmuch as Khadafi remained in power. But it soon appeared that he had underrated the long-term consequences of being branded an outcast. While the Tripoli government continued to harass exiles from Libya (there were reports of the abduction of a human rights activist in Cairo and a murder in London), these occurred on a much smaller scale than before. Tripoli continued to give some help and shelter to the most extreme Arab terrorist groups, particularly those unwilling to contemplate peace with Israel under any conditions, but reduced its support of non-Arab terrorism. Libyan propaganda was almost as violent as before, but there was one considerable difference: hardly anyone in the outside world paid it any attention. Prior to 1985, Khadafi seemed to have almost gained the stature of a world leader. By the 1990s he was virtually ignored, not just by the outside world but even by his fellow Arabs. He had started his career with far-flung schemes to promote Arab unity, and terrorism had been one of the main means to that end. By the 1990s he had reached the conclusion that Libyan expansion to the south, towards Africa, was more promising and certainly less risky. The Khadafi saga demonstrates what should have been clear from the beginning: that an unscrupulous and relatively unimportant government could buy influence by investing heavily in international terrorism, but once it became more than a mere irritant, a backlash was inevitable and its power would wane.[1]

LIBYA'S GEOGRAPHICAL CONTEXT

Libya has a Mediterranean coastline of 1,200 miles, with a fertile coastal strip giving way to the desert, the Sahara, which stretches eastwards to Egypt and the Sudan, southwards to parts of Niger, Chad and the Sudan, and then to Algeria and Tunisia in the west. Its sheer size is impressive (two and a half times that of Texas, seven times that of the United Kingdom), and its strategic importance is momentous as a natural trading route between Africa and Europe. It is not a crowded land, with just over five million people, mainly Sunni Muslim Arabs, settled there since the seventh century AD. What is significant for this case study, however, are the ways in which certain aspects of Old Libya have been transformed by its people into a New Libya, a process regarded perhaps superficially and not too objectively by outside observers.

A revolution that is geographical as well as political is outlined historically by Henri Pierre Habib (1975), a Canadian scholar:

When Libya was granted its independence by the United Nations on December 24, 1951, it was described as one of the poorest and most backward nations of the world. The population at the time was not more than 1.5 million, was over 90 per cent illiterate, and had no political experience or knowhow. There were no universities, and only a limited number of high schools which had been established seven years before independence. All this had been the result of centuries of Turkish domination and Western imperialism. Every effort was made to keep the Arab inhabitants in a servile position rendering them unable to make any progress for themselves or their nation. The climax of this oppression came during the Italian administration (1911–43) when the Libyans were not only oppressed by the authorities, but were also subjected to the loss and deprivation of their most fertile land which went to colonists brought in from Italy. The British and French who replaced the Italians in 1943 attempted to entrench themselves in the country by various divisive ways, ultimately to fail through a combination of political events and circumstances beyond the control of any one nation.

Despite the attempts made by a number of powers to keep Libya divided and weak after 1951 by establishing a federal system in a homogeneous state, the Libyans amended their own constitution in 1963, established a unitary state and removed a major obstacle to the unity of the nation. This obstacle was an administrative or structural impediment to the fuller evolution of independence which the Libyans sacrificed so much to achieve. More important than this administrative change, there were two major events which were to change fundamentally and drastically the Libyan make-up, and challenge the post-independence Libyan generation. The first event came in 1959 when highly marketable oil of superior quality was discovered in large commercial quantities. The impact of this oil discovery was to change within a decade the whole economic potential of the nation. This was the first challenge of the post-independence period. It meant that for the first time Libya was in a position, without outside help, to remove and eradicate poverty, raise the standard of education, and give itself the first real opportunity to face the challenges of the twentieth century. It was essentially the first step taken towards a still larger and more vital change that was to come and transform Libya into a modern state.

This larger and more significant change constitutes the second major event which was to revolutionize Libya and give it a new and dynamic face. This was the Revolution of September 1, 1969. It was a political, social and economic revolution permeating all facets of Libyan life. It was to rid Libya of the remaining vestiges of colonialism and endow it with a truer and fuller independence than nominally achieved in 1951. It would also allow the country to pursue its authentic Arab–Islamic vocation and perform its special role on the African continent. For Libya belongs to the Arab, Islamic and African world.

The new Libya has established relations with the African continent to an extent never seen before. It has also created closer rapport with Islamic nations and peoples all over the globe. And it is anxious to consolidate these policies particularly with the peoples of Africa and the Islamic world.

Since 1969 Libya has become a challenge to its own people in attempting to modernize itself and to create a viable nation with its own values and traditions independent of alien influences and pressures. It is providing its people with the benefits of their own natural resources, transforming the raw wealth of the country into services in agriculture, education, housing, health and welfare. Rarely has a nation done so much for itself in such a short time.[2]

QUADDAFI: THE ARCH-TERRORIST PERSONA

Muammar al-Quaddafi was born in a desert tent, 20 miles south of the seashore town of Sirte in the spring of 1942. The family were illiterate herders of camels and goats, Bedouin Arabs, who passed on to their son stirring stories of tribal heroes and memories of harsh Italian rule ever since the annexation of Libya in 1911. Primary and secondary schooling followed and Quaddafi struck all his teachers as gifted, serious, rather taciturn and a most devout Muslim.

Libyan independence in December 1951 led to a flow of books, magazines and newspapers from the wider world, above all from Egypt. Young students now listened eagerly to the radio and to the impassioned rhetoric of the Egyptian leader, Gamal Abdul Nasser. The following year, Nasser's 'army officer's club' overthrew a weak sovereign in Cairo and, reasserting Arab nationalism, unity and pride, replaced King

Farouk with a republic. Many Libyan students, dubbed 'irresponsible hotheads' by their teachers (Quaddafi was expelled for his outspokenness), saw their own ineffectual and corrupt monarchy as needing the potent medicine Egypt had distilled. Quaddafi's zest for change (Muammar means 'he who builds up') is summarised by David Blundy and Andrew Lycett (1987):

He had soaked up the Arab revolutionary ideas which poured out of Egypt under Nasser and, although he seemed to have no clear ideology of his own, he had produced a potent cocktail of revolution and Islamic fundamentalism. He was disciplined and immensely hard-working, and he had tapped into the reservoirs of underground discontent that existed in Libya under King Idris. He was poised to plan the revolution and he decided that the most fertile ground lay in the Libyan armed forces.[3]

As an officer cadet in Benghazi, Quaddafi's charisma was strong enough to persuade others, interested in sedition, to join his 'Free Officers Movement'. In 1966 the future leader was given permission to attend a four-month training course in Britain. That experience disappointed him as he sensed all around social and moral decay and racial prejudice. His return to Libya put into fast gear the planning for an overthrow of the weak government of King Idris, who was overly dependent upon imperialist oil companies. The revolutionary coup, when it finally happened in September 1969, was a remarkably bloodless one. (There is still debate over how far Washington and London knew in advance of the revolutionary intent. They may well have felt that the oil and strategic interests of external powers would be more secure in the hands of a strong and popular Libyan regime.) Quaddafi as head of state promoted himself from captain to colonel as Blundy and Lycett recall:

He quickly developed a political style, based on the rhetoric of Nasser, but with disquieting echoes of Benito Mussolini. His watchwords were liberty, socialism and unity, and always, incessantly, 'the people'.
    In one not particularly long speech in Sebha on 22 September 1969 he used the word 'people' seventy-seven times:

> The armed forces are an integral and inseparable part of this people, and when they proclaimed the principles of liberty, socialism and unity they proclaimed nothing new. It is the people which believes in liberty, socialism and unity and inspired them to the armed forces, its vanguard, which imposed them on the enemies of the people with the force of arms, thus, the people is the teacher, the inspirer and the pioneer.

As there were no elections, unions, free newspapers or even opinion polls, what 'the people' thought was entirely dependent on what Quaddafi decided they would think.[4]

With Quaddafi safely established as head of state, his ministers competently and confidently settled down to negotiations with the great international oil concerns as a prelude to their wholesale nationalisation in 1971 of all the Western oil companies operating in Libya. The economy was now clearly in the ascendant, as Blundy and Lycett note:

Quaddafi had every reason to feel pleased with himself. He had taken on the Western imperialists and won a resounding victory. Foreign troops had left Libyan soil and the most powerful corporations in the world, the oil companies, had been forced to play his game. The Libyan national coffers, already packed with oil revenues, were overflowing.

The money paid by the West was to be used, in part at least, to undermine it.[5]

LIBYA'S REVOLUTIONARY IDEALS AND POLICIES

Master of the Libyan revolution, Quaddafi is generally presented in the media of Europe and the United States as a political prima donna – devious, untrustworthy and prone to using violence capriciously. All too often, the foreign policies of someone the *New York Times* described as a 'warring, whirling dervish' are stated as degenerating into terrorism at its worst. Less frequently is Quaddafi described as a studious reader, a careful listener, and a pragmatist who with an ideological 'think tank' converts dreams into feasible programmes of reform.

The pronouncements of Libya's September Revolution may appear to lack logic, clarity and brevity; nonetheless, they have been powerful stimulants to Libyan action, at home and abroad. A brief outline only must suffice for this case study. Habib has this to say about the cardinal precepts of the revolutionaries:

The basic ideals of the September Revolution can best be described in the triple slogan of: Freedom, Socialism and Unity. It is by turning to the three slogans that the Arab would rediscover his dignity and his place in history.[6]

Freedom is a human need that goes back into history. Freedom is one of the basic objectives and ideals of the Revolution. The Revolution believes in the freedom of the nation and its citizens, in the freedom of the individual, in the freedom of the Arab in Libya in political, economic and social matters. The individual is to liberate himself from past centuries of oppression, emancipate himself from humiliation, injustice, ignorance and serfdom. He is to liberate himself from the domination of poverty and backwardness, from the nightmare of injustice, and from oppression. This is the freedom needed to emancipate the Arab from his intolerable position. Freedom is the natural right of each individual.[7]

But political freedom which was achieved on September 1, 1969, was not enough in itself. It was a means to achieve social freedom and a social revolution, that is to say, a revolution in agriculture, industry, legislation, laws, justice, etc. 'To fulfil social freedom,' says Quaddafi, 'one must proclaim socialism in its Arab and Islamic context.'

Socialism as understood in the ideals of the September Revolution lies in the collective participation in production and work, and in the distribution of production with justice and equality. It is not to distribute poverty among people, but it is to give an equal share of prosperity to all. Above all, socialism in the Libyan–Arab context must be understood as the socialism of Islam which stems from the heritage of the Arab–Muslim peoples, their beliefs, and the events in their great history. It is a unique experience – it does not advocate class struggle but insists on harmonizing class differences.[8]

When Unity was raised as the third ideal of the Revolution, the leaders of the Revolution were not addressing themselves to national unity, which was taken for granted. They were addressing themselves to the larger question of Arab unity. Total unity of the Arabs is the ideal objective sought by the September Revolution.[9]

Most importantly, these socialist principles, the so-called Will of the People, represent the gospel of the *Jamahiriyah* in which the old entity of state is replaced by the concept of the people's 'command' or 'congress'. These principles are held to be unparalleled elsewhere, as Habib relates:

The political ideals of the September Revolution included a comprehensive political, social and economic system to be linked through the basic Islamic heritage of Libya as a fundamental point of reference. Libyans rejected the capitalist and communist systems in both domestic and international matters. They believed that Capitalism has failed because it elevated man without considering the collectivity, while the Communists failed because they emphasized the collectivity and forgot man. The Libyans came out with the Third Theory in order to correct what they believed were the shortcomings of both Communism and Capitalism. They called it the Third Theory not because it was the third in order of importance but because there already existed two other theories.[10]

This collection of principles, gathered together in 1975 as a Green Book and elaborated as the Third Theory, is seen by Quaddafi himself as 'a humanitarian theory, not an aggressive theory [. . .] it serves humanity, unlike Capitalism, Communism and Zionism'. Yet, on numerous occasions, in Quaddafi's own rhetoric and that put about by his disciples, there is less stress on universalism and more on watchful guardianship. The Third Theory, part catechism and part manual for good governance, is to be protected and defended resolutely against, by implication, a host of unbelievers and adversaries. There are frequently rallying cries for urging unity for 'battles yet to be fought'. Moreover, 'if war has to be fought it should be fought on enemy territory', and above all 'there must be no lost battles'. These remarks, with Israel or imperial Anglo-American interests in mind, do raise questions as to Libya's preparedness to use violence for political ends. Libya's 'sacred duty towards all revolutions' is understood as firing enthusiasm for aiding national liberation movements in Angola, Northern Ireland, the Philippines, Latin America and South Africa – places where sectarian protest has become terroristic. Consequently, Libya has earned a reputation as a political troublemaker on a global scale. Revolutionary zeal is considered by most outside observers as leaping beyond the boundaries of the state, exporting intolerance, virulence and aggression. Readiness to use lethal violence, the bullet and the bomb is thought to be both deliberate in its targeting and on occasion indiscriminate.

STATE-SANCTIONED VIOLENCE

An account of Libya's resort to terrorism is introduced with reference to the sense in which Libyan revolutionaries use the term 'violence'. One of their publications (Ahmed 1983) has a two-part discussion of the term, although the meaning is not clear at times. First, they ask, what do Libyan revolutionaries understand by 'violence'? Is it not justifiable as a tool against those who would destroy a hard-won revolution?

According to our concept of violence, it does not constitute a doctrinal issue, it is no more than a stage which circumstances impose at a moment in which the complications of these circumstances become very critical.

We do not think that violence is important and inevitable as Marxism claims. In our opinion, the conflict may be settled without violence – in the Marxist sense. But this does not mean that violence is not necessary as a sole means and way of reacting against anti-revolutionary violence.

We think that, in the dialectics of revolutionary struggle, there are stages with which it is wrong to deal without violence.

Yet, reactionary forces will have to face another discovery which is more horrible for them than the previous one: they will find out that revolutionaries are determined to answer violence with violence.

[. . .] If violence will be practiced in the future, it will be total and all-inclusive; it will be exercised by peoples (societies) incited by revolutionary committees; it will be an organized violence, popular and overwhelming; it will be conducted by the people and for the people.[11]

A second question is: do revolutionary committees practise violence? The practice is justified only when it consolidates revolutionary advance and that is the responsibility, it is inferred, of revolutionary leaders. This point, however, is expressed somewhat quixotically when the leaders

lead the masses throughout the stages of revolution and this implies leading them also in the practice of violence so that this practice be psychologically and culturally fruitful, effective and human.[12]

The last statement in this part of the rhetoric may suggest to some observers that violence will very likely be action-beyond-words, aiming to bring tangible achievements and possibly taking the action on to the 'enemy's' ground as the chosen arena.

Quaddafi and his associates never secured effective political roles on the international stage; humiliated, they turned to instruments of violence. The Libyans went on to back insurgents in Uganda, Morocco and the Philippines and to support them with money and military hardware after 1972. There seemed every chance that such initiatives would establish Libya as an exporter of violence, and usher in a wave of state-sponsored terrorism. P. Edward Haley (1984) considers the inevitable question: at what point does the support given to foreign revolutionaries by an internationally recognised government become criminal? This is Haley's argument:

Qaddafi failed to extend his influence and win agreement with his ideas in 1973 in the two critical areas of oil and the Arab–Israeli conflict. Sadat, Faisal, and Assad shut him out of the October War, and he was unable to stop Egypt and Syria from entering direct negotiations with Israel. In regard to oil diplomacy, it was the Gulf producers that called the tune both as to the imposition of the embargo and its termination, which plainly was in preparation as the year ended. As humiliating as it must have been for him to be forced aside and ignored in this way on the main issues, Qaddafi none the less possessed other weapons that could be used in other policy arenas. He had toyed with them from the beginning of his regime; now he turned to them in earnest. The policy arenas lay for the most part in Africa, Asia, Europe, and even the United States, places far from the cockpit of the Eastern Mediterranean and the Gulf. The weapons on which Qaddafi began increasingly to rely were those of terror, subversion, and intervention. It was not simply that Qaddafi had been denied a more conventional role. His passionate hatred of Israel and the West and his strong convictions about Islam, not to mention his exalted conception of his own role in the scheme of things, would undoubtedly have pushed him into opposition sooner or later. Rebuffed in a humiliating way, he turned all the more wholeheartedly to the dark sides of power and politics and clung to his ambitions and expectations.[13]

Although it is a violation of international law to intervene in the domestic affairs of another country, governments regularly support armed rebellions in other states. This support certainly falls within accepted international diplomatic and military practice, and Qaddafi's backing of revolutionaries in Morocco and the Philippines accords with it. But Qaddafi did not stop with this kind of aid. He went on to give money, arms, and sanctuary to terrorists who committed random acts of horror. The activists in every cause will claim to represent the 'will of the people', and in the absence of a supervised plebiscite the validity of their competing claims is difficult to assess. The appropriate standard, in my view, is whether or not the assistance is used directly in support of the revolutionary cause on behalf of which it was given in the first place. The critical responsibility of the donor is to ensure that the recipients of his aid are not swept away by the fanaticism and moral relevatism that permeate desperate life-and-death struggles in every part of the world. If they are, the donor must stop the aid or become an international outlaw. It is difficult to make simple judgments because of the unavoidable dependence of most revolutionaries on outside help. What is difficult to judge in the abstract becomes far easier to discern when one examines specific concrete cases. As one considers example after example of the uses made by revolutionaries of outside government assistance, it becomes clear that the use is sometimes so tenuously connected with the original revolutionary cause as to be merely criminal. When the donor government declines to halt its aid and in fact even increases it in face of the obvious criminality and irrelevance of the violence it has helped unleash, then the government has become no less an outlaw than the terrorists it has nourished.[14]

Beginning in the early 1970s Qaddafi began to support terrorist and revolutionary groups and to initiate terrorist violence without regard for prudence or proportion. There was, of course, a consistent pattern to the acts. They were anti-Western and anti-Israeli, and they were designed to weaken the democracies of Western Europe and North America, to reduce their international influence, and to destabilize the countries bordering the Mediterranean. No acts of terror were launched or sponsored by Qaddafi in Eastern Europe or the Soviet Union. For a year or two before the October 1973 War Qaddafi criticized the Soviet Union for allowing Jews to emigrate to Israel. Once he decided to seek massive Soviet military aid even this feeble criticism stopped, and Qaddafi began to align Libyan foreign policy with that of the Soviet Union. This was particularly noticeable on matters of great importance to the Soviet Union, such as Soviet intervention in Ethiopia or, later, the invasion of Afghanistan.[15]

Qaddafi continued his support for terrorism, and within two years vastly increased his involvement. According to the former Libyan minister of planning, Omar el-Meheishi, Qaddafi had set aside $580 million for terrorism and paramilitary activities in 1976. At this point, of course, Qaddafi had passed beyond supporting terrorism – although he continued to do this – to the subversion, destabilization, and overthrow of foreign governments.

The motives for Qaddafi's extensive support for and practice of terrorism are clear. He wished to strike at Israel, the West, and enemies of his regime, domestic and foreign. Moreover Qaddafi's public, rhetorical diplomacy is not the most important problem he poses for the United States and its allies in the Middle East and Western Europe. Terrorism sponsored or initiated by Libya is one part of the problem. The other part is foreign intervention – the systematic training in Libya of thousands of guerrillas to be used to destabilize or overthrow neighboring governments.[16]

Haley quotes the observations of John W. Amos II (1980) that Libya went out to enlist the operational help of a range of terrorist groups:

Qaddafi's strategy of attacking Western positions in the Middle East, Israel, and all Arab states perceived to be pro-Western, logically led to a theory of targetting Western countries in their 'own backyard', meaning attacking them in their own territories. Tactically, this required the creation of an ability to hit targets located in Western countries as well as elsewhere. For this Libya did not possess a sufficiently extensive and sophisticated intelligence organization (at least at the outset) to carry out clandestine foreign operations. This lack, plus Libya's oil wealth, led to the obvious conclusion: utilize existing terrorist groups; coordinate, finance, and supply them [. . .] The selection of these groups, while seemingly random, was actually very carefully done to further the goals of the larger Libyan strategy [. . .] By 1976, the list of groups armed and trained [by Libya] had grown to encompass FROLINAT, Philippine Muslims, Thailand Muslims, Eritrean groups, and a variety of African organizations [. . .] The arms supplied were usually Soviet, and Libyan embassies served as supply and communications centres. Tripoli itself became the meeting place of almost every terrorist or insurgent group in the Middle East, Africa, and Asia.[17]

Laqueur's overview of the Libyan scenario, found on pp. 84–7, outlined the scope and intensity of terrorist incidents generally ascribed to Libyans. Precisely pinning blame on a Libyan has, however, frequently proved difficult, largely because Quaddafi moved into terrorism by means of his own 'hit-men' (whose identities were carefully shrouded) and also by entering the multi-representative terrorist network. Haley comments on this strategy of Quaddafi:

He opened his land and his treasury to existing terrorist organizations. In May 1972 the PFLP played host in Tripoli to a terrorist summit attended by representatives of Black September, Fatah, the IRA, Baader-Meinhof, the Iranian National Front, and the Turkish People's Liberation Army. This meeting was followed by others, such as the conferences in Baghdad (sponsored by the Soviet Union) and Trieste in 1974, with Libyan and Algerian officials in November 1976, at Larnaca in July 1977, and in South Yemen in 1978. These meetings are important because they facilitate joint planning and the sharing of organizational, intelligence, material, and intelligence resources. This in turn extends the reach of any single group – using Portuguese terrorists to attack an Israeli official, for example – and makes the attacks harder to anticipate.[18]

In general terms, Haley adds, 'the terrorist network, of which Libya was and is an integral part, significantly increased instability in the Middle East including Iran and the Arabian Peninsula and arguably in Western Europe as well'.

Terrorism sanctioned apparently by an irresponsible (and irrepressible) Libyan Government was to flourish for a whole decade between 1978 and 1988. The world watched, with growing distaste and alarm, Quaddafi's adventurism abroad, ending as it generally did in a welter of violence. In 1978 Tripoli dispatched commandos and tanks into neighbouring Chad to aid a National Liberation Front and to 'take out' any members of the legitimate government they came across. Twelve months later there was a symbolic, ultimately futile, expedition to back the maverick Ugandan dictator, Idi Amin. Quaddafi then turned towards civil strife in Algeria and Tunisia and in the guise of mediator used guerrilla bands to intimidate all sides in the conflict. Libyan embassies in Vienna, Prague, Bonn, Athens and Berne were converted into 'people's bureaux'. Western governments, confronted with fortified revolutionary cells in their own domain, anxiously wondered where the next terror outrage might strike as aircraft were hijacked, buildings were bombed, and 'death squads' hunted their victims in London and the United States. What were the implications of Quaddafi's mission-statement that Libyans must ensure 'the physical elimination of the enemies of the revolution abroad'?

During all this time Libya remained steadfast in support of the Palestinian liberation movement (though not of Arafat himself) and its hatred of Israel and of their United States backer went undiminished. Haley reports a declaration of Quaddafi aimed at Washington:

It is your attitude that drives the fedayeen to die and to kill the Israelis in Palestine. Your giving of arms to Israel! Your unwillingness to understand the Palestinians, your refusal to help them! You Westerners are the ones who make war the only possible solution.[19]

Inevitably, as the intensity of Libya's state-sponsored terrorism grew, governments came together to treat Libya as a pariah state with whom they could not continue to exercise civilised relations. In Haley's view, it was now clear that Quaddafi was 'running out of room' as he acknowledged a consensus refuting his policies:

Libya's increasingly aggressive and militant international actions in 1980 produced an astonishing series of foreign policy setbacks for the North African country. No less than thirteen nations in Africa and the Middle East as well as the United States either broke diplomatic relations with Libya or expelled Libyan diplomatic personnel. In addition there were tensions or a serious deterioration of relations between Libyan and eight other governments, from Uganda to France. During the months from July 1980 to January 1981 Libyan diplomats were expelled from four West African countries: Gabon in July, Ghana in November, and Niger and Nigeria in January. Much more serious were the tensions between Libya and Gambia, Senegal, the Central African Republic, Iraq, and Saudi Arabia.[20]

INTERNATIONAL COUNTER-TERRORISM

Libya's reputation as a nest of hornets did not always elicit a uniform response from outside. Blundy and Lycett in 1987 inferred that politico-strategic objectives were not consistently spearheading the counter-actions of the United States and of Britain. There were commercial factors to take account of, although, of course, these would not override response to violent attack:

Western leaders are [still] inclined to see a kind of schizophrenia in Qaddafi's foreign policy. Qaddafi the diplomat carries out energetic and often successful initiatives, dealing with such issues as trade and oil competently and sometimes brilliantly. Then there is the Qaddafi who funds terrorists and revolutionaries. Qaddafi himself sees no contradiction, although he is often puzzled by the reaction of Western governments who criticize his policies, condemn him as a lunatic, but are still prepared to do business with him. He believes that conventional diplomacy and revolutionary politics can operate in a complementary, not a contradictory, way and be means to the same ends: Arab unity, a Palestinian state, and the overthrow of imperialist or monarchist governments. He believes that if other rulers do not take the revolutionary path then they should be overthrown. He has no doubt that the United States acts in a similar way in its efforts to destabilize such regimes as Castro's in Cuba and the Sandinistas in Nicaragua.[21]

US policy towards Libya, perhaps a little less than its policy over nuclear arms limitation, is a battleground of conflicting views between different agencies and between departments of the same agency. The CIA, for example, contained at least two schools of thought, according to a Middle East analyst with special responsibility for Libya, who worked for it. The mainstream CIA analysts on the Libya desk saw all the information about Libyan terror but, like the members of the British Foreign Office, they were not impressed. They did not deny that Qaddafi funded, assisted and often instigated terror. They simply thought that among the players in Middle East terror he was not as significant as their masters in the White House believed. Their strong recommendation in dozens of memoranda was that the best policy towards Qaddafi was to ignore him unless he seriously increased his involvement in terrorism. They noted that Qaddafi had been cautious about hitting US targets and had only on rare occasions exported terrorism to the mainland United States. Their analysis of the majority of raw intelligence material about the movement of personnel and materials was that it really did not amount to much.

The clandestine services of the CIA, which are concerned more with covert operations than analysis, thought differently. They argued, in this war of memoranda, that the best way of dealing with Qaddafi was to confront him. They believed that from the raw intelligence a real threat to the US could be pieced together. Their counsel held sway with the President when he decided to launch the raid against Libya, and the clandestine services urged that action should be taken after the raid to topple Qaddafi.[22]

At last, in April 1986, the United States launched a punitive air-strike against Tripoli and other targets. Laqueur, as we have seen, believes that this operation had a lasting deterrent effect. On the other hand, a good deal of European and Arab opinion was outraged judging from public demonstrations and opinion polls in Britain, Spain, Greece, Germany and Egypt. The strike was regarded in some quarters as an over-hasty, badly thought-out response by the Reagan administration determined to show 'America strong'. Richard Falk (1986), an international law professor at Princeton, discerns a strange relationship between terrorism and counter-terrorism:

There is an odd convergence of motives between the terrorist who seeks to paralyze the adversary society and the counter-terrorist who seeks to mobilize that society in support of unilateralism and retaliatory violence. To break these linkages is crucial.

One observation stands out. If we seek to deprive terrorist activity of its impact, and therefore weaken the incentives to practice it, then we must put its exploits in proper context, and provide reassurances about safety and security. No counter-terrorist politics can succeed unless they include an appreciation of why terrorist preoccupations have gripped the body politic to such an extent.[23]

Another opinion from the United States is that of Bruce Hoffman (1998), who considers that state-sponsorship of terrorism has not been forestalled by certain counter-terrorism measures:

Today, state sponsorship of terrorism continues unabated. In 1996, for example, the US State Department designated seven countries as terrorism sponsors: Cuba, Iran, Iraq, Libya, North Korea, Sudan and Syria. With the exception of Sudan, which was added in 1993, each of these countries has remained on the list of terrorism's patron states for more than a decade. The reason, as noted above, is that neither economic sanctions nor military reprisals have proven completely successful in effecting positive changes to these countries' policies on terrorism. Even seasoned US government counterterrorist analysts are somewhat dismissive of their effects. A recent high-level discussion paper circulated within the American intelligence community noted that

In theory, the threat or imposition of embargoes and sanctions would appear to be a powerful leveraging tool in the conduct of foreign relations between countries. In practice, no state sponsor of international terrorism against which the US has enacted an embargo or sanctions has renounced it[s] role of sponsorship or denounced terrorism as a tool of its foreign policy. Nor has any state once placed on the state sponsors list ever been removed.

Military reprisals against state sponsors of terrorism have arguably proved no more effective; worse still, in some respects they have been counterproductive. For example, the aforementioned 1986 US air strike against Libya is frequently cited as proof of the effectiveness of military retaliation; yet, rather than having deterred the Qaddafi regime from engaging in state-sponsored terrorism, it appears that it may have had precisely the opposite effect. In the first place, so far from stopping Libyan-backed terrorism, the US air strike goaded the Libyan dictator to undertake even more serious and heinous acts of terrorism against the United States and its citizens. Indeed, after a brief lull, Libya not only resumed but actually increased its international terrorist activities.[24]

Terrorist incidents of Libyan origin are seldom reported in the contemporary press. From time to time there is discussion as to the best way to bring to justice those suspected of responsibility for the Lockerbie disaster. Libyan terrorism is an 'irritant' to be guarded against watchfully in the hope that one day it will disappear.

Already in 1990 there was eased tension between Libya and other countries. The *Financial Times* commented that Quaddafi's new-found international respectability was a reward for his decision to return to more conventional foreign and economic policies. Quaddafi was reported as admitting that Libya had founded some terrorist groups but that, when their aims and role had been discovered as leading to more harm than benefit, then support had been withdrawn. It was in 1991 that Libya had found, in its isolation, an opportunity to resume diplomatic normality. Oil revenues were rising by 40 per cent as a consequence of the Gulf War crisis and a world fuel shortage and the time seemed right to renew international trade contacts and investment. The terrorists donned new clothes and entered the marketplace.

For the next two years, Libya's new pacific countenance was not widely thought credible and tough sanctions were implemented by United Nations member states. Quaddafi now seemed more mercurial than ever, strongly condemning his brothers-in-violence among Islamic fundamentalists as 'mad dogs' and 'terrorists'. At the same time, in 1994, as he approved of President Clinton as 'a good man and a man of peace', he uttered a sombre warning that Washington should never interfere in Tripoli's affairs. Libya was capable of being a 'safety-valve' for peace in North Africa yet capable also of removing the safety-valve and blowing up the whole of North Africa along with itself and its enemies. In 1995 Libya applied to join the United Nations Security Council, declaring an interest in international work for peace. While Council members were considering the request of this penitent state, the applicant withdrew, observing tartly that the Security Council was a tool of US imperialism.

The position of Libya in 1999 was, indeed, that of a state slowly regaining its respectability despite the unpredictable manoeuvrings of Quaddafi, 'Leader of the Revolution'. United Nations sanctions were lifted in April 1999. The Lockerbie issue was eventually settled when two suspected Libyan terrorists were indicted and extradited with Libyan permission to be tried under Scottish law in the Netherlands in a court located on soil temporarily designated part of Scotland. In February 2001 three judges found one of the Libyans guilty and jailed him for life. His co-defendant was acquitted and returned to Tripoli to be welcomed by Quaddafi, once more voicing vituperation against Western powers.

Most people now live in towns with motorways, ring roads and a car for every seven Libyans. Erstwhile terrorists own restaurants for tourists, sell clothes and television sets, or study diligently in universities. Women ex-freedom fighters now have full sex equality in the army and in civilian life. Libya now has to fight drug addiction rather than foreign interference. The revolutionary slogan, 30 years old and a mantra for terrorism, was 'No future without unity'. A new gloss was put on this in September 1999 as Quaddafi, the former and foremost arch-terrorist, addressed 20 African presidents at a summit in Tripoli:

Now that [Libya's] liberation stage has ended, the world wants to know Muammar Gadafy as the leader of peace and development in Africa and other countries.[25]

In the case of Libya, terrorists have come out of the cold in a dramatic fashion. Already in 1999, as we have noted, United Nations sanctions were lifted. Five years later, the arch-enemy of the United States completed long and never easy negotiations, and on 21 September 2004 trade and transportation sanctions were lifted. Crucially, this was in recognition of Libya's commitment to eliminate its Weapons of Mass Destruction programme, which, according to the White House, 'significantly altered a potential threat to US security'.

Earlier, in March 2004, Britain was offering military aid in return for the scrapping of Libya's WMD work. Talks between the two countries explored further contracts in civil aviation and the import from Libya's very large gas fields. Britain's Prime Minster Blair visited Quaddafi in Tripoli and spoke of a new understanding: 'Let us offer to states that renounce terrorism and the development of weapons of mass destruction our hand in partnership to achieve it, as Libya has rightly and courageously decided to do.'[26] Out of the cold and into the warmth, it seems, as there was to be an accolade for Libya in May 2006. Washington and Tripoli were to renew diplomatic relations. Secretary of State Condoleezza Rice sounded the new notes emphatically: 'We are taking these actions in recognition of Libya's continued commitment to renunciation of terrorism.' Tripoli's cooperation had been excellent, she added. The efforts of America and its allies had brought a pariah state back into the world mainstream. Quite clearly, she put it, 'Today marks the opening of a new era in US–Libyan relations that will benefit Americans and Libyans alike.'[27]

GETTING OFF THE LIST

It was in May 2007 that the United States removed Libya from its list of state sponsors of terrorism. The move was in response to Libya's expressed intention some years before to abandon both terrorist activity and the development of a WMD programme. Talks between Washington and Baghdad had begun in the late 1990s. They were protracted, sometimes evasive and fiercely argued, at times various difficult issues went into secretive conclaves to one side of the main parleying. Outsiders such as South Africa's Nelson Mandela and United Nations Secretary, General Kofi Annan, leant a hand to resolving the disputation.

It has never been easy to gauge Libya's broader concern for human rights alongside a readiness to lay aside the use of violence. Certainly there were hopes that resumption of normal diplomatic relations together with being voted on to UN Security Council non-permanent membership might encourage a former pariah state to act more responsibly and liberally.

Bringing the renunciation of violence into practical terms has been a slow process. In May 2008 the United States and Libya began negotiations on a comprehensive claims settlement agreement to resolve outstanding terrorism-related death and physical injury claims against Libya. Eventually the agreement was finalised and implemented legally.

Throughout 2009 and 2010 extensive talks were arranged to deal with counter-terrorist strategies and tactics, nuclear non-proliferation, trade and investment, economic redevelopment, human rights. In May 2010 Gaddafi was received as an 'honoured visitor' by the White House and the US State Department. Gradually, step by step, the villains of Iraq were coming out of the cold into something a good deal warmer.

Libya's transformation from outcast to penitent to more responsible and responsive political player is remarkable though never straightforward. Speculation is vibrant as to which internal and external forces helped to shape the country's remustering. How crucial was it that by the mid-90s Iraq was struggling to cope with a fast-growing population, a notoriously mismanaged core oil industry, diminishing revenues, a turning away of former Arab allies, a freezing of hitherto generous support from the Soviet bloc, the grip of sanctions imposed by the USA and by the United Nations? There was always the chance that the US Air Force bombing of 1981 and 1986 might be resumed. Was it so that the contradictory impulses of the charismatic leader of an 'authoritarian democracy' at last were focusing on the likelihood of disaster if violent action was not done away with? Talking, peaceful movement forward should save the day. At least one observer, Bruce Jentleson, a former US foreign policy adviser, has concluded:

The backdrop of force was a factor, but not nearly the factor Bush and Cheney have portrayed it to be. The real story was the diplomacy.[28]

Lebanon I

LEBANON GRIPPED THE WORLD'S headlines in the summer of 2006 as a centre of conflict between the state of Israel and a guerrilla group, the Hizbullah, based in Lebanon. In June 2006, Hizbullah had abducted two Israeli soldiers and followed this with a provocative launching of rockets at its southern neighbour. Inevitably, Tel Aviv retaliated with several weeks of aerial bombardment and with Israeli Defence Force sorties across the northern frontier, in order, it was said, 'to exterminate a menace'. Civilian loss of life and the destruction of much of Lebanon caused much anguish in the West and led to feverish attempts to bring about a ceasefire, and, more basically, to move towards a comprehensive peace settlement for the Middle East. Impelling an international drive for regional peace and stability is always the realisation that Lebanese fratricide and forceful support for suffering fellow-Arabs will keep many millions of people suspended very close to the abyss. Indeed, ever since Lebanon emerged in 1943 as an independent state rather than as a French mandated territory, the country has been rent by civil strife and by continued hostilities with Israel. For almost 30 years, since the 1970s, Lebanon has been bombed and blasted periodically as Israel has attempted the removal of the Lebanese guerrilla irritant. At the same time there have been periods, not of reconciliation, but of politico-strategic withdrawal by Israel from its 'security zone' in south Lebanon as United Nations mediation and despatch of peacekeeping forces have eased tensions temporarily.

Out of the divisiveness of Lebanon a militant group was sure to arise. Hizbullah (also known as Hizb'allah or Hizballah), the Party of God, was formed in June 1982 as part of a religious group, the Shi'a (also known as Shi'ites, Shi'i, Shi'ia or Shiites), to provide an activist front in protest against social and political marginalisation and deprivation. Hizbullah goals, expressed cogently and emphatically, were the creation of an independent, Islamic Lebanon together with the ousting of corruptive foreign influences – the Great Satan. Muslim clergy, secular politicians, students and firebrand journalists all voiced strident, demonic opposition towards the United States and, in particular, towards Israel. They soon gathered support, funds and eventually weaponry from Syria and Iran. Within Lebanon itself, Hizbullah set out to design a system of welfare and public service provision to enable their Shiite half of the country's population to assert identity and their rights. Three members of parliament in Beirut were their elected representatives. More extreme elements within Hizbullah, however, lost no time in moving beyond propaganda broadsheets, impassioned rallies and personal intimidation to the use of violent, terrorist tactics such as selective assassination, the harassing of Israeli settlements and transport, the hijacking of aircraft, and suicide car bombing. As an instrument of revolutionary violence, Hizbullah has inevitably acquired a high media profile. Less well studied in the West, beyond condemnation of its violence and inhumanity, are the complexities of its origins and development. It seems necessary to go beyond the declaration of President George Bush that Hizbullah are merely 'a bunch of terrorists'. Interestingly, the notion of 'terrorists' and 'terrorism' seems to have the widest currency, as a recent statement on a Lebanese website sympathetic to Hizbullah makes clear:

. . . we call on the peoples of the world to distinguish between aggression, which is none other than terrorism, and the honest resistance that is the only way to deter the aggression and confront the terrorism resulting from that aggression. Israel is an aggressive entity that practises terrorism, occupation is one of the forms of terrorism. Hizbullah of Lebanon is a popular resisting trend against occupation and terrorism.[1]

THE REACTIVE NATURE OF HIZBULLAH VIOLENCE

In numerous respects Hizbullah is an idiosyncratic movement. A French political scientist, Elizabeth Picard (1997), argues that the origins of Hizbullah are best under-stood within the historical context of political mobilisation and violence and within the Lebanese community. Thus, she regards their violence, first, as largely reactive, taking the forms of extra-institutional protest, revolutionary insurrection, and terrorist acts, and, second, as a dynamic for dealing internally with Lebanese dissension and externally with Western interference. Hizbullah's violence is seen to raise four main questions: the distinction between terrorism and liberation struggles; the relation between terrorism and foreign sponsors; the effects of terrorism on Lebanese society; and the ideological linkage between terrorism and Islam. These were questions debated internationally in July 2006 as conflict flared into major violence.

In the Middle East, indeed throughout the entire Arab-Muslim region stretching eastward from Morocco to the Gulf and from Caucasia down to Sudan, few countries offer a better example of political violence than Lebanon. Not even Algeria which has suffered a large number of deaths in recent years. The only exception, it could be argued, is Iran.[2] [. . .]

. . . The birth and acceleration of this [reactive] violence can be explained by demographic, sociological, economic, legal and constitutional, as well as strategic and military, variables. Three phenomena in particular are especially significant. First, the Lebanese Shi'ia, as a group, was transformed in the space of forty years from an under-developed and submissive group to a community capable of rapid economic mobility and social mobilization. Second, because the Lebanese communitarian system is governed by a set of rigid rules, there was no continuity in the Shi'i transition from social mobilization to political mobilization. Consequently, the Shi'a saw their identity reinforced, their borders established, and their mobilization as a 'community' strengthened. Third, by using to their own advantage the failure of a new consensus within the Shi'i community and the impossibility of expanded political participation, outside forces – not only armed but 'arming' – intervened and propelled the discourse and practices of the Shi'ah [sic] towards conflict and violence.[3] [. . .]

At the outset of the 1970s, the Shi'a showed all the signs of readiness for social mobilization. Their contact with other, more prosperous segments of Lebanese society made their unfavorable situation, and their lack of social mobility, all the more painfully obvious. Indeed, it did not result in a process of assimilation, but on the contrary, one of rejection.[4] [. . .]

One of the paradoxes of Lebanon's civil violence during the 1970s and 1980s was that the discourse of all the Lebanese groups squarely laid the blame for internal dissension on foreign elements: either the *ajnab* – the West, and particularly Israel – or the *gharib*, those who do not share Lebanese bloodlines. Not only was the notion of *gharib* instrumental at de-emphasizing the internal cleavages in Lebanese society, but it also stirred up local passions against non-Lebanese and protracted the life of an indecisive political system that was mainly threatened by its own internal divisions. The belief in a foreign 'plot' (American, Syrian, Saudi, etc.) thus allowed the Lebanese to forge some semblance of a 'national' consensus. Seeking to avoid mutual accusations and self-criticism, they preferred to deny the existence of an internal dimension to the violence in their country. But in doing so, they are rendered incapable of understanding the real causes and the function of this violence – which of course meant that they could not heal its causes.

The Picard analysis of 1997 has a notable salience almost a decade later.

What must be underscored is not so much the phenomenon of foreign interference itself, but rather the juncture between international conflict and internal violence. After 1975, it became difficult to distinguish, concretely and analytically, self-defensive violence, deliberate political violence, and violence resulting from international conflict. External and internal violence became interactive.[5] [. . .]

Besides the defensive and competitive community violence, a third form of violence, qualified as 'terrorism', emerged during the revolutionary phase of the struggle. Bomb attacks aimed chiefly at spreading terror (such as the 1983 attacks against American and French army barracks of the Multinational Force in Beirut), hostage-taking (more than twenty Westerners were held in Lebanon between 1984 and 1990), and suicide missions were carried out (Israeli headquarters in Tyre were destroyed by an automobile packed with explosives in 1983). This form of violence, spectacular though marginal, raises four main questions.

First, at what point does one cross the line between 'struggle for liberation' and 'terrorism'? These acts of terrorism were acknowledged and interpreted by Shi'i militants, ideologues and tacticians as acts of war against an occupying power, Israel, and its allies, both local (the Christian militia in Lebanon) and international (the Western powers). The Shi'a, who constituted the majority of the population in South Lebanon, were the principal victims of the Israeli–Palestinian war after 1970 and the Israeli occupation after 1978. They were thus the first to adhere to the armed struggle against foreign enemies. Neither the Lebanese government nor the international community contested in principle their struggle for liberation. The issue was rather the use of violence against foreign civilians as part of the conflict, which raises the casuistical question of legitimacy as well as the existence of unequal forces between local militia groups and an over-armed state.

Second, putting terrorism in an international perspective, the relation between terrorist groups and the foreign states that sponsor must be examined. Both the study of the Fu'ad Ali Saleh's 'Shi'i' terrorist network in France and the process of liberation of the last hostages in 1991 following the end of the Gulf War show that most of these groups are financed by those states, including Iran and Syria, which opted in favour of a terrorist strategy in the second half of the 1980s. When, at the outset of the 1990s, they abandoned this strategy due to a changed international situation, they quickly and with almost total success imposed a return to international legality.

Third, the instrumental use of terrorist groups by foreign states raises the question of the relation between the Shi'i social movement and such groups. Here, the problem is not so much the organizational aspect of this relationship. On the one hand, the testimony of liberated hostages and the biographical information on certain of the authors of anti-Israeli attacks in South Lebanon indicate a definite social, even psychological, alienation on the part of extremist militants, as well as their doctrinaire rigidity. They show the characteristics that can be found among similar groups in Europe (Red Brigades, *Action Directe*), whose implacable logic led to their self-destruction. But on the other hand, the hagiographic literature, and the number and strength of popular demonstrations commemorating the memory of the martyrs, indicate that the action of terrorists, even if criticized by those in the Shi'i population who are victimized by reprisals, was in line with a majority political vision, all the more so that this action fit [sic] into a culture of violence. In this sense, 'terrorism' does not involve an inversion of the social movement but rather the extreme accomplishment of its aims.

Finally, we must question the relationship between terrorism and Islam. This link has been denounced by rightists in the West for whom the confrontation with Islam, and above all with Shi'i Islam as embodied by the Islamic Republic of Iran, has replaced the struggle against Communism. Shi'i publications such as *al-Ahd* and *al-Badil*, and the sermons and writings of religious authorities, show the contradiction between, on the one hand, a doctrine committed to the respect for life (by condemning suicide, for example) and the realization of earthly happiness and, on the other hand, the casuistry invented in the context of *jihad* in order to justify terrorist actions, including martyrdom.[6]

Issues raised by Picard have been discussed at length recently by Judith Palmer Harik (2004), at one time a professor of political science at the American University of Beirut. Picard's view of Hizbullah violence as 'largely reactive' and internally 'dynamic' has something in common with points made by Harik, though the latter's presentation of Hizbullah's strategic management appears controversial (especially in the light of the intense debate over the Lebanon–Israeli crisis of July–August 2006):

During the course of Hezbollah's 17-year struggle with Israel along the Lebanese/Israeli frontier in southern Lebanon, it has never been established by any party directly involved (including the United Nations contingent on the ground) that the Party of God has perpetrated a single terrorist attack against Israeli civilians. Highly conscious of the fact that accusations of terrorism would be used by the Israelis to try to halt the war of attrition being waged against them, Hezbollah leaders adopted and pursued a military strategy against Israeli military forces inside Lebanon's borders in which attacks against civilians meant to demoralize the government – a common definition of terrorism – had no place. Instead, guerrilla warfare techniques were used by the Party of God to achieve its primary mission – the removal of an illegal occupation. This strategy significantly undercut Israel's capacity to generate outrage against Hezbollah as a terrorist organization, while its successes elevated the Party of God to almost heroic status in Lebanon and throughout the Arab and Muslim worlds.[7]

The military strategy used against Israel, however, could not succeed on its own. It required the development of an interrelated political strategy that would sustain popular support during the lengthy period when Hezbollah's hit-and-run missions were slowly taking their toll and beginning to provoke massive retaliations from Israel. This popular support was vital in terms of countering Hezbollah's terrorist image, which was also founded on its links with Iran and Syria. Since a certain section of the Lebanese population opposed Syrian influences in their country after the civil war ended and feared Iran's influence on Hezbollah, the Shiite leaders recognized that something like a sustained public relations campaign would have to accompany the ongoing confrontation in South Lebanon. In fact, the Lebanese population would have to be persuaded that Hezbollah was no longer a radical Islamic militia that might try to replace the state with an Islamic republic if given any leeway. Hezbollah would therefore have to take every opportunity to prove that its transformation into a mainstream Lebanese party was authentic rather than opportunistic. Since this was a difficult undertaking in a country with a large Christian population, where secularism was well advanced among religious groups, Hezbollah's integration process required careful management to overcome the obstacles in its way.

I argue that this process was aided by various factors. First, Hezbollah's transformation and integration advanced the foreign policy goals of Iran, Syria, and Lebanon and therefore the Party of God received a great deal of support of varying kinds from these governments. However, that support was not sufficient to effect the party's thorough integration into Lebanese society, since many Lebanese were unhappy about the arrangement between their government and Syria or were fearful of a fundamentalist group in their midst that might try to change their country's secular status.

Second, Hezbollah leaders tried to overcome this hurdle by developing simultaneous strategies and tactics of accommodation with the Lebanese authorities and other Lebanese groups, and militancy toward Israel. This approach was helped by the fact that Hezbollah leaders chose to use considerable ideological flexibility to allay the suspicions of the liberal component of Lebanese society, by presenting their organization as a moderate, national party while still retaining its Islamic appeal and pious supporters. Moreover, projection of Arab and Lebanese identities and goals in addition to Islamic ones attracted new and diverse sympathizers, while deeply religious convictions, acts and Islamic discourse retained the loyalty of core constituents.

Third, pragmatic Hezbollah leaders were also able to adapt their organization to Lebanese political traditions and exploit the realities that imposed themselves after the 1989 Document of National Reconciliation achieved peace.

Fourth, the adoption of modern political techniques and new technologies to spread their message and expand their reach in many domains of national life and on the battlefield suited the psychological and material needs of the varying constituencies Hezbollah wished to mobilize. This eventually earned the party tolerance and respect.

Fifth, Hezbollah's development of a Media Department and satellite-connected television channel allowed it to constantly beam its message of resistance in Lebanon and throughout the Muslim and Arab worlds, where popular support for its fight against Israel was needed to insulate it from terrorist charges.

Sixth, strict adherence to 'rules' established by Syria to govern state/Hezbollah relations during conflict periods were an important means of warding off Israeli and American pressures on the Lebanese authorities to halt the party's military activities.[8]

Factors such as those above, Harik believes, may provide 'a greater understanding of why Hizbullah is lionized in the Arab and Moslem worlds and condemned as a terrorist organization in Israel and the West'. For Harik, moreover, Hizbullah is an organisation deliberately seeking to change its face.

HIZBULLAH'S RELIGIO-POLITICAL IDEOLOGY

Hizbullah ideology, welding fundamentalist religious belief and political observance, usually leftist, has been surveyed by A. A. Khalil (1991). In common with Picard, Khalil sees Hizbullah's emergence as the product of Lebanese tensions and conflict, which converge with external policy orientations, especially those of Iran. Hizbullah goes beyond the Qur'an (Koran) to emulate Leninist thinking, discipline and organisation. For Khalil the mosque becomes a rallying point for alienated Shiites who move towards campaigning as a jihad. Inevitably, and radiating beyond Lebanon, Hizbullah's assertiveness is viewed in the West as uncompromising 'terrorism', relying on sacrifice, suicide missions and martyrs. In many parts of the Arab world, though, the terrorists of Hizbullah are venerated as leaders of the 'faithful'.

The study of Islam and Islamic political movements has become a popular enterprise in the West. The religion and the world of Islam are still exotic and are hence a sensational topic. What made the study of Islam suddenly fashionable in the West is not an intellectual trend, but is rather a result of the belief that Islam is intrinsically responsible for the surge of 'international terrorism'. Western studies of Islam, however, are shrouded in generalities and reductionism. The rise of Islamic consciousness cannot be understood without specific references to the concrete conditions in every geographic area witnessing the emergence of Islamic fundamentalist movements. Islam does not mean the same thing to the people of Islamic countries; the practice and interpretation of the religion differ from one country to another. Consequently, the underlying causes behind the rise of the various fundamentalist movements are not standard or universally uniform. The subject should be approached with much more specificity.

Lebanon is one of those countries that is witnessing an intense resurgence of Islamic identification. It is the country which – in the eyes of the West at least – has made the study of Islam and 'international terrorism' indistinguishable. Yet, the causes behind the rise of Islam as an ideology are complex and not necessarily religious in nature.

Two words can sum up the deep social conflict in Lebanon. They are *al-Ghabn* (prejudice) and *al-Khawf* (fear). *Al-Ghabn* is used by Muslims to express their sense of injustice, and *al-Khawf* is used by Christians to express their fear of Arab-Muslim hegemony. While Muslims call for the redistribution of national wealth and political power, the Christians consider the privileges that they have enjoyed since the founding of the Lebanese republic in 1920 as 'guarantees' (*damanat*), as factors contributing to their psychological and political security. In other words, the National Pact, which set the official arithmetical formula for the distribution of political power on a sectarian basis, is a constant that is not subject to change according to Christians; while it is an invalid doctrine that time and reality had long transcended, in the eyes of Muslims.

This paradoxical view of the foundation of the Lebanese political system accounts for the deep tensions in society. Any diminution in Christian powers adds to the powers of the Muslims, and vice versa. Moreover, who is to say how to distribute power within the Muslim community? Relations within the Muslim faith are far from harmonious. It is almost impossible to come up with a formula that pleases all the sects at once.

Hizballah is the product of the tensions and conflicts within the Shiite community. The underlying causes for its emergence are deeply rooted in indigenous Lebanese conditions and in the aftermath of the Israeli invasion of Lebanon in 1982. Thus, it is inaccurate to maintain that Hizballah is an Iranian creation. It is also inaccurate to maintain that the idea of Hizballah 'was the brainchild' of Muhammad Husayn Fadlallah [a religio-political leader and writer]. Rather, it emerged as a result of the convergence of Lebanese Shiite interests with Iranian foreign policy orientations. [. . .]

The word *hizb* in Arabic does not have the same connotation that the word party has in English. According to the classical origins of the root of the word, *hizb* means a community, sect, or a group of followers. However, Hizballah ideology emphasizes the Quranic origins of its political terminology. Almost all of the political terms that the Party uses in its political literature are derived from the Quran. [. . .]

Hizballah is not an Islamic stipulation. It is an Islamic adaptation to the era of Leninist revolutionary organizations. The model of Leninist party organization was convenient to all those groups in the Arab world who favoured one-party rule and who are based on absolute self-righteousness and intolerance. Nasserism, Ba'thism, and some Islamic fundamentalist groups benefit from the undemocratic party structure of the Leninist organization which undermines the ability of the party members to bring about change and restructuring. Thus, any change has to emanate from above in a manner that suits the interests of the leadership in a given situation. Ironically, the Party of God, which professes a strong enmity to communism, emulates the Leninist model of party organization and borrows some of its political terms with some necessary modifications. [. . .]

In Leninist theory, the factory should be the major venue of political agitation and mobilization. In the ideology of Hizballah the mosque occupies the central stage. The mosques are transformed into arenas of political, cultural and Jihad actions, in addition to being places of worship of course, in which the decision-making process is based. The mosques are also places that provide their occupants with relative safety and security in countries where there is no freedom of expression and association. [. . .]

In Hizballah's ideology, injustice is caused by people; it is the result of what some people do to others. Like Leninist thought, Hizballah believes that justice and equality can be achieved through human efforts, through a revolutionary process. Hizballah represents a revolutionary version of Shiite Islam. [. . .]

Like the Leninist global outlook, Hizballah's ideology splits the world into two camps, the exploited and the exploiters. According to its vision, Lenin's 'international imperialism' becomes 'international arrogance', in reference to the USA. But some Hizballah ideologists deny the existence of a similarity between the ideology of the Party and Leninist ideas, and maintain that Islamic revolutionary thinking is far more comprehensive than Marxian analysis which is confined to the realm of economic exploitation while Hizballah ideology is more encompassing as it takes into consideration all aspects of human life.

It is ironic that a Shiite fundamentalist party should borrow ideas and organizational principles from the Leninist tradition. But this is not surprising when viewed within the context of the Lebanese situation where Hizballah emerged. In many ways, the rise of Islamic fundamentalist groups in Lebanon is the by-product of the failure and perceived bankruptcy of the Lebanese and Palestinian left. Slogans of change and revolution were monopolized by the left at a time when religious movements in Lebanon were generally conservative. The Shiites were until the late seventies drawn into leftist political organizations because they were alienated from the political system in the country.[9]

As Harik notes, once again there appears to be some multivariate management in Hizbullah's ideological campaigning:

Looking more closely at [this] ideological ambiguity as an important strategy to broaden support, we see that Hassan Nasrallah, Hezbollah's present Secretary-General, actually uses four different contexts or 'frames' in presenting his ideas about Hezbollah's struggle against the Israelis, choosing one or another to suit the particular audience he is addressing. For instance, when speaking at a rally in the dahiyeh where the gathering is mainly Shiites and most are likely to be partisans, Jihad is presented in its purely religious context as already described. Jihad is spoken of as a sacred religious duty that transcends all other aims. In this context the Israelis are referred to as infidels and heretics to be driven off Muslim soil. The present conflict is presented as but the first part of a campaign aimed at liberating Jerusalem and the other Muslim holy places.

On the other hand, when addressing a wider Lebanese audience of mixed faiths, Nasrallah presents jihad in nationalistic terms – as a patriotic duty to liberate the homeland and drive the Israelis out of Lebanon. In this context, Hezbollah represents the Lebanese people who are 'all resisting the enemy'.

A third frame of reference used in the Hezbollah leader's discourse is trotted out when the target group is more likely to respond to an Arab nationalist context than any other. Then the struggle against Israel is promoted with reference to the harmful inroads of the West in the region as an effort to stand up to and defeat America's imperialistic designs. In this frame, Israel is identified as an American lackey or agent that must be resisted by the spearhead of the Arab nation – Hezbollah.

Jihad is placed in yet another context when Nasrallah addresses an international or global audience, as he often does on broadcasts by his organization's international television channel, al-Manar (the beacon or lighthouse). Here he expresses the idea of his organization's jihad as an internationally recognized right enjoyed by all peoples whose countries are illegally occupied. In this frame of reference, the Israelis are said to be violators of international accords, such as the several United Nations Security Council resolutions that have demanded Israel's withdrawal from Lebanon since 1978.

One fact stands out very clearly from this discussion: Hassan Nasrallah is an adept politician and a confirmed pragmatist when it comes to promoting his cause – quite a contrast indeed from the irrational terrorist his enemies try to portray him as.[10]

THE PERVASIVE SENSE OF MISSION

The concept of Jihad has been misunderstood in the West (Khalil believes); it has also been misused by contemporary Islamic organisations.

Under the name of Jihad, hostages were taken, battles have been fought, and suicide missions have been ordered [. . .] The revolutionary ideology of Hizballah broadened the definition of Jihad to include all facets of party activity. [. . .]

The Islamic (religious) dimension of the concept of Jihad as practised by Hizballah should not be exaggerated. The Jihad of Hizballah should be equated with the concept of *an-Nidal* (struggle) as used by leftist parties in Lebanon. While Leninist parties attribute working-class motivations to their actions, Hizballah attributes Islamic motivations to its activity. The word also adds 'revolutionary credibility' to the practice of the Party because the word has been associated with spectacular bombing attacks against the enemies of fundamentalist groups. But Hizballah broadens the definition of the word to legitimize and 'Islamize' all of its alleged activities, from suicide bombing to kidnapping.

The notion of martyrdom in Shiism is often presented as an explanation for the military activity of Hizballah. While it is true that the promise of heavenly reward motivates some of the suicide fighters of Hizballah, suicide operations have been initiated by Palestinian groups in Lebanon long before Hizballah came into being. Thus, the 'martyrdom' of Hizballah is an 'Islamized' version of the Palestinian notion of *al-Fida*' (sacrifice). It should be remembered in this respect that Hizballah was not the only party in Lebanon to send fighters on suicide missions against Israeli targets. The Syrian Social National Party, the Lebanese Communist Party, the Arab Socialist Ba'th Party, the Progressive Socialist Party, and the various Palestinian organizations, have all launched suicide attacks against Israeli targets in South Lebanon.

Moreover, all Parties in Lebanon, from right-wing parties to ultra-leftist communist parties, use the word *shuhada*' (martyrs) to depict all those members who died in the course of the civil war. The religious significance of the term is often exaggerated. Of course, it could also be argued that certain religious trends and terms have permeated most political parties in Lebanon, including those who ostensibly espouse secular ideologies.

Hizballah benefits from the international attention focused on its activities. Even the depiction of its attacks as terrorist does not necessarily affect negatively the image of Hizballah in the eyes of its supporters and in the eyes of the Shiite community in Lebanon. The excessive focus on Hizballah by the USA and Israel adds to its reputation of effectiveness and combativeness. Moreover, the criterion by which the USA and Israel judge whether an act is 'terrorist' or not is not shared by people in the Arab world, particularly among Lebanese and Palestinians. A Hizballah leader, Shaykh Ibrahim al-Amin, did not even reject the 'terrorist' label of his party. He believes that the Quran 'ordered' them to engage in the fight against the USA and Israel. To support his argument, al-Amin cites a verse from the Quran which states: 'Muster against them [the believers] all the men and cavalry at your disposal, so that you may terrorize the enemies of Allah and the faithful'.[11]

Khalil equates the concept of Jihad (mission) with that of a struggle to earn 'revolutionary credibility'. Primarily, most followers of Islam would regard a jihad as a directly sanctified mission: this confers an obligation, partly religious and partly political (political in its broadest sense), to campaign on behalf of principles and to combat disbelief and heresy. Hizbullah's violence, seen in these terms, is proactive as well as reactive. That Hizbullah as a movement is something other than a mere political party is a point that Martin Kramer (1998) considers:

Hizballah's official spokesman maintains that the movement is 'not a regimented party, in the common sense', for the idea of an exclusive 'party' is foreign to Islam. Hizballah is a 'mission' and a 'way of life'. Another Hizballah leader has insisted that Hizballah 'is not an organization', for its members carry no cards and bear no specific responsibilities. It is a 'nation' of all who believe in the struggle against injustice and all who are loyal to Iran's Imam Khomeini. Still another Hizballah leader maintains that 'we are not a party in the traditional sense of the term. Every Muslim is automatically a member of Hizballah, thus it is impossible to list our membership'. And in the mind of Iran's chargé d'affaires in Beirut, Hizballah is not 'restricted to a specified organizational framework [. . .] There are two parties, Hizballah or God's party, and the Devil's party'.[12]

The cause of warding off those who would thwart Hizballah's mission has been embraced by Islamic Jihad. Islamic Jihad claimed credit for the spectacular bombing attacks that helped to drive US and Israeli forces out of Lebanon. Islamic Jihad has done much to purge Lebanon of foreign influence by waging a campaign of kidnapping against foreign nationals. It is difficult to say much that is authoritative about Islamic Jihad or to do more than speculate about the precise relationship between Hizballah and Islamic Jihad. Leading figures in Hizballah, as well as Hizballah's spokesman, disavow all knowledge of the persons behind Islamic Jihad. Western intelligence sources regard Islamic Jihad as a group of clandestine cells run by several of Hizballah's military commanders, in most instances in collaboration with Iran. But conventional thinking on this matter has changed more than once. Those communications issued by Islamic Jihad that are deemed to be authentic are too brief to open a window on this closed universe of belief and action.

But Islamic Jihad need not interpret itself to the world, for this is done on its behalf and with great effectiveness by the leaders of Hizballah. Whatever the relationship of accountability between Islamic Jihad and Hizballah, their ideological compatibility finds daily expression in the public statements of Hizballah leaders.

Two categories of action have posed unique challenges to these leaders, precisely because they employ methods that on their face seem to violate some principle of Islamic law – the very law that Hizballah has championed as a solution to all of Lebanon's ills. These are the suicidal bomb attacks and the kidnappings of foreigners. The arguments within Hizballah over both these extraordinary means provide much insight into how morality, law, and necessity may be distorted and remade under the relentless pressures of great collective distress.[13]

THE TAKING OF HOSTAGES

The act of hostage-taking, a common manifestation of political terrorism, has been something that Hizbullah has frequently resorted to. In the glare of media publicity, hostages have been taken where the players in the scenario are besieged or where they are known to have been forcibly detained in a secret location. Generally, this is followed by a credible threat to kill, injure or continue detention of a victim. The terrorists' threat faces a third party with the anguished choice of either meeting the hostage-takers' demands or submitting to blackmail. Hizbullah's relentless employment of hostage-taking and the management of the hostage-crisis by Western powers has been examined in detail by Magnus Ranstorp (1997), who believes that Hizbullah's motives are complex and easily misunderstood. The complicity of Iran is evident despite it being subject to volatile political developments in Teheran. The response of Western governments to Hizbullah's abduction of their nationals was considered by Ranstorp to demonstrate firmly held no-concessions positions in public, while in private there may be a resort to secret negotiation.

In a ten-year period, between 1982 and 1992, a number of enigmatic and obscure organisations, seemingly loosely or indirectly affiliated with the Hizb'allah organisation in Lebanon, not only launched spectacular and deadly suicide operations against the Western presence but also engaged in political acts of hostage-taking of Western civilians. While the shadowy Hizb'allah movement has denied any active involvement in these acts of terrorism, though applauding these operations in concert with Iran, its self-proclaimed main enemies of the United States, Great Britain, and France, collectively sustained casualties of over 300 individuals killed by the organisation while it has held over forty-five citizens in captivity for various lengths of time over a ten-year period. While the chaos and insanity of the fifteen-year protracted civil war in Lebanon contributed to the difficulty in extracting the Western hostages from among a multitude of confessional militias, it also led to the association and image of Hizb'allah in the West as a crazy and fanatic religious group, bent on martyrdom through suicide-operations and engaged in the random abduction of foreigners, under the assumed strict control and direction of Iran's clerical establishment.

Although the West crossed paths in Lebanon with the radical and militant aspects of the Shi'a community and the Islamic Republic of Iran through Hizb'allah's abductions of foreign citizens, the highly complex nature of the internecine conflict involving an array of confessional warring factions, with foreign patrons, prevented a clearly defined understanding of the Hizb'allah's motives and organisation from emerging. In the murky underworld of Lebanon's civil war, where conduct was regulated by regional, national, sectarian and family interest, the nature of the shadowy groups, acting under the umbrella of Hizb'allah, further compounded the complexity of the hostage-crisis and the involvement of Iran. The ambiguous nature of the organisation itself and its affiliation with Iran led to an array of misperceptions by Western governments and outside observers in their attempts to both understand and confront the prolonged hostage-crisis in Lebanon, at times with disastrous consequences.[14] [. . .]

Analysis of the hostage-crisis in Lebanon yields that Hizb'allah was indisputably responsible for the aforementioned abductions of Westerners despite attempts to shield its complicity through the employment of cover-names. Its organisational framework was not only sophisticated and assimilated according to Iranian clerical designs but also integrated with several key Iranian institutions which provided it with necessary weaponry and training to successfully confront self-proclaimed Islamic enemies and invaluable financial support for it to generate as well as sustain massive support and recruitment among the Shi'a community at the expense of other confessional groups.[15] [. . .]

The responses by the American, French and British governments to the abduction of its citizens in Lebanon have underlined the inherent difficulty in striking a balance between their moral obligation towards providing safety and protection for their citizens abroad without having to sacrifice national interests in the conduct of foreign policy. While all three states have pursued a firmly held and coordinated public position of no-negotiations with terrorists and no-concessions to their demands in the Lebanese hostage-crisis, the reality of actual conduct behind this façade has revealed not only the conduct of secret negotiations, either directly with the Hizb'allah, Iran, and Syria or indirectly through third party intermediaries, over the release of hostages, at times resulting in complex and murky deals, but also that the hostage-issue was intimately influenced by the conduct of foreign policies by these Western states in the Middle East. Although the two Western states and the United States have shared similar types of problems and challenges in efforts to manage and secure the extraction of its citizens from captivity in Lebanon, each individual state has pursued its own overt and covert policies to accomplish this task. Apart from their almost equal standing in Hizb'allah's Western demonology, largely due to their colonial past and present involvement in the Middle East, the divergence of approach to the hostage-crisis reflected not only the individual experiences of these Western states in confronting terrorism within their own borders, but also the nature and status of their relationships with both Iran and Syria as well as their policies in the Middle East, driven by different sets of political motivations as well as economic considerations. The differences from state to state in the frequency, time periods, and number of its citizens abducted by the Hizb'allah, coupled with the specific nature of demands, also contributed to the way in which the Western governments have crafted individual or concerted strategies to the problem of obtaining the release of their citizens from captivity.[16] [. . .]

The responses by the United States and the two West European states to the hostage-crisis in Lebanon have been governed by a uniform policy of refusal to negotiate or make concessions to terrorists under any guise. This policy of no-negotiations and no-concessions to terrorists has been embodied in a series of unilateral or joint declarations of principles which reflects not only the previous experience of liberal democracies in countering terrorism at home, based on the principled position that hostage-taking constitutes an unforgivable act that must not be rewarded through concessions and that a readiness to negotiate as well as a willingness to concede to demands only encourages further terrorist acts, but also that state support for terrorism in any form constitutes unacceptable international behaviour subject to punishment. While principles of US no-concessions policy have been unilaterally proclaimed by policymakers on countless occasions in response to new hostage-takings of American citizens, as outlined by public policy statements and documents, the European states have adopted not only unilateral policies in alignment with the uniform principle of no-concessions but also a concerted European approach to the hostage-problem, as evident by their solemn promise to make 'no concessions under duress to terrorists or their sponsors' at the 1986 European Community (EC) summit in London. The inconsistency between the declaratory policy of not negotiating or conceding to any demands and the actual conduct by Western governments in dealing with the hostage-crisis in Lebanon can be attributed to the often incompatible nature of firmly held counter-terrorism principles as an integral component of foreign policy in the Middle East towards Iran and Syria, who exercise any [sic] degree of control over the Hizb'allah. Despite the fact that both Iran and Syria have concealed the exact nature of their close relationship with the Hizb'allah, the recognition of Iran and Syria as intermediaries for Western governments in dealing with the Hizb'allah posed problems in upholding a non-flexible no-concessions policy as these states benefited indirectly from concessions made to influence the movement despite their own complicity in some of the movement's terrorist acts.[17] [. . .]

THE TERRORISTS' CONTINUING DIALECTIC

Hizbullah, in the minds of Western political leaders, remains part-enigma by virtue of its complex origins and its labyrinthian development. It is not easy to face down such a vigorous and violent movement. In January 1995 the Clinton Administration forbade its nationals to have any transactions that might imperil the Middle East peace process. World pressure has been increased recently against states suspected of sponsoring international terrorism and on all sides stern trading sanctions have been levied. Nevertheless, Iran and Syria have not relented and Hizbullah remains one of the world's most deadly terrorist organisations. There is no straightforward answer to the double question: what does Hizbullah gain by its terrorist activities and when are these likely to cease? There is no doubt that Hizbullah's 'culture of violence' will endure so long as the movement yearns at all costs strategically to promote a pan-Islamic cause and tactically to reinforce its own revolutionary identity as defender of the Shi'ite community. Moreover, Hizbullah willingly acts as a 'conduit' for Iran's own revolutionary message to the Islamic masses. Ranstorp believes that Hizbullah is unlikely to abandon its missionary zeal, directing its militancy and violence towards the goal of eradicating Israel and its Western associates.

For the Hizb'allah movement itself, the hostage-taking activity has served many important functions which reinforced the movement's ideological and political *raison d'être*, assisted in the expansion of its influence within the Lebanese Shi'ite community as well as defined and forged the movement's ties to Iran's clerical establishment [. . .] In a wider sense, Hizb'allah's hostage-taking activity also served to enhance its revolutionary credence and image as the true defender of the Lebanese Shi'a community against the enemies of Islam, especially as it played an instrumental role in expelling foreign forces out of Lebanon and through its tireless armed campaign against Israel. In this revolutionary struggle, the Hizb'allah was very successful in achieving not only its practical goals but also in accomplishing a psychological atmosphere of fear in the West of the actual threat and capability of the movement which served to enhance the status of the movement within Lebanon and beyond as a major nemesis of Western governments.

While Hizb'allah activity served to consolidate Iran's material assistance to the movement, its rapid transformation from a rag-tag militia into a tightly organised movement with an impressive military and extensive social services programme for the Shi'a community meant that the Hizb'allah positioned itself as a true political, ideological, and economic defender of the Shi'a community, filling the vacuum in place of the scant protection and assistance provided by the Lebanese government and other militias [. . .] While Hizb'allah's terrorism stereotyped the image of Lebanon's Shi'ites as religious fanatics bent on martyrdom in the Western world, the profound role and service of the Hizb'allah movement, fighting and buying its way into the hearts and minds of the Shi'ite community, far outweighed the consequences of any non-Islamic moral constraints imposed by Western public opinion. Apart from the fact that Hizb'allah veiled its justifications of violent activity solely to Muslim believers and according to Islamic law, the movement also provided the dispossessed Shi'ite community within a lawless civil war environment with a divine Islamic purpose and mission, which transformed from revolutionary struggle to a political vehicle aimed at addressing Shi'ite grievances and enhancing its wider agenda in Lebanon.[18]

Ranstorp sees the Hizbullah terrorists as a well-organised movement able to reinforce its ideological and political identity through a strong sense of mission and a succession of violent strikes, regarded by the West as atrocities. A different view is that of Kramer, who is convinced that in some respects Hizbullah lacks agreement, certainly over the question of hostage-taking, apart from other aspects of violence:

Hizballah is divided over the question of hostage taking. That is perhaps inevitable, for Hizballah began as a coalition and it remains one. The movement is devoted to one purpose: the eventual establishment of an Islamic state in Lebanon. But its leaders continue to debate among themselves the morality and legality of the means to that elusive end. The extraordinary means employed by some within the coalition have prompted an extraordinary debate. It is unusual because in Shi'ite Islam, only the cleric can morally disengage the common believer from his acts. In that limited sense, bombers, hijackers, and hostage takers are morally dependent on Hizballah and Iran, and the verdicts of their learned scholars are hardly academic. Yet their interpretations of Islam's dictates often differ in important and even fundamental ways. The evidence for their debate in interviews and speeches only hints at what must be an intense internal disputation over the future course of the 'nation' of Hizballah.

   As a coalition, Hizballah is liable at any time to split. Yet Lebanon's tribulations seem only to strengthen it. Hizballah has seen its enemies retreat time and again, reinforcing its view that Lebanon's crisis will be resolved through Hizballah's ultimate triumph. But Syria proposes a very different resolution to that crisis, one in which Hizballah has no place. The movement cannot confront Syria in conventional ways and expect victory. Hizballah is also unlikely to succeed in its bid to rid South Lebanon of all Israeli political and military influence if it resorts only to conventional methods. The debate over extraordinary means will not soon end.[19]

With the year 2000 introducing a new century, there was increasing international dismay and conjecture as to the outcome of the Palestinian–Israeli conflict. Would Hizbullah, a main player, ever renounce violence (terrorism)? The despatch of suicide bombers to Israeli cafés and markets was widely condemned as 'evil'. Would there be an end to this and to the taking of hostages, now less frequently resorted to by Hizbullah? Above all, what might be the attitude of Hizbullah to a peace settlement on the lines of the mediation attempts by the governments of the United States, Saudi Arabia and Egypt?

   These issues and many others have been addressed recently by Amal Saad-Ghorayeb (2002), a professor at the American University in Lebanon and one who is able to tune into contemporary thinking in Lebanon and among Hizbullah leaders. Concerned to confront simplistic definition of violence, Saad-Ghorayeb regards Hizbullah's rationale in regard to violence as a consequence of a 'moral equation and dictum'. (Readers will realise that there may be an element of partiality in her conclusions.)

Insofar as any premeditated act of violence against innocent civilians that seeks to create an atmosphere of fear in order to influence a specific audience can be defined as terrorism, the Hizbu'llah clearly advocates the resort to terrorism by armed Palestinian groups. For Hizbu'llah, however, whether civilians are killed as a result of conventional warfare or as a result of so-called 'terrorist' attacks, the moral equation remains the same, since both means of violence produce the same end result, neither means can be considered any more moral than the other.

Therefore, the party upholds the conviction that the principal determinant of the terrorism of an act lies in the circumstances that surround it, and not in its conformity to conceptual definitions. In line with this situational ethic is the belief that violence cannot be viewed in absolute terms, but must be perceived in a relative sense. Hizbu'llah's conception of terrorism hinges on the essential goodness or badness of a cause, irrespective of whether the means of violence employed were conventional or unconventional ('terrorist') ones.

According to this moral dictum, Israel's successive invasions, its occupation of Lebanese territory, its indiscriminate, and often surgical bombardment of civilian areas, in addition to its unlawful detention or 'kidnapping' of Lebanese civilians, render it a terrorist state in the eyes of Hizbu'llah (as has been pointed out earlier). But from Israel's standpoint, and that of much of the Western world, such acts are considered part of Israel's conventional warfare against Hizbu'llah and the Lebanese state.

On the other side of the coin, Hizbu'llah does not view Palestinian suicide attacks against Israeli civilians as terrorist acts, on account of their situation context, which consists of two principal extenuating circumstances. First is the party's perception of Palestinian violence as legitimate self-defence in the face of Israeli oppression. Not only do Israel's current oppressive policies vindicate the acts of violence against civilians perpetuated by Hamas and Islamic Jihad, but Israel's very existence also warrants such violence.

Because the Israeli state was founded on the displacement of an entire people, Israel is ultimately responsible for the Palestinians' attempt to retrieve their land through violent means. The perpetuation of the Israeli occupation of Palestine, coupled with the Israeli state's 'practice of the worst kind of aggression and violence against the Palestinians, necessitate all kinds of self-defense', which are the 'natural right' of the subjugated Palestinian people.

Viewed through this relative moral lens, suicide missions that are universally deemed terrorist become 'great *mujahidin*' and 'heroes'. So glorified are these attacks, that in Hizbu'llah's disclaimer of one of these suicide missions, the party finds it necessary to add, 'this is not something we have to exonerate ourselves from'. Over and above this, the party unabashedly and regularly enjoins the Palestinians to kill Israeli civilians, though always with reference to the instrumentality of such violence in defending Palestinian rights. More than anything, suicide attacks are perceived as the 'solution' to the Palestinian predicament in that they are the only 'way' of 'reminding' the world of the Palestinians' grievances. For Hizbu'llah, the exigency of such acts of violence is even more pronounced when the futility of diplomacy in effecting the required level of international awareness is taken into account.[20] [. . .]

Saad-Ghorayeb acknowledges that Hizbullah, as a religious body, places a different meaning upon suicide and martyrdom from that conventionally adopted in non-Islamic countries. As such, meanings may be puzzling, even contradictory to those 'outside'. Within Islam, martyrdom is both an exemplar of a defensive jihad and a model of virtuous self-sacrifice. There will always be the possibility that 'defensive' martyrdom may be abandoned as political circumstances are judged to have changed. Hostage-taking, too, seems to have been a temporary Hizbullah measure. Again, for Saad-Ghorayeb, it is the 'situational context' that rules and possibly modifies tactics when something so much resorted to is dispensed with:

Hostage-taking was therefore perceived as something 'forbidden' (on both moral and religious grounds), which nonetheless had to be resorted to under certain 'extenuating circumstances'. Accordingly, Hizbu'llah does not believe that the kidnappings should be viewed in abstraction but in their proper context, with an eye towards the 'causes' which provoked them rather than the 'consequences' they generated.[21]

Finally, Saad-Ghorayeb is not at all optimistic that Hizbullah can find itself able to accept the consequences of peace mediation:

Hizbu'llah may be willing to temporarily countenance an Arab-Israeli peace (*salam*), which it most probably conceives of as a transient lull but it is definitely not willing to condone a full-scale reconciliation (*sulh*) with Israeli state and society, at any phase of time. Viewed from the perspective of the party, the normalisation of economic, social, cultural and political relations with Israel would extirpate the existential foundations of the conflict with it, and would be tantamount to an approval of Israel's continued occupation of Palestine.[22] [. . .]

Even so, there is room for debate, manoeuvre and the prospect of final peace. Reliance on violence (terrorism) is a 'precarious' instrument. More moderate elements in the pan-Arab world may yet help Hizbullah to bridge peacefully what is seen to be a yawning gulf between the idealism of resistance and martyrdom and the political reality of practicable coexistence.

Kramer, writing about Hizbullah, 'the Party of God', and their lack of consensus about some of their activities (e.g. hostage-taking, hijacking, kidnapping, car-bombing), concludes that lack of agreement does not vitiate their enthusiasm and dedication:

It is certain that there is disagreement within Hizballah over how Lebanon's Islamic revolution should be hastened and whether this is an opportune moment to articulate a full plan. There are also differences on this score between certain leading figures in Hizballah and the movement's Iranian guides, who themselves are divided over how best to transform Lebanon. But for Hizballah's rank and file, these debates are of no great importance. The young men and women of Hizballah are fired by the pure image of a future Lebanon that will regain stability through Islamic law and justice and embark on a redeeming struggle against those who would banish Islam from this Earth.[23]

The fighting between Israel and Hizbullah was brought to an end in August 2006 as a consequence of delayed and contentious Security Council deliberation, eventual arrangements for a ceasefire tolerable to both parties, and moves to promote the outlines of a broader political settlement. Urgent international parleying between heads of state sought to bridge the gap, particularly between United States and Israeli positions and those of many other countries unhappy about the 'dispro-portionate' retaliatory action of Israel. Very much at the heart of stern disapproval and debate was the issue of whether a certain terrorist group, located as they appeared to be within the confines of a closely settled civilian community, could be 'dealt with' by 'surgical air strikes'. Israel's counter-terrorist action resulted in large numbers of deaths among villagers and townspeople and devastation on a horrendous scale. Might negotiating probes have been employed by Tel Aviv at an early stage in the conflict, granted that Israeli 'security' had already been lanced by Katyusha rockets? Once again it seems likely that counter-terrorist strategies and operations, if they lead to mayhem, are likely to recruit effectively among those made sympathetic to a defensive, liberationist cause.

Chapter 10

Lebanon II

THE LAST CASE STUDY featured Lebanon and its militant force, Hizbullah. Very much the concern of those following the crisis events of July–August 2006 was the question of how far other states might be sponsoring Lebanese terrorists. Might it be Syria or Iran? The question is a complex one and it can only be dealt with here in suggestive outline.

HIZBULLAH AUTONOMY

Whatever the extent of others sponsoring Hizbullah activists, there appears to be little doubt of their feelings of innate self-regard. The pronouncements of Hizbullah leaders in parliament, in the press and at public gatherings are quite clearly full of confidence. Interestingly, a contemporary Lebanese website, sympathetic to the terrorists, quotes the opinion of a well-known authority, A. R. Norton (1987):

Like it or not, Hizbullah is a serious player in Lebanon [. . .] The party's organisational roots now penetrate the Shia community and they are not easily uprooted. Even after the guns and Katyushas are collected Hizbullah's reputation will benefit from its leading role in the resistance which like it or not is widely admired in Lebanon, especially among the Shia. Hizbullah has been able to build an efficient and responsive organisation that meets many of the needs of its constituents while avoiding the tag of corruption that taints its parliamentary rivals [. . .] All of the facts seem to underline that while Hizbullah's future as an armed element may be somewhat uncertain, its survival as a viable political player is not.[1]

Hizbullah's terrorist identity appears to be acknowledged widely. Its guise as a 'viable political player' seems perhaps open to argument. Is this player to a large degree a puppet manipulated from elsewhere? Some will have it that Hizbullah in its motives and methods is a proxy – a pawn of the anti-Israeli interests of Syria and Iran, fighting at third hand the militant scheming of two larger, not altogether allied powers. Training, weaponry, funds and tactical assistance are all in the gift of Damascus and Teheran. Others assert that Hizbullah, in contrast, represents formidable Shiite opposition to Israel's strategic designs. Their leaders, it is thought, listen attentively to approaches from Syria and Iran from time to time, all in the process of shaping their own decision process. The truth must lie somewhere within these parameters.

LEBANON 'ON HOLD'

Until the crisis of 2006 broke, a number of informed observers considered Lebanon to be 'on hold', itself inchoate and unstable, while it grimly faced up to Israel's public and military frustration, Syrian and Iranian preoccupation with their own inclination, and a United States too partial towards Tel Aviv.

Richard W. Murphy (1996), one-time Ambassador to Syria, is one of those who have watched for 10 years or so the 'waiting game' of Hizbullah, one of its eyes on Syria and Iran; one of its hands, as it were, nibbling away at its southern Israeli-garrisoned flank, the other poised to see what might come along next:

The Hizballah militia attacks Israeli targets in a spirit of dogged exaltation, to challenge the occupation of south Lebanon. Hizballah is able to keep up hostile activity because it has been in the interest of both Syria and Iran that it do so. Damascus will await satisfaction in the Syrian-Israeli negotiations, suspended by Israel since early March, before considering it worthwhile to suppress the Hizballah militia once and for all; Tehran will probably continue to do all that it can to derail the Arab-Israeli peace process. In the meantime, the forced exodus of the 400,000 Lebanese has surely enlarged Hizballah's recruiting base among Lebanese Shia and served to silence critics of Hizballah among all the Lebanese communities. In sum, Israel found that its actions this time were no more successful than in 1993 in forcing Beirut to control Hizballah or in eliciting Syrian cooperation to achieve this end. Syria once again demonstrated that it can comfortably bear Lebanese pain.[2]

Another observer, Patrick Seale (1996), has no doubt that when Israel launched its punitive operation, the Grapes of Wrath, in April 1996, the prime political target was not only to parry Lebanese influence, it was to tackle head on the Syrian benefactor. He quotes Israel's Ambassador to Washington, six days after the start of the campaign, in regard to Israeli strategy:

'I would define it as negotiations with Syria so that it will help the Lebanese government to impose on Hizballah an effective ceasefire [. . .] If Syria wants to, it can prevent Hizballah from operating [. . .] Iran's ability to influence Hizballah depends on a Syrian readiness to permit the Iranian channels of influence to operate in Lebanon via Damascus. Syria, at a certain price, can end the activity. *What we have to do is to make the Syrians motivated enough to use their influence, which they have not been prepared to do over the last two or three months.'*

'Motivating' Syria was the name of the game. In less diplomatic language this meant that, by attacking Lebanon, by stampeding half a million people out of their towns and villages and thereby putting intolerable pressure on the Lebanese government, Israel planned to force Syria to curb Hizballah and grant immunity to the IDF in southern Lebanon.[3]

HIZBULLAH: PAWN OR POWER?

The issue of how far Hizbullah and Lebanon's government in Beirut are willing proxies of Syria has certainly shifted around in many minds over the last decade. One political analyst, Hussein Agha (1996), sketched some time ago the implications of what he terms 'the Syrian-Iranian axis' in Lebanon:

Between 1986 and 1989 Syrian-Iranian relations in Lebanon faced a number of near-crisis tensions. Each side was wary of the role played by the other's allies and proxies. The growth of Hizballah as a potent military force was matched by its emergence as an effective and energetic patron of an extensive network of social, educational, health and welfare services unavailable from any other source. Hizballah's challenge to Syrian dominance and its proxies among the Shia in Lebanon thus went beyond operational differences over the Palestinians and the war in the South, and began to strike at the very foundation of Syrian influence and prestige.

Agha goes further, apropos Syrian readiness to exploit the Hizbullah challenge:

Syria was not ready to stand idle as radical Sunni and Shia forces with powerful external patrons expanded their power and influence in Lebanon. In February 1987 Syrian troops clashed directly with Hizbullah in Beirut's southern suburbs, leaving no doubt who had the upper hand.[4]

Would Hizbullah's identity in its robust armed struggle be endangered by any Israeli–Syrian exploration of possible compromise? Once again, Agha is fairly sure of his findings:

The leadership of Hizballah has long been aware that the national consensus in support of its armed struggle against Israel's occupation of south Lebanon (a consensus that also strongly reflects Syria's own influence and attitudes) does not extend to its other long-term ideological commitment to continued rejection of peace and coexistence with Israel. The major trend within Hizballah, with the knowledge and understanding of Iran, is aware of the need to conform to the realities of a possible settlement between Israel and both Syria and Lebanon. [. . .]

A settlement between Israel and both Syria and Lebanon will confront Hizballah with some difficult choices. Much of Hizballah's appeal and influence has been based on its sustained resistance to Israel's occupation of Lebanese soil for over a decade. Hizballah is careful to confine its attacks to occupied Lebanese territory, except when provoked into retaliation across the border, and has strongly intimated that an Israeli withdrawal from south Lebanon will end its armed activities against Israel. The movement recognizes that the post-settlement security regime will certainly preclude a military option in any case.

A transition of this nature in Hizballah's policy and posture will partly depend on the balance of opinion within the movement, as well as the ultimate position taken by Iran and Hizballah's overall relationship with Syria. The official leadership of Hizballah enjoys good relations with both Syria and Iran and is as likely to be responsive to the requirements and sensitivities of the former as it is to those of the latter. So far Tehran has not indicated by word or deed that its ideological opposition to the peace process binds it to a commitment to abort this process by military means. For both Iran and Hizballah in all its tendencies, as well as the major part of Lebanese, Arab and Islamic opinion, the movement's resistance activities will remain legitimate until agreement is reached on a full and final Israeli withdrawal.[5]

Is Hizbullah, though, a willing pawn of Iran? Daniel Sobelman (2003), of the Jaffee Center for Strategic Studies in Tel Aviv, has studied closely Hizbullah's 'rules of the game', as he puts it, in relation to neighbouring states:

Another key player in Hizbollah's 'working environment' is undoubtedly Iran. Iran drafted its Revolutionary Guards – a military force set up after the Islamic Revolution, in addition to the Iranian army, and considered more professional and loyal to the conservative religious establishment – to be the main driving force behind Hizbollah's founding after Israel's June 1982 invasion of Lebanon. It was the Islamic Republic of Iran that supplied the embryonic Shiite organization in Lebanon with both the logistical assistance and the ideological mantle that has characterized it throughout its existence (such as the 'the downtrodden of the earth' ideology that was first adopted by the Islamic revolutionary leader Khomeini). Over the years Hizbollah's development into a skilled force with sophisticated combat techniques made it increasingly dependent on Iran, and while in 2002 Syria began supplying Hizbollah with Katyusha rockets, Iran was and remains the main source of Hizbollah's fighting materiel, the 'tools' that transformed the organization into a deterrent force to be reckoned with. Although according to Israeli intelligence reports the long-range rockets now deployed on Lebanese soil were not handed over to Hizbollah and remain under the supervision of the Revolutionary Guards, these Katyusha rockets frame Hizbollah's deterrence.

For many years fighting materiel has been flown to Hizbollah from Iran via Syria, an arrangement that still continues. Without Syrian and Iranian support Hizbollah would never have attained its present status, and in many ways the organization owes its very existence to Syria and Iran. On the ideological level Hizbollah is the product of Iran's policy, adopted in 1979, of 'exporting the revolution'.[6]

Sobelman is inclined to think that Teheran's ability to use Hizbullah as an Iranian pawn is limited in view of Iran's guarded relationship with Israel:

Iran's official policy toward Israel continues to be non-recognition of its right to exist and support for the creation of a Palestinian state in all of Israel's territory. Therefore, the establishment of political relations between Israel and its neighbors clashes with Iran's interests and could isolate Tehran's position should peace agreements be reached between Israel, Syria, and Lebanon. On the other hand, would a military confrontation between Israel and its two northern neighbors be desirable from Iran's point of view? At this stage, the answer appears to be negative.

This is one of the reasons why Iran began curbing Hizbollah activity in April 2002. The Iranian foreign minister, Kamal Kharazi, arrived in Beirut and in light of Hizbollah's escalation declared that Israel should not be given pretexts to attack Syria or Lebanon. But the picture is more complex. Although Kharazi performed a restraining role on the eve of the Hizbollah-initiated escalation, it was Iran that had prodded Hizbollah to act in the first place. Furthermore, Kharazi's statements earned him both criticism in the Iranian media, as well as sympathy and support, conflicting trends that bear witness to the fact that in recent years support for Hizbollah has become entangled, at least to a certain degree, in the internal struggle between the conservative bloc in Iran and the reformists. But the ties between Hizbollah and Iran's conservative establishment continue, and Israeli officials even claim that a 'direct channel' exists between Secretary-General Nasrallah and Iran's spiritual leader, Ali Khamanei.[7]

There is general agreement in the eyes of government in Lebanon, Syria and Iran that Hizbullah is an armed force to be reckoned with. Eighteen months before the 2006 crisis, Sobelman wrote of the threat-in-being in very clear terms:

Hizbollah's mushroomed rearmament with thousands of Katyusha rockets sends an unequivocal deterrent message to Israel and other parties. The organization's newly-gained military empowerment is a key factor in preventing the banishment of Lebanon's Shiite community to the political backwaters where it had long been relegated. As such, its enormous power is also aimed at the Lebanese authorities, who would find disarming Hizbollah a formidable task, one commanding a high price for the organization's consent.

One decisive feature of Hizbollah's strategic weapons – Katyusha rockets and long-range rockets – is that their deployment could produce grave consequences. Therefore, other than a deterrent role, their actual use would be very problematic for Hizbollah, and is reserved, in the meantime, for worst case scenarios. A Hizbollah-initiated rocket attack deep into the north of Israel would be an intolerable provocation, one that would most likely invite an Israeli invasion of Lebanon or some other form of massive strike.

At present Hizbollah prefers to avoid this; therefore it defines its rocket arsenal as a deterrent safeguard against an Israeli attack, and apparently it would resort to these weapons only after a deterrence failure and Israeli offensive.[8]

A TERRORIST CHANGE OF FACE

If there is awareness that Lebanon's terrorists represent a significant force, there is growing acknowledgement that that significance may be the result of forces making for deliberate change in form and function, as circumstances are seen to alter. This could be an illustration of Hizbullah self-dependence rather than of subservience to others. Supposing that there were to be an agreement for both Hizbullah and the Israeli Defence Force to withdraw from face-to-face engagement (as happened when by arrangement the IDF evacuated South Lebanon in 2000), would there not then be a need for the terrorist to change clothing or, as Sobelman puts it, to 'invest' in other 'channels':

One channel it has invested a great deal of effort in is the infiltration of agents into Israel. Hizbollah has also increased its intelligence gathering inside Israel, smuggling in fighting materiel, and making contact with other terrorist organizations. Today Hizbollah acts more as a long-range military force than a terror organization carrying out attacks on a daily basis. Hizbollah has prepared a file of potential targets, but is not satisfied just with collecting files and preparing the intelligence infrastructure for carrying out attacks. It is also developing the operational infrastructure for implementing them. Hizbollah works one step ahead [of events], that is, it advances its operational ability toward the actualization of these attacks. It does this by infiltrating agents who know how to consolidate the human infrastructure for executing the strike and how to obtain fighting materiel. In this way Hizbollah shortens its response time from the moment a decision is made to the moment the strike takes place. This pattern of activity is characteristic of an organization with institutionalized operational thinking.[9]

Hizbullah changes would be understood to be not only modification of military tactics but also initiative and vigour translated into the domestic political arena. Sobelman outlines what he considers to be the marks of this adaptive process:

The preoccupation with Hizbollah as an organization with military and terrorist dimensions tends to overlook the economic and social dimensions to the organization within the Lebanese domestic arena, which in fact may be expected to increase in importance the longer the status quo abides between Israel and Hizbollah and a glaring deterioration does not ensue. Hizbollah's public announcement of its concern for Lebanon's economy and tourist industry is only partially representative of its interests since, as a movement with social dimensions, it is careful to champion Lebanon's economic plight. Indeed, the leader of the Hizbollah faction in parliament, Muhammad Ra'd, announced that in addition to the struggle with Israel, Hizbollah and Lebanon are waging war on the socio-economic level:

> We face another confrontation and struggle in the domestic arena, namely, the economic war, the embargo, the budget deficit, recession, cash short-age, and rising unemployment . . . This is a war that requires planning

and everyone's cooperation since we are struggling on two fronts simultaneously, and the loss of one means the loss of the other.

The question raised here is to what extent Hizbollah's political strength serves its military prowess and ability to preserve the option of an armed struggle against Israel. Apparently by anchoring its roots in Lebanon's parliamentary, social, and economic arenas, Hizbollah has built itself a safety net of organizational legitimacy independent of its military dimension. The preservation of Hizbollah's legitimacy depends on its degree of success in supporting economic recovery and in providing welfare services to its constituency and to other needy publics. Hassan Nasrallah [Hizbollah's mullah leader] has noted that providing for the families of fallen comrades serves as 'the backing and continuation of the resistance option'.[10]

HIZBULLAH – PARTNER FOR PEACE

As we have noted earlier, Hizbullah's striving for preservation of legitimacy, its refurbishment of acceptable image, has gathered ground certainly since the year 2000. Once more, Sobelman is rather sure of his deductions:

The loss of the main arena of Hizbullah military activity that had formerly won the organization its legitimacy, prestige and national consensus has forced it to alter its modus operandi. Parallel to this, Hizbullah is trying to find alternative anchors of legitimacy in order to continue its declared military activity.[11]

This reads ironically, no fault of Sobelman, as the summer of 2006 brings the terrorists into tremendous armed conflict with the Israeli army.

Reality governs war, reality governs peace, reality governs change, it could be said. The last word from Sobelman underlines this thought:

Basically, Hizbollah is succumbing to the demands of reality. No organization, regardless of its ideological fervor, can survive unless it is able to respond and adapt itself to the dynamics of change around it. The more that an organization remains fixed in its conceptions and behavior patterns in the face of a changing reality, the greater the existential danger that it faces. Hizbollah is aware of this.[12]

Constraints imposed by a reading of reality, until very recently, were suggesting that Lebanon's terrorists must prepare for wholesale accommodation to changed scenarios. Habib Malik (2000), an American Near-East scholar, takes the view that Syrian–Israeli relationships, and a possible accord, bear directly upon Lebanon, proxy or not.

Hezbollah has already given oblique indications that it is beginning to prepare for a post-peace process political role in Lebanon. [. . .]

In an interview with Die Zeit (December 20, 1994), Hezbollah Secretary-General Sheikh Hassan Nasrallah said that resistance to Israel would end with the signing of an Israel-Syria peace agreement. This change in Hezbollah's policy orientation was further demonstrated by its participation in the 1992 and 1996 Lebanese parliamentary elections, in which several of their candidates were elected on both occasions. Hezbollah broadcasts constantly refer to the peace process as the *taswiya* (settlement), suggesting a recognition that a new situation is unfolding. (However, the choice of *taswiya* also indicates that the organization regards the approaching peace as essentially provisional.)[13]

Finally, in the light of a point made in the preceding case study, where President George Bush scorned the Lebanese activists as 'a bunch of terrorists', such a simplistic equation falls far short of the complicated nature of a group such as Hizbullah. The shaped growth of this group and above all its relationships with Syria and Iran pose a number of intriguing questions. A French political scientist, May Chartouni-Dubarry (1996), goes so far as to assert that Hizbullah is the only militia that has converted successfully into a political party.[14] If there is any mileage in that opinion, then a group such as Hizbullah deserves to be studied most carefully. Demonising terrorists is no way to examine their motives and methods.

STARING INTO THE ABYSS

It was in the latter half of the year 2010 and the beginning of 2011 that dissension in Beirut became a focus of international attention. For a good five years already the Lebanese had quarrelled over this issue: who had been responsible for the assassination of their Prime Minister Rafik Hariri and 22 others in February 2005? Surely, in most minds, it was Hizbullah's fanatics ('gun-toting, hoodlums' in White House parlance).

It took some months for the Lebanese government, headed now by Saad Hariri, the slain leader's son, to decide what to do. It was to call upon the United Nations to set up an independent tribunal to investigate the outrage and to prosecute those found responsible for it. Established in March 2009 there would be a final report two years later in March 2011.

An initiative on these lines was sure to polarise a community already coming apart at the seams. Interestingly, though, rival parties maintained stance and voice which lacked the customary antagonism. Their moves were cautious though never conciliatory.

1   Hizbullah was not condemned outrightly by government as an irresponsible terrorist. If its guilt was not established at Geneva it might be allowed eventually a fuller parliamentary role.

2   Hizbullah, for its part, had everything to lose through indictment both regionally and internationally. Hassan Nasrullah, its head, needed to dismiss a tribunal he saw as never impartial and quite clearly an American–Israeli tool. But if Syrian or Israeli murderous intent were revealed then the Party could show clean hands.

3   Further for Hizbullah, in the matter of cultivating public image, no tribunal report must ever counteract the Party's work for legitimacy and autonomy, something that only progressed inch by inch. Very positively the Party must stand clear as protector of the Shia oppressed. Definitely to be expunged must be the Shi'ite militancy of creating 'a laboratory of martyrdom'. Demonstrated, too, must be an interest in 'citizenship' rather than a resort to violent activism together with 'giving priority to the "logic of unity"'.

4   Further afield, Syria and Saudi Arabia had tried mediation of Lebanon's conflicts but found peace brokering rebuffed by contesting groups. A thorough United Nations investigation could usefully clear the air and ease the way for renewed attempts to mend a ruptured part of the Islamic world.

What is happening in Lebanon offers scope for reflection and hope, and a far more peaceful transition. Certainly the course of violent altercation, tragedy and destruction has served to concentrate minds. In a recent article in *The Guardian* (31 December 2010), Fawaz A. Gerges, director of the London School of Economics Middle East Centre, described a Lebanon teetering on the edge of crisis as 'staring into an abyss'. For government, for the 'terrorists', we may well ask, which is it to be – disaster or slow change for the better?

On 18 January 2011 the United Nations announced that the Special Tribunal for Lebanon judge, Daniel Franzen, had received the long-awaited results of the investigation into the Hariri assassination of February 2005. Return of the submissions might even take two months before final legal opinion is pronounced. As expected, Hizbullah was quick to show displeasure. Its partisan TV station put it thus: 'Washington pushed the indictments in order to light the fuse that will blow up the bridges that were built in order to find a solution.' Less trenchant criticism and a great deal of exhausting tension are evident in Beirut's streets. What most people expect is that at least three of the Hizbullah front rank and particularly Ayatollah Ali Khameina will be indicted. Will any Iranian participation be identified?

The year 2011 has begun amid universal uncertainty and despondency. What price, though, for the better? The 'National Unity' government collapsed after just 18 months in office when Hizbullah members pulled out in January. Might initiatives from Syria, Saudi Arabia, the United Nations restore calm? Could Barack Obama or Nicholas Sarkozy help? Hassan Nasrullah has sounded a warning note: 'Should one expect that Israel or the United Nations will allow an Arab political process to end smoothly? Never!' Is the yawning abyss-edge that near?

Sri Lanka

S RI LANKA, formerly the island of Ceylon, is a state lacerated by two bitter conflicts. One is that of the state versus the People's Liberation Front (JVP or Janatha Vimukthi Peramuna, the name of its founder), a Sinhalese extreme nationalist organisation anxious to bring down the moderate Colombo government. The other is that of the Tamil Tigers, whose demand is for an altogether separate state. JVP have largely been contained by vigorous counter-terrorism; the Tamil Tigers continue to rage unabated and it is with them that this case study is mainly concerned.

As the smoke cleared away from another bomb explosion in downtown Colombo, Sri Lanka's capital, in March 1998, an excited radio commentator was heard to declare, 'There are another seventy million terrorists out there.' This is perhaps the chief difference between Sri Lanka's Tamil Tigers and those we have already studied in other case studies, namely that this group claims the adherence and financial backing of an international web of supporters. They recruit additional disciples and well-wishers and radiate propaganda through the sophisticated publicity channels of six internet sites, radio and television. The so-called Tamil Tigers (the Liberation Tigers of Tamil Eelam (LTTE)) represent a terrorist faction whose activities have been a growing source of concern to 30 states over four continents. Nor is there any sign that the conflict that is devastating society in Sri Lanka shows any convincing prospect of reconciliation. Most worrying of all is that few commentators can find an explanation for the Tigers' suicidal and indiscriminate violence.

SRI LANKA'S CONFLICT: A GENERAL OVERVIEW

Walter Laqueur (1999) has compiled a factual and objective overview of Sri Lanka's conflict with the Tamil Tigers. It ends on a note of conjecture: what really is the explanation of the Tamil Tigers and their fanaticism?

Sri Lanka, an island just south of India formerly known as Ceylon, became independent of British rule in 1948. Its politics have been turbulent almost ever since. The Sinhalese majority faces a Tamil minority of less than 20 per cent (about 3 million people), who are concentrated in the north of the country. However the Tamils, some of whom were originally brought to the island from India as labourers, have the backing of a much larger Tamil population in South India, concentrated in the state of Tamil Nadu. The policy of the Sinhalese majority ruling the country has been less than enlightened towards the minority; this manifested itself in an illiberal language policy (Sinhalese only), the refusal to give all Tamils in Sri Lanka citizenship, and the attempt to repatriate some of them to India, even though they had been born in Sri Lanka. Sri Lankan politics, furthermore, has had a strong radical element; this was one of the very few countries in the world in which the Communist and Trotskyite parties had been strong simultaneously. At the same time, there was equal militancy on the right wing; when the then prime minister Bandaranaike was assassinated in 1959, the murderers were two Sinhalese monks for whom Bandaranaike was insufficiently nationalist.

The Tamil majority felt itself threatened once the British left, and various militant organizations developed in the 1950s and 1960s. Originally the inspiration was revolutionary, and the writings of Castro and Guevara, of General Giap and Regis Debray, which reached them by way of India, had a powerful impact. But gradually the Marxist element faded, and what remained was militant separatism pure and simple. The tension was fuelled by economic stagnation and a high unemployment rate, especially among the young. For an enterprising young Tamil, there seemed to be little to do but become a terrorist. But this explanation is not entirely satisfactory, as unemployment was equally high in Sinhalese and Muslim parts of the island. The fact that religious inspiration was not decisive among the Tamil should be stressed, because religion has often been thought to be the decisive factor in suicide bombing. The Tamil Tigers had the highest rate of suicide missions in the world, with many hundreds of victims over the years. Their motives were not to be found in their religion or ideology but, like Colombia, in their cultural and social traditions – in brief, in their history.

Conflicts between Tamil and Sinhalese continued throughout the 1960s. At the same time, various Tamil groups were fighting each other in a struggle for leadership. The Tigers fighting for Eelam, a homeland, developed out of a revolutionary student's association in Britain, and in 1976 the LTTE (Liberation Tigers of Tamil Eelam) was founded. It became one of the most effective guerrilla/terrorist groups in the world within a year. Its ideological guru was a Marxist–Leninist turned extreme nationalist named Balasingham, but the undisputed political military leader was Prabhakaran. From the very beginning, he was less influenced by Marxism–Leninism than by various Hindu thinkers. One of these was Vivekananda, who taught him to concentrate on training and indoctrinating the very young; another was Gandhi (short of nonviolence but with an emphasis on sexual abstinence); and above all, Subhas Chandra Bose, a chameleon-like man who served as a left-wing Congress leader and strongly supported the Japanese and Nazis during World War II.

What is commonly referred to as the 'Insurgency' began even earlier, in 1973, but during its first phase fighting was on a relatively minor scale. Growing Tamil militancy produced a Sinhalese backlash in 1981, resulting in riots and the murder of imprisoned Tamil leaders, which in turn led to a far bloodier Tamil campaign. This came to a halt only in July 1987, when Indian army units landed on the island in a peacekeeping effort. But the Indians faced Sinhalese resentment in addition to constant attack by the Tamil, who rejected the peace accord that had been worked out by Rajiv Gandhi, then Indian prime minister, and the Sri Lankan president. The Indians had little stomach for guerrilla fighting, and though some twelve thousand Tamils were killed, much of the Jaffna peninsula destroyed, and the Tamil Tigers forced to retreat to the jungle, the Indians decided to withdraw their troops from the island once they realised that peace between the two communities could not be achieved. Ever since then, civil war has continued on the island, with ambushes in the countryside as well as terrorist attacks in the towns, and while the Tigers have not achieved a significant victory, the Sri Lankan army has been unable to stamp out the insurrection.

The Tamil Tiger leadership committed two major political blunders: one, when they assassinated Rajiv Gandhi in 1991, and, two, when they rejected a generous autonomy offer by the Sri Lankan government in 1995. Despite the rebels' countless acts of indiscriminate violence, often against innocent civilians, the Tamil Tigers somehow preserved the reputation of an underdog, and thus attracted a certain amount of sympathy from the outside world. But much goodwill in India was lost following the assassination, and whatever sympathy was left disappeared when the Tigers showed extreme intransigence. It took six years for an Indian official inquiry committee to disentangle the circumstances of the assassination (its report was published only in December 1997); it appeared that not only had Tamil Nadu officials been involved, but that at an earlier stage in the insurgency the Tigers had been helped by the Indian secret services. The appeal of the Tamil Tigers was from then on restricted to the Tamil diaspora in foreign countries and their contributions, whether voluntary or forced, dwindled.

The Tamil Tigers, in their long fight against the ethnic majority, have shown inventiveness and extraordinary persistence. Mention has been made of the indoctrination of young Tigers in a spirit of national fanaticism, spiritualism, sexual ascesis, and a cult of suicide. The last usually involved cyanide, and is said to give the Tigers extra confidence in that they have an alternative to capture and imprisonment. They have been waging a guerrilla war based on the Chinese and Cuban pattern, and for a number of years they virtually ruled the Jaffna peninsula as a little state of their own, just as Mao had run Yenan. They had modern high-tech weapons, such as Soviet-made SA 7 ground-to-air missiles obtained from Cambodia, and dozens of tons of RDX, a powerful explosive, obtained from the Ukraine. They operated their own small navy, which plied between Sri Lanka and the Indian mainland, as well as Myanmar (Burma) and Thailand. They operated in large units of several thousand fighters, some of whom received their military training in Tamil Nadu and others in Lebanon [. . .] and for years they maintained a military base in Myanmar. Like the IRA, they ran corporations and businesses, and have smuggled arms, drugs, and other commodities.

Despite the relative weakness of the Sinhalese army, and for all the Tigers' proficiency in guerrilla warfare, they have been unsuccessful in fighting in the open. They lost their main base in the Jaffna peninsula as the result of a government offensive in December 1995, and had to abandon their last urban base in Kilinochi in September

1996. In the latter operation alone, about a thousand Tamil Tigers were killed or taken prisoner. But as so often before, they still had enough strength to inflict major blows on the government. In July 1996, four thousand Tamil Tigers attacked and seized a government military base northeast of Colombo. All 1,200 military personnel at the base were killed, and it was the most severe military defeat the government suffered since the beginning of the war. In addition, there were frequent bomb attacks. In January 1996, almost a hundred civilians were killed and 1,400 injured in the Colombo banking district. On another occasion four Tiger frogmen blew up two gunboats at the naval base of Trincomalee. On the other hand, a naval blockade imposed by India severely hampered Tamil Tiger arms supplies, which mainly came from across the sea. The small Tiger navy, consisting partly of speedboats, interferes with ships of other nations fairly regularly, committing acts of piracy against China, Malaya, and Indonesia, and this had not added to their popularity.

Tamil propaganda has been far more astute than government propaganda, and the Tigers have established a foreign service of their own with representations in thirty-eight countries, issuing daily news bulletins and running their own illegal radio station in Sri Lanka. Use is widely made of the Internet and video clips, which are distributed to leading media in foreign countries. Yet, with all this, the insurgency in Sri Lanka remains one of the most underreported in the world media.

The main bases of Tiger operations, such as the Jaffna peninsula, have been virtually destroyed; most of the peninsula's inhabitants have emigrated abroad. The war effort of the LTTE is mainly paid for by expatriate Tamil communities in Canada, the United States, Australia, South Africa, and several European countries. Some of the money has come in voluntarily, but the LTTE has also enlisted enforcers, extracting contributions from those reluctant to pay. This in turn has led to the arrest of the more aggressive collectors, and in some countries the Tamil Tigers have been banned altogether. The small Tamil community (some 25,000) in Switzerland allegedly contributed $8 million a year, a sizeable sum considering that most of them recently were very poor asylum seekers. In 1996, the Tiger leadership in Switzerland was arrested and charged with extortion.

In the shadowy world of drug smuggling there is little hard evidence of official LTTE participation, but there is some circumstantial evidence that individual Tamils have played a considerable role in smuggling heroin from Asia to Europe. The Tiger leadership has certainly tolerated it and in all probability benefited from it, but has not advertised its active involvement. The Colombo government, however, has claimed that drug smuggling constitutes the single most important item in the war treasury of the LTTE, and ships that smuggle arms and other commodities are also used to carry drugs.

In the guerrilla and terrorist war against the government, at least ten thousand Tamil Tigers have been killed. There has been enormous material damage to the north of Sri Lanka and the creation of many refugees. Nevertheless, the Tigers claim that despite these losses and many major setbacks they will continue to fight until they have a fully independent state of their own. The most they are willing to concede is a loose economic union with the majority patterned on that of the European Community.

What makes them fight with such tenacity and fanaticism? Religious and ethnic differences do exist but are not crucial; the Sinhalese hail from northern India, the Tamil from the south. The Tamil originally had the Hindu caste system; the Sinhalese are predominantly Buddhist. The Tamil claim that they cannot possibly live with the Sinhalese in the framework of one state; they always had a state (a kingdom) of their own, and it was against their wishes that they were fused into one country under British rule. This state of affairs is obviously true for a great many nationalities and tribes all over the world, and it would be impossible to reconstitute all of these kingdoms, duchies, and principalities. The Tamil militants are not, however, impressed by considerations of this kind. Their leadership, originally Marxist–Leninist, has transformed itself into an intense nationalist group, preaching a fanaticism and a ruthlessness that in Europe could be found only in the fascist movements of the 1930s.

The extraordinary ruthlessness of the campaign waged by the Tamil Tigers has shown itself in the indiscriminate killing of Sinhalese and Muslim peasants in addition to the political murders committed against rivals within the Tamil camp. The Tigers were originally only one of several militant groups among the Tamil community, and their rise to power left a bloody trail of assassinations in their wake, including, for instance, the elected mayor of Jaffna, who was killed by the young Prabhakaran, who in later years became the undisputed commander of the Tigers. In 1998, yet another elected mayor of Jaffna, a Tamil woman, was killed by terrorists. By this time it was no longer clear whether the assassins were Tiger surrogates or a smaller group competing with them. Such internecine warfare has weakened the cause of the Tigers and other militant separatists.

The virulence of Tamil terrorism and its proclivity to suicide cannot be blamed on social and political circumstances. While it is true that their treatment by the Sinhalese majority has often been unjust, only a feverish imagination can refer to it as 'genocide'. Learning from bitter experience and its own mistakes, the Colombo government has made far-reaching concessions to the Tamils over the years, and Tamils have been represented in prominent positions in the government. (The Sri Lankan foreign minister, at the time of writing, is a Tamil by origin.) It is true that the rate of suicide in Sri Lanka is among the highest in Asia, and indeed in the world, and has been steadily rising, but this seems not to be true with regard to Tamil Nadu in India. Poor economic conditions (some 40 per cent of the population live in absolute poverty) are largely the result, not the cause, of the civil war. The combination of a relatively well-educated young generation and youth unemployment can make for political radicalism and possibly even terrorism, but not necessarily for suicide. Hate is not directed against a foreign occupant or members of a religion distasteful to the Tamils, and the difference in language alone cannot explain the deep division, especially since the central government has made Tamil its second official language. Rather, there is a veritable 'cult of the martyrs' among the Tamil. One day of the year is celebrated as Martyrs' Day, but this is recent; it is not part of Tamil history or Hindu religion. It seems more Christian or Muslim than Tamil.

It is certain that the Tigers would not have lasted so long and been able to inflict so many losses on their enemy if it were not for their fanaticism. Assistance from Tamil Nadu and the Tamil diaspora, from Norway to Botswana, has also played an important role. But this, again, does not fully explain the riddle, because while there is Tamil solidarity in Tamil Nadu, there is no intense fanaticism equal to that found in Sri Lanka, nor has there been a movement for separatism in Tamil Nadu. Therefore, in the final analysis, there is no satisfactory explanation for the Tamil Tigers and their fanaticism.[1]

THE TAMIL 'GROWING TOGETHERNESS'

Laqueur might have stressed that Tamils regard 1972 as a 'crunch-point'. It was then that a new Constitution was drawn up by the Sinhalese majority who now grouped together in a new Constituent Assembly. The island's name was changed to the Sinhalese 'Sri Lanka'; Buddhism would be the state religion. Meagre safeguards relating to language use, welfare provision and employment went deliberately unobserved. As Tamils began to see themselves as second-class citizens in the land of their birth, riots erupted. Many thousands sought asylum overseas. Enthusiastic crowds of young men rushed to enrol as a liberating phalanx. Out of ashes and despair, the Tigers of Eelam were taking the field. Ruthless and dedicated, they marked down government officials and any Tamil they thought a 'collaborator'. Their fanatical single-mindedness and unquestioning peer loyalty was proclaimed by the mantra 'TERRORISM RULES – TERRORISM WILL WIN'. The reality of this was soon to cause much apprehension in government circles.

David Whittaker (2004) has written a short, concise account of the Tamil resurgence:

The Liberation Tigers of Tamil Eelam (LTTE) have brought 21 years of despair, destruction and misery to Sri Lanka. In several respects they are quite different from the other groups described.

- They are a separatist, liberationist group unlike the international al-Qaida and the Hizbullah fighting for the Palestinians.
- They rely on techno-terrorism using the Internet (www.tamilnation.org) to pump out propaganda and to recruit their ranks, radiating programmes from their own radio and TV studios, marketing widely videos and CDs.
- They claim adherence and financial support from a worldwide network of backers, reputedly 70 million in perhaps 40 countries.

These terrorists are a puzzle. Why do they go on with terror when there are attempts to secure a compromise and ceasefire and when some autonomy must be awarded even fanatical separatists? What is it that drives a group towards armageddon when their watchword is 'destroy everything that destroys you'?

The Tigers see history as making their case a well-founded one. Sri Lanka, formerly a British possession known as Ceylon, and Eelam to Tamils, achieved independence in 1948. The Tamils, living mainly in the north and east of the island of Sri Lanka, were a minority, one in five of a total population of 17 million. An ancient people, linked ethnically with Tamil Nadu, a province in south-east India, they were largely Hindu and rural workers. In their view, independence had asserted the domination of the Sinhalist majority, chiefly Buddhist, in the capital Colombo and the chief towns. Strong feelings of oppression on the part of the Tamils led to turbulence and riots. They were not, in fact, the only protestors against an intolerant government. There was also a Sinhalist faction, the Sinhalese People's Liberation Front, which struggled against both the government and the Tamils. Inevitably, a Tamil fighting leader emerged, one Velupillai Prabhakaran, whose early Marxist orientation became increasingly nationalistic and uncompromising. He it was, in 1976, who enlisted willing volunteers into a separatist striking force, the Tamil Liberation Tigers. To begin with, they used guerrilla tactics, concentrating on military not civilian targets. As always, though, inferiority at arms brings on frustrated wider violence. It was at this point that conventional lines of warfare merged into limitless destruction as casualties on government and terrorist sides began to mount. The neighbouring state of India, in 1987, decided that something should be done to insulate its south-eastern provinces, Tamil Nadu and Karnataka, from Tamil insurgency. The first approach would be by means of exploratory talks and a peacekeeping force sent across to Sri Lanka. If this were to fail, and eventually it did, then the Indian Army would field an expeditionary force. This intervention failed either to pacify the island or to induce Tamil Tigers to show any interest in laying down arms. Savage fighting ensued. Although the Indians gained the upper hand, occupying the Tigers' principal heartland of the Jaffna peninsula, there seemed no point at all in continuing an endless siege, and India withdrew after two years of disheartening involvement. There followed a return to a bloody civil war with the Tamil Tigers wreaking havoc on military and civilian personnel. The terrorists were increasingly seen as devilish and reckless, by the Sinhalese in Colombo. What was the point of showing any understanding of those who assassinated an Indian Prime Minister, Rajiv Gandhi, in 1991, and the Sri Lankan President Prendesa in 1993?

The Tamil Tigers, tenacious and barbarous, certainly, claim fervently that they have a rightful cause to defend. They have always been harassed and alienated, they say, by the Sinhalese. Imperial Britain disregarded them. Independence did nothing for them. Indeed, the harshness of government repression strikes them as 'genocide', violating the most basic human rights and their response has to be via armed resistance.[2]

[. . .] There is one thing that Tamils and Hizbullah and even the IRA in Northern Ireland have in common, namely, the significance of myth and tradition. A myth that proclaims that only revolutionary struggle can reassert group identity, restore inalienable rights and promote self-determination is worth fighting for regardless of cost. A myth such as this reinforces the credibility of a group. It inspires recruits. It consolidates the zeal of those who aspire, those who campaign and those who survive. The myth of invincibility gives purpose to a struggle through terror. The myth of victory-through-destruction has persuaded 17,000 Tamil Tigers in the last 20 years to resort to suicide and to seek martyrdom. 'We are', say the suicide cult, 'married to our cyanide'. In some rather strange, deep way, Tamil myths and hopes sustain 6,000 Tigers in a remorseless wave of terror despite savage losses. Terror, too, is unisex. Half of the 'Black Panthers' are women, the 'freedom birds', who are supposed to simulate pregnancy carrying high explosive charges under bulging skirts. Terror is sophisticated using speedboats and frogmen in harbours, and the latest missiles and mortars from sources in Libya, the Ukraine and Thailand.

The tally of terrorism in Sri Lanka is horrific. No town dweller, villager, policeman or priest is safe from being gunned down or bombed. Sixty thousand Sinhalese have been slain, including a score of prominent civil servants. Tamils have suffered grievously, 10,000 of them have been killed and they have lost 32 of their front rank leaders. Counter-terrorist measures by the government have been undeniably brutal.

Rampant terrorism in Sri Lanka is slowly decimating the island. After 35 years of bitter warfare, there are now signs of stalemate. In a contest for power, both sides are beginning to see the dream of complete separatist fulfilment as shattered by the march of events. Is there not room for a federal solution giving, say, autonomy to Tamil regions as a step towards autonomy and representation in Colombo's parliament? A prelude to negotiation would be a ceasefire followed by a lifting of the ban on the LTTE, and some arrangement for Tamils to meet a government deputation for exploratory peace negotiations.

A dramatic turn of events came about in April 2002. The LTTE leader, Prabhakaran, broadcast a notice saying that he would hold a press conference in rebel-held jungle on 10 April. The government cleared the main road for the access of eager journalists. Guides would escort the visitors to a secret location. No satellite phones were allowed. An excited huddle of correspondents saw the leader, not in fatigues, but a smart shirt, emerge from his bunker to face microphones and cameras. He spoke directly. 'We are seriously considering renouncing armed struggle if a solution acceptable to the Tamil people can be worked out'. He went on to state that the LTTE had been misrepresented. 'We fight', he declared, 'for the liberation of our people. You must distinguish between what constitutes terrorism and what is a liberation struggle' (*Guardian*, 10 April 2002).

[Were] the Tigers [. . .] walking away from terrorism?[3]

THE TAMIL DIASPORA

The term 'diaspora' is commonly understood to refer to the forced exile of the Jews from the Roman Empire and to their scattering throughout the lands of the Gentiles in the first two centuries of the Christian era. In the case of the Tamils the dispersion is mainly a voluntary one. In modern parlance it might best be described as a 'supporters club', which actively disseminates the case for Tamil self-determination within Sri Lanka and which has a cardinal role in accumulating funds (one estimate is that of $1 million a month) to support the cause.

It is the global growth of the Tigers that makes their case distinctive. They see themselves as a transnational entity [. . .] Their world presence is the LTTE International claiming a supporters' club of 70 million and backing, with vast funds and weapons procurement, the suffering and purpose of the Tamil struggle. *The Times* in 1997 spoke of the LTTE International as able to keep going indefinitely 'funded by the biggest international financial empire ever built by a terrorist organisation' (23 October 1997). One estimate of the Tigers' global income (much of it from North America and Europe) is of the order of £1.25 million a month, with about a fifth of that coming from the 50,000 Tamils resident in Britain. Nevertheless, it must be emphasised that many of the 150,000 Tamils living outside Sri Lanka have never supported terrorist activities.[4]

Business collectives and a rather secretive network of financial concerns and law firms in the United States, Australia, Canada and Britain supply a dependable monthly income. Freighters flying the Tamil flag regularly bring in foodstuffs and arms dealers' sophisticated weaponry for the Sri Lankan guerrillas.

Britain, particularly, in Sri Lankan eyes, is a gathering ground for Tamil expatriates who are surely standing four-square behind the LTTE. In October 1997, *The Times* carried this report about terrorist financing:

The Tamil Tigers, who have been waging a civil war against the Sri Lankan Government for the past 14 years, can keep going indefinitely, funded by the biggest international financial empire ever built by a terrorist organisation. Most of their money comes from Europe, the US and Canada. London is the propaganda headquarters, feeding information – much of it more credible than Colombo's accounts of battlefield developments – to Tamil organisations, embassies and newspapers worldwide. The failure of the international community to stem the Tigers' activities demonstrates the ineffectiveness of the global fight against terrorism.

Britain has all but admitted it is powerless to curb the Tigers, who raise, according to Sri Lankan estimates, £250,000 a month from Tamils living in Britain. The worldwide income is believed to be about £1.25 million a month, some of which goes to humanitarian causes, but most of which funds a sophisticated war machine.

More than 450,000 Sri Lankan Tamils live abroad, many of them victims of ethnic riots, especially those in 1983. They are thus inclined to support armed rebellion. There are 50,000 Tamils in Britain, most of them relatively prosperous, and many Tamils actively support the cause.[5]

THE POWER OF THE MAKING OF MYTHS

This case study of the Tamils and the one of Northern Ireland in Chapter 13 both touch on the apparent significance of myth to terrorists. The process of making myths assumes a realistic shape in order to lend credibility and force to LTTE rhetoric has been closely examined by Bruce Kapferer (1997). One Tamil myth suggests that there must be played out 'an age-old conflict: that the present situation is merely the reproduction of annual events established in pre-colonial contexts'. There is, by inference, a tradition of violent struggle that may be necessary to attain definable ends. Kapferer believes this to be a distorted premise; the current conflict, he argues, is entirely the result of recent colonial and post-colonial circumstances. Another Tamil myth, soon accepted by them as credible, was to present the state as thoroughly decadent and corrupt – an impersonal bureaucracy threatening the freedom of an individual and even that of a local village community. The myth reinforces the notion of opposable threat and of legitimate active response. Self-respect and rightful autonomy had long been eroded by the alienating policies of a government and of an intolerant majority; only struggle – the process of revolution – could restore basic human rights. Building myths was, as one might expect, a deliberate strategy to inspire the revolutionary cadres, to fortify their resolve, and to consolidate their strength in numbers. For Kapferer there is an inevitable linkage of cause and effect where myths help to heighten identity, and violence, ultimately terroristic, affirms identity where any confrontation contains an ethnic element:

Thus, Tamil guerrilla attacks in the interests of ethnic autonomy sparked violent anti-Tamil rioting much of which received the support of agents of the state [. . .] The violence of the riots created a deepening of ethnic division which gave the myths of ethnic identity greater relevance. Moreover, the riots generated the expansion of Tamil resistance.[6]

Violence, then, may move towards the objective of annihilation, Kapferer points out, towards the point when terror ousts terror, in a contra-terrorist campaign to 'rub out' suspect supporter groups. The picture is a familiar one: what happened in Sri Lanka has been seen in South America and the Middle East:

Thus, in government action, evidence of individual JVP [Janatha Vimukthi Peranmuna] activists in a village area occasionally became a pretext for action against the village as a whole. Government forces engaged in mass killings: 'guilt' via category-membership and the grim evidence is now being revealed in public enquiries. The bureaucratic/technical order of the state is not just the means or the instrument of state violence, it becomes itself generative of an expanding situation of violence.[7]

Another point characteristic of the Sri Lankan conflict is, for Kapferer, its 'religiosity'. Tamils are chiefly Hindu, observing the distinctions of the caste system; the Sinhala majority are Buddhist in the main. In regard to the Buddhist faith and its followers, Kapferer detects a marked distortion of value and a paradox that is grim in its implications:

Moreover, in the current context of intra-ethnic and inter-ethnic violence officers of the state make intense appeals to the key Buddhist value of non-violence. Further, there is, in the current situation, an implication that the state as constituted in reference to the Buddha ideal of non-violence is the supreme agent of Buddhist morality, a morality which is even present in the exercise by the state of extreme violence. It is a violence in the interest of the order of a Buddhist state.[8]

ETHNIC WAR AND ITS TALLY

Manoj Joshi (1996) has traced the terrorist tactics of the Tigers since 1975:

The 'honor' of carrying out the movement's first political assassination belonged to a young 17-year-old Tamil called Vellupilai Prabhakaran, who managed to shoot the Tamil mayor of Jaffna, Alfred Duriappah, in July 1975. The following year, Pirabhakaran had another 'first', a successful bank raid that netted him over half a million rupees. He then founded the Tamil New Tigers, which became the Liberation Tigers of Tamil Eelam (LTTE). In September 1978, another first was credited to the outfit, a time-bomb blast in an Air Ceylon passenger jet.

A key impetus to Tamil militancy was provided by the anti-Tamil riots of July 1983 and the massacre of a number of militant leaders [. . .] This led to a stream of refugees fleeing to India across the narrow neck of water dividing the two countries. Most, if not all of these refugees went to the Indian State of Tamil Nadu just twenty-eight kilometers across the Palk Strait. India therefore has been an important reference point for the groups for cultural as well as logistical reasons.[9]

Kapferer has made a detailed study of state and insurrectionary violence in Sri Lanka. He is chiefly concerned with the Sinhalese JVP (the People's Liberation Front) but most of the points he makes and the conclusions drawn are also directly relevant to Tamil terrorism and are well worth reproducing here. Kapferer's argument isolates a number of significant factors leading to conflict: the contrasts between affluence and poverty, above all in towns; the unconvincing assurances of the Colombo Government; the messianic and symbolistic postures and resolution of a liberating force (such as the LTTE and the JVP); the part played by motives of vengeance; and the prevalence of rumour and confusion. There were too many 'contradictions' in Sri Lankan society to lead to anything other than disruptive protest, aggression and terror:

The ethnic war exacerbated contradictions at the heart of the Sri Lanka state and in the political and social worlds of the Sinhala population. The JVP revolt of 1989–90, and its furious suppression by government forces, was a violent expression of the forces, emergent in such contradiction and the engagement of violence as the key weapon of resolution. The JVP drew on the energies of increased class suffering, especially among the rural and urban poor intensified by the economic strains of the war. The timing of the revolt coincided with the apparent emptiness of the Sinhala nationalist rhetoric of the government (evidenced in the Sri Lanka–India Accord which occasioned serious mass rioting). The state appeared weak, too, in its confrontation with the Tigers whose fighting capacity had reached legendary proportions among the Sinhalese population. In the representations among numerous Sinhalese, the Tigers are depicted as messianic in their commitment and, for many, present an aura of invulnerability. Prior to the JVP uprising rumour had circulated in Colombo that the Tigers were planning a surprise attack on the city and this had led to a small panic among the city's populace, some fleeing towards the countryside. There was wide belief that the ranks in the armed forces were highly sympathetic to the JVP and this undoubtedly encouraged the JVP leadership to embark on its final terror drive, in August 1989, to take over the government. It is generally understood that a JVP mistake (the enormity of which was almost unbelievable at the time and even more so in retrospect) in its discourse of violence at this time was responsible for its failure. The JVP leadership announced that it would attack the families of the armed forces if they did not disobey government directives to move against the JVP. This remarkable error is regarded as being instrumental in the turning of the tide against JVP fortunes and impelling a period of massive human destruction. This destruction often expressly took the form of 'righteous' vengeance.[10]

The conflict in Sri Lanka is much more complex than A versus B – it was a 'total situation of violence' in Kapferer's words:

The distinct dynamics of JVP and government violence expanded the dimensions of the violent context to create for a while a total situation of violence [. . .] As much as a struggle for controlling power, the violence was a vital element for constituting a social world in which a particular kind of dominating power was possible. Thus the Sinhalese population as a whole was increasingly drawn into the conflict and consumed in its fury.[11]

Moreover, in a very rough and quixotic way, the terrorists assumed the role of moral arbiters:

People executed by the JVP were not only identified as government stooges, or as behaving in defiance of JVP authority, they were also presented as offending local moralities. The JVP executioners often presented themselves as exerting customary or rightful justice, as asserting the justice that the agents of the government had ignored or themselves had abused. People killed by the JVP included rapists, seducers, thieves, etc. The killing occasionally followed the course of long-standing village disputes and exhibited the passions of local enmities and the desire for revenge.
    Broadly, the violent discourse of the JVP engaged the dynamic of the war-machine. It expanded through social relations and to some extent became driven by the violence already integral within them. Thus, its energy of destruction joined with the enmities already present and often of a long-standing nature in local areas. The JVP violence became part of pre-existing structures of vengeance and a vehicle for the settling of old scores. The government's need to destroy the JVP and to attack it at base progressively involved government forces in similar processes of local vengeance which expanded the destruction as a whole.[12]

The Sri Lankan tally of terrorism is enormous among a relatively small population. Estimates of the number of terrorists vary but are likely to be in the region of 6,000 fully armed and desperate fighters. They include women guerrillas, the 'freedom birds', and perhaps half of the Tigers are still in their teens. They have their own highly organised intelligence service. An élite brigade, the Black Tigers, operates a battlefield strategy known as 'Unceasing Wave', targeting key members of the government and the armed forces, public buildings and important parts of the economic infrastructure, such as power stations, fuel depots, commuter trains and stations. Terrorist strikes will be launched carefully before the security forces are called or when most people are asleep. The terrorist arsenal and methods are substantial and lead to horrendous damage and casualties. People are gunned down in the streets, and bombs are detonated in vehicles, trains and ferry boats. Mortars and heavy artillery are launched at public buildings. Muslim and Buddhist clergy and worshippers have been slaughtered. No village community can feel safe. Something causing much disquiet in Colombo is the extent of terrorist linkage between their 'front-line' operations in Sri Lanka and a supply and communications base in peninsular India. Joshi has a note about this:

Safe houses and communications centres were purchased in Tamil Nadu and Karnataka. The LTTE used local contacts for the purchases, but insulated their organization from them. Likewise the LTTE used small workshops and industrial facilities in Tamil Nadu to manufacture uniforms and even items like rifle-fired grenades. Communications were of great importance, and the LTTE had a sophisticated network using high frequency and very high frequency wireless sets, international direct dialling, all with security provisions. This network linked Indian safe houses with each other and with Jaffna and provided real-time control of shipping and smuggling operations.[13]

Sri Lanka's terrorism has known no bounds since 1983. The loss of life that terrorists have caused since 1972 is reckoned to be some 58,000 civilians and military personnel, two-thirds of whom died in the years 1984–97. Seventeen prominent political leaders have met their deaths. In the course of violent dissension within the LTTE's own ranks, 32 Tamil leaders have been killed.

FANATICISM AND SUICIDE

Laqueur acknowledges the searing fundamentalism of aggression–hate–fanaticism in members of a group such as the Tamil Tigers but warns that their 'political' beliefs and attitudes should not be simplistically defined. The old definitions of 'revolutionary' or 'reactionary' or 'left wing' or 'right wing' are inappropriate or inadequate in helping us understand terrorist motives and the degree of emotional involvement. As for the Tamils' fanaticism, Laqueur suggests that suicide by Tamils, while appearing horrific and pathologically extreme to others, may have for the individual activists and for their collaborators a positive value where martyrdom is a rational terminal decision demonstrating a worthy and invincible cause. (This seems to be the case with the Hizbullah in Lebanon.)

Being absolutely convinced of the rightness of his cause, the fanatic needs an enemy, and he is bound to have enemies since the majority will seldom agree with him. Hate plays a central role in his personality structure; paraphrasing Descartes, he can rightly say *Odio, ergo sum* – I hate, therefore I exist. The substance of his belief system may vary greatly according to history, culture, or the influence of charismatic leaders. But the burning passion is primary; ideological content is secondary.

Where does the fanaticism, the passion, originate? To what extent are biological factors involved, and to what degree social and cultural factors? Is there a biochemical trip wire that is set off by a childhood trauma? These issues have been widely but inconclusively discussed for many years. But it is not helpful to define radicals of this and similar persuasion as right wing or left wing, as is often done. The usual defining characteristics such as 'reactionary' and 'revolutionary' get mixed up in these mindsets. Some fanatics are simply nihilists, even though they will seldom admit it.

To argue that the Algerian terrorists, the Palestinian groups, or the Tamil Tigers are 'left' or 'right' means affixing a label that simply does not fit. Taken from early nineteenth-century Europe, these terms have little meaning in other times and parts of the world. The Third World groups to which we refer have subscribed to different ideological tenets at different periods, and it is as wrong to take Leninist slogans seriously as it is to subscribe to fascist rhetoric. The foundation of their movements is extreme nationalist orientation, frequently including religious motives in recent times. Such a religious-nationalist-populist movement can to Western eyes appear to be left wing one moment and right the next, as history has shown time and again. Why should one even try to classify terrorist groups using categories that are no longer relevant?

To begin to understand the mind-set of this new breed of terrorist, his cruelty and hate, the shedding of all moral restraints, the great rage about everything and nothing in particular, the joy generated by killing and destruction, one has to go, initially at least, over familiar ground: fanaticism and paranoia.[14]

The indoctrination of the positive value of suicide has been especially intense in Sri Lanka where almost all the candidates among the Tamil Tigers are in their teens. Carrying cyanide on their persons is considered to be an expression of their commitment to their cause: 'We are married to our cyanide; it makes us clear-headed and purposeful'. This commitment to self-destruction is combined with training in the commission of acts of the greatest cruelty.[15]

COUNTER-TERRORISM

Understandably the Sri Lankan authorities, like most governments, have sought to contain and then eliminate anti-state terrorism by means of a mixture of political and diplomatic moves allied to the employment of force. Joshi has examined particularly the course of Colombo's attempt at enlisting a mediator, in this case India. There was an element of force to be used in the approach:

In an important interregnum, between July 1987 and March 1990, the Indian Army, constituted as an Indian peace-keeping force, fought the LTTE in a bid to compel it to accept the Indo–Sri Lanka Peace Accord that had been signed by Indian Prime Minister Rajiv Gandhi and Sri Lankan President J. R. Jayawardene in June 1987.

Beginning as a two-brigade force to enforce the Indo–Sri Lanka Peace Accord, the Indian Peace Keeping Force (IPKF) confronted the LTTE in an aborted two-and-a-half year campaign which left twelve thousand dead and over five thousand wounded. In this period the LTTE showed themselves to be adaptive as well as innovative as guerrillas and terrorists. They first took on the IPKF from their urban redoubt of Jaffna and then, when forced out, from the jungle stronghold of north-central Sri Lanka.

The principal reason for Indian intervention in the affairs of Sri Lanka was to prevent the aggressive assertion of a Tamil identity in Sri Lanka from having a reflex influence in Tamil Nadu. Following Mrs Gandhi's assassination at the hands of her Sikh bodyguards in October 1984, India shifted gears in Sri Lanka. It first attempted to play honest broker between the Tamils and the Sinhala-dominated government of Sri Lanka. After two futile years, at the behest of both sides, it inserted itself as a party, as well as a guarantor, of an Accord signed with the Sri Lankan government on July 29, 1987.

However, in reality, the LTTE was relentlessly opposed to the deal and began a systematic campaign to sabotage the accord. This led to a confrontation with the IPKF, who launched an assault on the town of Jaffna. The Indian Army built up a four-division force that kept Jaffna free from major hostilities for eighteen months and bottled up the LTTE in the Wanni jungles of north-central Sri Lanka.

The 1987–1989 period was the most dangerous for the LTTE, but it adapted well to jungle fighting after being forced out of Jaffna. In some ways the organization actually became stronger and gained greater depth and experience. It was able to exploit the three-way relationship between itself, the Sri Lankan government, and the government of India.

By late 1988, badly bruised by the IPKF actions, the LTTE realized the imperative of getting the Indians out of Sri Lanka. The elections, unrepresentative to the interim northeastern state, boded ill for them in the long run. Neither their attacks nor the casualties they could inflict could compel the IPKF to pull out. The only way the Indians would go out was the way they came in, at the request of the government in Colombo.

The beginning of the end had arrived, as the new foreign minister of India, Inder Kumar Gujral, gratuitously declared in early 1990 that Indian troops would 'never again' be sent to Sri Lanka. India now was left with no leverage to insist on even a token implementation of the Indo–Sri Lanka Accord.[16]

Wider perspectives engaged the Sri Lankan Government in January 1998, when the United Nations completed the draft of an International Convention for the Suppression of Terrorist Bombings and opened it in New York for signature. As chairman of the Ad Hoc Committee working on the draft, Sri Lanka had played an important role in moving discussion into print, declaring frequently and vigorously that only concerted international action could combat terrorism, especially where, as in Sri Lanka, a terrorist group could call on backers and funding elsewhere. Effective action against terrorism had been frustrated, in Colombo's view, by too much sterile philosophical debate about the nature of terrorism. The Convention with its legislative and practical proposals had to be adopted and implemented without delay.

A concluding question is: what future is there for any resort to force among the Tamils of Sri Lanka? In May 1997 there appeared in a newspaper, the *Indian Express*, a number of points certain to exercise minds in contemporary Sri Lanka. The heading reads: 'Tamed Tigers Add to Tamil Trauma':

Just as the war can never end as long [as] the LTTE remains a force, Tamil aspirations for equality and political autonomy will certainly remain an unfulfilled dream if there were to be no LTTE.

[. . .] Tamil political parties are desperate that a solution must be found and finalised before the Sri Lankan army brings the LTTE to its knees. Third party assistance is urgently required more to push a political deal for the Tamils through the maze of Sinhalese politics but this must happen before the Tigers are eventually crushed by the Sri Lankan army, because sadly, the LTTE is the only lever that the Tamils have now.[17]

Taming the Tigers has certainly been an enormously traumatic experience for Sri Lankans. The civil war, flaring most obviously in 1983, has brought 24 years of misery and despair. There are today slight signs of moves towards settlement, provided LTTE and Colombo can agree on what must be a compromise for a minority even though that minority disputes the term. A real sticking-point in most negotiations is the Sri Lankan Government's fear that giving autonomy to six or eight mainly Tamil regions might shift a possible and acceptable federal solution towards an unacceptable full independence for the Tamils. Many Tamils among the 70 million believe that sometime, somehow, their claims for equality of representation and opportunity must be met and there can be few of them who believe that a continuation of terrorism in Sri Lanka will do anything other than prolong two decades of civil war and add to a toll of 65,000 lives lost. There seems no alternative to Colombo's pressing ahead with strategies that build on concessions already offered together with a disarmament programme monitored by an outside agency.

More recent developments show a dramatic process of on-off peace-dealing between government and rebels. In August 2005, the first major high-level negotiations for two years took place in an atmosphere of bated breath on all sides. Three months later the first steps to discussion were still warily tentative, with hopes that felt a way towards a federal solution.

Unfortunately, the Tigers were soon provoked once more into violence after one of their leaders, Colonel Karuna, with 3,000 men, veered away to make separate overtures to the government. After a brief exchange of fighting, April 2006 brought a chance of peace talks, possibly in Geneva, if both sides could square their demands through the mediation of a Norwegian peace envoy. (Four years earlier, in fact, an impartial body, the Sri Lanka Monitoring Mission, had managed to broker the ceasefire and truce of 2002.) This opportunity was to collapse within weeks because the Karuna faction split the Tiger front. Yet again, in 2007, faint hopes of peace are emerging despite the hard-line positions of 'no talks before peace' and 'no peace before talks'. Colombo must have rebel assurance of a stop to all killings; the rebels expect no less than clear concessions from a government federal in nature. Meanwhile, Norway's ambassador is waiting in the wings.

Four years after the 2007 faint hopes of peace, Sri Lanka is still a state in suspense. The contestants of earlier years seem unmoveable. The Tamil Tigers (LTTE) on the one hand still include fanatic secessionists as well as those more liberal in rhetoric and deed. The former continue to harry and burn opponents; resort still to suicidal martyrdom. The latter – an unequal mix of workers and professional people – decry stark violence and ethnic discrimination. If liberals do not readily reject Tamil myths they publicly work to devalue its hold on their untameable militant brothers. Important to Tamil campaigners of every intent is a reliance on tacit support and ready financing from Tamil cells in more than 30 foreign states. In this regard the 'techno-terrorism' of websites beams out messages generally intelligible but sometimes all too nihilistic and uncompromising.

In some senses Sri Lankan terrorism appears contradictory. A cease fire was negotiated between Tamil envoys and the Colombo government in May 2009 yet a State of Emergency is still rigidly in place. Security programmes are clear –

expounded but only patchily enforced by Sri Lankan 'task force' commanders who consider the government divided and irresolute, unable to get a firm hand on the 37 militant groups the Cabinet has listed. Not surprisingly given the confusion over enforcement there are instances of ruthless state-terrorism and resort to beatings, torture, rape, summary internment and forcible eviction. Something of the mayhem of now 60 years has evaporated but an essential question and dilemma is there for many Tamils. Are not our violent tactics 'legitimate' given the circumstances in which we live? That is a query once frequently voiced in Belfast, Cape Town and Beirut.

Spain

S PAIN DIFFERS FROM ALL other Western democracies, not only in strength of provincial nationalism, but also in the level of violence brought about by conflict between Madrid and the provinces. This case study looks at the ETA movement in the Basque homeland of north-west Spain, which has led to 40 years of violence. Although the Basques have only a weak and recently conferred political identity, they are nevertheless an ancient nation with a unique non-Indo-European language. The proud traditions and customs of former times have, however, been drastically affected, as subsistence farming in the hills gives way to large-scale mechanised agriculture in the southern plains and as sleepy seaports and inland market towns have been transformed by the introduction of shipyards and steel plants, magnets to immigrants from lower Spain.

OVERVIEW

At the time of writing (February 2007), a ceasefire tentatively arranged in late 1999 shows little sign of permanence. As an example of terrorist campaigning, what has happened among the Basques of Spain (and may happen still) poses a number of intriguing questions, as Goldie Shabad and F. J. L. Ramo (1995) relate:

ETA [*Euzkadi ta Askatasuma* – Basque Homeland and Freedom] was founded in 1959 by a coalition of radical youth groups, one of which had split from the historic Basque Nationalist Party. Its primary aims from the beginning have been Basque independence and recuperation of Basque culture and language. These objectives continue to be at the centre of ETA's ideological program, the five-point KAS Alternative, which it set forth in the mid-1970s as the minimum conditions to be met by the Spanish state in exchange for ETA's abandonment of political violence. Most of the five points are radical nationalist demands. The first of these is reform of the 1978 Spanish constitution to accept the right of self-determination; a second is the assertion of the territorial integrity of all Basque provinces in Spain, which means the revision of the 1979 Basque Autonomy Statute to allow for the incorporation of Navarra into the Basque Autonomous Community; a third is the demand for the institutional predominance of Euskera (the Basque language); the fourth point calls for the unconditional amnesty for all political prisoners and the withdrawal of all Spanish police and armed forces from Basque soil. The last refers to the conditions of labor and expresses solidarity with the working class. Apart from this, no other mention is made of leftist ideological principles.

ETA's strategy of armed struggle was adopted in 1962, but in the 1960s and early 1970s ETA engaged in only sporadic acts of violence against the authoritarian and ultra-Spanish nationalist Francoist regime. The most dramatic and consequential of these was the assassination in 1973 of Prime Minister Carrero Blanco, heir apparent of Franco, an event that helped to bring about the demise of the authoritarian regime. After Franco's death in 1975, ETA violence increased dramatically, particularly during the transition to democracy and the granting of regional autonomy to the three Basque provinces (Alava, Guipúzcoa, and Vizcaya) in 1979–80. Of the more than 600 deaths attributable to ETA between 1968 and 1991, about 93 per cent occurred after Franco's death; about 27 per cent took place in 1979 and 1980 alone, during which time the Basque Autonomy Statute was being negotiated and elections to the first Basque regional government were being held. Thus, despite the rebirth of democracy in Spain and the achievement of autonomy for the Basque region, ETA continued to act as though 'nothing had changed'.

But things had changed. Civil liberties were restored, political competition became legitimate, autonomous trade unions were permitted, and open expression of ethnic nationalist sentiments – even of demands for territorial independence of ethnically distinct regional populations – was allowed. Why then did ETA violence not only persist but escalate after the restoration of democracy? Was this part of its original plan? Did political and social circumstances in the Basque Country make possible a continuation of ETA's activities? Or 'are members of terrorist organizations, once assembled, like the sorcerer's apprentice who, unwilling to be dismissed when the job is done, continues the violence?'

The endurance of ETA in the context of the rebirth of Spanish democracy and the granting of autonomy to the Basque Country presents an interesting puzzle. Why did the armed struggle go on, and what were the effects of ETA violence on the new democracy and on Basque society and politics?

First, however, we should specify the geopolitical limits of our research. According to Basque nationalists, Euskadi – the Basque Country, or the Basque nation – is composed of seven territories or provinces: four in Spain and three in France. Thus conceived, Euskadi has about 2,900,000 inhabitants living in an area of 20,644 square kilometres. But this notion of the Basque Country, which originated in the late nineteenth century, conflicts with a more complex reality. On the administrative level, the three French provinces (8.2 per cent of the whole Basque population and 14.3 per cent of its territory) are little districts of the larger so-called Pyrenees

Atlantiques region. The four Spanish provinces are presently divided into two autonomous, or self-governing, regions, each having different social structures, institutions, and party systems: on the one hand, there is the unprovincial autonomous community of Navarra with 17.6 per cent of the Basque population and 50.5 per cent of the territory; and on the other, there are the three provinces of Alava, Guipúzcoa, and Vizcaya, which make up the autonomous community of the Basque Country, or Euskadi. Neither Navarra nor Euskadi, it is important to note, is ethnically homogeneous. In the latter, about 30 per cent of the population were born outside of the region and an additional 11 per cent are first-generation Basques. The frame of reference for our analysis is the Basque Autonomous Community, in which Basque nationalist parties are dominant and ETA has drawn most of its militants, focused most of its violent activities, and received its greatest popular support.[1]

BASQUE NATIONALISM: THE SOCIO-ECONOMIC CONTEXT

Basque nationalism, as an ideology and movement, emerged during the 1890s mainly as a result of various social developments associated with rapid industrialisation. Shabad and Ramo survey this regional transformation and see it as promoting ethnic solidarity:

Explanations of Basque nationalism and of ETA violence, in particular, focus on the interaction of several distinct, but related, characteristics of the Basque Country and of its relation to the Spanish state. These range from structural characteristics, to the cognitive, evaluative, and affective orientations of different groups involved in a centre–periphery conflict, to the ideological views and personal motivations of those who choose to engage in violence rather than pursue more 'normal' political activities.

During the course of its economic transformation, traditional Basque society, founded on small-scale agriculture and commerce, was changed to a society based on mining, heavy industry, shipbuilding, and banking. Between 1842 and 1868, industrialization was first localized in the provinces of Vizcaya and Guipúzcoa where the resultant dramatic growth in population size and urbanization provided favourable conditions for the later rise of Basque nationalism.

Two other developments associated with industrialization were also of great importance for Basque ethnic mobilization. Industrialization created a different system of social stratification in which a new class of Basque industrialists and financiers became dominant and were soon incorporated into the Spanish oligarchy. Efforts by this group to integrate the Basque provinces economically and politically with Spain provoked intense hostility from the traditional *petite bourgeoisie*. In addition to the emergence of a new financial and industrial oligarchy, a working class also developed, as thousands of farmers from impoverished areas of Spain moved to urban areas in the Basque Country. With the rise of this new immigrant working class, Spanish trade unions and anticlerical leftist parties became major social and political protagonists in the Basque Country. These changes in class formation and their political expression posed serious threats to the socioeconomic and political status of the traditional urban middle class and to the hegemony of Catholic and rural Basque culture. It was among these segments of society that Basque nationalism developed and flourished.

Another period of rapid social and economic transformation occurred during the so-called economic boom between 1960 and 1975. The population of Euskadi increased by 44 per cent, and this time all three provinces experienced growth. Once again, immigration from other parts of Spain was an important factor contributing to population growth (40 per cent in the 1950s and 48 per cent in the 1960s). By 1975 only 51 per cent of those living in the three provinces were natives born of Basque parentage; 8 per cent were of mixed parentage; 11 per cent were first-generation Basques; and 30 per cent had been born in other parts of Spain. Sixty per cent and 40 per cent of residents of urban and metropolitan areas, respectively, had some Basque ancestry; this compares with 85 per cent of the rural population.

As a result of this 'second' industrial revolution, the active population in Euskadi increased by 25.2 per cent between 1960 and 1975; the increase in Spain as a whole was only 9 per cent. The sectoral distribution of this expanding work force once again radically altered Basque society and had important implications for Basque nationalism in the late Franco period and the transition to democracy. The native Basque population became increasingly middle class and urban, and in time the political and social influence of this nationalist bourgeoisie supplanted that of the Basque, but Spanish-oriented, oligarchy. The nationalist movement itself became increasingly interclassist.

The immigrant proletariat remained a distinct, but increasingly substantial, segment of Basque society. Rather than undermine ethnic solidarity, these major social and economic changes helped to promote it. They did so not only through the creation of modern infrastructures for ethnic mobilization but also by the very threat they posed to the declining, but increasingly idealized, traditional Basque culture. Indeed, during the 1950s and 1960s it was primarily traditional institutions, like the church and family, that sustained ethnic solidarity.

The transition to democracy coincided with an economic crisis in Spain. Because the Basque Country was a region of early industrialization and heavy industry, this economic crisis was felt most acutely in Euskadi. Policies of industrial restructuring, combined with ETA actions against Basque industrialists (in the form of assassinations, kidnappings, and the imposition of a system of 'revolutionary taxation'), resulted in high levels of unemployment, particularly among the young. This provided additional fertile ground for complaints about economic exploitation of the Basque Country by Madrid, as well as for recruitment of new ETA members.[2]

BASQUE NATIONALISM: THE POLITICAL CONTEXT

Politically, relations between the Spanish capital and the Basque Province have been those of conflict for centuries. Franco sought to eradicate Basque distinctiveness by removing what autonomy they had achieved. This and Madrid's reluctance to loosen its grip after the 1936–9 civil war was seen as justifying a Basque resort to violence, as Shabad and Ramo relate:

Although Spain was an 'early' state, the political, social and cultural integration of its territorial components – nation building – was not fully accomplished. Several provinces (including those of the Basque Country and Catalonia) had for lengthy periods of time enjoyed considerable political autonomy from Madrid. This in turn allowed regional minority cultures and languages (like Euskera and Catalan) to persist despite efforts by the centre to promote a single Spanish (or Castilian) language and national identity.

To preserve their traditional culture and historic political rights (the *fueros*), Basques figured prominently in the two nineteenth-century Carlist struggles against liberal and centralist governments in Madrid. The Carlists were defeated, and seven hundred years after they were first established, the Basques lost their *fueros* in 1876. The Basques' struggle against centralism and their ultimate defeat coincided with the dramatic changes associated with industrialization. Thus, in the late nineteenth century numerous segments of Basque society perceived threats to their collective identity coming both from Madrid and from new groups within the Basque Country itself. It was at this time that Basque nationalism as an ideology and a movement arose.

Just as the civil war was about to erupt, the Second Republic granted political autonomy to the Basque provinces. Basque nationalists, despite their religious and conservative views, allied themselves with the Republican forces against Franco. Once again they were on the losing side. Franco branded Vizcaya and Guipúzcoa 'traitorous provinces' and, in the process of creating a highly centralized regime, abrogated the last vestiges of their autonomy, the *conciertos económicos*.

In order to eradicate Basque distinctiveness once and for all and to create 'a single personality, Spanish', the Francoist regime engaged in physical and symbolic repression of any outward manifestation of Basque cultural and political identity. As a result, Basques, and particularly nationalists, came to view their territory as suffering 'military occupation' by an illegitimate Spanish state. Thus, the duality of 'us' (Basques) versus 'them' (Spain) became even further entrenched as a part of Basque political and cultural reality.[3]

Post-civil war generations of Basques grew up in a climate of physical and symbolic violence and repression, in which all things Basque were labeled by the authorities as 'traitorous' and as falling within the realm of social transgression. This climate was reinforced by the transmission from older to younger generations of historical memories of earlier periods of violence against the Basque Country, as had taken place during the Carlist and civil wars. The choice made by a segment of the Basque community to engage in violence against the violence of the 'occupying forces' of the Spanish state – a choice understood, if not wholly supported, by others – contributed further to the rise of a 'culture of violence' in Euskadi.[4]

Furthermore, by placing all expressions of Basque identity into the category of social transgression, the Francoist regime helped to make the formerly impermissible – including violence – permissible. More important, it made the resort to violence, in the minds of many Basques, a morally justifiable response: If the situation is to be defined in terms of violence, there is already an ever present institutional violence; any response to it, even pacificism, is violence. Violence, therefore, is the basic agent of social change; and whoever refused to participate in it lacks personal commitment.[5]

THE CALL TO ARMS

It was in 1962 that student activists in ETA, increasingly dissatisfied with the moderate nationalism of the rather conservative Basque Nationalist Party, whose rhetoric they contemptuously referred to as 'possibilism', took a more vigorous stance, defining ETA as the 'Basque Revolutionary Movement of National Liberation'. This signalled the taking up of a position of insurgency against Madrid's government. In 1963 ETA made its first contacts with the Spanish Communist party and suffered the consequences of police repression in the aftermath of workers' strikes. The following year, at an ETA assembly, a significant shift in ideology was announced and, again, Shabad and Ramo describe developments:

It was at this assembly [in 1964] that ETA approved 'Insurrection in Euskadi', a document written in exile in France for the political education of its militants. It was at this meeting, too, that the strategy of armed struggle began to take on sacral overtones and to be sublimated into the idea of messianic liberation led by a vanguard of the enlightened. With ETA's growth after 1964, three distinct, but often overlapping, tendencies emerged within the organization. The first, promoted by the founders of ETA in exile in France, stressed ethnolinguistic principles and was virulently anti-Spanish. The second had as its model anticolonial struggles and emphasized the importance of guerrilla warfare. The third was pro-worker in its ideological thrust. French actions against the first group and police repression in Spain against the second resulted in the dominance of the third faction in 1965 and 1966. This group replaced the strategy of national liberation with that of 'class struggle', to be based on Marxist–Leninist principles and collaboration with the burgeoning workers' movement (including 'Spanish forces' both in Euskadi and in Spain as a whole).[6]

ETA, in the late 1960s, was a fragile coalition in many respects, uneasily expressing the aims of neo-Marxists, national liberationists and extreme militants who modelled themselves on Third World anti-imperialist guerrillas. By degrees the split between 'the men of the gun' and the more 'intellectual' Marxists became impossible to bridge, the former accusing the latter of Spanish 'infiltration'. The idea of popular revolution was torn two ways with a growing tendency towards sporadic terrorism. Shabad and Ramo put ETA's internal dissensions in these terms:

Throughout its history, the sources of ETA's factionalism and instability have been intense conflicts over four main issues: the priority to be given to national versus social liberation; the emphasis to be placed on mass political activity and, after Franco's death, on participation in democratic institutions versus armed struggle, and how best to reconcile these two strategies; the relation between the political and military branches of the organization and the degree of autonomy to be permitted to the latter; and, finally, the desirability of links with 'Spanish' political forces. Divisions over these issues have never clearly demarcated one group from another. Rather, depending on time and circumstances, views on these issues have overlapped in different ways and have thus resulted in unstable and temporary coalitions among

ETA factions. But differences over ideology and strategy have not been the sole sources of internal conflict and instability. Power struggles among leaders have played their part as well, and divisions among the rank and file have often been determined less by differences over ideology and strategy than by friendship patterns and personal ties to one or another leader.[7]

Michel Wieviorka (1997), on the other hand, has no doubt about the extent to which ETA leaders decided to turn theory into practice:

Faced with a dictatorship which was itself violently repressive, which resorted to imprisonment for political reasons, torture and execution, faced with state violence which went far beyond straightforward repression of political activists and was aimed at prohibiting any expression of national sentiments, armed struggle appeared as the only possible response, one which had proved itself over time with the Algerian FLN or Mao Zedong's Long March, and one which was exemplified in many national liberation struggles and guerrilla movements all over the world.

However, like other left-wing activists in western Europe, for a number of years ETA did not put this principle into practice. Armed struggle was an objective, an idea, an aspiration, the subject of heated discussion and childish squabbles, not a practice.[8]

Wieviorka regards ETA's reliance on terrorism as counter-productive and as an inappropriate response to social problems in a region becoming increasingly prosperous:

Hence the movement relies more on violence to keep itself alive. The increasing use of terror is its chief characteristic. Yet such reliance on terrorism has changed the character of the movement itself. Indeed, it has become counter-productive. For as a method terrorism has become blind where it was purposeful. It confuses means and ends. It bears little relation to the expectations and experiences of the people in whose name it is carried out. Terrorism has in fact broken up the original 'synergistic' qualities of the three dimensions mentioned above. Basque nationalism then is increasingly dependent on violence for its own sake. The movement has lost its original meaning. As already indicated, when the principle of armed struggle was adopted by the first militants of ETA, they were neither desperate nor poor. The Basque region was neither an economically exploited region nor the victim of a centre which pillaged its wealth. On the contrary, industrially and financially, it was a major centre. It was indeed a key to economic growth in Franco's Spain. It was critical to the more over-all modernization process. Indeed, it attracted large-scale immigration. The recourse to violence, at least in its initial stages, was not therefore the result of crisis or poverty but rather prosperity and growth.

Precisely because of such prosperity there was a well-defined proletariat. What gave Basque nationalism its originally revolutionary appeal and impetus was its attractiveness to those who saw the future in terms of a radical 'repossession' of wealth by the proletariat. The revolutionary class, the class with radical 'brains', was neither poor nor excluded. The chief agent of nationalism was a strong labor movement capable of aspiring to the leadership of an already well-established industrial society. ETA's activities had always been based on strong nationalism. It was able to hitch this nationalism to the star of the labor movement.[9]

A point raised by Shabad and Ramo is that ETA did not neglect to build up an international dimension: there was nearby France as a refuge for terrorists on the run, and, beyond, there were sympathy and weapons:

As for ETA's connections to other terrorist organizations, some members have been given training in Third World socialist countries, such as Yemen, Algeria, Libya, and Cuba. Available data suggest that ETA's arms come from the Middle East, and some of its funds have been provided by the Libyan government. Purchase of weapons, mostly from Communist Czechoslovakia and the former Soviet Union, was coordinated with other European terrorist groups. Since the 1970s, the closest and most continuous links with foreign terrorist organizations have been with the IRA.

The international dimension of ETA violence has also been reflected in its various efforts to ally itself ideologically with and to model its strategy on Third World anticolonial insurgent movements. As it turned out, these foreign models were largely inapplicable to Basque society. ETA was never able to create a broad-based insurrection movement or to engage in full-scale guerrilla warfare. None the less, the adoption of anticolonial models of armed struggle in the early 1960s had significant repercussions for ETA and for Basque nationalism and society.[10]

THE NATURE OF ETA'S VIOLENCE

An account of Basque terrorism raises a number of issues as we have seen earlier. Cyrus Zirakzadeh (1991) believes that some discussions of this terrorism employ inadequate perspectives and so prove less than helpful to understanding motive and development. In his detailed account of that 'rebellious people', the Basques, he argues that many writers focus too narrowly on armed struggle and neglect to consider the wider, non-violent areas of social interaction leading to various forms of protest. To refer to all ETA members as terrorists-in-the-making clouds the picture and the result is a 'negative characterisation' of Basque political violence. Zirakzadeh's conclusions provide scope for discussion about some of the reasons for terrorist behaviour and the shape it may eventually take:

We began our reflections on the causes and characteristics of Basque political violence by recounting a common view of the subject, that we have called the modernization interpretation. According to this position, the violence was primarily an expression of Basques' intense feelings of cultural dislocation and personal stress brought about by unusually rapid and widespread social changes, including secularization, urbanization, and industrialization. Popular feelings of distress were also reflected in and reinforced by the antimodern ideology propagated by the Basque Nationalist Party, which strongly criticized the values and structures of industrial, urban and commercial society, and celebrated those of preindustrial times. Culturally uprooted, persons from rural and small-town backgrounds lashed out at the agents and symbols of modernity, but without specific grievances in mind and without thoughts of achieving particular goals. Violence principally resulted not from economic concerns and political calculations but from cultural unfamiliarity and acute personal pain. The expressive political violence in turn antagonized Spain's armed forces and thus indirectly endangered Spain's open, pluralistic political system.

This study has presented an alternative interpretation that places great emphasis on economic problems and grievances, the mediating influence of local social movements and political struggles, and the adaptation and modification of non-Nationalist as well as Nationalist ideologies to a complex political and economic situation. The book has viewed the members of ETA as rational actors who consciously gave meaning to their circumstances, and who adapted, refined, and readjusted ideas according to constantly changing political circumstances. Etarras' (ETA members) ideas, such as the spiral theory of violence [contra-violence begets violence], were not simply expressions of rage but attempts to calculate under complex, local circumstances how best to respond to economic crises. [. . .]

[Basque political violence] was not solely a consequence of intense nostalgia generated by rapid social change. It was also a consequence of strategic choices by a set of political activists enduring economic crises who believed they could launch a spontaneous social revolution from below through the calculated use of violence. The hope of ending (or at least greatly reducing) economic suffering, of course, does not absolve the activists of moral responsibility for their acts. Murder and kidnapping, even when undertaken for purportedly humanitarian ends, are still murder and kidnapping. But this book modifies the current modernization interpretation by emphasizing the purposefulness and intended effectiveness behind violent acts, and raising questions about the material interests, local social institutions, and theoretical reasoning that led to the violence.[11]

THE TALLY OF TERRORISM

Statistics of lethality and abduction by ETA terrorists have been compiled by Shabad and Ramo:

During the more than thirty years of its existence, ETA has been responsible for more than 500 assassinations, more than 1,000 injuries, 60 kidnappings, innumerable bombings, armed assaults, and robberies, and an extended regime of 'revolutionary taxation'. ETA has been responsible for more than 70 per cent of all people killed in terrorist actions in Spain during the last twenty years.

Basque industrialists were also the target of nearly 500 attacks (bombings, sabotage, robberies and armed assaults) between 1972 and 1983. The second prime targets of attack have been banks, firms in crisis or in the midst of strikes, and, since France's decision in the late 1980s to cooperate with Spanish anti-ETA efforts, French firms.

In recent years there has been a qualitative change in the kind of violence practiced by ETA. Violent actions have been more indiscriminate and fatal, more frequently directed against collective targets (e.g. supermarkets, police headquarters), more often staged in the largest Spanish cities (Madrid, Barcelona, Zaragoza), and more sophisticated in the use of weapons. One can only speculate, but such changes tending toward more extreme, albeit less frequent, violent activities may have been the result of a loss of support for ETA among the Basque public in the late 1980s and hence the result of the erosion of the ties between ETA and the community it purports to represent.[12]

The militants of ETA itself have borne serious losses: 100 of them have died, while 20,000 have been arrested, with 600 of them lingering in Spanish gaols and 700 of them in France.

TERRORISTS AND INTERNAL SECURITY

Something that continues to arouse violent dissent among Basques today is the largely unsolved question of who controls internal security in Euskadi (also known as Euzkadi) after the autonomy granted in 1979. Should it not be the Basques themselves with their own carefully recruited and trained police personnel – one lightly armed protector of the peace for every 500 inhabitants? Or should it be officers from the Civil Guard and the National Police, successors to those sent by Madrid in the 1960s to enforce a harsh state of emergency? That repressive contingent sent one officer for every 600 or so inhabitants and their operational orders and legal codes were rigorous. In the light of those circumstances, a 'terrorist' response by quick-triggered ETA guerrillas was to be expected, as Jose Trevino (1982) relates:

By far the typical ETA assassination however involves rank and file policemen. Most killings occur in broad daylight in the streets. On other occasions the terrorists calmly walk into a bar or cafeteria serving policemen on breaks from their duties. Often without even bothering to conceal their identities, the terrorists single out their targets and 'execute' them in front of scores of onlookers. Yet, when police investigators try to ascertain the facts, witnesses are almost impossible to find.

The reluctance of Basque citizens to cooperate with the investigators comes mostly from fear or apathy, although there are those who are truly sympathetic to ETA's cause. The fear of associating or collaborating with the police is well founded. There is little doubt that ETA has an effective intelligence network which pervades almost every segment of Basque society. Further, ETA has repeatedly demonstrated its ruthlessness against informants and 'collaborators'. Besides, the ordinary citizen is generally noncommittal. He wants to live in peace in his homeland. The policemen are almost all outsiders, recruited from other regions of Spain. They are largely unfamiliar with the local culture and customs and within a year they are normally reassigned out of the Basque region.

Consequently, in Euzkadi, a vicious circle sets in. The inability of the police to cope with terrorism undermines the already shattered confidence in the police. The public's reluctance to cooperate further undermines the police forces' ability to fight terrorism effectively.[13]

Today, 25 years later, ETA has agreed to a cessation of its terrorist activities under the terms of a ceasefire. The question of who supervises internal security – an external or internal force – remains a severe irritant and so a further explosion of violence at some stage cannot be ruled out despite, as we have seen, a general Basque hostility to continued terrorism.

THE WANING OF ETA

The death of the Spanish dictator Francisco Franco in 1975 ushered in a transition to democracy that was fairly rapid, with the legitimising of political parties in 1976, a new constitution in 1978, autonomy granted to the Basques in Euskadi in 1979, and elections for the Basque parliament in March 1980. Transitional developments did not dissipate tensions. Much opinion in Spain, in the parliamentary debates in the Cortes, in the Spanish press and generally among the public continued to describe Basque separatists as 'crazy' or 'criminal'. Most Basques revered their leaders as 'patriots' and 'idealists' whose right to bear arms in defence of Euskadi was a sacred duty. Beyond, though, the strident rhetoric of both sides and the drama of terrorist incidents, the 1980s opened with cautious feelers about an end to intolerance, fanaticism and violence and the chance of a defined and negotiated settlement. By 1985 even the Basque Government was ready to condemn for the first time the terrorists in their midst who were responsible for indiscriminate violence in which many innocent citizens had lost their lives. ETA members, their supporters and their tactics were now seen as inimical to democratic freedom and progress. Hundreds of thousands of Basques flooded the streets to demonstrate an appeal for an end to ETA's terrorist actions. Cooperation between the governments of Spain and France had, in any case, started to blunt the edge of militant ardour. According to Shabad and Ramo, ETA began to turn in upon itself with fragmentation and quarrelling:

ETA's behavior in the late 1980s was reflective of its changed circumstances. On the one hand, the willingness of ETA to cast aside its conditions regarding talks with the Spanish state indicated that the organization's leadership had come to realise that ETA's position had deteriorated in terms of its ability to recruit new members, to carry out sustained effective actions, and to enlarge, let alone maintain, its degree of popular support. Thus, it was best to 'negotiate' while ETA could still do some damage and extract some concessions from the state. But along with this changed stance toward talks, what the simultaneous acts of violence and abrupt withdrawal from negotiations also suggested was that ETA had become increasingly divided between hard-line and moderate elements. It was with the latter that the government pursued its discussions [. . .] What might such talks accomplish were they to take place? Most likely, ETA would be reduced to its most violent core, a group of militants concerned primarily with the very survival of the organization.[14]

There does not appear to be a readily acceptable explanation of ETA's enduring violence following the rebirth of democracy in Spain after 1975. Was it a consequence of a 'culture of violence' (political violence, that is) married to an idealised, romantic view of traditional Basque values, aspirations and mores? This seems to be a conventional summation by many writers on Basque terrorism. Few of them go on to attempt a definition of such a 'culture'. In the early days of ETA, impulses that were part nationalistic, part Communist spurred on a clandestine élite to work for revolution, undaunted even when the support of most Basques visibly drained away as autonomy became more credible. Euskadi was not relishing the prospect of another string of decades of conflict. That a democratic regime succeeded an authoritarian one in Spain did not make it easier to deal with ETA's overt terrorism and with the lingering suspicions and dissatisfactions of so many Basques.

Did terrorism among the Basques bring them a brighter future and do much to advance or retard the onset of liberal democracy? A tentative response to this question is that of Shabad and Ramo:

What can be concluded about the effects of ETA violence? Two primary goals of terrorist organizations, whether they be ideologically left or right, religious or nationalist, are to undermine the legitimacy and the stability of the existing regime. How effective such organizations are in achieving these goals depends on a number of factors. One of these is the nature of the regime itself, although the impact of regime type is itself conditioned by other variables. Authoritarian regimes, such as Francoist Spain, are by their very nature far less inhibited by legal and normative constraints from countering the violence directed against them. Moreover, clandestine organizations have fewer opportunities, particularly in more repressive periods, to get their message across to their intended targets and to acquire essential resources such as militants, weapons, funds, safe houses, and so on. But at the same time, grievances provoked by repression of class interests or of religious and ethnic sentiments may foster growing and increasingly radical popular discontent with existing rule. This, in turn, provides a favorable climate for oppositional violence.

Democratic regimes, on the other hand, have a greater ability to lay claims to legitimacy and loyalty. They provide opportunities for voicing demands and expressing dissent through peaceful means. But should political violence occur, democratic governments, unlike authoritarian regimes, are faced with an unenviable choice. They may choose to act within the boundaries set by the constitution – and risk failure and being made to appear ineffective in the eyes of the public and the military – or they may resort to extralegal means to combat threats to the regime; this would not only undermine democratic rule itself but also provoke that segment of society in whose name the terrorist organization acts. Either extreme – failure of democratic means, or state violence – may achieve the terrorist organization's goals of delegitimation and instability.

The choices made by democratic governments for countering political violence are conditioned by a number of factors. One, of course, is the particular mix of values of governing élites themselves, their assessments of the circumstances they face and the likely outcomes of differing strategies, and their perceptions of the pressures placed on them from rival political élites. These normative, cognitive, and affective orientations may, in turn, be influenced by other variables, such as the actual scope and frequency of violence wreaked by antisystem forces and the patterns of opinion of various segments of the population.

Another factor, which we have emphasized here and which differentiates democratic from authoritarian regimes and hence their possible responses to political violence, is the embeddedness of terrorist organizations in a pluralistic political environment. The interaction between the terrorist group and more moderate 'alegal' or prosystem political forces that also represent the relevant social group may have an effect on public opinion, the severity of political violence, and ultimately the decisions made by governing élites on how to combat terrorism. We have argued here that it is too simplistic to view the interaction between these two kinds of groups as one of rivalry alone. Although it is true that the existence of legal channels for the expression of group interests may undercut frustration and support for organisations like ETA, the presence of extremist groups willing to use violence may be implicitly encouraged and overtly manipulated by more moderate forces to strengthen their bargaining position vis-à-vis the state. The relation between the two, therefore, is apt to be one of conflict *and* collusion, and both types of interaction potentially serve the interests and objectives of each group.

Thus, there is a complex array of factors that determine the effectiveness of oppositional violence at any given time and under a particular type of political rule. It is difficult to say, based on the Spanish case alone, whether terrorism is more effective under authoritarian or democratic rule. The Francoist regime did not end because of ETA, nor did democracy fail to consolidate because of ETA violence. At the same time, ETA violence did hasten the demise of Francoism, if only through its assassination of the dictator's heir apparent, Carrero Blanco. And it did jeopardize the transition to democracy by reinforcing or provoking hostility to the evolving rules of the game in two different quarters. Basque nationalists refused to endorse the constitution and only gave it 'backward' and ambiguous legitimacy through subsequent support of the autonomy statute. And a segment of the military came very close to toppling democratic rule in its February 1981 coup attempt. Although ETA activities did not lead to the destruction of democracy, they did help to change the rules of the game in another way. As Basque nationalist leaders have argued, without the constant pressure exerted by ETA violence, political élites in Madrid may not have felt as impelled to grant concessions to demands for Basque autonomy and for a fundamental restructuring of the centralised state. Ironically, without such concessions, democratic consolidation may not have been possible.

To say that ETA did not prevent democratic consolidation is not to conclude that ETA had no serious negative consequences. But these were primarily confined to the Basque Country. The persistence of ETA after Franco's death helped to sustain a culture of violence and, in so doing, placed major obstacles to the evolution of more rational and secular patterns of social and political interaction. It polarized and radicalized public opinion in Euskadi and called into question the legitimacy of the new regime. And it significantly affected the behavior of other, more moderate nationalist groups, thus making the resolution of centre–periphery conflicts more difficult to achieve.

Given these negative effects, it is fortuitous that separatist violence did not occur in other ethnically distinct regions of Spain, such as Catalonia and Galicia. Had it spread to other areas and not been confined primarily to the Basque Country, Spanish democracy might have been stillborn.[15]

Recent developments in Euskadi, the Basque homeland, to some extent echo what has taken place in Northern Ireland. In London and in Madrid early government insistence on terrorist disarmament before admission to a legislature has given way after prolonged discussion to conciliatory gestures – a phased 'handing-in' of all weapons and the freeing of prisoners. ETA's peace resolve in September 1998 announcing a 'total and undefined ceasefire' must have taken account of growing public hostility to continued and profitless terrorism. Unfortunately, ETA's peace negotiators are still unable to rein in extremists on the flanks of the movement.

There appear more recently to be grounds for more guarded optimism. The Madrid bombing of 11 March 2004 ('Spain's 9/11'), when 10 small bombs left in four trains killed 191 and injured 1,900, powerfully concentrated Spanish minds. At the outset ETA was blamed but evidence absolved it. Would the group really want to decimate working people? An al-Qaida cell was thought to be the likely originator and many arrests followed.

ETA declared a 'permanent ceasefire', rather unexpectedly, two years later in March 2006, when the aim was 'to promote a democratic process in the Basque country and to build a new framework in which our rights as a people will be recognised'. This declaration was met with caution by Madrid's Socialist government recalling that two earlier ceasefires in the 1990s had collapsed. Any exploratory talks must be preceded by a renunciation of terror tactics and a laying down of all weaponry. Nevertheless, within six weeks Prime Minister Zapatero planned to ask parliament for permission to initiate dialogue between contending parties. He was willing to give some ground on the issues of regional devolution and fairer Basque parliamentary membership. The autumn of 2006 brought intensive ETA calls on the Spanish and French governments to make 'important decisions' about Basque independence. Could not parts of northern Spain and even south-western France contain autonomous Basque communities? Proposals such as this were put to the Prime Minister himself when visiting Basque enclaves. He had to brush aside hyper-nationalist charges that 'Madrid was giving in to terrorists'. Indeed, Zapatero strenuously put about the need to confer and understand those who resorted to violence. Perhaps, his advisers suggested, he should visit Dublin, and possibly Belfast, to see what he could learn from Ireland's peace process, where talk finally melted posturing and ushered in peace. Many in Spain at least welcomed the Premier's stated three-part approach to peace – first, a genuine cessation of violent action; second, a process of sustained dialogue; and, third, determined work for coexistence.

Spain and Sri Lanka have one or two things in common. Each country has terrorist activism in a state of suspense. Both have bands of armed insurgents campaigning for independent secession, for territorial integrity in certain provinces, for some degree of cultural autonomy, for unconditional amnesty for all political prisoners, for political representation. Madrid and Colombo have each negotiated for a cease fire, the one in 1999, the other in 2006. These were arrangements shakily observed and satisfying nobody. Sri Lanka's Tamils LTTE and Spain's Basque ETA accuse their governments of repressive state terrorism against what they see as a legitimate right to ethnic self-determination. And given the concessions allowed by government to these formerly outlawed groups questions are often asked: why are violence and illegitimacy a morally justifiable response to national order for many? If violence is always on the agenda is it not surely counter-productive?

Latest developments in Spain are particularly interesting. In mid-January 2011 ETA took cautious steps along a path to end 50 years of violence. On a dramatic main-channel television screen three men in white silken masks announced that the cease fire was now 'permanent'. It should be verified by international observers. The political price for this must be dialogue and negotiation and official acknowledgement of Basque self-determination. Government response was swift. Alfredo Rubalcaba, Deputy Premier, saw in this move no real renunciation of offensive armed action and no repentance for past misdeeds, indeed, there was evident an arrogant, distorted, partisan view of reality. No international verification was either necessary or allowable. In Rubalcaba's view ETA's proposals for disarmament showed a group on the run, weakened and split. As in the ineffectual cease fire of 2006 ETA's leaders' 'pacific intentions' could not be trusted although it was known that a dissenting wing of ETA, a sub-party known as Batasuna, had had earnest discussions with Northern Ireland's Sinn Fein. All in all, prospects of amity seem poor and Spain is in a state of suspense awaiting the completeness of a three-point approach to permanent peace – an end to terrorism, meaningful talks, and a framework for assured co-existence.

Chapter 13

Northern Ireland

N ORTHERN IRELAND HAS BEEN called many things – for example, the Land of Wide Sunsets or the Land of Dreams. For most of the present century, though, the romantic appellations have given way to tragic ones – the Land of Long Memories, the Land of Myth or the Land of Terror. Romantic associations of gentle fantasy and humorous irrationality have been displaced by the grim realities of unreconciled conflict and widespread violence. It seems likely that long memories of discrimination, confrontation and struggle reinforced by quasi-religious myths of victimisation and sacrifice have done much to shape attitudes and behaviour in a community divided by intolerance, suspicion and resort to arms, and that memory and myth played a role in decelerating the momentum of a peace agreement signed in April 1998. Northern Ireland's terrorism is in a state of suspense. This case study considers three things – the significance of shared memories, the significance of myth, and the controversy over disarmament, that is, 'arms decommissioning'. What will not be found in this case study, however, is any simplistic deduction of cause and effect. First, some historical introduction is needed.

IRELAND'S TROUBLES: HISTORICAL ANTECEDENTS

An outline of Ireland's conflict scenario and of the difficulties of settlement and reconciliation is given by David Whittaker (1999):

'The trouble with the Irish is the English' is a traditional Irish refrain shared more often by Catholics in the southern Republic of Ireland than in Northern Ireland. The English connection through history has brought them harsh oppression, tumult and tragedy, high-handedness from absentee landowners, detached and apathetic government from Westminster. Seven hundred years ago Anglo-Norman overlords forced the barbarous Irish tribes beyond the confines of their defended 'Pale'. Four hundred years ago Tudor monarchs exported rapacious nobility to Ireland once more to grab land. Three hundred years ago Northern Ireland was a battleground for the followers of William of Orange to establish Protestant dominance over Catholics, loyal to James II in England and very likely disloyal enough to favour Louis XIV of France. Two hundred years ago the English were intent on penalising the Irish for being influenced by the seductive egalitarian ideas of revolutionary France. Throwing off the yoke of a Hanoverian king and his Protestantism in the name of equality and liberty would invite remorseless retribution. There was a brighter moment in 1800 when the English Liberal Prime Minister, William Pitt, put on the statute book an Act of Unity uniting England, Scotland and Ireland, and granting 100 House of Commons seats to Irishmen – Protestant Irishmen. Catholics had to await any degree of emancipation for another twenty-nine years. Where now was the reputed British belief in democracy and liberalisation? Was the concept of 'British' a euphemism for the hypocritical and untrustworthy English? Victorian times did nothing to satisfy resentments in Dublin and the association between London and their dependency in Northern Ireland grew stronger. In 1886, W. E. Gladstone, the veteran Liberal at Westminster, campaigned eloquently and passionately for Home Rule to placate the troubled Irish.

Hostile Tories and the suspicious Unionists of Northern Ireland would have nothing to do with this proposed breaking of imperial bonds. Home Rule would turn out to be Rome Rule. Buoyed by the message to them from Winston Churchill's father, Lord Randolph Churchill, that 'Ulster will fight, Ulster will be right', they made preparations for manning defences against Catholics in north and south.

The First World War brought trouble in Ireland to breaking point. By 1915, among Catholics there was fury at the injustice and anomalies in English and Protestant ascendancy. Rifles were smuggled in from Europe, and German sympathies for Irish dissolution were evident. In the United States powerful Irish lobbies in New York and Boston voiced loud concern and this was amplified in the influential Hearst press. In Dublin, with its underground links to Belfast, Irishmen planned to cut moorings from London and to expel the English. There was an angry alliance of idealists within the Sinn Féin nationalist movement seeking a Celtic Revival and of armed men mustering determined forces. English excesses in the past, English prevarication against Ireland's contemporary demands, and the prospects of English curbs on future progress were not so much dreams as motivating forces pushing the Irish towards complete independence.

Against gathering clouds of conflict, part-religious, part-political, there were firm constitutional gains for Ireland. In 1920, the Government of Ireland Act conferred self-government on Dublin. Two years later the Irish Free State was born in Dublin, made up of twenty-six Irish counties. At the same time, Ulster was given six counties and a frontier drawn up between the two Irelands. Constitutionally this may have suited the English. For the Irish there were the beginnings of conflict here, with the south rejecting partition, hoping for eventual unification of the entire island, and with Ulster absolutely determined never to permit unification. For many hardened Protestants it was the 'no Popery' of their forebears again. A conflict of intention and will was inevitable. It was to be a conflict with deep historical roots.[1]

ULSTER'S CONTEMPORARY DIVIDE

Whittaker's outline continues looking at the battle for rights among rival elements, the political and religious affiliations of the contending groups, and the socio-economic contrasts at the heart of conflict:

The civil conflict in Northern Ireland reveals three components – a battle for civic rights, that is, socio-economic rights, a nationalistic North–South contest and a politico-military struggle mainly between extremists on the political flanks. These elements are interdependent, relating political controversies to the gulf between an oligarchy and a disadvantaged minority. There is a polarisation of religious affiliation in this conflict, which has made consensus difficult to achieve. There are strident voices in Ulster and vigorous, often bloody, action. Most conflicts have political leaders, their profiles highlighted by the media, their personalities often demonised. In Northern Ireland there is no Mandela to bring discordant elements together in another rainbow nation.

In Ulster the divide reveals most Protestants supporting Unionist or Loyalist parties – the Ulster Unionist, the Official Unionist, the Democratic Unionist. At the time of the April Agreement of 1998 David Trimble was the Unionist spokesman. (Dr Ian Paisley, a maverick to the hilt, headed his own creation, the Democratic Unionists.) These people play the 'Orange Card' of attachment to Great Britain. Two-thirds of their men belong to the fraternal, uncompromising Orange Order. Nine out of ten members of Ulster's own security force, the Royal Ulster Constabulary (RUC) are Protestant. Overall, Unionists feel themselves hemmed in politically and geographically. Catholics, in the main, are loyal either to Sinn Féin, whose President is Gerry Adams, or to the Socialist and Democratic Labour Party (SDLP) where John Hume has been active for twenty-five years. There is a small Alliance Party. Some idea of the proportionate representation of these parties may be roughly estimated from the voting patterns in the 1993 local council elections, which gained Unionist parties almost 50 per cent of the votes, the SDLP 25 per cent, Sinn Féin 15 per cent, the Alliance Party 6 per cent and other groups 8 per cent [. . .] Many Catholics, terming themselves Nationalists or Republicans, are wedded to the ideal of a united Ireland, and they see the Unionists as Disunionists and the Loyalists as Disloyalists. Threaded through the political stance of the Catholic protest are symbols of sacrifice, of martyrdom, of a 'colonial freedom' movement against imperial subjection.

Northern Ireland's other divide is its socio-economic diversity. Social contrasts are now less marked than they were when industry and commerce were booming and affluence and poverty co-existed uncomfortably. Protestant and Catholic now share unemployment (Europe's worst) and reliance upon welfare [. . .] the test of progress and the possibility of reconciliation for ordinary people in Northern Ireland will be the provision of fairer shares and fairer chances. Gerry Adams, in August 1997, put this squarely to a Sinn Féin meeting in Belfast: 'A settlement where the poor remain poor and the dispossessed remain dispossessed would not be a real change of lives. A cobbled-together political settlement and an end to killings are not enough.'[2]

THIRTY YEARS OF STRIFE

The upheaval of society in Northern Ireland remains the theme of Whittaker, an upheaval in which Nationalist and Protestant contestants have suffered grievous losses together with the general population. It is seen that there are many factors bringing about violence among sectarian adversaries and their military and paramilitary wings. Successive Whitehall governments never moved far away from supporting the Protestant Unionists and savagely condemning the 'terrorism' of the Catholic nationalists, principally that of their IRA. It was not until the 1980s that secretive exploration of the prospects for peace was steadfastly pursued between London, Belfast and Dublin. The peace agreement of April 1999 was to bring all sides together in a general ceasefire and round of negotiations. The ultimate fashioning of a definitive end to terrorism is still debatable and in the balance:

Contemporary Ulster has to look back over three decades of bloodshed. Mainly since 1969 Northern Ireland has been convulsed by sectarian violence as rival groups have taken arms against each other and against the British army which has been endeavouring to maintain the peace. In that time the casualties and damage have been horrendous, with 3,500 civilians dead, 30,000 injured and a loss to property totalling many millions of pounds. In a province with only 1.6 million people this is a toll that touches nearly everybody in some fashion. Northern Ireland's police force, the Royal Ulster Constabulary (RUC) has had 300 officers killed and over 9,000 wounded. Mainland Britain has tried to staunch the flow of dissolution, at times deploying 20,000 soldiers together with 8,000 armed police, all at a cost of £3 billion a year. Thirty years of carnage have prompted emotional responses in the rest of Britain, which span everything from outrage to scapegoating and, at times, feelings of utter inability to do anything in terms of pacification and conflict solution.

Armed confrontation has brought groups termed 'paramilitaries' face to face. The Nationalist (Catholic) vanguard is led by the Irish Republican Army (IRA) and three other splinter groups. Unionist (Protestant) forces, calling themselves Loyalists, are the Ulster Defence Association (UDA) and again three splinter groups. Altogether, there is an impressive armoury of thousands of rifles, home-made machine-guns and grenade throwers, anti-tank weapons, and a great deal of Semtex and other explosives.

The IRA has acquired notoriety as an agent of destruction. Founded in 1919 as a commando unit against British rule in Ireland, the organisation split three years later with the proclamation of the Irish Free State. The majority of these 'Freedom Fighters' rejected the new state, the minority accepted it with regret. With detachments of British soldiers Whitehall now had to fend off an armed band of insurrectionists who were to be outlawed in 1931 and again in 1935. During the Second World War there were even those in IRA brigades who regarded themselves akin to the French Resistance movement, fighting an army of occupation in the same way. Otherwise, the conflict in Ireland was low-key.

It was in the 1960s that the mood of many Irishmen changed. They became interested in United States protest movements, particularly those connected with the Civil Rights Movement and the Vietnam War. The thrust of their demands had to do with a better deal for Catholics in regard to local government reform and improved housing. As their agitation brought little response both from the Protestant majorities on local councils and from Whitehall, a largely peaceful demonstration by the working class turned sourly into a popular uprising. In Belfast and Londonderry (Derry) barricades went up and angry words gave way to priming of weapons and the making of petrol bombs. By 1969 there were running battles in the streets, a curfew had been imposed and arrests were widespread. The IRA was now on a war footing, though somewhat split between an extreme element, the Provisional IRA (Provos) forming assassination and punishment squads to deal with Loyalist opponents, and a more moderate Official IRA, prepared, so they said, to substitute talk for bullets.

The 1970s brought wavering fortunes for all sides. There was little prospect of any negotiation in a situation now aflame with destruction and death. British use of internment after the rounding up of suspected 'terrorists' merely served as a recruiting office for the IRA. Closing down the Belfast parliament at Stormont in 1972 and the imposition of Direct Rule from London of course angered Nationalists, who saw themselves condemned to live in a British fiefdom, and it also distressed those Unionists who championed the right to substantial self-determination within the orbit of a protective Great Britain. Direct Rule was reimposed in 1974. Violence soared and atrocities were committed by all sides. The English press, reporting outrage after outrage, soon voiced the questions: how can Britain deal with street guerrillas who appear to know what they are against but have little notion of what they are for? How far is it possible to dethrone the martyr-image? Apart from the confrontations with rifle and bomb there was the more political tactic of detainees who resorted to a hunger strike. How was Britain to deal with that?

The Northern Ireland conflict was beginning to enter a different phase as the 1980s brought bombing and murder to places in the Republic of Ireland and to the British mainland. Although the IRA and the Loyalist paramilitaries vilified each other and there was much wringing of hands in British government circles, there now began a series of covert probing by all sides as to the tentative possibilities of settling the conflict. Quite clearly, contestants, the protesters and the security forces, had underestimated the determination of others to keep the action going, and had overestimated the extent to which they could wear them down. The only rational way out of this was to initiate a peace process. Sinn Féin made clear that they distanced themselves from the violent tactics of the IRA.

Inching forwards, through enquiry and discussion, towards a prospect of peace received frequent hammer blows when town centres were blasted by high explosives and gunmen wreaked havoc. Attempts to bring about an unconditional ceasefire succeeded finally in 1994, only to be aborted two years later when London's prestigious business centre at Canary Wharf and the heart of Manchester suffered immense bomb damage. The British government now made the bottom line of its negotiating position quite clear: no talk without unequivocal repudiation of all violence. Only then would Sinn Féin be allowed a place at the table. Terrorism would never win anything. In South Africa and in the Middle East the ANC and the PLO had been permitted to engage in resolution discussion only when they had agreed to relinquish strategies of violence. As a first step to Northern Ireland's demilitarisation all weapons must be 'decommissioned'. A special commission to devise ways of doing this was to be set up under the chairmanship of Senator George Mitchell from the United

States. These moves did not find favour with Sinn Féin. Their simple retort was: remove the circumstances which lead men to resort to arms and the arms will then be laid down. In 1997 there seemed to be an impasse. Decommissioning must be implemented before peace talks began; no decommissioning would be started before peace talks were under way. In autumn 1997 good sense prevailed with the IRA militarists agreeing with their political allies in Sinn Féin that the issue of decommissioning and an end to violence should not block the beginnings of real conflict settlement. 'Speedy demilitarisation of the entire [Northern Ireland] situation' was their demand.

Efforts to design a peace process acceptable to all participants at last brought diminished violence and in April 1998 a peace agreement. There were times in 1997 and 1998 when the very real concessions made by the Nationalists were in danger of being derailed by Unionist disaffection and by the resentful opportunism of their extremists. Would a peace agreement be a sell-out? Would that be surrender? No conflict of interests should be resolved through selling short the basic rights of a majority.[3]

SHARED MEMORIES AS ENERGISERS

Paul Arthur (1997) argues that many in Northern Ireland 'use' memories of the past as agents of reinforcement, inspiration and consolidation, and as preludes to purposive action (which may not always be violent). Arthur begins by quoting the description of Denis Donaghue, a fellow-Ulsterman, that memory is 'agglutinative' – memories of the past are kept alive, the refreshed memories justify the events that occur:

> History is only one way of being significant. Memory gives the unofficial sense of history, effects an order not sequential but agglutinative. That is why we never ask our memories to line up rationally or sequentially, like soldiers on parade: they obey our orders, but not always or in the form we prescribe.

The uses of history as memory, not only to keep the past alive but sustain a sense of loss, deprivation, marginalization, not to speak of the affronts, discrimination, prejudice, and the like has sustained the tensed boundaries of the Irish working-class community extremely well and not only in places like Derry or West Belfast. Everywhere in the Six Counties there is evidence of the past. Handed out generationally, the stories of the fall, victimization, colonialization, pariahization, etc., are almost as deeply relevant as were myths of the eternal return among the Jews. Such memory was important not only within Northern Ireland but the Republic and the diaspora as well. For it fed the clienteles. To be sure, to keep alive, and use memory to intensify yearning, fresh events are required. And where the IRA was not the perpetrator, the various Protestant paramilitary organizations obliged. Between both sides, and of course under the watchful eyes of the British army, there were political events galore.[4]

For Arthur three things stand firm particularly in Ulster memories: the sense of shared 'victimhood', the feeling and fact of dispossession, and the concept of striving for emancipation. He finds agreement with David Apter (1997) in understanding compulsions towards a continuous resistance campaign, which becomes, in a black sense, a 'treasured' memory. Opponents are demonised, traditionally so:

The point of departure for contemporary emancipatory movements 'is not equality but *victimhood*. This is what distinguishes them from "old" social movements which fought for equality or greater participation. [. . .]'
    The IRA fits into this model in that they are [a] protest movement which is

> confrontational and violence-prone and relatively uninterested in rectifying this or that economic, social, or political ill, or providing greater political access to those deprived by reason of religion, gender, ethnicity, race, language, class, role, or other affiliations. Such affiliations are interesting only as provocations requiring the violation of standing jurisdictions.

    Viewed from below – and Ireland is essentially a bottom-up society with a demotic culture – in place of civilization and progress people read conquest and dispossession and a loss of patrimony and a historic sense of grievance. Theirs was not

> a world of choice from which some have been excluded but a universe of meaning in which insight is inspired by victimhood and confrontation [where] inversionary discourse is a means of altering prevailing boundaries and jurisdictions on the ground and in the mind. If they reject ordinary claims and demands and remain aloof from negotiation and the bargaining that accompanies democracy the intent is to create moral and symbolic capital in opposition to economic capital.[5]

[There is] a profound sense of piety, a deep sense of history and of grievance, and an essential sense of the contemporaneousness of the past. It is a narrative of dispossession overlaid by a fundamental religiosity secularized by a doctrine of manifest destiny. It is what has sustained Irish nationalism through centuries of failure.[6]

A shared memory of something denied, something lost, something to be fought for, stood proudly in Irish minds as their small independent state was established in the south in 1916. The Republican mission then and now goes further than passive 'remembering' – the past must be made to live and 'live forward', a strategy that Arthur sees the Sinn Féin leader, Gerry Adams, holding to fervently:

The Irish Free State was born with its national ideal unfulfilled, an embittered and armed minority within its boundaries, a humiliating economic reliance on its traditional enemy, the United Kingdom, and an economy which supported too many unproductive people. And yet it endured. Its very endurance was an affront to those who believed that the 1916 rising had been betrayed. They believed that the new political establishment indulged in what the Japanese call *mokusatsu*, that is killing with silence.

The mission of contemporary republicanism is no less than to restore that 'memory', to rediscover Ireland's soul. And that entails tackling all those vested interests who have recreated modern Ireland. It means moving beyond the status of double marginality – the loss of patrimony in the past and the removal of 'voice' in the present. It is a historic task in the heroic mold and it means returning to first principles. It works on the assumption of splendid failure within a characteristic Irish time-frame which

> inclines Irishmen to a repetitive view of history and that such a view inclines them – perhaps in defensive wariness and from fear of failure – to prize the moral as against the actual, and the bearing of witness as against success. The *locus classicus* of this cast of mind is the Proclamation of the Republic on Easter Monday 1916.[7]

In this century the 1916 Rising is the crucial event which explains all others. The President of Sinn Féin, Gerry Adams, has no doubts as to its significance and relevance to today's struggles:

> Oglaigh na hEireann (the IRA) today takes its historical and organizational origins from the forces which engaged in the Easter Rising of 1916, though one can trace its ancestry much further back if one wishes. But the circumstances which shaped the support for the IRA are above all the experience of the barricade days from 1969–72. These days are of continuing importance not just in terms of the IRA but because they saw the development of tremendous communal solidarity, more than a memory of which remains today.

'Memory' again and that umbilical link between 1916 and the barricade days of the 1970s!

The problem with 1916 is that the 'philosophers and political thinkers of the 1916 Rising did not survive it, and this set the stage for counter-revolution. What we have done is that we have taken a step towards reversing the effects of the counter-revolution'. There is an obvious tactical advantage in taking such a step. It removes republicanism from its conspiratorial ethos onto centre-stage as a mass movement built on communal solidarity. It combines the heroic failure of 1916 with the self-reliance and mutual solidarity created in the mobilization spaces of West Belfast, Free Derry and elsewhere. It has a wider *political* meaning:

> We are not engaged in any new departure. We are committed absolutely to the objective of Irish independence [. . .] In the past the republican movement was a separatist movement with radical tendencies. In its current embodiment the radical tendency is for the first time in control.

[The year] 1916 was a significant historical punctuation mark, an exercise in calculated martyrdom whereby the blood of the fallen would irrigate the barren soil and create the climate for a new generation to continue with the struggle. It was another step along the road to national liberation begun by Wolfe Tone in 1798 and continued by the Fenians in the nineteenth century. It was part of a *narrative* — 'the universal desire to make sense of history by retelling the story to ourselves'. Narrative can serve to release new, and hitherto concealed possibilities, of understanding one's history [. . .] the contemporary act of rereading (i.e. retelling) tradition can actually disclose uncompleted narratives which opens up new possibilities of understanding. That was what the 1916 Rising was about.[8]

Thus, for Northern Ireland's Catholics, the 'four glorious years', 1918–21, strike a note of justified martyrdom, going much further than nostalgia. What the British Government of the day in London condemned as the irresponsible terrorism of gun-battles and fire-raising was for the fighters of Dublin and for their allies further north the arming of a rightful nationalism. When protracted violence re-erupted in Northern Ireland in 1969, the Catholic community was to some extent taken by surprise at first, until past memories bore down upon present reality and in Arthur's words led to a 'circularity' of violence when each side mobilised to defend what it regarded as its civil rights:

[. . .] republicanism was unprepared partially because it had been engaged in its own internal debate. It lacked the resources to defend its community but, paradoxically, that meant a stronger sense of communal solidarity because often it was the ordinary citizen rather than a revolutionary élite which organized the barricades to defend the areas of Catholic west Belfast against an onslaught launched by protestant mobs with RUC complicity. It was in this milieu that the new generation began to assert themselves.

They started with several assets, the most crucial being that 'the whole process was so *natural* as to be beyond comment'. Attitudes were more important than weapons, and that was to be the key to republican strategy: 'Nothing had to be imported, nothing fashioned by ideologues, nothing sold to the people, nothing secretly arranged because of events. All that was needed was to exploit the existing reality'. That reality was based on a memory of past oppressions and the nature of an intimidatory culture with the emphasis on territoriality and the need for vigilance. Settler vigilance, whether in the form of loyalist mobs or locally recruited militias (official and unofficial), 'taught the natives that power and self-assertion were the property of those who could successfully inflict violence'. The result was a circularity of violence whereby 'vigilance of power perpetually generates the symptoms of rebellion it purportedly guards against; while rebellion on the principle of collective responsibility validates the anxieties of the dominant'.

[. . .] sections of Protestant Ulster perceived the civil rights campaign as a challenge to their very existence and entered into a form of public banding because they believed that state power could not monopolize coercive relationships. In that situation 'the whole system is one of threatened violence in which the state is a feeble pivot between its ostensible supporters [. . .] and the natives'.[9]

For the beleaguered Catholics in Northern Ireland there was the predicament that their violent politics of resistance and of sacrifice needed to find a more logical basis for conflict resolution, as Arthur points out:

They [the Republicans] were able to present politics as a narrative of oppression. They found no difficulty in revealing the state's hegemony in incidents like the introduction of internment in August 1971 when only republicans were lifted. They demonstrated their capability to resist compromise when the Northern Ireland government and parliament were prorogued in March 1972. Rather than accept that as a 'victory' they followed the predictable pattern of emancipatory movements 'to move from immediate ends to ultimate values and to define their objects in terms of the widest moral imperative'. But by standing outside the normal framework of politics 'using doctrine, ideology and theory to challenge the *doxa*' they confront the problem that adherents 'of violence as a political technique need to show that violent acts can have political consequences. They must demonstrate that some kind of exchange relation holds – or can be created – between the worlds of violence and politics'. Equally governments 'need to tread a delicate line between showing that violence is powerless to acquire any kind of political exchange value and formulating the political responses which demonstrate their commitment to its repression'. Irish republicans relied on two components: repression and the elevation of the symbolic side of political life.

It might be argued that Irish political violence of the past twenty years has moved from the extra-institutional protest of the civil rights movement through a politics of oppression to a politics of sacrifice in search of a logical project.[10]

Could it be that memory as an imprint of history and as an impelling force for defensiveness loses any logical thrust when confronted by the ambiguities of myth? This is a question that has caught the attention of a number of writers on terrorism and something to which we now turn.

MYTHS AS REINFORCERS

Two aspects of the concept of myth seem significant here: first, the conventional understanding of a fictitious story or legend embodying ancient beliefs and interpretations; and, second, and taking it further, what is known as a *mythopoeia* – the making of myths. We see in some of the other case studies, such as those of the Hizbullah, the Montoneros of Argentina, the Tamils of Sri Lanka and the German Baader-Meinhof group, that myths, perhaps refashioned, can be incorporated quite deliberately into a political repertoire. This is perhaps what Eric Hobsbawm had in mind when he referred to 'the invention of tradition'. For Richard Kearney (1997), what he terms 'foundational' myths disclose the original sense of the word 'tradition'.

Foundational myths disclose the original meaning of tradition – *tradere* – carrying the past into the present and the present into the past. So myths of tradition may be said to defy the normal logic of *either/or* by conflating not only opposite time-scales but also such opposed orders as living and dead, divine and human, redeemed and damned. Here we are confronted with another logic – that of imagination and dream – where laws of contradiction and causality no longer operate.[11]

Elsewhere, Charles Townshend (1995), writing about political violence in Northern Ireland (especially the terrorism of paramilitaries), sees the myth proving useful there in many ways. Primarily, it is used to mobilise both the revolutionary cadres and the mass of the people. Second, it assists the creation of social solidarity. Third, it may help heal the wounded heroes of a cause in the event of failure:

Mobilization for revolution has two elements that often prove to be as distinct in practice as they can be made in theory. The first is the organization of the revolutionaries; the second the mobilization of the people. Historically, the first has been more common than the second. Irish history contains plenty of examples of this discrepancy. Indeed, a mass rising of the kind expected by most nineteenth-century revolutionaries never happened, even in 1798. None the less, 1798, like 1789 and Year II in France, became a potent myth that mobilized successive generations of revolutionaries. The Anglo–Irish war of 1918–21 fell well short of the ideal type, but through the brilliance of republican publicity, it generated a myth that was at least as potent. These are myths, I would suggest, in the strictly Sorelian sense that they simplify the world sufficiently to make action possible. A nationalist contemplating any actual 'people' would be driven rapidly to loss of faith, if not suicidal despair. Simplification or idealization is the essence of the notion of the *Volksgeist* and the essential condition for nationalist activity. The myth of the nation provides the reason for action; the myth of popular mobilization underwrites the feasibility of action.

Anarchist terrorists had posited an alternative mechanism of revolutionary violence, propaganda by deed [. . .] Propaganda would arouse the people, who would ultimately triumph by sheer weight of numbers.

In Ireland, however, a quite novel mechanism for interlocking revolutionaries and people was emerging at this time – pragmatically rather than theoretically. Michael Collins's repudiation of traditional IRB insurrectionism in favour of guerrilla methods arose naturally out of Irish conditions. The IRA established the viability of the numerical formula first laid down in print by T. E. Lawrence and later the staple of counterinsurgency manuals: 'Rebellions can be made by two per cent active in a striking force and 98 per cent passively sympathetic'. The IRA did not dispense altogether with the old myth of the people. But the new relation provided a more sophisticated basis for the republican claim that they stood for the Irish popular will.[12]

[. . .] The 'four glorious years' of 1918–21 stand out as the climax of the nationalist myth of the 'risen people', a myth whose power has fueled republican intransigence ever since. Defeat in the civil war was accommodated by a cerebral sleight of hand that one penetrating historian has called the 'triumph of failure' [. . .] But it remains impossible to grasp the nature of the present armed resistance without recognizing the imprint that history lays on it.[13]

[. . .] Even 'total devastation' has proved transient, noiselessly repaired by the deep and steady force of republican sentiment, historically armored against the shock of failure.[14]

Reliance on myth has played some part in influencing the attitudes and actions of Northern Ireland's Protestant Unionists according to Townshend, who instances the mythical association of eighteenth-century Protestant victories when the Orangemen routed the Catholicism of James II, a feat of arms commemorated today (in an oddly derivative style) by asserting a provocative right to march through Catholic housing estates in Londonderry and Belfast. There is also the mythical claim that Ulster's Unionists represent a nation when the single issue of legitimate hegemony is trumpeted, a call which, in Townshend's view, is now less strident and less dependent on myth:

The loyalist incorporation of history has been, if anything, more vivid and concrete than that of the nationalists. For contemporary Protestants the symbolic weight of the Ulster Covenant and the Ulster Volunteer Force of 1912 is vast and seems to have been transmitted effectively through superficially different organizations like the 'B' Special Constabulary and the Ulster Defence Regiment.[15]

The unionist mobilization into violence at many points prefigured that of the nationalists. It would be hard to say which of the two is likely to prove the more irreducible. Currently, the prestige of loyalist paramilitary organizations (Ulster Defence Association, Ulster Freedom Fighters, Ulster Volunteer Force) is not high, but the Protestant community has its own myths of popular mobilization, which parallel those of the nationalists.

Yet despite pervasive and novel uncertainty about the proper mode of action in the present crisis, there is little sign that fundamental unionist attitudes have become less monolithic in their simplicity. The general notion of a Protestant 'way of life' retains wide currency, and though the visual symbol of King Billy on his white horse may be less in evidence, the old slogans – We will not have Home Rule; No surrender; Not an inch; and, more disreputably, No popery – remain powerfully expressive definitions of the ground on which loyalists are prepared to fight, or at least to threaten to fight by organizing in military fashion. The best observer study of Protestant activism accepted the view that modern paramilitary groups can be seen as products of traditional Northern Ireland society, not subverters of the old order but extreme versions of it. Those who formed and joined them were used to uniforms, punitive discipline, parades, and a system in which one gave and received orders. But they were unfamiliar with democratic organizations and unused to making their own decisions.

There have been a number of attempts to demonstrate that the components of Protestant identity meet the criteria of nationality and that Ulster unionists are thus a nation. None of these demonstrations has been wholly successful, though since in practice the ultimate proof of nationhood is the capacity to vindicate it by force of arms, there is a degree of circularity in all such analysis. Plainly, Ulster Protestants have come close to such self-assertion on several occasions over the last century but have never taken this collective responsibility. At present the principal barrier is lack of confidence in any specific outcome; exponents of United Kingdom integration (the original antidevolution position of 1886), Northern Ireland devolution à la Stormont (with or without power sharing), and Ulster independence vie for support. It is possible that in the future terrorist violence will be used in a bid for control by one of these persuasions, but so far Protestant paramilitarism has been limited to the traditional single-issue politics of communal ascendancy.[16]

While the myth of 'victimisation' is perhaps shared among activists on all sides, it must be among Catholics that it arouses most resonance. 'When it comes to myth', Kearney has said, 'the past is never past'. Above all, for Townshend, the hunger strikes demonstrated this. He quotes Apter (1997) about the making of myths as political symbols and goes on to present the imprisoned terrorists under the rubric of 'the egoism of victimisation'. In certain eyes, in Belfast and Whitehall, gunmen were audaciously pressing for status as political prisoners. Surely, though, these terrorists were deservedly locked away as common criminals? Arthur makes the point that starvation to death was not an unknown form of sacrifice in Ireland and in its modern version it conferred a sacrificial ideology upon a revolutionary one. The prisoners had gone to the Long Kesh gaol not to win but to die:

Apter (1997) may well have had the hunger strikes in mind when he wrote that endowing 'confrontational events with political symbolism is itself a strategy which changes the political process from accountability and consensus to a politics of spectacle, theatre, violence, drama [. . .]'. Here was a confrontational event imbued with political symbolism which challenged the *doxa* in a highly theatrical manner. While the republican campaign had been launched against the prevailing accountability and consensus no one single incident or event invested as much spectacle as did the hunger strikes. They raise fundamental questions about the place of the IRA in a typology of violence-prone movements; about the extent to which it is an archetype of emancipatory movements; about whether we can 'read' the strikes as a version of the authenticity paradigm which challenges the impersonality of man-made mass deaths and, as such, as an inversion of the death-world; and finally, once again, whether contemporary republicanism has a logical project.

If any one episode explains the resilience of republicanism it is the hunger strikes of 1980–1. The background is simple: since the introduction of internment in 1971 a battle has been waged between the prisoners and the authorities over the question of political status inside the prisons. Republicans considered they were not criminals. Adams (1986) [. . .] insists that the importance of political prisoner status 'has nothing to do with any contempt for the "ordinary criminals" who are so often the victims of social inequality and injustice. From Thomas Ashe to Bobby Sands the concern has always been to assert the political nature of the struggle in which the IRA has been engaged'. Generally the Catholic community shared Adams's belief that the profile of the prisoners was not that of a criminal class. The emotional reaction by the Cardinal (O'Fiach) after a visit to protesting republican prisoners in 1978 was a precursor of things to come: 'they prefer to face death rather than submit to be classed as criminals [. . .] anyone with the least knowledge of Irish history knows how deeply rooted this attitude is in our country's past'.

By putting it in this historical perspective the Cardinal was drawing attention to the fact that before 1980 no less than twelve republicans had starved to death for their beliefs in this century. It was a practice which flourished in pre-Christian times in Ireland [. . .] Sean MacBride, former IRA Chief of Staff and Nobel Peace Prize winner in 1974, argued that 'it was not some isolated political happening of our time but a deep symptom of a historically recurring persecution: "a fall-out resulting from the cruel interference by Britain in the affairs of the Irish nation"'.

More importantly the prisons' campaign made the distinction between a *sacrificial* ideology and the *revolutionary* ideology of the military campaign.[17]

Kearney also takes up sacrificial ideology as demonstrated by the hunger-strikers:

The most dramatic instance of the myth of sacrificial martyrdom in recent times has been the hunger-strike campaigns of republican prisoners in Northern Ireland, culminating in the death of Bobby Sands. The hunger-strikers in the H-Block at Long Kesh were driven by politics but inspired by myth. The distinction is, I believe, important. If asked why they were doing what they were doing, the prisoners would invariably reply – to defeat the British. But if asked why they saw the self-infliction of suffering and hunger to the point of death as a way of doing this, they would point to mottoes by Pearse or McSwiney on their cell walls. The republican hunger-strikers sought to escape their actual paralysis by realigning their plight with a mythico-religious tradition of *renewal-through-sacrifice*. [. . .]

The invocation of this sacrificial rhetoric was to become a conspicuous feature of the Long Kesh campaign. But it was something which operated largely as a pre-reflective password of the tribe, frequently escaping critical analysis. The IRA's ideology of martyrdom inverted what went by the name of normal political logic (at a parliamentary or military level); it subscribed instead to a mythic logic which claimed that defeat is victory, failure is triumph, past is present. [. . .]

The IRA's ideology was sacrificial to the degree that it invoked, explicitly or otherwise, a 'sacred' memory of death and renewal which provided legitimation for present acts of suffering by grafting them onto paradigms of a recurring past. It thus afforded these acts a timeless and redemptive quality. By insisting in 1978 that their prison campaign was 'not ten years old but sixty years old', the IRA were clearly identifying with the long nationalist tradition of the 1916 and Fenian martyrs. On the one hand, to be sure, the Provisionals presented themselves as a highly modernised and pragmatic paramilitary movement. But on the other, they confessed to taking their 'inspiration and experience from the past', that is, 'from the native Irish tradition' founded on 'our Irish and Christian values'.

[. . .] Hunger-strikes were better recruiters than bomb-strikes.[18]

A final point about myth as an energising force is illustrated by a warning of Kearney that reliance upon myth as a motivating and legitimating element may help the process of emancipation, say, when it is related to the myth of a motherland (to be defended at all costs), yet it may also lead to a hyper-defensive reluctance to engage in dialogue and contemplate concessions towards others. This seems a possibility where so many outside observers deplore and condemn what seems to be the obduracy of Sinn Féin or of the hardline Protestant factions to 'give up the gun'. Those who maintain unwavering loyalty to particular myths tend to exclusive rigidity of outlook and behaviour and this excludes dialogue:

Myth is a two-way street. It can lead to perversion (bigotry, racism, fascism) or to liberation (the reactivation of a genuine social imaginary open to universal horizons). If we need to demythologise, we also need to remythologise. And this double process requires a discrimination between authentic and inauthentic uses of myth. For if myths of motherland are often responses to repression, they can also become repressive in their own right. That is why it is necessary to see how myth emancipates and how it incarcerates, how it operates as an empowering symbol of identity and how it degenerates into a reactionary idol. At best, myth invites us to reimagine our past in a way which challenges the present status quo and opens up alternative possibilities of thinking. At worst, it provides a community with a strait-jacket of fixed identity, drawing a *cordon sanitaire* around this identity which excludes dialogue with all that is other than itself.

Without mythology, our memories are homeless; we capitulate to the mindless conformism of fact. But if revered as ideological dogma, and divorced from the summons of reality, myth becomes another kind of conformism, another kind of death. That is why we must never cease to keep mythological images in dialogue with history.[19]

TERRORISM AS A LEGACY

Arthur also has in mind the generative force of memories, myths and symbols in deepening the attitudes and the resilience of sectarian combatants and the mainly passive, wider society supporting them. For him the length and intensity of this civil strife suggest that history 'has been fashioned as a weapon' and that it represents a 'culture of violence':

This has not been simply a low-intensity 'war' but also a campaign of attrition visited primarily on civilian communities conducted often by their *soi-disant* defenders (and often with the complicity of the community). But they also mask the degree to which the violence is 'controlled' as if it operated under strict rules of the game – unlike Lebanon from the 1970s or former Yugoslavia where ethnic conflict had been kept under artificial wraps for a generation or more and then exploded with an intense ferocity.[20]

Thirty years of sectarian divide and violence in Northern Ireland have caused most observers to ask: 'why does it go on?' For Townshend, at least, this three decades-long persistence of 'latent civil war' calls for continuing investigation and he suggests that political violence persists because public perceptions come to regard it as an end in itself. It conveys a message and a clearly understood one, more within Ireland than outside. Yet, the configurations of the conflict are never entirely clear and there is a mesh of relationships between explosive militarism and cautious political moves that probably begs the question of how effective terrorist violence really can be. Some of the momentum is carried forward often in a loose and episodic fashion by paramilitary elements on both sides of the divide. Townshend's question in conclusion is a troubling one: has terrorism assumed a 'normality' in Ulster that seems in some respects permanent without ever offering a solution?:

Political violence persists because it is effective. Its efficacy is the primary condition of its adoption, readoption, legitimation, and containment. This is not to deny that at certain periods or levels of conflict there can emerge what has been called a subculture of violence, in which for organizational or psychological reasons violence becomes self-validating, or autotelic. Walter put the distinction with typical lucidity: 'As long as terror is directed to an end beyond itself, namely control, it has a limit and remains a process [. . .] Under certain conditions, terror becomes unlimited and therefore no longer a process but an end in itself. [. . .]'

So the crucial question about the process of terror is not How much damage was caused? but What message did the damage convey? The message may or may not approximate the one intended by the terrorists. A longish list of possible messages could be drawn up without much difficulty: it would include We are strong enough to do this; We mean business; Our opponents cannot protect you; and so on. In the case of the IRA it is evident that all these kinds of statements made by acts of violence were grasped at quite an early stage, certainly by 1921. Despite many vicissitudes in the intervening years, the IRA has never lost sight of this deliberate application of harm as communication. Most important, such messages were on the whole clearly understood by their principal audience, the Catholic community in the six counties.

By contrast, these acts have communicated radically different messages to their secondary audiences, the British public and the northern unionists. [. . .]

The theoretical capacity of terror to fracture the state as the symbol of public order and clamorously to break the monopoly of legitimate coercive power (which organized criminals also break, but quietly) has been effective only within ethnic limits. Outside them the paradoxical outcome has been, if anything, reinforcement of the attitudes and policies the IRA needed to undermine. This has been as clear at the practical, administrative level – where the suspension of the devolved Northern Ireland legislature and its replacement by direct British rule in 1972 looked at first like a republican success but has come in time to be a larger obstacle to their aims – as at the attitudinal level, where an ingrained British reaction has been the refusal to 'give way to force' whatever its cause.

[. . .] Any complacent notion that the level of violence has become 'acceptable' to either the authorities or the communities is soon ruptured by periodic outrages, but sheer force of habit has made many of the trappings of guerrilla terrorism practically invisible. It is possible that basic assumptions about the nature of normality have altered over the twenty years of irregular warfare; certainly nobody in Britain in 1969 would have believed it possible for troops to maintain public order for more than a few months at most. Force of circumstance may be driving the six counties to a form of political life that is permanent and yet in no sense a solution.[21]

THE PEACE AGREEMENT

In the wake of 30 years of terror, April 1998 brought a breakthrough in the shape of all-party consensus. This was the so-called April Agreement, which is summarised by Whittaker:

The April Agreement has three strands: a democratically elected assembly with executive and legislative authority protecting the rights and interests of all; a North–South Ministerial council for consultation, cooperation and action on matters of mutual interest; a British–Irish council representing Belfast, Edinburgh and Cardiff. Human Rights are to be protected through a possible Bill of Rights. Arms are to be decommissioned within two years. Provision is to be made for improved security liaison and for prisoner release.

Throughout Great Britain the settlement of April 1998 was greeted with immense relief. Was the conflict of thirty years now brought to an end? Apart from understandable hyperbole there remained areas of concern and controversy. As in all moves towards conflict settlement, it is difficult for negotiating participants to encourage their followers to accept the compromises and concessions they feel bound to make.[22]

Given that the April Agreement remains in the fullest sense unratified, the opinion recorded above seems something of an understatement. There is an ominous shadow unless arms are finally 'decommissioned'. There remains some dismay that the promise of settlement and of reconciliation is not yet certain.

THE PROBLEM OF DISARMAMENT

The prospect of an end to terrorism in Northern Ireland raises many debatable issues in regard to timing, intentions and the extent to which a final and pacific laying down of arms can be guaranteed. Three questions, especially, seem difficult to answer. First, which sectarian groups can be relied upon to bring objectivity and consistency to the implementation of peace? Second, what is the extent of the usable weapon stocks held by rivals in conflict? Third, how far is general disarmament likely to be successful?

First of all, it is very clear that the sectarian divide is fragmented. Catholic Sinn Féin's militarists in the Irish Republican Army (IRA) have broken away into such groups as the Dissident IRA, the Real IRA and the Continuity IRA, or Continuity Army Council. Then there is the Irish National Liberation Army (INLA). Recently, members of Catholic Reaction Force have been associated with arson and targeted killings. Altogether, these groups account for possibly 600 well-armed men with doubtless many hundreds of tacit supporters in Catholic areas. On the Protestant Unionist flank there are half a dozen identifiable groups, by no means all committed to violence – the Ulster Unionists, the Ulster Democratic Party, the Ulster Volunteer Force (UVF), the Loyalist Volunteer Force (LVF) and the Ulster Defence Association, or Ulster Freedom Fighters. Numbers may approximate those of their Catholic rivals. Again, there is a tenuous observance of the ceasefire by the vigilante elements in the two last-named bands. (A much more liberal (and pacific) Third Force is made up of the Labour Coalition, the Socialist and Democratic Labour Party (SDLP) and the Alliance Party.) What is unpredictable and, of course, worrying is the degree to which latent terrorism is, as it were, under wraps. While all parties declare that it would be inadmissible to reject disarmament, few seem ready openly to give up their arms. Even if terror is completely dispelled, embittered extremists may step up violence.

Second, the resumption of terrorism is always a possibility so long as considerable weapon stocks are covertly kept in being. Dependable figures are hard to come by, at least in public revelations. There is every reason to credit the existence of many thousands of assault rifles, handguns, machineguns, several tons of Semtex and other plastic and commercial explosives, mortars, grenade launchers, flame throwers and large amounts of material for Molotov Cocktails. Reportedly, the IRA has fair supplies of anti-tank weapons and several rocket launchers.

Third, there is the problem of disarmament or 'decommissioning'. This has been a complex affair despite the loudly voiced statements of numerous Ulster politicians putting the situation in simple, non-negotiable terms. Sinn Féin's wish has been to put the arms matter to one side until they were allowed to sit in the new power-sharing executive the April Agreement envisaged. Unionists would have No Truck With Armed Terrorists. Neither party was comfortable with the British Government's compromise suggestion in 1998–9 that talks about disarmament and representation could proceed in tandem. There has always been an element of the zero-sum game in the rhetoric: 'If it's good for them, it must be bad for us.' Certainly, for paramilitary activists, the IRA and the Unionists any handing in of arms, without firm guarantees by others, represents 'surrender'. There is little understanding of the position taken by South African and Israeli guerrillas, who realised they had to make sacrifices for the sake of peace.

Already in January 1996 there were firm recommendations from the Mitchell Commission set up in Belfast to frame proposals for disarmament. It was a three-man body, composed of US senator George Mitchell, Canadian general John de Chastelain, and former Finnish premier Harri Holkeri. Their advice was that the British Government abandon the demand that paramilitaries give up their weapons before all-party talks could begin. Unequivocal negotiations and independent verification would call all bluffs.

Two years later, in April 1998, no discernible progress had been made in getting rid of weapons. The Mitchell requirements for the laying down of arms were made very clear in their contribution to the 67-page text of the April Agreement – that 'Moment of History' as the Irish press saw it:

All participants reaffirm their commitment to the total disarmament of all paramilitary organisations. They also confirm their intention to use any influence they have to achieve the decommissioning of all paramilitary arms within two years following endorsement in referendums north and south of the agreement and in the context of the implementation of the overall settlement.

The Independent Commission (the Mitchell Commission) will monitor, review and verify progress in the decommissioning of illegal arms, and will report to both governments (London and Dublin) at regular intervals.[23]

The position about decommissioning has always been one of waiting for things to begin. Ulster Unionists partnering Republican Sinn Féin in a new Northern Ireland executive temporarily left the executive in February 2000, since complete IRA decommissioning had not been started by February 2000 and would not be completed by May 2000. Whitehall and Dublin prefer the term 'putting the weapons beyond use' to 'decommissioning' as a spur to convincing terrorists on all sides that laying aside weaponry is a voluntary and trustworthy act. In May 2000, two independent 'inspectors', from South Africa and Finland, were to inspect IRA arms dumps, sealed but not finally destroyed. For the first time in 30 years tension in Ulster became dramatically lower and British army numbers were much reduced.

Sanguine expectations and plain speaking were to rid Northern Ireland of violence. They have not entirely done so at the time of going to print. One suspects that memories and myths have some consequence in this shortcoming. US Senator George Mitchell in 1999 finished a five-year term in Belfast as mediator. His patience and diplomatic ingenuity are now legendary. In April 1996, when terrorism was still rampant in Northern Ireland, he spoke of the violence around him in very direct terms:

There is a powerful desire for peace [. . .] that desire creates the present opportunity [. . .] All sides must forget their vast inventories of historical recriminations [. . .] What is really needed is a decommissioning of mind-sets.[24]

Month by month, Northern Ireland is inching back to stability. The IRA leadership formally ordered an end to its armed campaigning. Henceforth, there was to be development of purely political and democratic programmes 'through exclusively peaceful means'. Writing in *The Guardian* in August 2005, Roy (Lord) Hattersley regarded the uniting at least economically of north and south Ireland as inevitable, 'courtesy of the global market, economics and the European Union'. So, 'where economics leads, politics is bound to follow'. Sinn Féin had the strongest possible interest in preserving the peace and sharing in prosperity. It was, indeed, a Farewell to Arms.[25]

The Canadian General de Chastelain, responsible for decommissioning arrangements, confirmed in September 2006, that the IRA had now put all its weapons 'beyond use'. (Even so, there was no very clear sign that any one of the other loyalist paramilitary groups was following this example.)

Institutional democracy in Ulster remained frozen in September 2006. The Northern Ireland Assembly set up by the April Agreement of 1998 and then suspended in October 2002 was still closed, despite confirmation of its establishment under Whitehall's Northern Ireland Act of 2006 and Royal Assent of 8 May 2006. Meanwhile, Britain's two parliamentary houses were to attend to legislative business. The later autumn months brought brighter news. The Northern Ireland Assembly was to reconvene, after all, and would sit for 12 weeks. This arrangement is being seen as a 'Virtual Assembly' in that it may debate but have no lawmaking powers. There was now to be a deadline for full restoration of the Assembly, namely 24 November 2006. Not negotiable as a fixture, it was envisaged that the convention of 108 Assembly members would succeed in furthering trust and hope. (Behind the scenes there continues to be a great deal of intensive political and/or governmental discussion between London, Belfast and Dublin.)

The parties in dispute now have to decide whether to implement a blue paper – a 'road map' – for Northern Ireland, which means tough decisions about power-sharing and confidence-building, particularly for Sinn Féin in acknowledging the rule of law, so often seen as a set of Unionist handcuffs.

The Armalite rifle brought terror to Northern Ireland. Unarmed, Irish 'straight talking' will be the only way to open gates and smooth out the road.

It was on 26 March 2007 that the old rivals, Ian Paisley and Gerry Adams, met in Belfast in face-to-face discussion. Confronted by this momentous step towards peaceful resolution London has put aside the threat of resumed Direct Rule and gives Northern Ireland ten weeks to seek accord. Dr Paisley and Martin MacGuinness would then work together as head and deputy of a resurrected, autonomous Stormont.

POST-CONFLICT

In the post-conflict scenario of Northern Ireland the old constraints of memory, myth and the usefulness of violence are still there. Nor is the conventional polarisation of political and religious affiliation at all radically diminished. Looking, though, at contemporary developments in a time of sectarian coming together it is best to remind readers – there can be no simplistic deduction of cause and effect.

Generally, today, Irishmen are striving to dissociate and disengage. Overall, the process attracts a great deal of research, discussion and controversy. Much useful work in the domain of forensic psychology is being done by John Horgan in Cork. Two careful rejoinders preface his scrutiny:

'Leaving terrorism behind might suggest leaving behind the shared social norms, values, attitudes and aspirations so carefully forged while a member of a terrorist group. On the other hand, it might indicate some adherence to these values and attitudes, but perhaps no longer engaging in actual terrorist activity.'[26]

Put basically one may understand the IRA activist leaving his rifle in the corner of the room. For him Horgan's 'supportive qualities of involvement' no longer sustain belief and action and leaving may be voluntary or involuntary. Horgan sees this as personal abandonment of what has gone before when 'goal attainment needed psychological, physical and organizational "investment"'. This may be desirable for the public and for security officialdom. Will life for the returning terrorist now be limited, void of meaning and intention? So the rifle cannot be left to rust 'beyond use'. Organisational disengagement is much debated publicly. Articles in the press from time to time voice some cynicism. For Conor Cruise O'Brien there is in the 'Irish Mind' too much 'passion and cunning' to guarantee unviolated progress.[27]

Interestingly, Paul Wilkinson in St Andrews, is particularly concerned with 'individual pathways out of terrorism' set against organisational bonding. Rejectionist wings in the IRA have renamed their watchkeeping Continuity IRA and Real IRA, keeping their powder dry as it were. For Wilkinson

there is no previous case in Western Europe of a terrorist movement succeeding in transferring into a peaceful political party.[28]

Transferring into a more peaceful guise is being undertaken with studied seriousness by former activists. 'Strong in the fight, strong in peace' must illustrate the relict toughness and present determination of the former protagonists. Press coverage shows pictures of Unionists holding both a banner 'Prepare for Peace' alongside their battle gear and cocked rifles. Old loyalties are not for below the surface.

Yet, particularly both in Northern Ireland and elsewhere, for Wilkinson

there is reason to believe that the terrorist who has been subjected to intensive political indoctrination and conditioned by the terrorist training and way of life when under the direct influence of fanatical terrorist mentors, is potentially susceptible to determined skilful and well-planned re-education and rehabilitation techniques if only we could make these available within our penal systems.[29]

Given the long history of dedicated patricide in and around the Province this hope may well raise a few eyebrows there.

Nevertheless, reconciliation and rehabilitation programmes are being devised through institutional building and development. On 8 May 2007 devolution of statutory power definitely came back to Northern Ireland. The office holding of Ian Paisley and that of Sinn Fein's Martin MacGuinness was confirmed. The putative 'road map' became Northern Ireland's 'Normalisation Plan' in March 2010. The Northern Ireland Assembly now met confirmed on the Stormont legislative estate and members could now draft and debate bills for enactment.

Paisley and MacGuinness represent the Assembly in a North–South Ministerial Council bringing together (at first warily) Eire and Northern Ireland. The stated goal across the whole range of community provision and enterprise is 'to promote the harmonious and mutually beneficial development of the totality of relationships among the peoples of these islands', an affirmation incomprehensible to the street fighters of only a few years ago. Assembly elections in early 2011 will certainly transform the public image of contending parties now preferring dialogue to weapons handling. And their deliberations will also consider inter-European relationships. By degrees, in Conor Cruise O'Brien's view 'rampant militarism' gives way to ordered, slowly uniting progress. Is not 'terrorism then finally "outed"'?

CONCLUSION

It is sad to read the foregoing discussion written in 2007 when more stability and reassurance were surfacing in troubled Northern Ireland. Four years later, in the spring of 2011, things are very different. Over the four years there has been a relatively low level, spasmodic occurrence of violence to mar the apparent movement towards peaceful settlement. Conor Cruise O'Brien would deplore, of course, without too much evident surprise, the descent into 'rampant militarism'. Bombs, mortars, the murder of policemen, machine guns and booby traps have been brought back in each of the four years. Tentative talks between government and 'dissidents' (still so-called) have come to nothing. Today's threat level is once more rated as 'severe' and on 'high alert'. O'Brien, thinking of the 'Irish Mind', would associate with continued weapons handling what *The Times* in February 2011 termed 'the fissiparous tendency of the Irish to disassociate'. The IRA splits into Real IRA, the Continuity IRA and a Gaelic-speaking unit. The Unionists, long a loyalist core, are splitting into smaller groups, too. All too obviously, unless serious talking together displaces lethal terrorism, Northern Ireland will remain fractured, disrupted and dangerous.

Algeria

THE BITTERNESS AND BRUTALITY of terrorism in Algeria have made world headlines for almost 50 years. To understand the origins and development of turmoil in that country it is necessary to look rather closely at its political landscape. The lethality of the struggle there owes much to feelings of failure and futility among Algerians. The ending of the Second World War in 1945 brought for many colonial territories expectations of increased self-determination. In Algeria the French colonial administration failed to pay attention to articulate demands from the non-French population for social and economic reform. The liberation movement failed to frame a convincing popular campaign and to communicate it to a wide, eager constituency. Successive administrations, largely French but with Algerian membership, failed to address political, social and economic issues and to establish any legitimate authority acceptable to those who felt disenfranchised. They fell short of building any tolerance between secular governance and the Islamic observance of the majority of the population. Failure to deal with manifestations of protest and to use the possibilities of discussion and compromise led to irrepressible frustration and growing violence. Lack of leadership, irresolution, disunity and confusion resulted in widespread lawlessness and a recourse to terror tactics among malcontents. These latter are organised into a number of groups: the FLN (Front de Libération Nationale), the FIS (Front Islamique de Salut), the GIA (Groupe Islamique Armé) and the MIA (Mouvement Islamique Armé).

THE POLITICAL BACKGROUND TO ALGERIA'S CONFLICT

There are many written accounts of the origin of Algeria's chaos and a useful outline is to be found in the report of a visit to Algeria by a panel of 'eminent persons' who were appointed by the Secretary-General of the United Nations in June 1998. The panel report contained the following historical account:

On 1 November 1954, the principal Algerian nationalist movement, the FLN, began a struggle for independence. A ceasefire was agreed to in March 1962 and independence was declared in July 1962.

In August 1962, the Algerian provisional Government transferred its functions to the Political Bureau of the FLN [the Front de Libération Nationale] and in September a National Constituent Assembly was elected from a single list of FLN candidates and the Algerian Republic was proclaimed. A new government was formed with Mr Ahmed Ben Bella as Prime Minister.

A draft Constitution providing for a presidential regime, with the FLN as the sole party, was adopted on 28 August 1963. In September 1963, the Constitution was approved by referendum and Mr Ben Bella was then elected President. In June 1965, the Minister of Defence, Col. Houari Boumedienne, deposed Ben Bella in a military coup. Former President Ben Bella was first imprisoned and later allowed to go into exile.

In June 1975, Mr Boumedienne introduced plans for: creating a socialist system, maintaining Islam as the State religion, the drafting of a new Constitution, and the holding of elections for a President and National People's Assembly. A National Charter was adopted by referendum in June 1976, by 98.5 per cent of the electorate. In November, the new Constitution incorporating the principles of the Charter was approved by referendum.

Following the death of President Boumedienne in December 1978, Col. Chadli Ben Djedid, commander of the Oran military regime, succeeded him. Within two years, President Chadli and his government began to gradually reverse the socialist economic policies pursued by President Boumedienne.

Liberalization of the economy and an overhaul of State machinery gained pace in the period after the oil price crash of 1985/86. In 1987, in response to the decline in the price of petroleum and the increase in Algeria's external debt, the Government introduced austerity measures and began to remove State controls from various sectors of the economy. The acceleration of efforts to open the economy to the free market was accompanied by steps towards political pluralism. The country remained a one-party State until 1989.

After his re-election in 1984, the Chadli presidency had been marked by periods of unrest especially in 1986 and 1987. Severe unemployment, high prices and shortages of essential supplies, resulting from the austerity measures, provoked, in 1988, a series of strikes led by the Union Générale des Travailleurs Algériens (UGTA) and in October of that year riots erupted in Algiers, spreading to Oran and Annaba. A six-day state of emergency was imposed and according to official sources, 159 people were killed and 3,500 were arrested during confrontations with the government forces.

In response to the unrest, President Chadli proposed constitutional amendments allowing non-FLN candidates to participate in elections. These reforms were approved in November 1988. A new Constitution signifying the end of the one-party socialist State was approved by referendum in February 1989, allowing the formation of political parties other than the FLN.

Other legislation adopted in July 1989 further reduced State control of the economy, allowed the expansion of investment by foreign companies and ended the State monopoly of the press. Despite these changes, strikes and riots continued during 1989, in protest against alleged official corruption and the Government's failure to improve living conditions. A programme of economic liberalization was announced and the first multiparty municipal and provincial elections scheduled for December were postponed to June 1990.

In April 1991, President Chadli announced that the first multiparty general elections would take place in June. The FIS argued that a presidential election should be held simultaneously, or shortly after, and in protest against the electoral law proposed by the Prime Minister, Mr Mouloud Hamrouche, the FIS incited an indefinite strike and demonstrations, demanding the resignation of President Chadli. Violent confrontations occurred, and in response President Chadli declared a state of emergency and postponed the general elections.

The National People's Assembly was dissolved by presidential decree on 4 January 1992 and on 11 January President Chadli resigned. The High Security Council cancelled the second round of voting and on 14 January a five-member High Council of State (HCE) was appointed to act as a collegiate presidency, until the expiration of Chadli's term of office in 1993.

Amid sporadic outbreaks of violence and terrorism, the security forces took control of the FIS offices in early February 1992, the High Council of State declared a 12-month state of emergency and in March, following a court decision, the FIS party was formally dissolved.

On 26 August 1992, a bomb explosion at Algiers airport indicated a shift in terrorist methods: from then on, violent acts were directed not only against the security forces or Government officials and civil society figures, but against people who were not specifically targeted.

Political efforts and attempts at reconciliation continued against a background of escalating violence throughout the country, and in December 1992, against a background of severe economic and social problems, a curfew was imposed in the capital and in the six neighbouring departments. In February 1993, the state of emergency was renewed for an indefinite period.[1]

THE ERUPTION OF VIOLENCE

As a consequence of so much political volatility, contemporary Algeria is a 'state in agony' according to Martin Stone (1997). Islamic insurgents target state employees and supporters, even foreigners. Algeria's military-backed regimes, unable to cope with their citizens' economic and social distress, continue to lash out savagely at all dissenters, many of whom are being recruited by the FLN as guerrillas. Thus, terror tactics have had a long history whether they are the result of political extremism or of clan vendettas:

3.30 p.m. Monday 30 January 1995: a car loaded with TNT explodes in front of the Algiers headquarters of the Sûreté Nationale on the boulevard Amirouche.

At this time of day carnage is inevitable. An overcrowded bus passes in front of the car at the moment of detonation, and the street is crowded with shoppers buying food for the start of the holy fasting month of Ramadan, which starts later in the evening. Blood, limbs, clothes and papers litter the pavement; severed limbs have to be removed from the roofs of nearby buildings. Forty-two people are killed, more than 250 injured. Although this is the worst single bombing in the history of independent Algeria, it has taken place in an unexceptional week: in addition to at least thirty members of the security forces being killed, gunmen have kidnapped and killed the four children of a hero of the war of independence and murdered a French resident in Algiers.

Algeria in the mid-1990s was in a desperate condition. Between 1992 and 1997 some 120,000 people were killed in a terrorist insurgency characterised by staggering cruelty on both sides. Fanatical Islamist insurgents pursued a dirty war to topple the state, fighting fearlessly against their numerically superior foe and literally terrorising the population. In the mountains and the countryside, an informal guerrilla army laid ambushes for a security apparatus reliant mainly on conscripts; in the cities and towns killers, some in their teens, assassinated thousands of 'liberals' who were considered supporters of the state: schoolteachers, doctors, lawyers, journalists, academics, civil servants and former fighters in the war of independence against France. More than 100 foreigners were killed, mostly French, of whom more than thirty were men and women of religion – priests, nuns, monks. The Bishop of Oran was among them.

Algerians grew accustomed to unexplained explosions and bursts of gunfire at night; to news of yet another colleague or relative being knifed to death or gunned down while on the way to work or out shopping; to constantly coming across security force roadblocks and checkpoints that could always turn out to be a dreaded *faux barrage*, a 'false checkpoint'. Across northern Algeria, guerrillas raped and murdered women, some merely for refusing to wear the veil. In certain villages guerrillas even tried to enforce the highly questionable practice of *muta*' (temporary) marriage, which is tantamount to legalised prostitution. Individuals who considered themselves at risk were forced to live the life of a fugitive, furtively staying with friends or in protected compounds surrounded by the security forces. Those who could afford it left to live and work abroad, mostly in France.

Algerians had learned to read between the lines of the terse reports of security encounters published in the government-monitored press. They had become accustomed to reports of startling military successes against the guerrillas in the mountains and of 'key' terrorist leaders being killed in raids, understanding that, in reality, summary justice had been meted out. Many Algerians, even members of the security forces, accused members of the state itself of being behind the terrorist actions as a means of prolonging the violence for their own ends. Policemen secretly complained of being ordered to participate in death squads, shoot-to-kill raids and the torture of suspects.

The factors that underlie this appalling situation are complex and hotly disputed. Having lost virtually all legitimacy, Algeria's military-backed regime clung to power in the face of a savage terrorist war. Thirty years of rural depopulation had resulted in overcrowded cities where unemployment was rampant and the living conditions of the majority were intolerable. From being an elegant colonial port in 1962, Algiers had developed into a sprawling overcrowded metropolis. Most of the population were under thirty years of age, their parents having moved from the more socially conservative rural areas to the city in the 1960s and 1970s. Thousands of families were crammed into crumbling old apartment blocks or into modern soulless high-rises, with children often forced to sleep in beds by shifts. Unemployment and under-employment were high; the quality of life poor for most; and a sense of hope absent. The pattern was repeated in most towns across northern Algeria – Blida, Medea, Constantine, Skikda. Economically Algerians were paying the price for the mistakes of the past: the grand industrialisation schemes of the 1970s; over-reliance on oil and gas revenues; and the effects of a crippling foreign debt. [. . .]

A nation-state in Algeria as defined in European terms came into being during the latter half of the nineteenth century. In the first six decades of the twentieth century the indigenous Muslim populations re-evaluated their own societies and over time determined to suppress their inherent divisions and coalesce together to eject the occupying colonial power. This suppression of social segmentations spawned new factions and frictions within society that re-emerged immediately after independence in 1962, only to be swept aside as a small westernised élite seized power.

This élite used the imperatives of nation-state building, the assertion of political independence, national development and stability to suppress debate about the political, cultural, religious, social and even linguistic identities and directions of the independent state. One of the key questions left unaddressed in the early 1960s was the religious orientation of the Constitution. The regime's adoption of a blend of Third World socialism, Western European social democracy, pan-Arabism and Islam was a compromise designed to appeal to all sectors of society, but which in fact was rejected by all.[2]

RELIGIOUS AND SECULAR RIVALS IN CONFLICT

Ever since independence was won from the French in 1962 government opponents, religious and secular, have remained bitter rivals with divided allegiances in the view of Stone. He emphasises that Islamic fundamentalism in Algeria and elsewhere is not in itself disposed to using violence, though frustrated zealots may feel bound to adopt it:

Since independence, Algerian politics has been dominated by the interaction between various factions, clans, interest groups and ideological tendencies. Until 1989 the official ruling organisation, the Front de Libération Nationale (FLN) was merely a political façade behind which these various groups vied for power and influence. Although the one-party state was formally demolished in 1989, the four main political tendencies within the FLN – the dirigistes, the liberals, the secularists and the Islamists, each of which held conflicting conceptions of Algerian society – became locked in a bitter rivalry. This dangerous interplay grew apace with the introduction of political pluralism and the legalisation of the Front des Forces Socialistes (FFS) and the establishment of the Front Islamique de Salut (FIS) in 1989. As with previous groups, there was considerable blurring and flexibility of the groups' memberships and ideologies, with some public figures considering themselves as belonging to more than one camp. Although the FFS and FIS had supporters in government and in the political parties, their efforts were principally directed at gaining the ear of the ultimate power in Algeria, the military. The military was itself divided over the Islamist 'problem', broadly forming two camps – the 'eradicators', who favoured liquidation of the Islamists, and the 'conciliators', who sought to bring them into the establishment.[3] [. . .]

Algeria's struggle for independence lasting eight years was one of the most bitter and bloody wars of self-determination in history. To describe the war as merely a struggle between colonisers (the French) and colonised (the Muslims) would be misleading and incorrect. Parallels with South Africa are more appropriate as the conflict was principally between the *pieds noirs* (Algerians of French descent) who wanted to remain in their native land under French protection, and the indigenous Muslims, who demanded initially an end to their second-class status but ultimately full statehood and complete control over the reins of power. The war also involved feuds and disputes between rival Muslims and between the *pieds noirs* and the French authorities. Acts of barbarism were committed on all sides. [. . .] Thus it was that the population of newly independent Algeria was overwhelmingly disoriented, bewildered, displaced and hopelessly ill-equipped for the task ahead.[4] [. . .]

Muslim activists often turn to violence out of desperation as so-called modernist regimes seek to suffocate the evolution of political Islam to protect the interests of the ruling élite. Sometimes the regimes themselves create and protect activist groups in order to besmirch the reputation of more mainstream Islamists whom they perceive as representing a greater threat.[5]

There were around sixty Islamic extremist groups active in Algeria in the mid and late 1990s. They ranged from tiny cells operating in cities to militias boasting as many as 50–60 armed guerrillas active in remote mountainous areas. The Algerian regime was anxious to present the groups as posing a serious though not terminal threat, and thus the Algerian media often distorted reporting on their activities and composition. Such distortion also characterised the greater part of contemporary foreign, and particularly Western, reporting on Islamic extremism in Algeria. By July 1997 at least 100,000 people had died in terrorist violence over the previous three and a half years, though the real figure may have been as high as 120,000. The inclusion in this figure of at least 115 expatriates killed during this period rendered Algeria statistically the most dangerous place in the world for foreigners, most of whom were murdered by the GIA [Armed Islamic Group] or its allies. However, the blood feud and the vendetta have traditionally played a major role in Algerian society and a considerable proportion of murders and other attacks ascribed to terrorists in fact represented the settling of scores originating in times of greater security and stability. [. . .]

The phenomenon of Islamic extremism in Algeria should be considered against the wider background of the Muslim world and the non-Muslim world's perception of it. Violent Muslim groups stepped up activities in several Islamic states in the early 1980s as the Iranian revolution and the Lebanese civil war increased the non-Muslim world's awareness of the growing importance of political Islam. Indeed, Western observers have found it difficult to distinguish extreme Islamism from its merely political or fundamentalist manifestations. As in other Muslim countries, the vast majority of Islamists in Algeria vigorously reject the use of violence to achieve their aims. A comparative study of countries where Islamic extremism has developed would produce a number of common factors. In Algeria, as in Egypt and Tunisia, extremism grew in an environment where the regime simultaneously rejected radical Islamism on one level while adopting parts of its agenda on another. At times these regimes appointed Islamist figures to government posts as a means of opposing leftist influence, particularly among students. [. . .]

Broadly there are two strands of Islamic extremists in Algeria: religious zealots and frustrated Islamists. Religious zealots were active in the 1960s but only rarely in the 1970s, and the first significant attacks did not begin until political Islamism was gaining momentum in the early 1980s. [. . .]

The distinctions between the FIS [Front Islamique de Salut] and the extremist fringe became increasingly blurred as the violence worsened throughout 1992 and 1993. Even allowing for the regime's readiness to ascribe almost every act of violence in Algeria to Islamic extremists, many party members and officials within and without Algeria were directly or indirectly involved in extremist activities. In the first six months of 1992 the organisation grew rapidly as thousands of frustrated FIS supporters went underground in the weeks after the cancellation of the elections. The sight of relatives and friends rounded up and transported to the Saharan internment camps was a major incentive for many to join the MIA [Mouvement Islamique Armé]. Official reports of 'terrorist' trials frequently mentioned the alleged perpetrator's former – or in some cases – current membership of the FIS.[6]

ALGERIA'S GUERRILLAS: ORGANISATION AND FOREIGN SUPPORT

Stone continues his account:

The MIA was organised on the triangle system developed by FLN guerrillas during the war of independence. Under this system each member of the cell knows only two other members of the network, though not their rank or status within the organisation as a whole. If detained and tortured an activist's objective is to remain silent for at least twenty-four hours to allow the other members of the cell to go to ground and inform the network. This allowed the network to continue functioning effectively even when the presumed leadership of the organisation had been arrested or temporarily incapacitated. The network was highly decentralised: cells were based on apartment blocks or *quartiers* and no activist ever came into direct contact with the leadership. Although there is strong evidence to suggest that the leadership took policy decisions on strategy and targeting, the cell commanders themselves made the day-to-day decisions. [. . .]

There is no reliable data on the numerical strength of the Islamic extremist groups. The authorities in April 1993 claimed that there were no more than 175 active guerrillas (most of whom were members of the MIA) with a network of 925 supporters. These figures were almost certainly gross underestimates, and the true number of active guerrillas was more likely to be as high as 10,000 or even 15,000, with perhaps as many active supporters. The estimated strength of the GIA's [Groupe Islamique Armé] armed forces was some 2,500. Guerrillas were predominantly under twenty-five, unemployed and lived in towns or cities, though many were older and had long criminal records. The groups raised money among Islamist supporters in emigré Algerian communities in Europe and North America, particularly from wealthy Algerian businessmen with Islamist sympathies. Armed robbery of banks was an additional source of finance; in March 1993, for instance, there was a five-day siege of a bank near Blida. [. . .]

Iran and Sudan have often been demonised as the grand international patrons of Islamist organisations, and Algeria has repeatedly singled out the two countries as foremost among foreign governments that support its extremist groups. In March 1993 Algeria severed diplomatic ties with Teheran. Although the extent of Iran's support of Algeria's extremists has probably been exaggerated, there is considerable evidence pointing to official Iranian support as part of its policy of exporting the Islamic revolution throughout the Muslim world. There is reason to believe that Iran was involved in the Algiers airport bombing of August 1992 and there were occasional reports of Iranian 'agents' being deported from Algeria. The Algerian press described the Iranian embassy in Algiers as a 'nest of spies' and claimed that Iran paid for a group of Algerian Islamists to travel to Lebanon to receive military training in Hezbollah camps. Evidence of Sudanese involvement, however, is less convincing and rests mainly on the established links between Islamists in Teheran and the Sudanese capital, Khartoum. Sudan's Islamist-backed military government has earned a reputation as a haven for numerous foreign Islamist groups, particularly Egyptians, and the Algerian authorities probably feel compelled to denounce Sudan as well as Iran. [. . .]

ALGERIA'S GUERRILLAS: THE PATTERN OF TERRORISM

Remote mountainous regions provided the ideal terrain for the extremist groups, as they did for the FLN and the followers of Bouyali before them. Both the MIA and GIA formed *maquis* groups in the mountains of the Tellian Atlas, from where they could mount ambushes on the security forces along roads and in nearby population centres. Official figures for terrorist-related incidents in the period February 1992 to April 1993 showed that of approximately 860 casualties, 315 were security-force personnel and soldiers; 370 presumed Islamic extremists; and 170 were civilians. The guerrillas would often terrorise the local population into concealing their whereabouts from the security forces. An operation in May 1992 provides a good illustration of the size and organisation of a typical guerrilla force. Five army battalions were mobilised against armed extremists who had installed themselves in the remote mountainous region near Lakhdaria, south-east of Algiers. The MIA-linked group had planned to use its remote base on Mount Zbarbar to attack the security forces and symbols of state authority in the area. Abdelkader Chebouti was also reported to have established a training camp on the mountain to shelter a number of Islamist army deserters. At least 150 would-be *maquisards* were arrested in the operation.

In the autumn of 1992 the extremists began an assassination campaign against their enemies. The motives behind the killings were a combination of classic terrorist tactics ('kill one to scare a thousand') and religious zeal. As Francis Ghilles has observed, the killings were often redolent of sacrificial acts. 'Honour can only be washed with blood, [and] witnesses must be present at the sacrifice'. Cassette tapes of sermons in which extremist imams ordered the faithful to kill anyone collaborating with the authorities began to appear in September 1992. Those under threat ranged from members of the government to civilians perceived as supporters of the regime in a wide range of professions and who were therefore enemies of the Islamist movement. This included civil servants, local government officials, *mudjahidine*, party politicians and officials of state-run authorities. The assassinations were usually well planned and executed, and the periodic waves of attacks on particular targets were intended gradually to increase pressure on the regime. By 1995 most politicians and senior civil servants had been forced to flee their villas on the hills above Algiers to take refuge in the well-guarded seaside resort of Sidi Fredj to the west of the city, from where the most important travelled to work by helicopter. [. . .]

In 1993 the extremists broadened their interpretation of their enemies to include relatives of government officials and 'anti-Islamist' civilians. While many victims had some family connection with the security forces, such as fathers or uncles in the gendarmerie or police, others had no apparent reason for being targeted. Scores of merchants, shopkeepers, engineers and labourers were knifed or shot to death. The assassins also struck at minor employees in local or central government. Although they were technically civilians, the MIA singled them out because of their vulnerability and their connection to the state. In March 1995 the GIA issued a warning that it would kill the wives, sisters and daughters of state functionaries, and followed it up with a spate of murders of women. In one such incident, a young secretary in a state-linked institution was shot in the back of the head as she entered her apartment. She died in her brother's arms. The extremists later imitated the tactics of the FLN by carrying out random bomb attacks in public places. In 1994 the GIA began to plant bombs with the aim of terrorising the population into pressing the authorities to negotiate with the Islamists. Among the most serious of these incidents was the blast outside Algiers central police station in March 1995, in which more than forty people lost their lives. In June 1995 the GIA began a campaign of suicide car bombings in Algiers.

The zealots also struck at journalists writing in 'anti-Islamist' publications and working for the state broadcasting corporation. [. . .]

Infiltration of the armed forces was an important element in the extremists' armoury. Scores of incidents were planned with the knowledge and assistance of security-force personnel, acting either voluntarily or through direct or indirect intimidation. [. . .]

In September 1993 the GIA began to murder foreigners, and by mid-1997 more than 115 had died in Algeria, though, as with all other aspects of the post-Chadli crisis, there was a large degree of falsification in the reporting of the murders. [. . .]

The GIA staged more attacks on foreigners across Algeria over the years that followed. The incidents were a combination of opportunism and sophistication. Most victims were long-term expatriates with no security and thus easy to target. Other victims were nationals of socialist or former socialist countries (such as Vietnam) with which Algeria had cemented cooperative alliances. [. . .]

By 1995 the leading Western countries, particularly the United States, had identified Islamic extremists as the most significant threat to Western interests worldwide, citing Algeria as the most visible 'proof' of this development. The threat of terrorist attack decimated Algeria's foreign business community, and those expatriates who remained did so from the safety of a guarded company compound, or were likely to be long-established residents who refused to leave Algeria and were unable to afford any protection.[7]

COUNTER-TERRORISM MEASURES

In 1998 the report of the United Nations 'eminent persons' was to acknowledge that terrorism in Algeria had passed through four stages. The report went on to describe the counter-terrorist measures being put into effect by the Algerian Government:

In the first stage it was aimed at security forces and government employees; in the second stage it was aimed at intellectuals, journalists, lawyers, artists and foreigners; in the third stage it was aimed at the general infrastructure of the country, e.g. bridges, schools, railways, and electricity supply; and in the current stage, it is aimed at the entire population. [. . .]

The authorities, on 30 September 1992, had created 'special courts' to try cases of terrorism. A terrorist act was defined as 'any violation of State security, the territorial integrity of the country or the stability and normal functioning of institutions by any act having the object of sowing terror among the population and creating a climate of insecurity by attacking persons or property.' [. . .]

Between October 1992 and October 1994, 13,770 persons had been judged by the special courts and 3,661 of them, or 25 per cent of those appearing, had been acquitted. There had been 1,661 sentences of death, 1,463 of which had been passed *in absentia*, and 8,448 sentences of imprisonment. [. . .]

In the light of experience with the struggle against terrorism at the judicial level, judicial procedures had been standardized in February 1995 through the abolition of the special courts and abrogation of the decree on terrorism and subversion. 'Terrorist and subversive crimes' are now legally defined and are to be dealt with by the ordinary courts. However, some lawyers with whom we met told us that some of the features of the special courts had been passed on to the regular courts. This allegedly had the effect of qualifying many acts as terrorist acts, although this might not always be the case. [. . .]

We were told that with the rise of terrorist violence, the civilian population, especially in the remote rural and mountainous areas, had been increasingly exposed to wanton acts of violence and brutality. The population of these villages and communes had requested that they be allowed to possess and retain arms and ammunition for their self-defence. Accordingly, legislation had been passed providing for the establishment of self-defence groups in villages and communes. The legislation authorized each household to have a gun and some ammunition. The self-defence groups operated under the control of the army or the gendarmerie, whichever was nearer. Ammunition provided to a household had to be accounted for and was intended to be used only for self-defence.

The Government had been able to reverse terrorism and to bring it to the stage where it had almost been eliminated largely because of the existence of these self-defence groups. The Government estimated that about 3,600 terrorists remained in widely scattered isolated areas. The Head of the Armed Forces, General Lamari, told us that wherever self-defence forces had been established, attacks by terrorists had stopped in 99 per cent of the cases. It was pointed out that the backbone of the self-defence group was represented by former fighters in the independence struggle, 'the patriots'.

We were told that the self-defence groups had indeed played a decisive role in the fight against extremist violence; however, it was alleged that they were also sometimes responsible for excesses committed against the civilian population. Bearing in mind the atmosphere prevailing in Algeria, in which there is simultaneously a transition to an open society and a fight against terrorism, we asked about monitoring arrangements and procedures to ensure that the self-defence groups did not commit excesses. The authorities told us in response that the self-defence groups came under the authority of the gendarmerie or the army, whichever post was nearer.

Some of those with whom we spoke told us that the Government needed to improve the ways in which it responded to terrorism and in which it dealt with charges that excesses are committed by security forces. We asked repeatedly about the arrangements in place for preventing excesses from being committed by these forces, about how they were implemented and with what results. For the most part we received only general answers. The authorities did, however, provide us with lists of around 140 cases in respect of which action had been taken against members of the security forces. We think that this is an area where the Government should be more open.

We met one of the self-defence groups when we visited the village of Igujdal in the Kabyle region. Officials, members of the self-defence group and the population of the village were present. In our discussion with members of the self-defence group, they informed us that they had had to face extremist violence for six years. Their village had been attacked and they had had to defend it with their own arms. After they had repulsed the attacks, the authorities had come and offered help. They had then organized a self-defence group in the village. The self-defence group was headed by a committee, and every night some members of the group kept guard over the village.

Asked whether they were united in agreement on the organization of the self-defence group, they answered in the affirmative. However, a member of the group said that whereas the vast majority had served on it for almost six years without any recompense, they had discovered that some members were being paid clandestinely by the authorities. When we asked how payments were made, the answer given was that they were made through the regional office. The President of the Regional Assembly, who was present, acknowledged that when the regional assembly had voted funds for the budget it had decided against a provision for such payments; however, the Minister of the Interior had reversed that decision.

Asked whether they felt that their security would be threatened if the self-defence groups were abolished, they answered that the villagers did not know what would happen if extremist violence continued. One speaker stated, 'We are fed up with extremist violence.'[8]

The 'eminent persons' report concludes with a direct recommendation to the Algerian authorities:

It is crucially important, at the same time, that the Government give serious consideration to programmes of social reform that would reduce the sense of hopelessness that we were told was very widespread among large sections of Algerian youth. Unless these pressing social problems are tackled urgently and effectively, Algeria could experience more social dislocations and tension in the future.[9]

There are a number of disquieting circumstances in the case of Algeria's terrorism. In the first place, the scale of violence has led to frenzied butchery as referred to above, where terrorist targeting has been superseded by wholesale slaughter chiefly of villagers. One estimate is that 75,000 lives have been taken during the period 1992–8 alone. Another 20,000 or so Algerians have 'disappeared'. Second, the Algerian Government has rebuffed all help from the outside for the homeless and the traumatised. As we have seen, a panel of United Nations visitors was allowed some freedom to survey and report, but Algeria has not been ready to facilitate monitoring of a destabilised situation and offers of help from any other quarter. Terrorism in Algeria is to be dealt with by Algerians alone. Third, and doing nothing to reduce the impression of failure on all sides, is the apparent existence of a logistical network of sympathisers among expatriate Algerians elsewhere in Europe, chiefly in France. Fourth, there is the determination of armed Islamic groups – much splintering has taken place – never to enter into dialogue or truce with the force for law and order in an all-out struggle against an illegitimate and secular Algerian government. Finally, there is the suspicion, aired in the Western press from time to time, that a defeatist government often turns a blind eye to the brutal activities of rebel groups. There is, indeed, much about the Algerian scenario that prompts the question whether we have here the twisted possibility that the means is becoming the end.

Something of a dramatic change seems evident in the instance of Algeria being more cooperative in its counter-terrorism approaches. The information below comes from the US Department of State's International Information Programs and is dated 28 April 2004:

Algeria continued to be a proactive and aggressive regional leader in the global Coalition against terrorism. Algeria's support of US counter-terrorism efforts on a case-by-case basis demonstrated its strong overall support of Coalition efforts against al-Qaida. In May 2003 Algerian security forces secured the release of 17 of the 32 European hostages kidnapped by a faction of the Salafist Group for Call and Combat (GSPC) in February and March [. . .] On 11 September 2003, the GSPC issued a statement declaring allegiance to several jihadist causes and leaders including al-Qaida and Usama Bin Ladin. Algerian law enforcement and security forces continued to pursue GSPC terrorist operatives disrupting their activities and capturing or killing several of them. Algeria participated in a pan-Sahel regional counter terrorism seminar in Bamako, Mali in October.

Algerian officials have stated that the number of active terrorists within the country has fallen from 25,000 in 1992 down to a few hundred today, due in large part to a series of successful offensives undertaken by Algerian security forces. Algeria has, in fact, made great strides toward eliminating terrorism in most parts of the country. The Algerian Government has focussed much of its counter terrorist efforts on the international level toward creating international consensus for an international convention against terrorism. This would include defining what constitutes an act of terror as distinct from an act of 'national liberation'. To this end, Algeria hosted a summit in September 2002 of the African Union (formerly the Organization of African Unity – OAU) aimed at ensuring the implementation of the OAU's 1999 Convention on the Prevention and Combating Terrorism. Algeria has strongly condemned acts of international terrorism.

With regard to enforcement and international agreements, Algeria has ratified all but one of the international conventions and protocols relating to terrorism. Algeria is gradually implementing, in its domestic legislative and regulatory systems, the requirements of these instruments, which may result – among other changes – in extradition of wanted terrorists.

Algeria was among the first states to criminalize the financing of terrorism. The Finance Act of 2003 expanded these efforts by lifting banking secrecy regulations and formalizing procedures that banks and insurance companies must follow in reporting suspicious transactions [. . .] In addition, Algeria is seeking an extradition treaty with the United States, and President Bouteflika has proposed an international treaty under UN auspices, that would replace the need for individual bilateral extradition treaties. Algeria is a party to 11 of the 12 international conventions and protocols relating to terrorism.[10]

As we have already seen there has been a general transformation into a more peaceful and stable Algeria. Terrorism, though, remains as something which has external perspectives. In today's parlance it is 'export-led'. What particularly troubles Algiers and its state neighbours is the recruitment, training, and exodus of would-be terrorists, mainly men, keen to join in with outlawed dissidents elsewhere. The intending militants feel alienated and disenfranchised in a Algeria unstable much more economically than politically. The messianic visions of Al-Qaeda and Osama bin Laden and in many cases the jihadic urges of Islam fuel their ardour. Some will even join the training camps in Afghanistan. They are ready to spill over from opposing their own army-baked administration to fixing on targets, in Europe and North America even, that coincide with Europhobian impulses.

In 2010 Algeria began to work alongside the African Union in an attempt to reduce the activist outflow. An African Centre for Study and Research in Terrorism located in Algiers, the capital, has put in hand research projects studying terrorist motivation and factors that trigger violence.

Algerians who embark for Europe will hope to make contact with like-minded individuals some of them expatriates precariously resident there. Possibly they will be able to locate a supply of arms and high explosive. Algiers has conferred on the subject of terrorist export with the European Union in Brussels. The United Kingdom, France, Spain, Italy and Germany all have deportation procedures arranged.

A consideration of Algerian terrorism ends on a rather worrying note. Egypt in early 2011 is flooded in anti-government protest and rioting. A good number of Arab scholars and journalist observers have predicted that reverberations of the happenings in Cairo and along the Nile will soon be felt dramatically in other Mediterranean lands.

Peru

CONSIDERED BY MANY to be the most dangerous and violent terrorist organisation in the world, the Shining Path group (Sendero Luminoso, or Sendero) of Peru is unique in many ways. After more than 20 years of violent disruption of civilised order, it remains today a menace to Peruvian society despite the attempts of successive governments to defeat it and despite a general revulsion at its message and its methods. Christened by Marxists as 'a shining path to the future', it represents for most Peruvians something that is archaic and destructive. Originating as an educational enterprise in the Indian-settled lands of Peru and directed by academics anxious to reinvigorate a community, it has twisted away into authoritarian rigidity, contemptuous even of the poor it set out to benefit. Insurgency, as a thrust for liberation – power to the people – is not hard to understand where it has arisen in many other countries: in Peru it has broken down into an illiberal, obsessive reliance on violence. There is a messianic insistence on the part of a leader and acolytes on power (only) for the Party. 'Everything other than power (for the Party) is illusion', is Sendero's apocalyptic claim. Peru has been lacerated by the toll of 18,000 dead, 3,000 'disappearances', and well over 2,500 terrorists captured. Violence continues. This case study will attempt to throw light on the origins and development of a vicious form of terrorism. Following that, the question will be put: what can contemporary Peru do about its 'time of terror', now more than two decades old?

THE ORIGINS OF SENDERO

A detailed and very systematic account of the birth and development of Peru's terrorism is provided by David Scott Palmer (1995). He isolates a number of key factors in the context surrounding the rise of Sendero.

First, we should use the label 'terrorist' advisedly – the group would disown it:

Sendero does not see itself as a terrorist organization, but rather as a revolutionary movement fully engaged since 1980 in a people's war. Actions that others call terrorist, Shining Path militants justify as a necessary part of a long-term struggle to take power in a country in which the élites have always violently exploited peasants and workers. By labeling the movement terrorist and by emphasizing counter-terrorism in its response, the government may well be playing into Sendero's hands. Its actions make the peasantry more fearful of authority; provoke local, national and international revulsion against the government; and foster conditions that contribute to the generalization of violence in Peru by provoking others on the Left and the Right to carry out their own terrorist actions.[1]

Second, Sendero began in a small provincial university in the 1960s:

[They were] one more group on the Marxist Left within a pluralistic Latin American academic context. In 1963 and 1964 there was no reason to believe it would ever be anything more than that. The activist young professor who led this particular 'study group', Abimael Guzmán Reynoso, was one of several at the university at the time who covered the political spectrum from radical to government supporters to conservative. Like the others, the university group identified with Guzmán, developed ties with national political movements in the 1960s and competed for influence in universities and unions around the country. Guzmán's organization was affiliated first with Castroite groups and then with the Maoist party breakaway after the 1963 Sino-Soviet split.

Sendero did not grow out of a national context of systemic and official repression or a systematic thwarting of opportunities for access to national politics. Shining Path in a real sense made the revolution in Peru. Inappropriate government responses then contributed to creating the conditions that Sendero had already posited to justify its actions. The terrorism engendered by Guzmán's organization was one component of its deliberate action to force a repressive state response that would alienate the populace and make them more receptive to Sendero's message; it was not a reaction to standing state-terrorism practices.[2]

Third, the place where the movement began was an inauspicious locale:

Sendero got its start in one of the most isolated and poorest regions of Peru, where central government access had been historically intermittent, communications difficult or virtually impossible, poverty generalized, and Indians and Indian communities very predominant (the region of Ayacucho).

Fourth, the university where it all started was launching an innovative extension movement (after closure for some years):

Most significantly, the University of Huamanga was designed to serve as a catalyst for social and economic change in the region by offering to local youth an array of specializations most needed to address the problems of the Ayacucho area. Instead of the traditional schools of law, medicine, and engineering, there were programs of education, applied anthropology, rural and agricultural engineering, and nursing. Instead of immediate specialization upon entering the university, students spent their first two years in 'basic studies', a type of interdisciplinary liberal arts education, to broaden their knowledge of the world around them. In another major departure from previous higher education practice in Peru, the faculty was contracted on a full-time basis with salaries set high enough during the first few years to attract some of the country's best academics.

Furthermore, a specific mission of the university was to reach out to the wider community with an array of services in health, education, and local development [. . .] the distinctive contribution of Peru's first 'new' university – active participation in various aspects of local development in one of the poorest regions of the country – was gradually infused with a radical, sectarian political content. Under the leadership of Professor Guzmán, first as education-program teacher, then as director of the teacher-training school, and finally as director of personnel of the university, the goal of forging an institution committed to the teaching and extension of Marxist principles in all of the university's activities was realised between the mid-1960s and the mid-1970s.[3]

Fifth, the region of Ayacucho had been a field for an array of government development programmes since 1963 that had materially improved the local economy, the infrastructure of settlement and housing, public health, and literacy. Inevitably, though, overlap in provision and some disagreement was sure to occur:

The growing sectarianism of the University of Huamanga's extension activities in the late 1960s and early 1970s was counterbalanced for a time by this array of government programs, with generally positive consequences for the local, mostly peasant population. University students were active with their political agenda in some communities, while the government and its affiliates were involved with theirs in many others. By the early 1970s, however, the dynamic shifted markedly, largely due to inappropriate new government programs. The resulting decline in the well-being of many Ayacucho peasants made it even harder for them to cope after the earlier improvement in their situation, however modest. It set the stage for Sendero more easily to expand its access to and influence with a peasantry increasingly disquieted, disillusioned, and discontented.[4]

Sixth, and again perhaps inevitably, the academics in the University of Huamanga began to pull away from any state enterprise towards their own ingrained philosophical stance that no better deal for the peasants could be anything less than a revolutionary transformation of society and that the ideology sustaining that must be principally Maoist:

They were advancing their Maoist vision of Marxism by action as well as by study instead of being satisfied by merely talking about it. The emerging conviction that they alone had discovered the keys to Marxist theory and practice by years of diligent study, conscientious application in the field, and the building of close ties between some Ayacucho peasants and the intellectual vanguard gradually produced a virtually unshakable faith in their uniqueness, even within the larger Marxist revolutionary community. They saw themselves, if you will, as the equivalent of the reborn Christian, the true carriers of the faith and, therefore, destined to eventual triumph no matter how daunting the odds.[5]

Seventh, the pinnacle of responsibility must be that of the leader (Guzmán):

Professor Guzmán went on to hold key positions in the university. The directorship of the teacher-training school permitted the introduction of a more partisan political criterion and the use of his considerable academic and personal skills to attract and radicalize many enterprising students of humble origins. The patronage and influence involved with this position enhanced his already demonstrated ability to attract a substantial number of the most able students and faculties in the university and commit them to his radical course.

Though already a Communist party member, part of his militancy and revolu-tionary conviction, like that of his closest circle, might have been derived from the impact of the poverty and isolation of Ayacucho, with which he had daily contact through his students, the extension programmes to outlying communities, and the city itself. Another key element is the personal magnetism Guzmán projected, his dedication to the study of Marxist writings, and his ability to synthesize his insights in a pedagogical way that made everything seem so clear and correct. In a university in which the student body had grown enormously by the early 1970s and in which most of the outstanding Peruvian intellectuals originally attracted to Huamanga had departed, Guzmán's talents stood out even more.[6]

Eighth, and very significantly, Sendero's initiators waited for the government to make a move. What turned out to be a long-term military regime (1968–80) focused on the need to change the country in order to save it:

The government [military, 1968–80] adopted an aggressive Third World stand. A number of large private corporations, both domestic and foreign-owned, were nationalized. The state expanded dramatically in size, from being one of the smallest in Latin America to one of the largest. The Marxist Left was legalized and legitimated, particularly labor unions, which proliferated at historically unprecedented rates even as the government was attempting to construct a competing social-property structure combining workers and management in industry, mining and agriculture. A major agrarian reform was undertaken, starting in 1969, that over the next ten years dramatically restructured Peruvian agriculture.

However well intended and however significant their benefits for some sectors of Peru's population, the changes introduced by the military government also facilitated the rise of Sendero in a number of ways. Encouraging Marxist groups provided alternatives to Shining Path on the Left, on the one hand, which proved to be a major obstacle to the advancement of Sendero's guerrilla war. But on the other hand, by letting the political dynamics within the universities largely take their own course in the 1970s, the military regime allowed the Sendero centre at the

University of Huamanga to become much stronger than it would have been had it been subject to closer review. The reformist phase of the military government, 1968–75, coincided with the period of Sendero control of the university and the concomitant expansion and deepening of radical study groups there.

In addition, the application of the agrarian reform in the Ayacucho area proved disastrous. This was mainly because this region had a much higher proportion of Indian communities to private haciendas than most other parts of the country, and the haciendas were both smaller and poorer for the most part. As a result, the agrarian reform broke down the old system without providing an alternative that would generate new resources in its place. Historic animosities and tensions, previously moderated by the weight of the status quo and government mediation, increased, and most of the peasantry wound up worse off as a result.

The overall effect was a substantial decline in production and peasant well-being in the area even as alternative avenues of recourse were also being reduced. Shining Path's ongoing activities in the communities became more and more important, partly as a direct consequence of the application of central-government policies in the Ayacucho area.

Sendero, given its years of preparation and expanding presence in the area, was particularly well positioned to take advantage of the government's problems and the growing distress of the local population. Sendero Luminoso's historic decision to launch the people's war in early 1980 was, thus, far from fortuitous.[7]

SENDERO'S STRATEGY

Scott Palmer has traced the evolution of Sendero's strategy as a response to the opportunities just outlined:

The Sendero strategy is, at root, a prolonged war of attrition over an increasing expanse of the national territory, a war that is intended to force the government to increase its expenditures on military actions, thus making it less and less able to satisfy basic popular demands. In addition, militants work to create an increasingly chaotic situation in the cities that authorities will eventually not be able to control. Over time, the population, especially the third that lives in Lima, will lose its capacity to cope and will see in Sendero 'the only authority capable of restoring order'. Military success is not Sendero's goal, according to some analysts. Rather, it is to paralyze the economy, destabilize the government, and force authorities into making unpopular decisions.

However, the organization does pursue a long-term military strategy designed to take military advantage of the government's growing inability to manage the country. Following Mao, Sendero's prolonged people's war is to develop in three strategic phases in its relation to government forces: defense, equilibrium, and offense. Each is determined by the relative size and operational capacity of Sendero forces vis-à-vis those of the government. In the 'strategic defensive' phase Sendero wages 'guerrilla war' with small armed units; in the 'strategic equilibrium' phase the armed struggle becomes a 'war of movements' with much larger military forces, up to battalion size, capable of engaging government forces on equal terms.

Given this strategic assessment, for Sendero the role of terrorism is central to attaining its objectives [. . .] Terrorism for Sendero has the specific objective of reducing the scope and capacity of government authority, thereby causing the centre to lose legitimacy in the minds of the population.

SENDERO'S ORGANISATION

To work towards its objectives, Sendero has constructed an elaborate political and military structure:

The basic unit is the cell. Each cell has five to nine members, including a leader, called the *responsable político*, as well as two explosive experts, a physical training instructor, and a person responsible for ideological training. Cells do not normally operate in their home regions, and members are not apprised of orders given to other cells, or of the identity of other members. Only one member, usually the *responsable político*, has direct communication with the next higher level of leadership. There is also a hierarchy of commitment and responsibility broken down into five distinct groups – premilitants, militants, military personnel, organizers, and leaders – of which the first three operate in separate cells. These cells are, in turn, coordinated by the leader of the subsector who answers to a zonal director responsible to a regional committee. Planning and coordination between zones is carried out by a coordination committee, ultimately answerable, along with its regional counterpart, to the National Central Committee, the ruling body of Sendero.

The country is divided by the Shining Path leadership into six regional committees. In the Metropolitan Region there are also four 'special squads' with specific and distinct duties related to 'annihilation', 'assault', 'containment', and 'razing', which carry out selected terrorist operations in a coordinated sequence.

Much of the responsibility for the selection and implementation of specific operations rests with the regional committees and their commanders, giving the organization a substantial degree of local autonomy. This means that the dynamic of Sendero activities in one part of the country may in many cases bear little relation to that in another. It also gives to the movement a flexibility that rests with those who presumably know more about local situations than those at the top.

Overall control remains firmly in the hands of the National Central Committee and, before he was captured, most particularly in those of Guzmán himself (whose *nom de guerre* was Comrade, then President Gonzalo). In addition, there are periodic party congresses (believed to have been held in 1979, 1982, 1985 and February 1988) to assess and critique the movement's progress.[8]

Sendero organisational capacities have been improved by carefully tailoring strategies to peasants' concerns about personal security and economic survival, a risky way of proceeding in view of government counter-insurgency and the fragile nature of any alliance with frightened *campesinos*. Cynthia McClintock (1984) has this to say about Sendero methods:

In tailoring its strategies to the peasants' concerns about personal security and economic survival, Sendero has been a much more calculating guerrilla organization than its predecessors. The movement has reduced its risks in various ways. Most Senderista militants are indigenous to the region and thus do not stand out physically from the rest of the population. Also, members' identities are carefully concealed. All members use aliases, and during terrorist activities they are masked with large woolen hoods. Few Senderistas know more than four others: each guerrilla cell has a maximum of five members; one is the leader, joining the committee at the next higher level.

Sendero has also reduced risks to the peasantry by restricting the presence of governmental authorities in the Ayacucho region. As early as the 1970s, officials who sought to enter Senderista territory were shot. Since 1980, Sendero has targeted civilian authorities assiduously. Between 1980 and August 1983, eighteen civilian officials were assassinated, and many more wounded or threatened. As a result, virtually none are left in the area.

Sendero has provided significant benefits to its supporters. Of course, it promised a better life. But the movement has also taken action – violent action – to benefit the peasants materially. After blacklisting relatively well-to-do landowners, shopkeepers, and intermediaries, and either killing them or causing them to flee, Sendero distributed their property among villagers, and cancelled debts to them. To recruits, Sendero has offered basic subsistence (probably possible as a result of Sendero's economic levies on the drug trade). Sendero's terrorist actions are also apparently perceived as daring by some Sendero recruits, a disproportionate number of whom are mere adolescents.

Since January 1983, with the onset of the government's counter-insurgency offensive, the political cost–benefit equation has blurred somewhat. Sympathy for Sendero has become much more dangerous. The toll of the struggle has mounted. By early 1984, the government admitted that about 3,500 people had been killed; 1,500 'disappeared'; and 4,000 had been arrested. Although the government reports most of the dead as Senderista militants, it is known that villages considered sympathetic to Sendero were raided and even bombed; Amnesty International and other independent observers believe that most of the dead were civilians.

Sendero's own actions during this period may have alienated the peasants. It has been reported that Sendero became more ruthless and wanton in its attacks, and that the guerrillas tried to reduce agricultural production and to stop weekly markets. Probably most important, Sendero was unable to protect its peasant allies from counter-insurgency offensives; when Ayacucho's pro-Senderista villages were assaulted, the guerrilla leaders fled elsewhere. At the same time, Sendero's ranks have become less disciplined and coordinated, and may even have been infiltrated by 'pseudo-Sendero' criminals.

Yet, it does not appear that the security forces won many peasants to their side during 1983. As we have seen, the subsistence crisis in the southern highlands was worsening at this time, and peasants were especially angry at the government. Moreover, the behavior of Peru's security forces in Ayacucho, like the behavior of most militaries amid such conflicts, was generally reported to be poor. The counter-insurgency personnel were regarded by many as arbitrary, brutal, and corrupt. While the security forces did attract some peasants to their side – most clearly, the

Iquichanos – economic inducements were rumored to be of considerable importance to the peasants' decisions.[9]

Scott Palmer has attempted an estimate of Sendero growth over the years 1980–92 and also a tally of reported incidents and casualties for which the guerrillas have been held responsible:

Although estimates vary widely, Sendero is believed to have grown from about 100 militants in 1980–81, to 3,000 to 10,000 in 1987–88, to 3,000 to 4,000 armed cadres, as many as 10,000 militants, and some 50,000 premilitants (sympathizers and occasional contributors or members of front organizations) by mid-1992. Guerrilla casualties, mostly Sendero, have been high: the number of 'presumed terrorists killed' through 1992 was 10,655. Among the casualties are many important Sendero figures, including entire cells, regional committee members, and members of the Central Committee. Even so, the number of reported incidents exceeded the thirteen-year average of 1,814 every year between 1985 and 1992. The ratio of deaths per 100 incidents also rose sharply during the four-year period beginning in 1989, even though both incidents and deaths declined by 30 per cent through 1992, after both hit historic highs of 2,779 and 3,745, respectively, in 1990. Over 62 per cent of all police and armed-forces political-violence casualties have occurred since 1989 (1,420 of 2,278). These gruesome data make abundantly clear that Sendero as an organization has clearly been capable of maintaining its destructive course in spite of increased pressure from government forces.[10]

THE GROWTH OF SENDERO EXPLAINED

Once again, Scott Palmer has listed what he considers are crucial factors, both inside and outside Sendero, which help to explain the movement's growth. First, there is the ideology:

A complete system of values and beliefs from a basic Marxist conception of the class struggle (Marx), the dictatorship of the proletariat (Lenin), rural revolution (Mao), and nationalistic domestic Third World revolution (Mariátegui), with Guzmán as the living guide. The Sendero ideology provides a recognizable alternative value system in a group-solidarity setting that, when combined with actions, enhances one's self-worth.

It may be compared with a religious experience, an alternative to Catholic or Protestant activism, because of which the individual 'convert' changes personal behavior and feels much better about himself or herself. It can also be an alternative to activity in a more moderate Marxist party or union, which Shining Path leaders view as a violation of radical orthodoxy because these parties or unions stoop to participating in what SL militants believe is a totally corrupt system. The myth of invincibility and of the inevitability of eventual triumph that SL training and flyers espouse appeals to an idealistic youth's inclination to self-sacrifice for the larger and longer cause. Purity is achieved and maintained by aloofness, discipline, intense training, spartan living, following the lead of the superior, and putting the movement ahead of self. Ideology is inculcated through the 'popular schools' or through militant teachers trained at the University of Huamanga while the education programme was under Sendero influence, teachers who are now working in other teacher-training programmes or in public schools [state schools].

Second, there is an array of supportive fronts and organisations:

[These are] designed to support and publicize Sendero activities at the grass roots or to defend, protect, and help militants or family members.

Third, recruitment of sympathisers has been taken in hand most efficiently:

From among the most able of these activist Sendero sympathizers can come the replacements for the premilitant and militant cells of the party. A third important factor, then, is that a recruitment hierarchy begun with this group of legal (until 1988) organizations at the base has been capable so far of keeping a flow into the clandestine cell structure and so on up the ladder to the top.

Fourth, a factor helping to explain why the movement was able to sustain its violent momentum through 1992 despite government pressures is the large number of women involved:

[Women appeared] at all levels of the organization, right up to the top positions in both the regional commands and the National Central Committee. Sendero's MFP [Women's Popular Movement] was formed in 1975. During the early 1980s all the known secretaries of the Lima Metropolitan Committee were women, along with at least half of the leadership of the other regional committees. Large numbers of women participate in Sendero's major military operations, and a woman is frequently charged with responsibility for delivering the fatal shot in the assassination-squad operations. In 1987 alone, 491 women of the 790 captured were charged with 'terrorist crimes'. It is speculated that women overcome the subordinate role and status historically ascribed to them in Peruvian society when they participate as equals in the Shining Path apparatus and lead many of its initiatives.

Fifth, Sendero has made a deliberate effort to recruit very young people as 'iron militants':

Militants in rural areas are often only fourteen or fifteen years old. The youth are perceived by the leadership as more idealistic and more easily formed. Without the outside commitments and experiences of their elders, they are also more easily and more completely committed to the Shining Path cause. Sendero thus secures strong and unquestioning supporters by attracting and educating them while their personal perceptions and values are still in flux. Older people are considered to be much harder to work with, less predictable in their commitment to the organization, and less trustworthy. Today's fifteen-year-old militant, if he or she survives, will be tomorrow's twenty-two-year-old commander, organizer, or leader.

Sixth, there is the overarching importance of the leader:

In Guzmán, the Communist Party of Peru had from 1963 until 1992 [his time of capture] a very special combination of intellectual and tactical ability. The image projected was that of an aloof but charismatic individual of remarkable powers of comprehension, interpretation, and capacity for prediction, totally sure of himself and of the rightness of the cause. His analysis of Peru and the revolution is considered by his colleagues to be the equal of the great Marxist leaders, Marx, Lenin, and Mao, and thus worthy of elevation as 'the fourth sword of Marxism'.

What impressed many observers of Sendero's development in Peru was the total dedication of members to the leader.

A seventh and final factor strengthening Sendero's operative capacity is a profitable connection with certain aspects of the drug trade in Peru and in particular:

[. . .] access since the mid-1980s to a portion of the significant resources generated by coca and cocaine paste production and trafficking, largely in Peru's upper Huallaga valley. Though not conclusively proved, it is believed that Sendero garnered a minimum of $10 million a year (some estimates range as high as $100 million) between 1987 and 1992 from 'taxes' on a large portion of the valley's 80,000 coca growers and from levies of up to $15,000 a flight on the mostly Colombian traffickers as they landed on the scores of clandestine runways in the valley to pick up their cargoes of cocaine paste. Many analysts have concluded that this income is used to pay salaries to Sendero militants, provide financial support to families of cadres killed in combat, and to pay for arrested comrades' jail maintenance and legal fees for court trials.[11]

In any case a key factor making for Sendero strength, apart from the secrecy of gathering and movement, was its self-sufficiency in deriving what was needed from the locality:

Food and sustenance came from the peasants who supported them, arms from the military and police by taking them, and dynamite from the mines and road building crews. In this fashion the revolution did not become dependent on outside sources, with their own agendas and objectives, which might subvert the local dynamic of the revolutionary process.[12]

Finally, in Peru, a progressive erosion in economic opportunities as a result of gross inflation, unemployment, and increasing poverty presented Sendero as a radical and desirable alternative to what was not being afforded by the state:

[There was] a certain appeal – employment, restoration of self-respect, a coherent, fully defined belief system, and specific solutions to Peru's current problems.[13]

SENDERO LUMINESCENCE BEGINS TO FADE

Despite the receptiveness of peasants, the *campesinos*, and of poor urban workers to the revolutionists' promises and plans, Sendero momentum has been uneven and halting since 1990, though its menace is always in the shadows. Frustration on all sides has led to much appalling violence. Mayors have been assassinated, government cooperatives destroyed, and *hacienda* (estate) owners and government officials ambushed, altogether a cycle of disruption seemingly without much object. Sendero appears to have taken little account of the insight and common sense of the *campesinos*, as a Peruvian sociologist, Carlos Izaguirre, commented in 1996:

Guzmán underestimated the resilience of the survival mechanisms that the Peruvian people have developed over decades, and the faith in progress that underscores their Sisyphean efforts. He failed to appreciate the true dimensions of this age-old game of resistance and adaptation, of scepticism and expectations, and of simultaneous rejection and acceptance of the rules and the predominant institutions.

The idea of radical rupture is profoundly alien to Peruvians. Shining Path sought to implant it through the use of terror. They killed hundreds of *campesinos* for bettering themselves as traders and sellers, for serving as state officials, for voting in elections, and for being mayors or grassroots leaders opposed to the armed struggle. They tried to boycott elections, development projects, and the markets where *campesinos* sold their products. They wanted to turn every protest march into a general 'armed strike'. They tried to impose the fiction of their own authorities and popular committees. Shining Path had some success, but it was precarious. In the end, they invited military repression and intervention in the areas where they organized.

In this way, the spiral of terror grew from both sides. But the pragmatism of the *campesinos* eventually led them to forge an alliance with the army, since it had both more power and the representation of the state. Despite the military's record of brutality, tens of thousands of *campesinos* began forming, under military tutelage, civil-defense patrols to fight off Shining Path.

Shining Path's insurrection thus became a revolution of *campesinos* against *campesinos* – a popular war against the people. Shining Path had most appeal among social groups located on the periphery of productive activity: students, teachers, unemployed young people from the shanty towns. With this membership, Shining Path developed more as a sect than as a movement with a popular base of support. This lack of consistent social support would prove to have dire consequences for the Party.[14]

GOVERNMENT RESPONSE TO SENDERO TERRORISM

Between 1989 and 1992 Sendero stepped up its terrorist activity in and around the Peruvian capital, Lima, badly shaking the government's confidence, as Izaguirre relates:

212 SIXTEEN TERRORISM CASE STUDIES

During this same period, after several years of striking out blindly against the population, the state began to reformulate its counter-insurgency strategies. Even though the police and the military did not coordinate their efforts – indeed, there was a great deal of rivalry between the two institutions – these shifts hastened Shining Path's demise. Through stepped-up intelligence efforts, the police were able to arrest a number of key intermediate-level leaders, weakening Shining Path's internal organization.[15]

Government response to the challenge of political violence and terrorism begun by Sendero and emulated to a lesser extent by other groups has taken a variety of forms since 1980. The haemorrhaging of economic growth, hyperinflation, spiralling unemployment and industrial strikes all diverted ministerial attention in the earlier years away from acts of violence and denied the security battalions the personnel and funds they needed. Counter-terrorist measures lacked force and coordination and were marked by indiscriminate search and arrest, summary interrogation, even torture – means of repression that often led to numerous casualties among bystanders.

By 1985 the Peruvian government was rooting out internal problems of corruption, maladministration and human rights violations within its own security department. A National Agency against Terrorism was set up, a state of emergency was proclaimed and intelligence work was made more sophisticated. In 1990 a political newcomer and professor of mathematics, Alberto Fujimori, surprised Peru by winning the presidency. Fujimori introduced a neoliberal reformist programme and a determined long look at the nature and extent of terrorism. By 1992 Guzmán himself had been arrested, along with 300 sector leaders in that year alone. Two years later, from his cell in a specially built impregnable prison, Guzmán put a peace proposal to Fujimori. There might have been some negotiating room here had not the leaders of Sendero still at large vociferously proclaimed their disassociation from any peace feelers and cessation of their terror campaign. The only course the government felt feasible was to try to turn the edge of terrorist ardour and recruiting by enlisting the support of *campesinos* for a policy of rural reinvestment and land reform. Security in the towns and the countryside was to be improved through mustering civil-defence patrols made up of volunteers and military advisers. Measured by the number of incidents and deaths, terrorism began to wane after 1995. Yet, as Scott Palmer sees it, the government of Peru has, year by year, frequently played into the hands of Sendero's strategists:

First it gave the guerrilla cadres time and space to grow. Then it applied military force in an often indiscriminate manner, thus alienating local, usually peasant populations. When the government finally began to get things right on counter-insurgency policy in 1985 and 1986, the momentum could not be sustained, due to disastrous macroeconomic policies that impoverished millions with runaway inflation. Government human rights violations multiplied as well. The drastic economic measures required to undo the damage at the macro level further increased human misery at the micro level, besides virtually guaranteeing two or three years more without economic growth.

Sendero took full advantage of the opportunities presented it. They expanded the organization and recruitment, especially in Lima. They increasingly invoked city-wide armed strikes in urban centres around the country. They continued to damage the country's infrastructure as well as, and sometimes simultaneously, set off car bombs for maximum psychological effect. And their agenda of highly selective assassinations and intimidation, in Lima shanty towns especially but also in other sensitive locations around the country, moved inexorably forward.

The result of government errors, on the one hand, and Sendero's adroitness, on the other, was, not surprisingly, an erosion over time of government capacity and legitimacy, particularly in those provinces and urban slum areas where the Shining Path converts had been most active. As the central government became more and more bogged down by severe economic constraints, more and more opportunities opened up for Sendero to advance, even though the guerrillas themselves lacked the installed capacity to take full advantage of them. Government authorities were further hampered by continuing the long-standing practice of focusing attention on the provinces, which frequently resulted in inappropriate or even counter-productive policy formulation and implementation. Bureaucratic rivalries among different government agencies and political parties that put narrow partisanship and short-term gain above the country's interests complicated the process still further.

Democracy should have been a major bulwark against the advance of Shining Path in Peru, but as it was practised in the 1980s, it contributed significantly to the generalization of violence and to its own erosion.[16]

After 20 years of furious campaigning in Peru, that bright, articulate message, Sendero Luminoso, Shining Path, is in most respects a dark and dangerous quagmire. Its premises and promises have opened few doors and slammed most of them shut in the estimated 80 per cent of Peru in which its desperate advocates operate. Terror and intimidation are the chief mechanisms to manipulate for influence and control, mechanisms that are counter-productive and destructive. Sendero, in common with other terrorist factions (especially in Germany and Italy), has to a significant extent become a prisoner of its own ideology. It was in 1996 that Izaguirre, with a sociological perspective, detected a movement ideologically pinioned and divided:

The cycle of political violence begun in 1980 came to an end during the brief period framed by two watershed events: Guzmán's arrest in September 1992, and the declaration by Shining Path leaders still at large of their opposition to Guzmán's peace proposal in February 1994. 'It is a norm of the Communist movement that Party leadership cannot be exercised from prison', said the dissident faction in direct allusion to Guzmán. The play's final scene is the division of Shining Path into Guzmán's pro-peace faction, and the faction that continues to wage war.

Both factions are trying to resolve the same problem: how to keep Shining Path alive and relevant after the many defeats the Party has suffered. For Guzmán, saving the Party requires halting all sabotage and guerrilla activities and engaging in unarmed political activities for several years. Those who oppose him, led by Oscar Ramírez Durand ('Comrade Feliciano'), believe the Party's only salvation lies in continuing its armed activities, though with less intensity than before, and emphasizing the reconstruction of its grassroots cells via the classic ant-like work of its clandestine militants.

Despite their opposing prescriptions for action, both sides perceive that Shining Path has entered a new phase of its existence. Guzmán has even said so explicitly in his new manifestos. Feliciano and his comrades, by reducing their activity and prioritizing underground political activity, recognize implicitly that times have changed. Aware that Shining Path has lost the leading role that it held in the early 1990s, both groups share the common goal of remaining in the wings, like understudies, in anticipation of better times.

It is unlikely that Shining Path will disappear from Peru's political stage any time soon. But given the reduced size of both factions, the violence will be low-key and will take place mainly in parts of Peru that are of little political or economic importance, such as shanty towns in Lima and towns in the jungle or Andean highlands.

Shining Path is no longer proclaiming – to audiences in Peru and the rest of the world – the existence of their popular committees or their impending overthrow of the state. Rather, they are hoping to exercise a combination of political hegemony and terror at the local level. Occasionally, they will carry out a spectacular act of sabotage or ambush a military patrol. These activities will not endanger the stability of the state or even cause foreign investors to leave Peru in search of safer pastures. The principal aim of such activities is to remind everyone of their continued presence on the political stage. Shining Path poses few risks to Peru's stability in the short term, but the risks may grow as time marches on.[17]

Are there any certainties at all as to security in contemporary Peru? Scott Palmer's conclusion in 1995 is sombre and entirely relevant today:

Since 1980, terrorism has become institutionalized in Peru, some without question state-sponsored, but mostly guerrilla-provoked. The consequences in human and material terms have been devastating for society and the country at all levels. Sendero may not win, but through its systematic, selective, and methodical terrorism, Peru is certainly the loser.[18]

Since defeat 10 years ago, Shining Path has been reduced to a rump faction of 200 or so, largely confined to jungle regions in eastern Peru. Elsewhere, sympathisers may resort to isolated car bombings in the capital, Lima, or assassinate police officers and authority figures from time to time. A government broadcast in June 2006 viewed the terrorists, once so powerful, as no longer a political group, 'but a band of thugs at the service of drug-trafficking organisations and coca farmers'. The latter, certainly, had a virulent grievance against Lima seeking to eradicate their crops.

More ominously, several thousand former rebels have been released from prison under presidential amnesty since 2005. All too frequently, they intone the old mantra of 'Elections, no, People's war, yes', the slogan that launched the 'people's war' two decades ago.[19]

As in Colombia, the US government is advancing considerable funding to endow a coupled programme of security improvement and socio-economic reform. Washington and Lima view with concern the unquenched luminescence of Sendero Luminoso.

While Shining Path's malevolent activities have somewhat decreased mainly as a result of more sophisticated police work and army patrolling there is much concern in Lima about wide-ranging terrorist involvement in narco-terrorism. Four powerful insurgent groups are reckoned to have almost unlimited finances resourced via money laundering, protection rackets and corrupt market manipulation. Some of the drug barons certainly have agencies in Colombia. The Peruvian guerrillas, never too obviously an ideological movement, are closer than ever to rapacious wheeling and dealing among coca farmers, drug handlers, and certain transport firms.

In January 2011 there began a sustained debate in the press and government and legal circles as to whether contemporary legislation about narcotics was at all tight enough or even sufficiently discerning.[20]

Colombia

B ETWEEN 1946 AND 1966 the Republic of Colombia was the scene of one of the most intense and protracted instances of widespread civilian violence in the history of the twentieth century. Known in Colombia simply as *La Violencia*, this episode claimed perhaps 200,000 lives, including 112,000 at its peak in 1948–50. Colombia, later, in 1960, had the highest violent death rate in the world.

The Colombian case study differs from the others in that here we have an entire nation torn by the horrors of 20 years of political strife. Nobody was able to escape the tensions and dangers. More than in other Latin American states seared by violence, such as Peru and Argentina, in Colombia terrorism took hold of all sides of the conflict. The state of Colombia has recovered from two decades of turmoil and there is an appreciable measure of reconciliation among those formerly at each other's throats. Unhappily, though, contemporary Colombia is struggling with an immense drug problem of production, addiction and trafficking – with, of course, its own component of violence.

This case study begins by examining the context within which protest, conflict and violence built up. Some explanations will be offered for causes and development of the terror, particularly in regard to the struggle with guerrilla forces. There will eventually be a close look at the peace process as it cautiously began and as it has gathered credibility and reliability. What this case study will not do – the point is stressed in conclusion – is to settle back on simplistic, cause-and-effect discussion. Colombia's terror was always too multifaceted for that. For the reader the facts of this terror will beg a good number of questions.

THE COUNTRY OF COLOMBIA

Colombia is the fourth largest of the Latin American countries and the third most populous. It is the only one to have coasts on the Caribbean and the Pacific; otherwise it is landlocked with Panama to the north-west, Venezuela to the north-east, Brazil to the south-east, Peru to the south, and Ecuador to the south-west. There are 31 million Colombians, of whom 58 per cent are *mestizos* (mixed Spanish and Indian), 20 per cent owe their origin to other parts of Europe, and 14 per cent are *mulatto* (black–white mixture). Spanish is the language of the majority and 96 per cent declare allegiance to Catholicism. Seven out of ten live in towns, the largest of which are Bogotá (the capital and a megacity of five million people), Medellin, Cali and Barranquilla. Even so, there are vast areas of rainforest (*selvas*) and plains (*llanos*). Colombia is rich in natural resources, such as hardwood forest, gold, precious stones, petroleum and coal. Agriculture provides a living for 30 per cent of those employed, 24 per cent are in manufacturing, and 17 per cent are in commerce. Great strides have been made in building a diverse and vibrant economy despite the boiling over of social conflict for many years.

TWO COLOMBIAS: ONE TERROR

Colombia, as a context for sustained political violence, is often described as having two faces – the 'formal' Colombia, the constitutional state, and the 'informal' Colombia, a 'real' and very different polity.

Jenny Pearce (1990) has written at length about the two-in-one labyrinth that Colombia presents:

There is a Colombia which is constitutional and legalistic, which boasts all the trappings of a modern polity. This is the Colombia which is often described in the world's press as the most democratic country in Latin America. But there is also a 'real' Colombia of the people, where the rule of law barely holds, deprivation and poverty are the norm and democracy is just a word on a historic document.

Loyalty to two traditional political parties for many years was the link between the two worlds; the people fought out the bitter party conflicts on behalf of the ruling oligarchy and their own allegiances to the two parties which divided that oligarchy were sealed through generations of bloody vendettas. A tradition of party political violence was established which culminated in the late 1940s and 1950s in the last great civil war between the parties: *La Violencia*. The final phase of *La Violencia* was one of social banditry and lasted until 1965.[1]

The same élite that had been in charge before *La Violencia* emerged, in full control, after it. The challenge from below had been defeated before it took hold, and this enabled the economy to function and prosper through most of it. The peasants, meanwhile, rather than concentrate on their own class interests which might have turned them against the ruling élite, instead killed each other on its behalf, fighting its party battles and other parochial conflicts that divided them from one another.

No expression of social conflict was permitted outside the control of the two traditional parties. The state could play no role in the mediation of such conflicts and, indeed, had no independent role of its own to enable it to look after the interests of society as a whole.[2]

The economy came to mirror the duality of the political order, between the formal and the real.

At one level it modernised over the years and enjoyed growth rates which made it one of the most successful examples of economic management in Latin America. At the other level, a 'people's economy' emerged, in which the majority of the population live and work, the so-called 'informal sector'. These two economies are by no means separate, but are distinct in many ways.[3]

The formal economy resembled that of every other civilised and sophisticated state with its bourse, its banks and insurance firms, its real estate, and its industrial and service sectors. This was the arena of pensioned employment, career-building, management strategies, and a wide array of responsibilities, loyalties and reasonable expectations. It was not the arena, generally, of hire-and-fire, of under-employment and unemployment, of seething conflict and proneness to violence. The contrast with the informal sector was gross and unsettling, in the view of Pearce:

The informal economy covers a wide range of activities, both legal and illegal, all unregulated by the state. By 1984, 56.6 per cent of employment in the urban areas was in the informal sector, involving 3.5 million people compared with 2.7 million in the formal sector.

The informal economy includes workers who earn their living on the streets doing odd jobs, washing cars, shining shoes, collecting rubbish for resale, the hopeful providers of services who will leap out at a traffic light to wipe car windscreens. It includes casual sellers of artefacts, cigarettes, newspapers and flowers and also prostitutes and thieves.

Also belonging to the informal sector are those employed in small enterprises outside the ambit of government control and regulation. About half the construction industry is in the informal sector. All are characterised by the precarious nature of existence. Long-term employment contracts, employment- and social-protection schemes, safety and health provisions are all absent, as is the payment of taxes to the authorities.

The sector operates at the margin of the formal economy of modern capitalist production and state provision.

But the low incomes generated in the sector make it difficult for informal workers to earn enough to provide the basic elements of life.[4]

The formal economic realm was the place of power, affluence and privilege, largely town centred, with a central core that remained exclusive and unready to admit any reform. Even so, in the Colombia of the 1950s there was a large increase in the 18–35 age-group, with growing uncertainties, a scramble for jobs, and much dissatisfaction. The frontiers of the informal economy encompassed thousands of acres devoted to large-scale beef-raising and coffee-growing where the *campesinos*, peasants, eked out a life of grinding poverty. Illegal activities flourished – embezzlement, bribery, tax evasion, smuggling for a black market, petty theft and drug trading. Characteristics of urban squalor on the other hand were appalling slums, delinquency, prostitution, malnutrition and the scrambling for survival of the *gaminismo*, the street children in their ragged thousands. As was to be expected here was the seedbed of eventual rebellion.

If this was the nature of the 'real' Colombia several decades ago, a third sector of the economy, very much an informal one, has developed, namely the narcotics sector. By the late 1970s marijuana was going out of fashion to be replaced by cocaine. Growing the coca leaf (imported from Peru and Bolivia) represented for the peasant an undreamed-of opportunity to improve his livelihood. The opportunities were a magnet for thousands of unemployed to leave the capital, Bogotá, and other cities; there were opportunities also for a few with cash and little conscience to 'muscle in' and amass great fortunes as 'drug barons'.

Thus, for Pearce, there are two Colombias, for most of half a century a society cut down the middle with discordant elements manipulating for survival and space and with a succession of governments, twin party or coalition, quite unable to adapt to destabilising circumstances or handle processes of inevitable change. *La Violencia* was inescapable.

LA VIOLENCIA: SOME EXPLANATIONS

Paul Oquist (1980) takes a broad view of this phenomenon and argues that there are clear social–structural explanations – at least four chief ones – namely, political rivalries, socio-economic causes, institutional aspects and psychological/cultural factors. In outline they are as follows.

First, political discord:

The 1946–66 violence occurred in a country whose historical context includes the Spanish conquest, the wars for independence, and the multiple civil wars that took place throughout the nineteenth century. Since the 1850s, social violence in Colombia has been closely associated with partisan rivalries between the two traditional political parties – the Liberals and the Conservatives – but, although party competition is an important element in the analysis, it cannot be stated that this factor alone caused the violence.

The immediate twentieth-century antecedents of the 1946–66 violence stem from the electoral violence that surrounded the 1922 presidential campaign, the transference of the presidency from the Conservative to the Liberal party in 1930, and the various manifestations of socioeconomic violence in the 1920s, 1930s and 1940s.

Forced abandonment of agricultural plots and coerced land sales at under-value prices spurred the political conflicts. Violence reappeared in 1946 during the electoral campaign. However, the most intense violence centered precisely in those areas that had been most affected by the partisan violence of the 1930s.

This local partisan violence soon became the overriding national political issue. Charges and countercharges of responsibility for the killing escalated the friction between the two political parties. An accelerated rate of inflation and numerous strikes also contributed to the general social unrest.

In addition to the partisan battles, agrarian conflicts of various types, struggles for control of local power structures, revenge raids, and banditry were common.

The social fabric of Colombia seemed to have disintegrated. Although the civil wars of the nineteenth century with their positional, battlefield warfare carried high death tolls, they were not comparable to the horror and lack of security for the entire population that resulted from decentralized battles, raids, and killings in village after village, year after year.[5]

After the failures of government coalitions and the ever-present threat of takeover by a military junta, a *Frente Nacional* (National Front) administration was formed in 1958 ostensibly to try to bring an end to the ferocity of *La Violencia*. The exhaustion and revulsion felt by Colombians had to give way to agrarian reform, innovative development in the towns, a wider measure of political freedom and 10 per cent of the state budget to go to state educational projects. Liberals and technocrats in government would work in harness with organised labour. The dream, though, failed. The feud between rival interests, basically a defensive posturing, never vanished. It was a sour feeling of stalemate – *plus ça change*, as Oquist recalls:

Some important party leaders sought continued coalitions to defend basic common interests of the dominant classes and/or to avoid a civil war. The dynamics of party competition proved unabatable, however, and the party struggle continued at all levels of society.

In sum, a division in Colombia's *clase dirigente* ('ruling class') occurred as a result of nonpluralistic, mutually exclusive partisan politics under socioeconomic circumstances where neither side would admit banishment from state power. The result of this conflict was a partial collapse of the state in a society with numerous potential social conflicts. The deflation, inefficacy, and, in some cases, absence of state power led to the exacerbation of these conflicts, and frequently to their violent expression. Many of these conflicts were of an interclass nature. This combination of different social processes in *La Violencia* accounts in good measure for the intensity of the phenomenon. Its geographical distribution was generally concentrated in those areas in which there occurred both the partial collapse of the state and the maturation of social contradictions into acute conflicts.[6]

Second, Oquist considers possible socio-economic causes of the prelude to communal violence. Again, he discerns an element of defensiveness:

Antireformist forces used violence as an instrument of repression to the point that it became institutionalized. Certain sectors of the Liberal party responded to this violence in an attempt to topple the reactionary groups from power. This intraélite conflict was accompanied by a revolutionary popular uprising without ideology that proved to be emotional, cruel and unorganized.[7]

Oquist quotes a Colombian sociologist probing social causes and seeing:

[. . .] violence as the product of a counterrevolutionary strategy elaborated by the dominant groups in Colombian society to crush a mass movement that threatened the basic legitimacy of the prevailing institutions.

The dismemberment of popular movement took place in three stages:

1   The probing of the capacity to resist followed by an offensive against the most powerful unions, and popular organizations.
2   A systematic offensive by means of the massive unleashing of violence and an implacable annihilation of popular leadership, including the assassination of Gaitán [a prominent Liberal].
3   The establishment and consolidation of oligarchical support structures with the application of a formula of economic liberalism and political absolutism.[8]

Fundamentally, then, as one Colombian understands it, La Violencia incorporated three basic types of violence:

(1) the counterrevolutionary violence that used the state as the prime instrument of repression; (2) survivals of the traditional confrontations between Liberals and Conservatives; and (3) a confusing, conflictive process of combined popular resistance and social decomposition.[9]

Violence, to become terroristic in time, broke out into general sectarian warfare, as a Colombian sociologist view it:

The political violence seems to have hidden class struggles but the latter, in reality, often assumed the form of the former [. . .] The violence in the cities and in the rural regions might have had electoral ends in the beginning; but later the ends became more complex, and in this complexity it was possible to perceive, in some provinces, the war of the landlords against the sharecroppers, squatters, and poor peasants, and, in the agrarian exploitations of the capitalist type, the persecution of the owners against the labor organizations.[10]

Third, there are institutional aspects leading to grave disequilibrium:

[These were] attributable to an entire series of dysfunctional institutions. The roles of the society were deformed as part of widespread structural cleavages in Colombian society. For example, the police, rather than being the guardians of order, became the agents of disorder and crime.

The principal dysfunctions were the following: impunity in the judicial institutions, poverty and lack of land in the economic institutions, rigidity and fanaticism in the religious institutions, and ignorance in the educational institutions.[11]

Fourth, for Oquist there are psychological/cultural factors. Many who follow this line of consideration, Colombians and foreigners, regard *La Violencia* as an irrational phenomenon with a degree of sensationalism, perhaps, in their putting of the case where such terms are used as frustration or uninhibited political passion or a need for aggression or status deprivation. Oquist is guarded in applying such concepts as causative factors:

Violence may be either rational or irrational. Violence is considered rational if it is a means utilized in the pursuit of potentially realizable goals. Conversely, 'irrational violence' is physical aggression or the credible threat of the same that is not oriented towards a goal, but that has violence itself as a goal (i.e. as in the case of psychological satisfaction derived from violence), or that does not have the potential to achieve the goal in question. Examples are a senseless killing, the elicitation of sadistic, maso-chistic, or cathartic satisfactions, violence employed in the pursuit of an impossible goal, or violence by which it is impossible to achieve a realistic objective. In sum, the violent conduct of psychotics, sadists, or *quijotes* ('rebels motivated by illusory causes') with tenuous relationships to reality constitutes 'irrational violence'.

Most instances of widespread, protracted social violence are not characterized by irrational violence. However, irrational violence does tend to accompany rational violence and increase in intensity with it.

In Colombia, the sociopolitical processes known as *La Violencia* were accompanied by much irrational violence. This is hardly surprising considering the intensity of *La Violencia* and the degree to which the repressive capacity of the state was deflated. [. . .] The irrational aspects of the phenomenon do not satisfactorily explain its origins or its intensity or its geographical distribution. To achieve an explanation of widespread, protracted, social violence, one must refer to the *social conflicts* that underlie such conduct and to the factors that condition whether a given conflict becomes violent or not.[12]

In Oquist's mind, whatever the significance of the factors outlined above, prime responsibility for Colombia's slide into chaos fell on the failure of its legitimate government:

A partial collapse of the state occurred as a result of intense partisan conflicts. The political élite was divided to such an extent that state authority was deflated. This took place at the national, regional, and local levels. It is this partial collapse of the state that explains the nearly simultaneous evolution of numerous conflicts into violence. This dovetailing of various physically coercive struggles is what in turn explains the intensity of *La Violencia*. The duration is in part attributable to the difficulty of reasserting state authority in some areas.[13]

THE COURSE OF VIOLENCE

By 1950 a full-scale civil war was being fought in some of Colombia's provinces. There were Liberal guerrillas in the field taking on the left wing, there were

Communist guerrillas fighting Liberals and anyone suspected of capitalist and entrepreneur leanings, and there were Government counter-guerrillas mopping up those branded as 'disloyal'. On the peripheries of action there were bandits out for spoil. From time to time there would be a truce agreed and a short ceasefire. So fierce and frenzied was the momentum of violence that the age-old arguments about cattle pasturing and access to water and trails were now settled not with fist and stick but with arson and gelignite. Even the priests, it was said, carried pistols to dissuade the more aggressive members of their congregation. The nation was steadily engulfed with violence – the *La Violencia* that was to last a good 15 years until its exhausted slackening in 1965.

The relentless, sad cycle of terroristic conflict has been chronicled and examined by Pearce, who divides it into two phases, namely 1949–53 and 1958–65:

La Violencia 1949–53

The first phase of *La Violencia* was its most violent. Three-quarters of its estimated 200,000 victims were killed between 1948 and 1953, more than 50,000 in 1950 alone. In these years the violence was generated mostly in the name of the parties; rural bosses mobilised their peasant clients in bloody vendettas against neighbouring villages; Liberal landowners organised peasant–guerrilla armies which engaged the Conservative forces of the state in 'hit and run' actions. A great mobilisation of peasant armies took place, with an inherent ambivalence. While they were led politically by sectors of the dominant classes through the traditional parties, the military leadership was in the hands of the peasants themselves.

Direct confrontation was rare; Liberal guerrillas carried out an act of sabotage and revenge exacted on any Liberal household. Paramilitary groups of civilians and police, such as the *aplanchadores*, the fearsome *chulavitas* and the infamous *pájaros* or assassins, carried out indescribable acts of violence which Liberals met with atrocities of their own. Decapitations, mutilations, sexual crimes and, with them, robbery and destruction of homes and land characterised *La Violencia* and earned it its name. Criminality and senseless violence intermixed with political and social violence. The barbarism unleashed was multifaceted and defies easy explanation. The army, reflecting the weakness of the state, was caught unprepared to deal with the guerrillas, but by 1951 it, too, was drawn into the conflagration.

La Violencia by no means affected all of rural Colombia but was confined to certain regions. It affected the coffee-producing regions with particular intensity, as well as Valle, the *minifundia* areas of Boyacá and the Santanderes (which had long histories of partisan violence) and also the cattle lands of the eastern *llanos*.

Within the coffee-producing departments, the region of Cundinamarca and Tolima became the centre of brutal partisan violence, as well as the place where landowners settled old scores against the local peasantry who had organised against them in the 1930s. The *chulavitas* spread terror and forced thousands to flee to the south of Tolima.

Elsewhere in the coffee-producing departments, complex developments took place. Many richer landowners chose to absent themselves. Liberals often fled on receiving the sinister *boleteo*, warning them to leave the region or face death.

Thousands of poorer peasants, as well as richer landowners, were dispossessed of their land or forced to sell it very cheaply. Land changed hands in a variety of ways; peasants were dispossessed by other peasants as a result of party conflict and some peasants gained access to land abandoned by landowners as well as *vice versa*.[14]

In June 1959 a *coup d'état* erupted. A period of military rule seemed to many to be the only way of putting out the blaze and doing something to retrieve social and political order. Almost predictably and in devious ways the generals moved swiftly to break up the urban political movement and to curb independence of political expression. Relenting their harshness a little, the army command offered an amnesty to all past dissidents save for those known to be Communist. Again predictably, a measure such as this brought few rebels out of their sanctuaries; it was cynically received by townspeople and by *campesinos* being 'pacified' by riflemen and curfew. Nor were the ultra-conservatives in the army and police pleased at magnanimity, which they saw as weakness.

La Violencia 1958–65

The formation of the *Frente Nacional* (mentioned on p. 183) as a life-support system did not achieve its objectives, as Pearce relates:

Although the formation of the National Front officially brought *La Violencia* to an end, it did in fact continue in a different form, namely that of banditry, in which over 18,000 people lost their lives, 75 per cent of them in the departments of Tolima, Valle and Viejo Caldas.

The bandits of this second phase of violence were peasants who had been called guerrillas in its first phase, but who lost their political legitimacy in the new era. These bandit/guerrillas had either not accepted the amnesty offered by Rojas, or had done so and found themselves still under attack by the army. They had subsequently refused to accept either the amnesty offered by the National Front in 1958 or the party pact and peaceful coexistence which was then established.

They were joined by large numbers of revenge-seeking adolescents who had grown up during the terror and seen their homes burned down and their families brutally murdered. No longer dependent on national political leadership, they now looked to local bosses who began to use them for local political purposes. Banditry flourished in areas where official terrorism had been widespread but where the peasants had not developed their own forms of resistance – in the north of Valle, north of Tolima and in Viejo Caldas, mostly coffee-growing areas where small and medium property coexisted with large estates. Here there were ample mountainous regions in which to hide and rich pickings from the estates from which to live. Some day-labourers on the estates were 'part-time' bandits.

The local peasants gave active or passive support to the bandit chiefs. 'Chispas', 'Capítan Venganza', 'Desquite', 'Sangrenegra', 'Pedro Brincos' and others were mythical and heroic figures. Once in a while the bandits would identify with the social antagonisms of rural Colombia, as, for instance, when they even began to attack property belonging to landowners in their own party. Although potentially a radical social force, they mostly remained loyal to their Liberal Party affiliation. Their enemies were peasants of the other party as well as landowners, and they carried out violence against both. They accepted the patronage of local party bosses while standing out against the national political project of the ruling class.[15]

The government's failing grip on the security situation induced them to deploy all available resources in a counter-insurgency offensive. They appealed to Washington for aid and secured $60 million and useful equipment for dealing with riots. The United States had been grateful that during the Korean War of 1950–3 Colombia had set Latin America an example by sending a well-armed brigade to General Macarthur's expeditionary force. Thus, they willingly despatched 'security advisers' to Bogotá and there they established the first counter-insurgency training school in Latin America. Counter-insurgency met terror with terror. There was now every reason to expect a guerrilla struggle of remorseless intensity.

GUERRILLA STRUGGLES

A detailed account of Colombia's guerrilla struggle is to be found in Pearce. She divides her account once more into two phases, the generation of 1964–mid-1970s and the generation of 1974–82:

The first generation 1964–mid-1970s

Only since the 1960s have independent guerrilla movements [the FARC (*Fuerzas Armadas Revolucionarias de Colombia*, the Revolutionary Armed Forces of Colombia) and the ELN (*Ejercito de Liberacion Nacional*, the National Liberation Army)] begun to challenge the domination of the traditional parties and propose an alternative structure of power.

The rupture with past struggles was incomplete. At least one guerrilla movement, the FARC, emerged directly out of peasants' experiences in certain regions during *La Violencia*. A handful of legendary guerrillas/bandits participated in the new movements – Fabio Vásquez, a founder of the ELN, was not the only guerrilla leader whose family had been wiped out during *La Violencia*.

But the new movements were primarily children of their times. As elsewhere in Latin America, but perhaps more so in Colombia where guerrilla warfare had been going on for ten years, the Cuban revolution made a big impact on the small group of left-wing students. They were impressed by the way in which, in little over two years, a tiny band of guerrillas had taken power in a small Caribbean island, and the belief that a revolutionary situation existed in Colombia soon took root among the urban radicals. Just under half the population still lived in rural areas and most believed that the revolution would start there.

Political exclusion had contributed to the rise of armed organisations that refused to form an allegiance with a political order that served only the interests of a profoundly conservative ruling class. Economic developments in the countryside, particularly in regions of colonisation or expanding commercial agriculture, encouraged peasants to turn to an option that offered defence against rapacious landowners and a political project in which they figured as actors and subjects.[16]

The FARC was born in the 1960s in the wake of army operations against peasants who had settled land during *La Violencia* and maintained their own armed defence under the leadership of the Communist Party. The party had organised the peasants and their armed defence, but as a party; 'armed struggle' in the rural areas was always subordinate to a broader political strategy, which included electoral participation, not armed struggle as a priority. This was the way they put their mission:

> Our party [. . .] nevertheless considers that there is no revolutionary situation in Colombia as yet. It does not consider armed struggle in cities because such a struggle can be little more than a series of isolated events accomplished by little groups [. . .] The guerrilla struggle is not at present the principal form of battle. [. . .]

Although it subsequently expanded its influence, the FARC remained for most of this period a defensive organisation, with roots among peasant colonisers for whom communism was less a political ideology than a strategy for survival. They faced the constant harassment of large cattle ranchers, backed by the army, only too ready to take over land the colonisers were forced to abandon through lack of resources and infrastructure. In these circumstances the FARC offered protection both from the ranchers and from unscrupulous middlemen, and also organised basic services.

In a number of areas the FARC took over the role of the negligent or absent state to become the governing authority for large numbers of peasants. Zones of self-defence became guerrilla fronts. In the Magdalena Medio, the FARC became a virtual rural civil guard, supported for a period by landowners as well as peasants as the only force to provide law and order. These roots enabled the FARC to survive the 1970s.[17]

A second group, the ELN, made its first public appearance on 7 January 1965. The ELN gained a great deal of publicity and sympathy when a radical priest, Camilo Torres, joined it at the end of 1965. Before taking up the armed struggle, Camilo had attempted to build a political movement, uniting all those hostile to the National Front. The 1963–66 period was one of recession and unrest. His programme, entitled 'A platform for a movement of popular unity', caused a great stir when it appeared in March 1965, bringing him into conflict with his religious superiors.

Camilo planned to build a United Front of popular movements to bring people with disparate political and religious beliefs together around a common revolutionary platform. He contacted the ELN in July of that year and began a long series of discussions. The ELN was interested in his work, recognising the need for a mass urban movement that might parallel the work carried out by the Cuban 26 July Movement in Havana.

Camilo's own charisma generated an initial wave of support. The first edition of his movement's journal, *Frente Unido*, cost about twice the price of a normal newspaper but sold 50,000 copies almost immediately. But the more Camilo spelled out his programme, the less unity it generated; too left-wing for some, such as the small Christian Democratic Party, and too liberal for the sectarian left, he abandoned the project at the end of the year. His decision to join the ELN caused a considerable stir, for he had won much respect for his political work, which was in fact more valuable to the ELN than his presence in the mountains. He was killed during his first action on 15 February 1966.

Many sought to follow Camilo's example; the ELN's military capacity grew and it extended its operations to the south of Bolívar. But it remained militaristic and did little organisational or political work among the peasants. Its authoritarian, vertical structure centred around a handful of key leaders. Tensions between them ran high and differences were often resolved through executions. Two basic conflicts emerged between those who began to stress political work in the urban areas, and those who stressed the military aspect and the peasantry. The urban work suffered a major blow in 1968 when the organisation's urban network was destroyed with the loss of many cadres.[18]

According to Walter Laqueur (1999) the FARC grew rich. Two-thirds of their wealth came from protection rackets among the growers of coca and opium poppy, and from extortion and robberies. These resources went towards survival – buying weapons and refuge, bribing informers, and the forging of documents. Terror, for terrorists, is an expensive commodity. ELN activists hit out at Colombia's capitalist oil syndicates, destroying their pipelines, refineries and offices.

The second generation 1974–82

A guerrilla movement with a difference, M-19 (Movimento 19 de Abril; the April 19 Movement) was founded in 1972 when there came together remnants of a popular national alliance (mainly urban middle class), a good many radical students, some enthusiastic Greater Colombia nationalists, and a hard core of Trotskyists whose extremism neither the FARC nor the ELN was prepared to tolerate. The recruits to M-19 quickly began to carry out a campaign of vigorous urban terrorism, for they felt rejected by a government that, on 19 April 1970, had defrauded a reform-and-trade union movement of a legitimate electoral victory. There was perhaps, in the beginning at any rate, something of a Robin Hood image – the robbing of the affluent to benefit the dispossessed. Pearce discusses M-19's distinctive approach:

M-19 never belonged to any left-wing tradition or Marxist orthodoxy. It is closer to what might be called 'armed populism', in which its folkloric leadership sought to build an anti-oligarchic and anti-imperialist mass movement with an armed wing. The Leninist vanguard was rejected in favour of broad mass fronts with a multi-class character.

It was not until 1979, however, that it really hit the headlines when in January of that year it stole 5,000 weapons from the armed forces' main arsenal at Cantón Norte outside Bogotá. Although most of them were later recovered, the army never forgave the guerrillas.

Turbay Ayala became president in 1978, following the first national civic strike in 1977. Strongly influenced by the armed forces, his response was to establish the most repressive government the country had known, beginning with a draconian security statute. Imprisonment and torture, never absent in Colombia, became systematic. M-19 members were soon filling the prisons, being subjected to terrible tortures and emerging as heroes.

M-19 began operating in the rural areas, particularly in Caquetá, in 1979. This was a conflict-ridden region, with peasant colonisers protesting against the assaults of ranchers and the neglect of the state; in 1972, 10,000 peasants had occupied the capital, Florencia, for eight days. The FARC's already solid roots were reinforced by army and police repression of the civilian population. In 1978, Turbay Ayala declared the region a 'war zone'.

Both the guerrilla movements associated with the coca boom (M-19 and the FARC) took a pragmatic position on coca. The FARC established law and order in its areas of control and, in return, the producers and traders paid a percentage of their earnings to the guerrillas. It also protected the peasants from the traders (it stopped them paying them in *basuco* or crack) and encouraged the growers to grow food crops as well as coca. The FARC was authoritarian and harsh in punishing wrongdoers, but it established rules in a situation where the law of the jungle would otherwise reign. Its law of the mountain, as it was called, gradually won legitimacy and support. Corruption ran high within the army and police, further reducing their authority among a peasantry already deeply hostile after years of abuse at their hands. If the peasants did not pay the guerrillas, they might have to pay the army and it was usually more threatening and arbitrary in its behaviour than the guerrillas.

The FARC expanded its influence considerably in the late 1970s. At the end of 1979 it had nine fronts, by the end of 1983 it had twenty-seven. At its seventh conference in May 1982 it conceded for the first time that a revolutionary situation existed in the country, and added the letters EP (*Ejército del Pueblo*, People's Army) to its name. It also decided to adopt more offensive military tactics. These significant shifts were an indication that the armed struggle was on the agenda as never before.

Serious political mistakes and abuses of power accompanied the growth of the FARC's fronts, perhaps as a result of rapid recruitment with insufficient politicisation. The tactic of demanding protection money from landowners began to look more like criminal extortion than politics, particularly when it was used against the less prosperous landowners.[19]

The FARC, in fact, went through such an expansion that its activists and their terror methods were welcomed among the rural poor in Venezuela, Panama and Ecuador.

THE POSSIBILITIES OF PEACE

After the general election in 1982 the new President, Belisario Betancur, a Conservative, had to cope with both severe economic recession and a crippling climate of insecurity. To bring about some degree of stabilisation he announced the formation of a peace commission on which all sectors of Colombian life would be represented. Even delegates from the Communist Party and from M-19 would be welcomed and all political prisoners would be offered unconditional amnesty save for those found guilty of atrocities. This brave attempt at national reconciliation never got off the ground. Army chiefs were hostile to any form of compromise.

Ranchers and big business feared irreparable breaching of their exclusive domains. What agreement there was turned out contradictory and ambiguous. Meanwhile, it seemed as though the guerrillas were not losing face. The situation ended in disaster on 6 November 1965 when M-19 occupied the Palace of Justice in Bogotá. Hundreds of troops and tanks went in, the building was destroyed and 12 Supreme Court judges and their assistants, 41 rebels and 17 soldiers were killed.

After the Bogotá battle the army was the only state institution with the capacity for strong and decisive action. Colombians watched this with foreboding. The political parties were rent with factionalism, while the drug mafia held sway in the towns and in huge tracts of coca-growing land. The Catholic hierarchy had to wrestle with the daring radicalism of priests preaching 'liberation theology' and 'freedom' for the poor and oppressed. Would terroristic methods, if sustained, bring about constructive change or initiate a tumble into further anarchy?

THE STATE'S COUNTER-OFFENSIVE

Pearce is in no doubt that by 1986 Colombia's political crisis had become acute with power fragmented throughout the country. The 'formal' constitutional state was menaced, broken even, by the 'informal', unconstitutional initiatives of the violent. Was Colombia now becoming 'a democracy without the people', she asks:

Marginalised economically and politically, the state has reserved for the majority the 'state of siege' and all the exceptional repressive legislation and procedures that can guarantee order where other mechanisms fail. Even that sector of the middle class that has been included economically remains on the margins of the existing political system. By 1986 'official' and 'unofficial' repression dominated and the ruling élite was preparing to go on the counter-offensive against the many challenges that now faced the political order.[20]

On 27 January 1988 the President of Colombia introduced a 'Statute of the Defence of Democracy'. Pearce declares that not one of the 78 articles in the statute referred, as one might have expected, either to drug trafficking or to extradition. To deal with 'political crimes' was the objective. Moreover, the wording of the statute struck an ambiguous note in places:

The statute defines a 'terrorist' so imprecisely that arrests can be made if an individual is under suspicion, or has participated in an act of civil disobedience which, in the judgement of the police, has provoked terror in the population or endangered lives or property. Radio broadcasts or articles about security problems can be taken as public or private incitement to participate in terrorist acts and penalised with up to ten years in prison.

Anyone suspected of participating in 'terrorist' activities can be arrested without a judge's order by a soldier or policemen and held for ten days before being brought to court – a period during which they are often subjected to torture or ill-treatment.

The police and the military were given the right to search homes and arrest people without a judge's order. Two months later, after a wave of army searches without warrant, the Supreme Court declared it unconstitutional, but the practice continued in many areas.[21]

Habeas corpus provision was modified and civil trials now included personnel seconded by the army. Military operations regularly involved house searches, overt intimidation, torture, killings and 'disappearances'. This continuous repression had much in common with the 'dirty war' practised by the government in Peru. As in Peru, the government's counter-terrorist measures included the arming of so-called self-defence groups as a means of legitimising paramilitary action.

Otherwise, counter-insurgency programmes sought out specific targets:

The government and the right all too frequently identified popular leaders with the guerrilla movements. Since counter-insurgency doctrine called for the isolation of guerrillas from their social base, 'draining the sea from the fish' as it was known, the government was able to justify the repression of all forms of popular protest. This kind of war bears heavily upon civilian populations – guerrillas are mobile and can more easily escape army operations.

The guerrillas and the popular movements therefore had a somewhat contro-versial relationship. The guerrillas could provide defence under certain circumstances, but in so doing implicated the popular movements in the armed struggle. The guerrillas supported the banana workers in Urabá and helped them improve their wages and conditions, but at the cost of the region being militarised. As they became more effective, though, the popular movements faced repression with or without the guerrillas' presence.[22]

REVOLUTION IN SUSPENSE

Colombia's revolution remains unachieved despite the ardour and desperate action of those hungry for reform. It is debatable whether the descent into terrorism has put significant reform into cold storage until government has security in steady hands. Writing in 1990 Pearce has no doubt about the delay and she quotes from one of Colombia's academic journals:

As Colombia's guerrilla movements began to build popular support, they found their spaces for political work starting to close. Defending the civilian population was difficult, but recruiting large numbers of civilians under threat into the guerrilla movements was logistically and politically impossible. They were too weak in the urban areas to claim that a revolution was imminent in the short or medium term.

The guerrillas had to respond to the political impasse, but the government had yet to recognise that it could not defeat them militarily. A massive army campaign during 1989 had failed to weaken the ELN and, within this context, the guerrillas had to decide how to use their armed strength. Should they, as the ELN wished, deepen the revolutionary process through a prolonged popular war? Or, as the EPL insisted, find political openings by uniting all forces against 'fascism'? Or, as the FARC and M-19 argued from their different perspectives, win reforms and the right to participate electorally? In 1989 arguments for peace or war, reform or revolution were once again being debated. William Ramírez Tobón (*Análisis Política*, no. 5, 1988) feels that the 'enemy in the peace negotiations is more than a military opponent or an opposition force. The guerrilla represents, whether we like it or not, a dream of a new society, a project different from the established order in existence today in Colombia. Behind the guns are voices that cry out for employment, education, health and the right to life'.[23]

Perhaps in an already confused community there were simply too many voices urging differing styles of reform:

Many progressive urban intellectuals rejected armed struggle and traditional left-wing politics and wanted to build a third force based on civic movements and broad social alliances. They formed a movement in early September 1989, called *Colombia Unida*. The UP hankered for a still elusive 'bourgeois democracy'. In some regions the guerrillas had simply replaced the state. In others they were emphasising grassroots politicisation and popular power, from which they could build a revolutionary alternative in Colombia.

No political project (right, left or centre) had national legitimacy and, though with insufficient bipolar conflict to generate civil war, this contributed to a sense of social and political decomposition. There were wars in regions such as Urabá and the Magdalena Medio, where class conflict was particularly acute, but in the cities, where there were no clear political options other than cocaine and crime, violence bred violence.

Meanwhile the traditional élite was still searching for a political formula that would restore its hegemony more permanently with a minimum loss of power. The modernisers wanted to strengthen the state further, reform institutions and pursue a peace plan on their own terms. The majority of the élite were concerned at the loss of political legitimacy but their main interest was the preservation of their own privileges. In that sense, a weak state served them best.[24]

To what extent terror incapacitated government in Colombia is arguable. The programmes of counter-terrorism could be thought over-reactive and negative as Pearce intimates:

The Colombian journalist Antonio Caballero once called Colombia a 'political time-bomb'. Can an economy that has created only 500,000 jobs in manufacturing, which a leaked World Bank report (July 1989) describes as closed and meeting the needs of only a minority, provide the majority of its population with a humane existence and the means to a livelihood? The archaic political order that has kept that minority in power has proved incapable of taking on this responsibility. The bomb will carry on ticking until it does, or until the left proves itself able to unite the people around an alternative social and political project.[25]

By way of conclusion one question needs to be asked as we begin a new century: what are the chances of a peace process, which has already stumbled over 10 years, ending 40 years of conflict? A brief outline of progress to date makes for sober reading:

- 1990–4: the Colombian government begins to soften its refusal to negotiate with 'terrorists'. Guerrillas, sensing the easier position, press for membership of the Constitutional Assembly as well as immunity for their leaders. Both sides explore some international monitoring of demobilisation and withdrawal but the FARC says 'No' to any United Nations mediation. Negotiations 'freeze', though delegates meet unobtrusively in Venezuela and Mexico.

- 1995: guerrillas are now strong and confident enough to line up as the National Guerrilla Coordinating Group (NGCG). Consequently, the government, fearful of lost ground and initiative, reopens prospects of army withdrawal and frames a programme for assisted reincorporation of former guerrillas into civilian life. Unhelpfully, these proposals collapse as major army offensives roll by and the NGCG recoils from Bogotá's 'ultimatum'. The FARC, over-confident, attacks Colombia's anti-drug task force.

- 1996–8: momentum quickens. The government now realises its popularity is being rapidly eroded by large-scale peasant protest; coincidentally, the NGCG see their own ranks denuded as former terrorists increasingly prefer peaceful protest to orchestrated violence. The NGCG is now willing to talk provided their arrested members are treated as Prisoners of War. Bogotá wonders how 'inhuman terrorists' could be accorded Geneva Convention rights.

- 1998: guerrilla schisms occur as the ELN and the National Peace Council (successor to the NGCG) meet in a monastery in Mainz, Germany (a German Catholic Church peace initiative) and together work out a framework for a convention enabling Colombian non-governmental delegates to press Bogotá continuously for widespread political, economic and social reforms. Preliminary outlines for army evacuation, amnesties and guerrilla resettlement are drawn up.

- 1999: begins with the ELN and the FARC differing as to how to deal with the army's continued punitive sweeps. The government now acknowledges that the embryo revolution 30 years earlier had no alternative than to adopt terrorist methods. Did weak governments too readily resort to insensitive strategies and over-reactive tactics? In May 1999 optimism and consensus are evident: in Bogotá disarmed terrorists and government ministers decide a Common Agenda for Change – to build a new Colombia with reforms of the bureaucracy, the army, the judiciary, new agrarian and environmental policies and codified citizens' basic rights.

- 2006: 'stalemate' between conflict and internal stability seems to mark the situation. The careful mediation of the United Nations, of the United States and of some concerned neighbours has not achieved very much. Drastic reform programmes to deal with the economy and social systems are still forerunners of sound peace and reconciliation.

Columbia and Peru, neighbouring states, each have an immense problem which has devastating consequences, namely, narco-terrorism – that is, the production and distribution of narcotics by terrorist cartels together with associated corruption and money laundering.[26]

Colombian society and economy struggles still with a problem by nature ingrained, violent and escalating. Measures to counteract narco-terrorism have shown progress where specialised units using sophisticated equipment have been fielded. There has been promising advance when Colombia has joined with partner nations under the aegis of the United States Southern Command (SOUTHCO) in detection, monitoring, tracking and interdiction of drug runners. Information sharing, maritime and aerial surveying, interception patrols are now very closely organised. Drug seizures in dismantling trafficking in Colombia trebled between 2007 and 2009. By the autumn of 2010 Colombia was a lead member of Latin American ongoing symposia and defence ministry collaboration.

Germany

THE SUBJECT OF THIS case study is the Red Army Faction (the Rote Armee Faktion or RAF), once known as the Baader-Meinhof group. During the 1960s and 1970s this notorious organisation terrorised what was then known as West Germany and operated as a number of hard-line cells carrying out a desperate terrorist strategy and recruiting a network of supporters. Its logistics of attrition and its propaganda were impressive until a determined German government and an alarmed public managed to reduce the conspiracy to its present-day secretive and much more heterogeneous remnant.

Essentially, political terrorism in Germany has illustrated an escalation from protest to violent demonstration and lethal action. It still raises many puzzling questions. How was it that the protest movement of young Germans developed into brutal and senseless terrorism? They were the first generation, after all, to enjoy life in a democratic community after the horrors of National Socialism. Many, too, were from affluent and privileged families. Were there distinctive socio-cultural or psychological factors to account for fanaticism in post-war Germany? Could some of the influences on their attitudes and behaviour have been imported from abroad, while others were perhaps the product of a nation divided unhappily into West Germany and East Germany?

PROTEST TO TERRORISM: SOCIO-CULTURAL ORIGINS

As regards protest, already in the 1950s students in German universities were kicking their heels at conservatism and authoritarianism among the staff, regarding them as infuriatingly slow in responding to the changing circumstances of society and to the great increase in student numbers. This cry for reform was linked with some degree of resentment of control by an older generation (somewhat tainted by Nazi memories). The growing student protest, chiefly led by the Socialist Student Association (SDS) was influenced by many external issues – America's war in Vietnam, the liberation struggles of Third World peoples, the anti-nuclear war campaign, the anti-apartheid movement, the vibrant mobilising appeals of Che Guevara, and the radical critiques of Herbert Marcuse and Jean-Paul Sartre. If reforms were not urgently implemented constitutionally, then youth would have to take reform measures into their own hands, for instance through extra-parliamentary opposition, Ausserparlamentarische Opposition (APO). Students increasingly despaired about the prospect of significant improvements and about any reliable alliance with what was for them a much too conservative left-wing front betraying student revolutionary fervour and ideals. When large student gatherings in Berlin, Frankfurt, Hanover and Marburg were addressed by such 'inflammatory' activists as Andreas Baader, Ulrike Meinhof and Rudi Dutschke, the tenor of these assemblies was swiftly regarded by the state security division as illegal and confrontational. Eventually, in 1967, police tear gas and live bullets were used to disperse 'terrorist agitators'.

PROTEST TO TERRORISM: PSYCHOLOGICAL FACTORS

An attempt to throw light on the origins of German terrorism from a psychological standpoint is provided in the analysis of Schura Cook (1982), a 'psychopolitics consultant' in southern California. Her hypothetical case (which may not convince everyone) is that some young Germans 'over-identified' with imported cultural elements, and political and social issues. American problems, so dynamic, counter-cultural and anti-authoritarian, became the problems of Europe's youth. At the same time, Cook argues, they 'under-identified' with the contemporary German system, for they were uncomfortably aware of the dictatorial past and although they were born and raised after 1945 there was for them the crucial need to resolve an identity:

The need of many young Germans to be totally different from their parents' generation resulted in identification problems. How could they identify with their parents' generation which exterminated millions in concentration camps and fought brutal and aggressive wars? Therefore, the German youth was characterized by a hypersensitivity towards all authoritarian structures in society. Anxiety and tension were the result of this identification conflict. Collective guilt feelings for the horrible deeds of the parents' generation predestined them for the anti-authoritarian role of the youth movement. In Germany this resulted in a generation conflict manifested in a particular 'hypersensitive' atmosphere.

The unrelieved gap between the subconscious need to identify with the German system and the conscious hate against this system created a large section of estranged hypersensitive German youth. They felt they had become chronic injustice collectors, constantly aware of the insincerity, hypocrisy and greed of their environment, which they had learned to hate with unmitigated passion. Providing a remedy for injustices is the basic motivation for terrorism and the hypersensitive Germans saw evidence of this injustice everywhere and reacted accordingly.[1]

Cook continues the argument with the supposition that many young people in Germany found it difficult to discern the difference between the former fascist Germany and the new democratic ambience that surrounded them. For them this was a 'reality loss', which became a key factor in regression from what Cook terms psychological and social 'sensitivity' through 'hypersensitivity' (strong views about political and social injustice) to 'hyposensitivity' (the complete negation of sensitivity and lapse into terroristic brutality).

The young terrorist reaction, Cook concludes, moved through uncertainty about themselves to a search for group solidarity, to preference for anti-conformist attitudes and behaviour, to a longing for 'kicks' and the excitement of violent action, and, all together, to a gradual loss of inhibition about using violence as a means of political protest. In their growing hatred and rage and in response to what they saw as a biased press and their elders' lack of understanding, a wave of violent protest in some quarters became virtually unstoppable:

The transition from an anti-authoritarian youth protest movement to a political movement that eventually deteriorated into a hard core group of fanatically determined terrorists was brought about as much by the role of the press and police actions as by any intrinsic characteristics of the movement itself. In the course of political polarization and violent escalation, determined terrorists, criminals and crazies succeeded in infiltrating the anti-authoritarian youth movement and used its moral prestige for terroristic violence. At this point, indiscriminate activism for the sake of action was eventually transformed into strategic terror.[2]

They had become action addicts, interested only in living out their fantasies. In their self-imposed isolation in the underground these fantasies had become realities for them, the only realities they knew.[3]

ORIGINS OF GERMAN TERRORISM: THE HISTORICAL DIMENSIONS

A wider and more historical interpretation of German terrorism is to be found in the political analyses of Geoffrey Pridham (1981) and of Peter H. Merkl (1995). Their reference points are: first, the historical origins of terrorism; second, the question of ideological orientation among German protest groups; and, third, sociological aspects. For them, historical factors in Germany's domestic politics are all-important in aiding understanding. Merkl, for instance, sees inevitability in the growing violence between West German police and students:

But the students' and other rebels' attitude towards the police, encouraged also by later clashes, remained impotent rage, frequently aggravated by the self-serving, hateful explanations of police conduct given by the press and by various Berlin establishment figures. It was very easy in this setting to feel that one had to defend oneself with lethal force against a lawless, violently repressive, and arbitrary authority that seemingly ignored its own legal and constitutional standards. It was also most plausible to perceive the established authorities as a crypto-fascist, or closet Nazi, force – in spite of democratic elections and majority support – which would inevitably reveal its true nature upon a little provocation. As Rudi Dutschke put it, 'If we were in Latin America, it's clear I would fight weapon in hand. [But here] we are fighting so none will ever need to take up arms.'

The use of police violence out of all proportion to a legitimate state interest removed much of the well-inculcated taboo against the oppositional use of similar violence in self-defense and lent legitimacy to the terrorist acts to come. Against the ugly pogrom mood among the West Berlin establishment, violence escalated quickly.

The genie of violence was out of the bottle, untrammelled by bourgeois inhibitions, ready for attack on the hostile media and authorities, and all this with an exhilarating sense of freedom after years of repression and frustration. Perhaps their very success and its reverberations brought about their undoing – on 1 May 1968 the SDS assembled a demonstration of 30,000 in Berlin; ten days later 50,000 demonstrated in Bonn against the acceptance of the Emergency Laws; and in Paris *les événements* broke out. Soon sober reflection set in, the 'manic phase' ended, and there was a renewed sense of impotence and frustration. The student movement began to disintegrate into many directions: Young Socialists, the newly founded Communists (DKP), Maoists, Trotskyists, trade-union activists, gay and feminist groups, child-care groups (*Kinderläden*), and rural communes.

As the mighty student movement died, following its most activist, even violent peak, it spun off small but intensely violent movements much as a dying hurricane might spawn tornadoes. The German literature on terrorism calls them the *Zerfallprodukt* (by-product of disintegration) of a brilliant social movement, and in a comparative context, I have called this the fire-sale theory of terrorism – after the revolutionary fire burnt out, its high-sounding, though fire-damaged, values became the easy rationalizations of trigger-happy zealots. Some critics of the German terrorism literature have warned against the tunnel vision of both the terrorists themselves and the conservative enemies of the student movement, who insist that the student movement directly and logically led to terrorist excesses, when in fact it had many and varied consequences, including political apathy and depression, a rueful return to the major parties, a 'long march through West German institutions', the citizen initiatives, the women's movement, and peace, ecological and alternative movements – all of them rather nonviolent. The same caveat, of course, applies to the logic of condemnation: it should be possible at the same time to condemn the later terrorist violence, to approve of most of the police measures to apprehend the guilty, to support the constitutional right of APO [Extra-Parliamentary Opposition] and the student movement to demonstrate, and to condemn the public hate campaign and police lawlessness unleashed on them by the Berlin Senate and the media.[4]

Pridham has reservations as to the extent that this early German terrorism was in any real way a unified movement:

Whatever the impact of German terrorists as a whole, especially with reference to their early years of involvement, they did not themselves represent a movement in any conventional sense. The New Left, or the Extra-Parliamentary Opposition

(APO) as it was formally known, faded rapidly before the 1969 change of power in Bonn, and its participants went in a variety of directions: a substantial number, so far as they remained in politics, were absorbed into the SPD [Social Democrats], a much smaller number into orthodox communism, some became anti-communist publicists and only a minuscule proportion became engaged in any way in terrorist activity. At the same time one should not underrate the symbolism of '1968', for whatever the APO's failure as a movement it was bound to have indirect political consequences of some kind. The student background of many individual terrorists and the involvement of some in the vogue habits of commune-living and the drug scene suggested a link with the mood of radical protest against conformist bourgeois society, but the specific relationship between APO and the later terrorists demands closer examination before any general points can be inferred.[5]

Looking at the domestic political context, Pridham adds student 'disillusionment' with the left's establishment as well as hostility towards what they regarded as rightist, authoritarian government:

While it is accepted there is no simple explanation for the appearance of terrorism, a number of different factors relating to its origins can be deciphered. One of these often neglected in the discussion of German terrorism and its causes is the domestic political context in which it arose. This is worth emphasising because, although the Vietnam question undoubtedly became a classic object for youthful indignation, the early terrorists spent more time in polemical attacks on the Federal Republic (albeit sometimes described as a 'colony' of the USA) rather than on 'American imperialism' as such. The desire to create a 'Vietnam feeling' did feature prominently in leaflets distributed by them in connection with the first actions in 1968–69. Some of them were later to claim that the motive for the Frankfurt department store fires of April 1968 had been 'to light a torch for Vietnam', just as Gudrun Ensslin, one of them, asserted: 'We did it out of protest against the indifference towards the war in Vietnam.'

All the same, the chief 'enemy' for the terrorists remained West Germany itself and its postwar system and this continued to be so once their actions became a trend from 1970. Various political developments inside the Federal Republic, as confirmed by some terrorist writings of the time, seemed to help ignite their determination to embark on their course of violent protest – above all, a general disillusionment with the constitutional left, as represented by the Social Democrats (SPD), which could be traced back to the break between the party and the Socialist Student Organisation (SDS) in the early 1960s but which came to a head with the Grand Coalition of the SPD with the Christian Democrats (CDU) and Christian Socialists (CSU) (especially over the issue of the emergency laws) and thereafter was fostered by the general failure of the much promised 'inner reforms' once the SPD became the principal governing party from 1969. Since the SPD's coalition with the CDU/CSU was clearly viewed by the radical student movement as a fundamental challenge, several later terrorist figures then involved in minority activist circles within the SDS (notably Horst Mahler and Ulrike Meinhof) were influenced by this viewpoint.[6]

ORIGINS OF GERMAN TERRORISM: THE IDEOLOGICAL DIMENSIONS

Most commentators on German terrorism have found some difficulty in making out the ideological content and orientation of the early terrorists. Pridham believes that divergence from conventional socialist principles in time widened the gap between terrorists and the broad left:

A first glance at German terrorism would certainly locate its ideological home on the left, or as more left than anything else in the sense that its main ideological targets and phobias were distinctly 'right wing', e.g. Nazism/fascism, American imperialism and Vietnam, bourgeois opposition to the 'class struggle', capitalist society. The historical link with the New Left, the political background of individual terrorists and the fact that their circles of 'sympathisers', both active and passive, all came from the political left suggested the same ideological location. West Germany did not undergo any phase equivalent to Italy's period of neo-fascist inspired violence in the early 1970s. Violent activities (for 'terrorism' is too strong a word here) deriving from the extreme right have occurred spasmodically in the Federal Republic through the 1970s, with some fluctuation and occasional growth in incidents, but they cannot *in toto* be considered and have not been perceived as presenting the same challenge as 'red' terrorism.

Yet, the problem of identifying specifically the ideological left-wingess of the German terrorists remains and is underlined by their complicated relationship, or really lack of it, with the constitutional left. A good illustration of this problem is Willy Brandt's commentary in his speech to the Bundestag during the debate on terrorist legislation in March 1975:

> It is customary to speak of the terrorists as of the 'left'. This is a use of speech which has been taken over only too thoughtlessly, also by me and therefore I criticise not only others but also myself. There is certainly a reason behind this in some cases – therefore two comments. Firstly, those who decree the terrorists the title of 'left' in the sense of the proper political spectrum of our country – I emphasise, political – are doing them an honour to which they have no right. This includes them in a schema – about which one can of course argue – that is taken from the parliamentary sphere. I say emphatically: the terrorists are everything other than 'left' in the sense of the political and parliamentary spectrum of parties. They have nothing to do with it. They are rather people who play into the hands of reaction. Secondly, those who nevertheless characterise them as 'left' in an ambiguous way are defining consciously or unconsciously the parliamentary left so as to place it, again consciously or unconsciously, close to the terrorists. In the name of the parliamentary left – and this is the role of Social Democracy, also when it is part of the new centre – I reject firmly these views.

So far as the terrorists themselves were concerned it could be said they represented unorthodox variations based on Marxism. This assertion is only possible because of the political divisions of the Marxist tradition in German history. The terrorists themselves laid claim to 'Marxist' or even 'communist' inspiration, firmly rejecting the 'anarchist' label, in which their ideological loyalty was to Mao-tse-tung or Che Guevara rather than Lenin – as in their criticism of the DKP for being 'embourgeoised' and not wanting to overthrow the state. Insofar as they had any German historical reference points, these were the 'purist' martyrs of Rosa Luxembourg and Karl Liebknecht. Yet it is also possible to add that insofar as they resembled features of German romanticism they were more akin to right-wing politics. All the same, by any usual standards it is still difficult to measure the ideological dimension of German terrorism. Various authorities or observers have commented that for the terrorists ideology has provided a 'camouflage' or that it is eclectic and taken at face value, that at best it is utopian (or 'criminal utopianism') and finally that it is theoretically weak as it offers no clearly defined alternative society, only the belief that the system should be 'different'. There is some element of truth in all these remarks but it still remains to identify more specifically the ideological content and orientation of the German terrorists.[7]

Three overarching leitmotivs may be said to have contained key concepts in terrorist thinking since they were regularly included in underground publications. Pridham considers these as central to motivation:

(a) *The concept of the 'armed struggle' and the model of Third World liberation movements.* This probably had the greatest individual influence on terrorist thinking, especially as it gave the groups a sense of international solidarity in the face of their lack of popular following in the Federal Republic. However, this leitmotiv had a definite history of its own deriving from the New Left (e.g. the hero-worshipping of Che Guevara), and it undoubtedly provided the salient 'theoretical' basis for terrorist activity. Numerous terrorist booklets, manuals or statements gave expression to it: 'The concept of the urban guerrilla' (1971, written by Ulrike Meinhof), 'Concerning the armed struggle in Western Europe' (allegedly authored by Horst Mahler), 'Serve the people – Red Army Faction: urban guerrilla and class struggle' (sent to *Der Spiegel* for publication in April 1972) and 'Lead the anti-imperialistic struggle – Create the Red Army – the action of Black September in Munich' (November 1972). It was repeated by other shorter statements from the RAF's two ideological leaders, Horst Mahler and Ulrike Meinhof, on various occasions. Briefly, while identifying with 'oppressed' people in the Third World in opposition to 'US imperialism', the theory involved following Carlos Marighela's application of guerrilla warfare to urban areas and drew succour from the theoretical blessing given by Frantz Fanon to violence as an intrinsic element of revolution. The terrorists' fervent adherence to these concepts had something of a simplistic ring when applied to German conditions [. . .] This clearly involved a fundamental rejection of legal methods and parliamentarianism, but two further points are worth a mention. The absolutist and cathartic view of violence, in asserting that the destruction of the existing order was an essential precondition for a 'free' society, was nevertheless hedged with conceptual ambiguities in a German context. The other point concerned the terrorists' idea of their relationship with the masses. These theories contained an automatic belief that 'armed struggle' would inspire mass support, but here they were criticised from

within the 'unconventional left' – Jean-Paul Sartre emphasised their failure to construct a mass basis, and eventually Mahler left the RAF on these grounds. In answer
to such criticism they argued that it was not a question of 'supporters' or
'fellow-travellers' but of the 'effects' of their politics in 'changing people's attitude
to the state' following the government's anti-terrorist measures.

(b) *The Nazi 'connection' and 'formal democracy' in the Federal Republic.* Although
Nazism was defeated militarily in 1945, it was in the view of the terrorists still living
'spiritually' and politically. This basic association of the postwar democracy with the
Third Reich – whereby the Federal Republic was only 'formally' a democracy
(a term borrowed from the New Left) because it served only the interests of the
'bourgeoisie' – was, of course, in the intensity with which it was applied, a special
feature of the German version of terrorism for obvious historical reasons. As an
emotively charged concept it involved not so much a theory as a theoretical assumption and it covered a variety of other or related attitudes, e.g. problems of generational
conflict, postwar Germany's 'neglect' of the 'spiritual' education of the young and
above all the thesis of 'structural violence' on the part of the existing system
(a concept elaborated theoretically by Galtung at this time) and the need to oppose
it with counter-force. This socio-political anti-Nazism, expressed through the frequent
use by the terrorists of the term 'resistance' to describe their own activities, was
said to be influenced by their personal complexes about the past, but it also clearly
drew on the revival of anti-authoritarianism in the late 1960s as a virtually sub-
cultural attitude of the younger generation by no means confined to the New Left.

On a more directly political level, the terrorists' main claim was that anti-
communism from the time of the Cold War had opened the way for 're-fascistisation'
in the Federal Republic, especially as Germany had unlike many other European
countries experienced no 'mass-scale armed anti-fascist resistance'. This particular
thesis of the terrorists predictably aroused more controversy in West Germany than
many of their other ideas, with perhaps the most pertinent argument coming from
the political historian Bracher that the terrorists were making the mistake of confusing
'totalitarianism' and 'fascism', so that the discussion centred around the confrontation
of fascism versus socialism while ignoring the difference between parliamentary and
totalitarian rule. It is worth noting that on a psychological plane the views of the
terrorists occasioned much debate focusing on the thesis of their being 'Hitler's
children'. This thesis worked in two different directions: on the one hand, that they
were reacting against the recent past and sought to compensate for it, and on the
other that they were subconsciously identifying with it. The latter interpretation
produced the idea that the terrorists were 'left-wing fascists', although as a concluding
point it is worth distinguishing in political terms between their ideological anti-
Nazism and the fact that their *methods*, violent as they were, resembled those employed
by Nazis.

(c) *The rejection of consumer society.* This leitmotiv overlapped somewhat with the
preceding two, both because of the terrorists' sympathies with the Third World
'proletariat' and because they were influenced by New Left theories about what
Habermas called 'a form of modern, noiseless fascism', above all Marcuse's critique
of capitalist society as having a 'fascist' potential sociologically speaking in its
'degradation' of humanity. This anti-capitalist leitmotiv again allowed an outlet
for generational conflict because of the terrorists' attack on the materialistic

preoccupations of the parental generations, and provided a further basis for over-throwing the established system. For this reason they have been called 'refugees from affluence' or 'the spoiled children of the economic miracle' (a reference to the prosperous middle-class background of many of them). Generally speaking, terrorist thinking on this matter hardly offered anything new or original.

This last point is certainly stressed by Pridham:

These ideological leitmotivs and the various concepts they included were largely negative, certainly utopian and very much second-hand. Because of these character-istics doubts have to be cast on how far terrorist thinking involved any integral or systematic assessment of the wrongs and deficiencies of West Germany. One particu-lar problem is that terrorist language, while familiar in its use of jargonistic terminology, has been both confused and confusing as a means of communicating ideas.[8]

Pridham goes on to refer to the organisational underpinning of the terrorists' ideological positions:

It is no secret, and obvious from the nature of their planned actions, that the terrorists have usually been well organised. Their methods of preparation have been systematic with various common features such as the procurement of arms from abroad or by stealing from military depots, the renting of so-called 'conspirative flats' usually in anonymous blocks, a strong mobility with the use of fast cars and other details like the forging of passports and driving licences. One key factor has of course been finance, a vital precondition of all these expensive modes of operation. Aside from the pattern of bank robberies (which produced DM 5.4 million during 1970–78 with another DM 6.2 million from other forms of robbery) as the main source, financial demands have been made on active sympathisers, there has been some blackmailing of those implicated in small ways with assisting the terrorists who prefer this not to become known and apparently material support from international terrorist contacts, notably the Palestinians. These international links have been an important backdrop to German terrorism for other reasons since various leaders have at times received guerrilla training in the Middle East, some German terrorists have participated in actions abroad (e.g. the attack on the OPEC headquarters in 1975) while, more notably, Palestinian terrorists have sometimes played a central part in German activities (the Munich Olympics massacre in 1972, and the Lufthansa hijacking during the Schleyer affair in 1977).

In the later 1970s this efficiency seemed less evident, for a principal change had by then occurred in the structure of German terrorism. Whereas in the first phase of 1970–72 the terrorist scene had been dominated by the centralised and nationwide RAF, in the latter half of the decade several autonomous groups were operating, although all committed to a form of 'strategic' agreement. The mere dynamism of terrorism itself, together with the fact that the West German security authorities were now 'biting', made it in any case unlikely that its structural nature would remain stable. This more hydra-headed leadership situation made it in turn more difficult for security to be effective in tracking down the terrorists. Already by 1975 a lack of contact and coordination was apparent between the different groups: the so-called

'Central Info-Office' had been disbanded, terrorists were more cautious in avoiding contact with other groups and there developed a preference for a strict division of labour through smaller units, which could easily disperse when necessary. One could add to this a further qualitative difference and speak of a second generation of terrorists, for many of them were distinctly younger than the original Baader-Meinhof group – born in the late 1940s or early 1950s rather than 1930s or early 1940s – and therefore had no direct experience of participation in the student protest movement of the late 1960s. It is possible to suggest that they were differently influenced, if at all, by the ideological assumptions of the New Left. The 'belief system' of the terrorists was seemingly inherited by later groups, but what is clear is that they drew inspiration from the very act of terrorism itself with the Baader-Meinhof acting as trail-blazers.[9]

ORIGINS OF GERMAN TERRORISM: THE SOCIOLOGICAL DIMENSIONS

Pridham does not find it easy to distinguish the social context within which early German terrorism was operating, since in many respects the cells were isolated on the left and were marked by shifting numbers of 'active' and 'passive' adherents to a cause. There are, however, some basic social elements:

First, the predominantly bourgeois background of the terrorists and the prominence among them of women accord with patterns in other West European countries [. . .] Second, the relative political isolation of the terrorists naturally had its social side. As we have seen, it has been necessary to differentiate between the various tendencies in the West German political left – between the constitutional/anti-constitutional left in general and among the extreme left between orthodox and 'unconventional' communists – because these historical divisions derive from conflicting aims for German society and divergent means of achieving them. The country's long background of fratricidal antagonism between these divisions created added pressures for the deliberate isolation of the radically activist minority within the left. Moreover, the terrorists' reminder of the Nazi past in such brutal terms was hardly comfortable to those outside circles committed unswervingly to their beliefs. Consequently, recruitment into terrorism involved an act of finality that expressed itself in the absolutist demands of the various groups.

One final question in this context is the degree to which the German terrorists as a phenomenon may be said to have social roots, that is with which social groups they have had any relationship and which may provide a potential recruitment basin.

The most valid point to make at this stage is to distinguish between the 'active' and the 'passive' among the 'sympathisers'. The former would include those involved in some form of practical assistance for the terrorists, notably in providing temporary accommodation; while 'passive sympathisers' comprised the much larger audience receptive of the terrorists' theories (which after all had never been confined to the terrorists) but who had reservations about or disagreed with their violent methods. Even this distinction had its weaknesses as a sociological description, not only because of inevitable overlap but also on account of the variety and complexity of motives that led some people into active support (and maybe even terrorism) and others close to its border but never actually across it. Various official estimates have been given at different times of the numbers of 'sympathisers', sometimes confusingly totalling them all together, with ranges of up to several thousand 'active' supporters around a hard core of some 60–200 terrorists. They have been drawn from the intelligentsia or academic and professional classes (e.g. doctors, lawyers, some priests, but above all students), but clearly they have been a fluctuating and unquantifiable number.[10]

Merkl interprets extensive analytical and statistical material published by the West German Government in 1977–8:

Quite illuminating and comparable to the findings and surveys in other countries are the results of the study of the life histories and individual case records of some 227 left-wing terrorists charged or sentenced by the end of 1978, most of them RAF and June 2nd members. Unlike the terrorists of the German radical Right, the 227 had four times the number of parents in the higher occupational categories (independents, higher white-collar and executive and civil service status, and the professions) as the population average. Female left-wing terrorists were to an even higher degree the daughters of the German upper classes: five times the average. Workers and farmers were distinctly underrepresented among the 227, which may help to explain the terrorists' disdain for the working masses of their country. Their ages were typically concentrated in the second postwar generation (born between 1941 and 1955), which also supplied most of the '1968ers' of the student movement, especially the birth cohorts of 1941–47.

About one-third of the left-wing terrorists of the seventies were women [. . .] Disproportionate numbers of the female terrorists had graduated from a *Gymnasium* and had attended a university. A much larger percentage of both sexes than the average population of comparable age were unemployed or employed only partly or intermittently. There are strong signs of downward social mobility between the fathers and their terrorist offspring, and disproportionate numbers left the university without completing their course of studies. From this basis the life-history research proceeds to the more revealing but also slippery areas of how the family and school background of the terrorists may be different from that of young people of comparable age.

No less than 69 per cent of the men and 52 per cent of the women reportedly had major clashes with parents, schools or employers – 33 per cent with their parents, 18 per cent with employers – of prior records of criminal or juvenile offenses, many of them repeated entries. Although there are no exact population averages or control groups with which to compare, the percentages are so large as to suggest in many cases a conflict-ridden youth aggravated by parental death, divorce, remarriage, and other misfortunes of modern societies. German social scientists sometimes refuse to accept such evidence, because it falls short of a theory of causation of terrorism, but the parallels to such information about other violent movements, for example, the Weimar storm troopers of 1928–33, are striking. Human behavior, of course, has never been subject to simple cause-and-effect relations. In spite of their socialization patterns, every German terrorist could just as well have turned away from terrorism, being a creature endowed with free will; and some did.

Why, then, did some terrorists desert the cause? Merkl adds a point to this:

Some of the researchers asked why some terrorists had turned away from their engagement and when. About one fourth did, most while in jail – a major reason for keeping them separated from each other – and most among those were specialized in a relevant skill rather than in exercising leadership. Although only a few indicated why they quit the group, usually because of the means employed or because of both means and goals, disproportionate numbers of defectors attempted suicide (11 per cent), and many appear to have been swayed by such factors as breaking off their education or job training, drastic mood swings, or the end of a significant personal relationship in their lives. They were generally less violent and somewhat less involved in the groups and had also exhibited better social integration in their personal backgrounds, suggesting, perhaps, the ego strength required for the turn-around.[11]

THE TALLY OF TERRORISM

Joanne Wright (1990) has enumerated the terrorist actions of the RAF and its affiliates over the period 1967–85. There were fierce demonstrations greeting the Shah of Iran's state visit in June 1967 and the shooting then of one student. (This was to give birth to the splinter group, the June 2nd Movement.) Ten months later part of Frankfurt's shopping area was burned to the ground. In May 1972 US army bases in Frankfurt and Hamburg were bombed, with four deaths. Judges, prosecuting counsel, prison governors and leading Christian Democrat politicians were ambushed and threatened between 1974 and 1977. These the RAF labelled as 'necessary actions', since any return of the police-state of the Nazi Third Reich must be aborted. Between 1970 and 1978 there had been 108 attempted murders (one in three succeeded) and 163 kidnappings.

It was in August 1975 that an RAF squad seized the West German embassy in Stockholm, demanding the release of 26 prisoners, among them Andreas Baader and Ulrike Meinhof. The Bonn government refused to concede: two embassy officials were shot, and explosives went off by accident.[12]

Jillian Becker (1989) takes the list of incidents further:

With the deaths by suicide of Andreas Baader, Gudrun Ensslin and Jan-Carl Raspe on the night of October 17th–18th, 1977, about a year and a half after the death of Ulrike Meinhof also by suicide, the 'Baader-Meinhof' terrorist group – as it was dubbed by the news media – may be said to have come to an end. The group had called itself the 'Red Army Faction' (Rote Armee Faktion), or 'RAF'. Some terrorists who had belonged to the group when Baader was alive continued to be active after his death, and new members joined it in subsequent years. They went on calling it the 'RAF'. Sometimes in news reports and commentaries the surviving group was still referred to as 'Baader-Meinhof', but the term seemed increasingly inappropriate. The character of the group changed with the changing circumstances of the late 1970s and early 1980s. The original impetus, that is to say the political atmosphere and particular issues which had stimulated the founder-members to mount their campaign of terrorism, was gone by then. The sort of young rebels who were attracted to the secret life dedicated to violent subversion changed too. Those who came to it later seemed less complicated, showed less need for self-justification, and carried out attacks ever more blatantly callous and brutal.

Yet it was not until 1984 that there was a resurgence of terrorist violence by the RAF. At the same time, newer groups struck with bombs and fire-bombs, and the number of explosive and arson attacks in cities and towns throughout the Federal Republic rose steeply over the next two years to well over 400 a year in 1986. Other acts of terrorist crime amounted to about 1,300 in that year.[13]

Wright and Becker agree that after 1981 the principal targets were connected with NATO and the United States. US air bases were bombed and officers, even civilian contractors, were shot at. In justification, the RAF used familiar themes of imperialism and liberation. Now West Germany and other states of Western Europe needed to be liberated rather than Vietnam or Palestine.

Throughout the two decades of terror those terrorists who were imprisoned went on hunger strike. In Wright's words:

The hunger strike can be a particularly effective weapon, as the state can be presented as barbaric if it lets the prisoner die, and barbaric if it intervenes to force feed. The purpose of the RAF's hunger strikes was to force the state to change the conditions under which it held the prisoner, and to recognize the political component of the RAF's crimes. The RAF prisoners invariably described themselves as political and demanded treatment as such.[14]

Deaths and injuries as a consequence of terrorism in Germany were insignificant compared with the number of road accident casualties during the same period. The terrorists were comparatively few in number yet their activity was effective when measured against the atmosphere of crisis and real fear that was widespread in the population at large. Again, their activity meant a massive deployment of counter-terrorism where there was a trebling of security forces and a five-fold increase in the budget of the Federal Criminal Police Department. Almost certainly, it was the vigorous and wide propaganda work of the terrorists that yielded them a profile never commensurate with their thin numbers.

THE PUBLIC'S RESPONSE TO TERRORISM

In general terms, as we have seen, the effect of German terrorism in its early days led to confusion, fear and even panic until it was seen that the counter-terrorism measures of the government were taking hold. More specifically at the outset, and taking into account the customary black-and-white, unanalytical style of press reporting, there was real perplexity as to the motivation and future intentions of bombers and incendiarists. Given the nature of unforeseen terrorist incidents with their destructive outcome it is hardly surprising that public response was over-whelmingly censorious as to effect and rarely enquiring as to cause. Pridham sees this as an understandable response:

Mass opinion was undoubtedly disturbed by the major terrorist crises. In this sense, the terrorists achieved one of their aims although with the opposite consequences they had predicted, for far from undermining the popular base of the Federal Republic the attacks on prominent figures produced a feeling of outrage in which one could perceive a certain attribution to the state of a sacrosanct quality.

The picture presented by the media, especially the press, was often one of unmitigated hysteria [. . .] It was commonly stated during the debate over terrorism that attention concentrated exclusively on its effects rather than its causes. This was not strictly true, as is already evident, but it is more apt to say that in searching for the causes political debate was very much more *geistig-politisch* than *sozial-politisch* orientated – that is, it was characterised by a moralistic and often abstract cultural–historical approach to the problem rather than one that followed a 'social–scientific' mode of enquiry and would have allowed a more differentiating approach. Hence, the historically coloured insistence on defending the *Rechtsstaat* at all costs and the accusations levelled against the liberal press of trying to 'understand' the terrorists.[15]

Like terrorists in other countries, the RAF and associated groups manufactured and transmitted a range of propaganda to clarify and expound their message. It is not at all sure that they were successful in putting their aims in terms easily grasped by the common man, especially where rhetoric was coated in violence. There is every indication that their own far-from-clear rationale not only failed to penetrate the target but also rebounded unproductively. Wright takes a close look at RAF propaganda enterprise. She conjectures that terrorist propaganda has specific targets and messages that are adjusted or emphasised according to the target selected or the particular tactic being adopted. Wright goes on to identify three target audiences – the 'uncommitted', the 'sympathetic' and the 'active', using these categories to aid definition:

Propaganda is not neutral; it aims to further the aims of the propagandist. One assumption of terrorist strategy is that violence will bring the terrorists mass support by provoking the state to adopt repressive counter-measures. Violence as propaganda 'by deed' is certainly instrumental in this, but accompanying it are themes designed to discredit the state and present the state as disadvantaging a particular section of society. These themes, and the channels through which they are promoted, are aimed essentially, although not exclusively, at an 'uncommitted' audience. Once the uncommitted actor begins to ask why an organization perpetrates such terrorist acts, propaganda shifts its emphasis and reclassifies the actor as at least potentially 'sympathetic'. Here propaganda concentrates on justifying the need for violence, and attempts to widen the sympathetic audience usually by focusing on issues much narrower than the overall objective. The objective as regards the 'sympathetic' audience can be said to be to provoke action, and once this happens propaganda again shifts its emphasis. Within the 'active' audience, propaganda aims to keep the individual bound to the cause, and stresses morale-boosting themes such as the inevitability of victory and the justness of the cause.[16]

This seems an interesting theory, but the reader may have difficulties with it (as Wright seems to). It is perhaps the 'uncommitted audience' that both Wright and the RAF see as elusive:

The Marxist terminology and communist utterances of the RAF were not credible reference points for a people who saw themselves as being in the forefront of the battle against communism. Therefore, it is not surprising that the RAF aroused hostility amongst most of the uncommitted audience, rather than encouraging any movement towards the sympathetic audience.

In the case of the so-called 'sympathetic audience' two major elements appear to have formed the foundations of RAF propaganda:

One is the expansion of the ideological appeal to an analysis of what is perceived to be wrong with the current situation, and a rejection of all nonviolent means of achieving it. The second is the use of specific issues to expand the base of support. Both components are very evident in the propaganda of the two groups involved in this study.

    The RAF argued that the capitalist mode of production had brought new forms of repressive terror. The people most subject to this terror had become so tied to the processes of production that they could not see their oppressed situation. The violence perpetuated by the RAF would itself help the oppressed see their true situation, and demonstrate that an alternative was possible. The RAF's violence would force the state to reveal its real fascist nature, and thus the people would rally to the RAF as their defenders and saviours. The parliamentary and extraparliamentary left had failed totally to respond to the situation, and therefore there was no option but to resort to violence, or in the RAF's terminology 'urban guerrilla warfare'.

    However, as the RAF's most general ideological appeal was rejected by the uncommitted audience, so was its more detailed one by the sympathetic audience. Orthodox communists had already given up the notion of a violent revolution within the Western democracies by the time the RAF emerged. Others on the Left also rejected the RAF's analysis, and the students' main concern proved to be university reform, not a violent revolution. The RAF clearly identified a potentially sympathetic audience and directed a considerable propaganda effort towards it. But this sympathetic audience was not generally the disadvantaged group defined by the RAF's ideology. It was, like the RAF, essentially middle class and educated. Those defined as disadvantaged by the RAF did not see themselves as disadvantaged, and were subject primarily to messages of violence and threat.

    None the less the RAF was at times able to discernibly increase its sympathy. This sympathy was limited to fairly specific objectives, and was more a result of government reaction than of actions by the RAF itself. As mentioned earlier, the climate of fear generated by the RAF led to increased police powers and to changes in the criminal code. The West German state also argued that even in prison the RAF presented such a danger to the state that special holding conditions were necessary. The actions of the police, legislative changes and the prison conditions were successful for the RAF because they were based on a credible derivation of fact acceptable to the target audience. The RAF's sympathetic audience was amenable to suggestions of increasing repression, which the state's treatment of the RAF seemed to show. But while many were critical of the police's behavior and of the legislative changes, and supported a considerable easing of the conditions under which RAF prisoners were held, the linkage with the RAF's overall objectives was inherently weak. In the early 1980s the RAF tried to strengthen this link by presenting West Germany as an American colony within NATO. Its 1984 strategy paper advocated attacks on NATO, but these attacks were to be accompanied by attacks on representatives of West German 'fascism', and a hunger strike by RAF prisoners.[17]

As for the 'active audience', in Wright's view, this is where terrorist propaganda must be directed 'inwards' to seek out adhesion to the group and to cement it:

The aim of propaganda as regards the active volunteer is to further bind the individual to the cause. Thus it is not surprising to find propaganda stressing the need for further action, and emphasizing morale-boosting themes such as the inevitability of victory. The organizational structure of the terrorist group also plays a part in isolating the individual from alternative propaganda sources. Ideology plays its part by providing further justifications for the need to commit acts of terrorism and reassurances that the 'cause' justifies such acts. Prisoners too seem to assume a role of some significance in propaganda directed inwards. Certainly prisoners and the state's treatment of them seem to provide the terrorists with the most tangible link to their sympathetic audience and ways to increase it, but how the terrorist group itself treats its imprisoned members has obvious internal implications. While successful operations freeing prisoners undoubtedly send messages to the uncommitted and sympathetic audiences, their primary effect is on internal morale especially if an 'experienced' volunteer is returned to active service.[18]

STATE RESPONSE TO TERRORISM

Three pervasive themes illumined the debate about democratic values and the challenge of terrorism from the start, according to Pridham. First, then and today, terrorism is regarded in the eyes of the state and by all sides of the political spectrum as presenting a threat to Germany's constitutional order or *Rechtsstaat* (state of law). Second, there was and still is the expectation that a German citizen has to be an 'active democrat' prepared to uphold and defend basic order. Third, a balance must be maintained between the individual rights of citizens within a liberal state and the need to implement security measures without infringing individual rights. Between 1971 and 1978 the German parliament, the *Bundestag*, enacted numerous restraining provisions. New laws were passed in respect of hijacking and abduction, and there was a tightening up of the searching for and arrest of suspected terrorists who would then be put into solitary confinement. In Bonn a new government department was created, the Federal Office for the Protection of the Constitution, with powers to obtain intelligence about the movements and activities of designated persons and, if necessary, to use informers and police *agents provocateurs*. Not all these devices were approved in liberal quarters. If trials were to be 'expedited' under a new code, might this limit the rights of the accused? Was it legitimate to put defence lawyers in treason trials under higher court 'supervision' because of the possibility of their being regarded as 'terrorist lawyers'?

A counter-terrorism measure arousing contention was the *Berufsverbot* (job ban) of 1972. This was a government edict to ban suspected terrorist sympathisers from tenured employment in all state-sponsored occupations. In the first four years of the ban nearly half a million people were officially screened not merely for supposed terrorist activity but also for any behaviour that might put their political reliability in doubt. By many this edict was alleged to be a tool of a repressive, fascist state. Not all Federal Government response was seen as hazarding constitutional freedoms. It could be said, apart from panic here and there, that a good many Germans were inclined to be reflective rather than obsessive about threats to their community, as Pridham indicates:

Yet, the debate over the effects of terrorism on the political scene has revealed an evident and often passionate interest in the *quality* of the democratic system and not merely its stability.

Two effects have been popularly attributed to the rise of terrorism in the Federal Republic: promotion of a strong internal security system and encouragement of a trend to the right. The first is without doubt, but the second demands some qualification. Other left-wing circles accused the Baader-Meinhof and later groups of provoking a right-wing reaction, but in conventional political terms this is difficult to establish. The Social and Free Democrats were in power in Bonn throughout the course of terrorism in the 1970s, but despite some political setbacks and security failures they have by and large managed to contain the issue in the party-political sense, this being confirmed by their image of competence in the area of law and order. Nevertheless, there is always the possibility of severe political repercussions in the event of disaster in another major terrorist attack, particularly in view of the widespread West German obsession with all matters of security.[19]

Law statutes, he points out, were unlikely to get rid of the malevolence, persistence and ingenuity of those who intended to mete out revolutionary terror:

Terrorism simply could not be legislated out of existence, an assumption that owed something to a traditional belief that political conflicts could be solved with administrative means and that quite ignored the sociological roots of this new phenomenon.[20]

It would be beyond the bounds of this brief account of terrorism in Germany to go too deeply into analysing motives and methods. (It is said that the analysts studying terrorists have always far outnumbered the terrorists themselves.)

The enigmas remain. We now know a good deal about the origins and the shape of German terrorism as a result of autobiographies, interviewing, prison confessions and seized documents. Nevertheless, there are numerous questions. How did a dedicated few suppose that their plea for a better deal for the downtrodden and their comradeship with the exploited in every land would ever have a magnetic appeal if it were accompanied by end-justifies-the-means violence? When terrorist propaganda shifted from warranting a genuine struggle to advocating deliberate attacks on persons and property was this not likely to be considered destructive self-indulgence and nihilistic? Were the would-be revolutionaries not in danger of being branded (even by the 'sympathetic') as irrational fanatics, or prisoners of unreality?

In conclusion, this case study seems to point up two common features of the terrorist – his defensiveness and his apocalyptic visions. Konrad Kellen (1998) has this to say about defensiveness:

In fact, probably all terrorists, whether of the religious, ethnic, nationalist, or political/social variety, believe that their targets, individually and collectively, are not only guilty because of what they do and represent, but because they oppress and mistreat the terrorists. It seems to be extremely difficult for Western observers to see and accept that terrorists, whom society regards as the ultimate aggressors, believe that they themselves act out of self-defense. How can that be in West Germany? Very simply, from the beginning, West German terrorists have regarded themselves as the innocent victims of an aggressive, intrusive, repressive West German state ready to use violence – structural violence, they call it – to keep itself in power and to repress them and other 'rightminded people'.

Most people and their leaders in the Western democracies refuse to accept this psychological phenomenon. In fact, it seems they are no more aware of it than they realize that the Soviet Union is honestly afraid of the West and generally acts from that impulse. Psychologically, however, by far the most important key to understanding terrorists is that they feel they are defending themselves against an aggressive, evil, intrusive and murderous world.[21]

Those in the Baader-Meinhof group who confidently awaited the Moment of Truth, the rainbow's end to the Right Way Forward, were millenarians. Becker quotes the scholarly conclusion of Norman Cohn about the nature of this predilection:

It is characteristic of this kind of movement that its aims and premises are boundless. A social struggle is seen not as a struggle for specific, limited objectives, but as an event of unique importance, different in kind from all other struggles known to history, a cataclysm from which the world is to emerge totally transformed and redeemed. This is the essence of the recurrent phenomenon or [. . .] persistent tradition – that we have called 'revolutionary millenarianism'.[22]

Given the earnestness and absoluteness of the German terrorist (similar to that met with elsewhere) there is no easy response to terrorist campaigning and outrage. As Kellen put it, terrorism is an intellectual challenge to us all:

In the end, as important as the penchants for ideology and rebellion are in provoking and shaping terrorist behavior, they are not all-important. At least as significant are the realities that infringe upon, and affect, the world that the terrorist experiences. And among the most affecting of these is the rhetoric that governments articulate in response to the terrorists' acts. Bombastic threats followed by abject cave-ins do more to sustain the terrorists than does any id or ego – or, for that matter, any ideology or rebellion.[23]

At the dawn of a new century in the year 2000 Germany was more united politically, more cohesive socially, more confident economically but rent through with unease as to a peaceful future. Increasingly there are anxieties as to the likelihood of terrorist incidents initiated either by young German radicals (the memories of 1960s and 1970s are there) or by Islamic immigrants. Over two decades, public, press and ministerial circles have intoned the word 'solution'. Surely there must be a determined response to those who threaten violence?

The eyes and ears of the state have to range from awareness to prevention through investigative activity tightly controlled by ministries, defence units, police, and intelligence services. An elaborate database feeds information readily since 2006.

Federal legislation has accumulated a power to charge, try and sentence suspects which has had some success yet incurs a good deal of criticism as to its specificity. Are the definitions of terrorism and terrorist too loose? Do they threaten civil liberties in the laws of 2001, 2002, 2006, 2007? Since much terrorist activity, suspected or carried out, is pan-European should not the Bundestag politicians and the lawyers work more closely with other states? This was much debated in 2008 and 2010 and remains a keen area of disputation.[24]

Italy

THE CASE OF TERRORISM in Italy is interesting in several respects. Social and economic deprivation are seen to breed violent agitation and response. A small group of determined students came together in 1970 to fashion an instrument to carry through political action-at-all-costs. This was to be known as the Red Brigade, the Brigate Rosse or BR. Unavoidably, the outcome was to be a violent one. Italian terrorism flourished between 1970 and 1989 on account of the tardy unresolve of governments rent by factionalism and corruption to frame consistent strategies of counter-terrorism. How, then, have Italians learned to live with 30 or so years of terrorism in their midst? Is it credible, as some believe, that Italy as a country is distinctive in harbouring negative millenarian tendencies – a culture of violence, which a well-organised group may exploit? 'Why did they do it, those Red Brigadists?' asks Alison Jamieson (1989):

Most of the Red Brigadists were intelligent and young, some of them genuinely dedicated to ideals of brotherhood and justice; they had acquired at university the political skills of analysis, communication and persuasion, skills which should have enabled them to contribute more than most to influencing peaceful progress in society. Why did they throw these skills aside and turn instead to the gun, killing people in cold blood, often preceding the killing with the prolonged and excruciating mental torture of kidnap – perhaps the most loathsome and inhuman of all man's inhumanities to man?

How did a few dozen such people, a hard core aided by a few hundred part-timers, dominate the political life of Italy for ten years, killing and kidnapping politicians, judges and industrialists, disrupting the process of law? And how, in the end, did the fragile, chaotic and corrupt system of Italian democracy, already bombarded by criminal gangs and constant economic crises, survive this onslaught and emerge with its rule of law strengthened by the ordeal?[1]

THE ORIGINS OF TERRORISM

The BR, originating in Milan in 1970, was an outgrowth of the Europe-wide radical student movement of 1968–9. A small circle of leaders directed political struggle in the belief that, against an authoritative state that often employed violence, a recourse to violence by subjects and victims was justified. Clandestine conspiracies and provocative action and what nineteenth-century anarchists termed 'the propaganda of deeds' were legitimate. As the leaders of the BR understood it and in numerous broadsheets proclaimed it, their actions were not those of a mindless class war. The BR would be the vanguard of proletarian resistance against its fundamental enemy, the Italian incarnation of a 'multinational imperialist state'. This was 'liberation' strategy in sour, uncompromising terms. 'Justificational violence' was to be the exercise of retribution for what the Marxist–Leninists among them considered to be injustices against the working class. Magistrates, industrial managers, political and social figures could be abducted as hostages in a move towards 'incipient Socialist revolution'. As means to an end, opponents would have to be marked down and 'terrorised'. Danila Salvioni and Anders Stephanson (1985) have studied the organisational permutations of the BR:

The most important elements stemmed from two groups of (former) northern Italian students: one (mainly sociologists) from Trento led by Renato Curcio, and the other from Reggio Emilia in which Alberto Franceschini was the most prominent. In 1969, they became part of the Metropolitan Political Collective in Milan, and it was from this experience that the Red Brigade was most directly to emerge. On the whole, these were students of middle-class or working-class background who had become part of the enormous expansion of the university system in the 1960s. There were notably few upper-class or upper-middle-class members. But whatever their social roots, they were clearly not 'marginal' people, social outcasts, as would often be the case with subsequent forms of left-wing terrorism. Nor, as is sometimes done, can their background simply be described as predominantly left-wing Catholic. The Trento group contained a fair number of old Catholics – some still practising – but the Emilia group was chiefly of Communist parentage. Neither fact is surprising. Catholicism and the Communist party have traditionally been the two outlets for personal activism in Italy, and the BR's founders had an extensive history of such efforts.[2]

Paul Furlong (1981) has looked at the social and economic preconditions of Italy's terrorism and at the national and political context within which they operate. Left-wing terrorism seems to depend upon international models; right-wing groups are close to earlier fascist traditions. Three strands in the political culture are: first, a classic state liberalism; second, tenacity derived from wartime resistance; and, third, a tradition of popular opposition to centralised government. Varied influences, often contradictory, help explain a minority feeling permanently excluded politically. Organised violence has been a predictable consequence of political confusion and economic malaise:

In Italy, recent history certainly from the Risorgimento is scattered with minority groups committed to political activism that finally issued into organised violence and sometimes into terrorism. Left-wing political terrorism in Italy in its contemporary form is in its ideological expressions and organisation very much dependent on international models, in some cases with explicit rejection of indigenous theories of political violence; right-wing political terrorism on the other hand is ideologically close to the fascist traditions of 1920–22, though in its operations it differs somewhat from that model. Despite these differences, the traditions of violence in Italy are important for an understanding of its modern political terrorism.

Italy presents us with conflicting and confused strands of political culture that result in a wide variety both of forms of political violence and of attitudes towards political violence on the part of political actors. There is the traditional authoritarianism of the Liberal state that developed after the unification of Italy, exaggerated and developed by the fascist state, which has residual survival in areas within the central administration, the judiciary and the armed forces. Second, the guerrilla warfare carried out with some success by the partisans against the occupying German forces is significant as a model for some modern terrorists, but not only for that. The idealism and tenacity of the resistance movement found only partial expression in the constitution of the Republic, but their tradition is claimed as a source of legitimacy by many contemporary political actors. Third, there is a specifically Italian tradition found in the violence, almost invariably unsuccessful, of those who opposed the Liberal state, whether in an organised form as anarcho-socialists or 'bourgeois patriots' or in a disorganised and spontaneous fashion as brigands and outlaws, particularly in the South. The modern Italian state is an amalgam of these strands. It has inherited both the tradition of centralised administration and the emphasis on the supremacy of the law that characterised the Liberal state, with its formalism, its authoritarianism and some of the practical failings, in particular its vulnerability to political pressure. The combination of this 'strong state' tradition with the relatively radical democratic and federalist state that appears in parts of the postwar constitution is uneasy, but it is these two together that influence in different directions both the development of organised political violence and the response to it by the state.

Against the 'redneck Marxism' of the left-wing terrorists and the grandiose operations of the neo-fascists, the Italian polity presents an ambiguous and polyvalent set of tactics, torn between its liberal–democratic constitution and origins and its authoritarian heavy-handed tradition. Political terrorism is implicitly an attack on the authority of the state, and may be closely connected with the development of a minority that believes itself to be permanently excluded from the political system; the questions that arise in the Italian case might therefore concern the authority of the Italian Republic and the economic, social and political conditions that have led to the emergence of a 'permanent minority'.

The social and political origins of Italian terrorism can be found in the contradictory influences that produced the Italian constitution and that resulted in the radical expectations engendered by the resistance movement; in the tempering of the populist democratic elements in the Constituent Assembly; and in the delays and lapses that accompanied the implementation of the constitution. The political system that has developed is characterised by the continuous occupation of power by one party, the Christian Democrats (DC), for over thirty years and the exclusion from ministerial posts since 1947 of the next largest party, the Italian Communist Party (PCI). The electorate, divided for much of this period into two hostile and exclusive blocs supporting one or other of these parties, is extremely stable in its voting patterns.

The continuous occupation of power by the DC has fostered the development of a system of government based on clientelism and petty compromise, known commonly as immobilism, in which unstable coalitions are cobbled together on the basis of distribution of ministerial posts with programmes nominally supported by the coalition parties rarely reaching the stage of implementation. The coalitions are beset by inter-party and intra-party wrangling, by personal feuds and ideological rigidities, by vacuous adherence to fine-sounding principles and by cynical opportunism.[3]

Thus, for Furlong political terrorism is a predictable consequence of so much malaise:

An economic crisis producing unemployment particularly among the younger age-groups, political parties that are unable to agree on appropriate measures, a social fabric severely threatened by the industrial mobilisation of the immediate postwar period, and not least a political culture that supports radical expectations and gives legitimacy to the unsatisfied hopes and programmes of the postwar political reconstruction.[4]

David Apter (1997) sees those who commit violent acts (such as the BR) seeking broad public support through confrontational acts, a moral crusade in a sense, but a presumptuous one to outside observers:

Mobilizing oppositional forces for the forcible overthrow of the state, or terrorism, in which small bands use acts of violence to render the state impotent, turn citizens into bystanders, and force the state to engage in violent retaliation which undermines both its credibility and legitimacy. [. . .]

The Red Brigades in Italy [. . .] played a cat and mouse game with the Italian state which it tried to make stupid and incompetent by daring acts which left the authorities helpless. It also revealed the corruption at the core of the state, a critique which was not as wrong as the solution. The Red Brigades, as a movement, represent other similar ones, like Baader-Meinhof (Red Army Faction), and Action Directe. These came to regard themselves as the last pure crystalline structure, the radical residue of the 'generation of '68', the others having become compromised and corrupted. For the Red Brigades, the story-telling includes a classic tale of betrayal, the proletariat betrayed by the Italian Communist Party. The hegemonic enemy represents world capitalism. Loss is double, the product of the proletariat to a hegemonic bourgeoisie, and the domination of that bourgeoisie, and the state itself, by NATO, the chief instrument of the American military–industrial complex. Terrorism is necessary to up-end the state and reclaim the national patrimony, returning it by means of revolution to its rightful owners.[5]

THE NATURE OF ITALIAN TERRORISM

Furlong, surveying the interwoven reaction and response to terrorism in Italy, considers that the incidence of terrorism developed largely in two phases. The first phase, 1969–73, begins with neo-fascist public outrages, then more selective and symbolic targeting by the BR setting themselves up as legitimate strong-arm defenders of the proletariat. Despite terrorist 'success' there is a sense of isolation among many *brigatisti* who doubt whether clandestine violence effectively promotes Socialist advance:

In the first years of terrorism post-1968, it was clearly the right-wing terrorists who dominated the scene with a series of spectacular gestures. On 12 December 1969 a bomb exploded in the Piazza della Fontana in Milan. There were fourteen deaths and eighty people injured. Three days later the police arrested Pietro Valpreda, a known anarchist, and the mass media loudly proclaimed his guilt. But it was nearly nine years before the case was to be closed with Valpreda acquitted on all charges, two neo-fascists convicted for the attack after having fled from house arrest, and damaging revelations made both in court and out concerning the involvement of security services in the manipulation of right-wing terrorism. In the five years from 1969 to the end of 1973 there also occurred a series of bomb attacks against political targets, an abortive *coup d'état* in December 1970, the long drawn out riots in Reggio Calabria fomented by the MSI, and the development of the so-called strategy of tension. This was the period of mass political terrorism operated by the neo-fascists in which the victims were indiscriminately selected from the target group – the general public – with the aim of producing panic prior to the armed takeover of power.

　　At the same time there was the steady growth of a more selective form of political terrorism, in which the target group was narrower and the victims therefore more limited: this was the terrorism of the Red Brigades, in this period overshadowed by the terrorism of the right, but later to come into its own. A major difference between the two forms of terrorism, which indicates their differing objectives, is the frequency with which the neo-fascist groups use bombs in crowded places, while the BR rarely use bombs and do not appear to have aimed any operations directly against the public at large. The activity of the BR began in August 1970 in Milan. They were a development of the Collettivo Politico Metropolitano (Metropolitan Political Collective), later termed Sinistra Proletaria (Proletarian Left), a group restricted to Milan some of whose leading members, in particular Renato Curcio and Margherita Cagol, had been together at the University of Trento and had their first known taste of political activity in left-wing Catholic groups there. Others who joined the BR at this stage or soon after, such as Alberto Franceschini and Roberto Ognibene, came from the PCI-dominated area of Reggio Emilia. Though the BR appear to have chosen clandestinity early in 1971, the terrorist attacks mounted by them were high in symbolic content and low on physical injury for a considerable period. Arson against cars belonging to managers of large firms or against known neo-fascists appears to have been their trademark, with occasional well-planned and well-publicised kidnappings that inevitably resulted in a 'proletarian trial' and the release of the prisoner. Throughout this period the BR showed a gradual increase both in expertise and in ambition. The arson attacks constituted bread-and-butter operations undertaken against representative targets with the aim both of inducing terror among the 'ruling class' and of stimulating the working class to take up arms. The BR also showed at this stage a great interest in and knowledge of factory conditions and organisation. Many of their 'proletarian trials' were little more than interrogations to extract information about suitable targets. Their purpose appeared to be to establish themselves as 'vigilantes of the workers', and their operations were usually explained in the inevitable leaflets as actions on behalf of particular groups of workers.

The experiences of those years, though not marked by any obvious success in achieving their overall objectives, may paradoxically have confirmed the BR and other left-wing groups in the validity of their strategy. Clandestinity and 'proletarian justice' may have begun as a reaction to the heady days of 1968 and the labour struggles of the 'hot autumn' of 1969 in the belief that the intensification of the class struggle was both desirable and necessary.

Furlong sees this first phase, despite its moments of terrorist 'success', as encouraging feelings of isolation (even a sense of futility) among many of the *brigatisti*. Clandestine activity was never to be altogether effective in promoting the advance of Socialism:

Because [it was] clandestine, it was the violence of an isolated group, unable to achieve any direct relationship with the masses it was supposed to be serving. Though to some extent BR has been able to overcome this isolation in recent years, the pattern of its activity is still characterised by reliance on clandestine violence as the single valid instrument of revolutionary activity. In this also it is to be distinguished from the revolutionary groups on the extreme left that have not chosen clandestinity, whose view of the BR is well summarised in the description of them as '*compagni che sbagliano*' − comrades who are in error.[6]

Furlong's second phase is given as 1974–9. The attacks of the BR on prominent political figures are seen as an armed struggle raising their horrific public image without any consequential increase in proletarian support. The BR's following may have been thin and erratic but the group is now mature enough to know how to strike at the government in Rome. (As we shall see later there is, among commentators, speculation as to how far the BR were prisoners of a myth about the centre when in reality Italian power was much diffused.) Generally, the discipline, expertise and confidence of the BR stand out in contrast to the shrill terrorist clamour of an indecisive left wing and a much weakened neo-fascist front. Even so, BR, in using both full-time and part-time terrorist members, does not coordinate activities easily. They cannot take for granted popular support for their violent methods. Yet BR confidence had its ups and downs, as Furlong relates:

The years 1974–79 were the boom years for BR with several major operations against their name and the clear assertion of their leadership over the pullulating left-wing terrorist groups. As well as the regular attacks on representative figures, the declared strategy of the BR was to strike at the heart of the state. This they attempted to do with the kidnap of Mario Sossi, a public prosecutor in Genova, on 18 April 1974, three weeks before the divorce referendum; the murder of Francesco Coco, chief magistrate in Genova, on 8 June 1976; and the kidnap of Aldo Moro, president of the DC, on 16 March 1978, who was murdered (presumably on 8 or 9 May) and whose body was found in the centre of Rome on 9 May. These grand manoeuvres appear to have been expressly designed to have the maximum political impact, since they invariably occurred either during election campaigns or at times of government crisis. Sossi was kidnapped during an extremely divisive referendum campaign, which pitched the DC against its governmental allies and the PCI and in which the issues raised spread wider than the single question of the divorce law to cover the fundamental political direction of the country. Coco, who had been responsible for the rejection of the terms previously agreed with the BR for Sossi's release, was murdered exactly a fortnight before the parliamentary elections of 20 June 1976 in which the PCI were expected to make large gains. Moro was kidnapped on the day that Prime Minister Andreotti, after a prolonged government crisis resolved with the considerable help of Moro's negotiating skills, was presenting his new government's programme to parliament, with the support of the PCI. But the dual strategy of the BR, comprising persistent attacks on middle-ranking officials, industrialists and police with the occasional grand attack, has so far failed to incite the working class to civil war or even to mobilise them against the state and the parties. [. . .]

The BR now [1974–79] have an articulated organisation with established groups – 'columns' – of full-time clandestine terrorists in at least four major cities and probably elsewhere. Each column consists of about six members, one of whom is in touch with the central control; the columns are kept strictly separate from one another. The BR are directed by a national executive known as the 'Strategic Control' (Direzione Strategica). Though the organisation is well able to preserve clandestinity, the isolation of the columns appears to have led to problems for the Strategic Control of keeping the operations of the individual columns under central direction. The BR are well equipped, well trained, thorough and determined. They are extremely careful in their recruiting and appear successfully to have resisted significant infiltration since 1975. They are not short of finance, which they obtain by robbing banks and from kidnappings. Unusually for groups of the extreme left they have survived for nine years under difficult circumstances apparently without major defections or divisions, and have not been deterred from their operations either by the overall failure of their strategy or by the increasing frequency of arrests of their members.

In an effort to avoid the isolation from which the BR suffer, their main rival group, Prima Linea, operate on part-time clandestinity. The members of PL are expected to hold ordinary full-time jobs and as far as possible live the lives of normal members of society, though any involvement in 'mainstream' politics is not feasible. PL operates therefore like a traditional 'secret society'. This 'part-time' clandestinity probably explains the restricted quantity of PL's operations; it does not appear to have increased their capacity to establish direct relationships with working-class organisations.

Despite the continued success of the anti-terrorist group led by General Dalla Chiesa, it is not a hazardous speculation that the operations of BR and PL will continue for some time to come and that they will be increasingly determined and ruthless. In January 1979 for the first time the BR murdered a member of the PCI who had notified the police of the presence of a BR informant in the factory where he worked. This operation could only be necessary if the BR had failed to win the argument with the PCI and other organised groups over the political direction of the Marxist left, and may be interpreted as indicating the reliance of the BR on terrorist tactics to achieve some control over the area they claim to be organising and leading.

At the same time, it must be acknowledged that left-wing terrorism attracts significant consent in certain sectors of society and sympathy in others. BR and PL both rely on the support and cover provided by 'irregulars', and both appear to have good contacts in some of the major industrial complexes in the North, as well as in the larger universities (in particular, Rome, Bologna, Turin and Milan). BR appear to recruit mainly from the universities, among the urban unemployed and in the prisons; PL, because of their different strategy, cannot be so reliant on the urban unemployed. These sources are likely to continue to supply the groups both with permanent activists and with irregulars. Administrative rearrangements have produced some change in the prisons, where the policy of establishing top-security prisons preferably on outlying islands, such as the Asinara, for long-term and dangerous prisoners appears to be having some success both in keeping captured terrorists behind bars and in preventing their proselytising activities in the ordinary prisons. The left-wing terrorists appear able at present to retain these links with limited sectors of society while the overwhelming majority of the population appear either to reject them completely or to prefer to ignore them. This is perhaps more a function of the failure of the political system adequately to cope with chronic social problems than a result of any great success of the BR in winning support for their strategy. The sympathy of the unemployed and the anarchic student groups is ambivalent and unstable. Political terrorism of both left and right is likely to lose sympathy and consent because of the increasing intensity of their methods; combined with the increased efficiency of the security services who now appear to be taking terrorism seriously, this means a bleak future for the terrorists, though the short-term prospects for the Italian citizen are not good either.[7]

Two distinctive features of Italian terrorism are emphasised by David Moss (1997). First, there is the reliance on working towards social-revolutionary objectives rather than ethnic nationalist ones:

A comparison with Northern Ireland suggests a further distinctive feature of the Italian case. In advanced industrial societies attempts to promote clandestine social-revolutionary violence have to contend with a difficulty not encountered in cases of ethnic-nationalist violence. The activists of ethno-nationalist violence at least share a clear set of religious or ethnic characteristics with the populations on whose behalf they are fighting, as well as some straightforward political goals, even if the identification of exactly which hostile group stands between the population and its goals may be a matter of controversy. But the social-revolutionary users of violence in liberal-democratic societies such as Italy have to make violence not only an instrumental technique for damaging opponents but also the symbolic basis of the community of activists. Solidarities have to be built around availability for violence in order to attract sympathizers, encourage affiliates and identify enemies. Whatever support for social-revolutionary violence may be claimed from class identification, the dispersed social classes of present-day capitalist societies can only on very rare occasions provide the kind of direct explicit solidarity that ethnicity or religion confers.[8]

A second characteristic of Italian terrorism is an element of 'exchange' of violence between the political left and right, ritualistic in that 'macro-violence' is displayed and exploited for different constituencies and contrasted political ends, especially in the main cities:

Most violence had occurred more or less openly in the course of the student and worker mobilizations, characterized by direct confrontations between extremists of the Right and Left and clashes with police in the course of mass demonstrations. Given the importance of the practice and discourse of violence in recent Italian history and the scale of mass mobilization and confrontations across all major institutions between 1967 and 1969, what is surprising about the first phase of clandestine violence is less its appearance than the reluctance to exploit it [. . .] both exploited the symbolic capital of the Resistance in creating a model for their actions and appealing for the support of the wider communities in which they claimed membership. As a result the violence which ensued fell rapidly into a predictable sequence of exchanges which reflected the dominant empirical and discursive opposition between Left and Right in post-war Italian politics.

The examples of macro-violence by the extreme Right and extreme Left revealed their different approaches to the distinction between politics and violence. The bomb massacres of the Right – four across Italy between 1969 and 1974 – were designed to create the sense that violence had become a pervasive element of everyday life. Making victims indiscriminately, the bombs demonstrated that violence was no longer a separate domain, remote from all but political extremists, but a potential threat to everyone. Trust in the governing parties to protect their electors and other citizens would be undermined. Similarly, by leaving their attacks unclaimed or trying to throw responsibility for them onto the Left, the extreme Right was also seeking to weaken the significance of the general distinction between Right and Left and the kinds of political strategy each was prepared to use. The disruption of these taken-for-granted distinctions was part of a general strategy to subvert the boundaries which had excluded the Right from full political legitimacy since the fall of Fascism.

A quite different relation between the fields of violence and politics was represented in the macro-violence of the extreme Left – the five bloodless kidnappings carried out by the Red Brigades between 1972 and 1974. They provided a carefully structured occasion for demonstrating the separate existence but mutual accessibility of the fields of open and clandestine politics by moving the victim across the boundary between them during his capture. His confessions – confirming the role of extreme Right violence in repressing working-class mobilization on the shop floor – were designed to transform the accusations of his captors into established knowledge for dissemination to the widest possible audience. Kidnappings – lasting up to several weeks — thus served as an elaborate mechanism for the production of knowledge about politics. In contrast to the incorporation of violence into everyday life and politics by the extreme Right, they represented a highly structured exterior site from which the reality of politics could be revealed.

Within the contrasting frames created by macro-violence, both Right and Left practiced the micro-violence of attacks on opponents and their property. Right-wing militants attacked the activists of the extreme Left; members of the Left retaliated [. . .] Their attacks were concentrated against neo-Fascist activists, accusing them of waging class war against the working class on the street and shopfloor, protected by the local representatives of an increasingly repressive state. To assess the results of their displays of 'counter-power', they sought direct reports from factory floor or sympathizers from the extreme Left.[9]

THE TALLY OF TERRORISM

The statistics of Italian terrorism are appalling. During the years 1969–87 there were 14,591 recorded terrorist attacks. One third of these incidents occurred in 1980. It was right-wing terrorism that ranged most widely and brutally in the first phase of terrorism – 9,000 attacks were attributed to them and one in four incidents featured the use of explosives. Left-wing terrorists belonged to 181 different groups. The BR captured most attention in Italy's press with the daring kidnapping of former Italian Prime Minister Aldo Moro in 1978 and of US Army Brigadier-General Dozier two years later. The BR also claimed responsibility for murdering Leamon Hunt, the US Chief of the United Nations Multinational Force and Observer Group, in Sinai in 1984. Nothing was left to chance by the BR, which may explain why their 'score' of vicious attacks between 1972 and 1986 was rather lower at 18 abductions and 69 murders. Even so, in one year, 1979–80, the BR admitted to 439 terror attacks. For Moss the tally of Italian casualties and property destroyed needs to be seen in broader perspective and he gives the example of Northern Ireland:

The Italian case, involving radical terrorism, did not exact its casualties from among the proletariat — the class of preference in keeping with the Leninist tradition of the Red Brigades. Nevertheless there was plenty of political violence. It was inaugurated by a right-wing bomb massacre in 1969; it ended with the murder of a Christian Democrat intellectual by the residual members of the left-wing Red Brigades in 1988. The damage to people and property in those two decades — circa 400 murders, 5,000 injuries, and 12,500 attacks on property — was certainly substantial; yet it amounted to only half the number of deaths from political violence in Spain and barely one-sixth of the deaths in Northern Ireland over comparable periods (Hewitt, 1988). Wider comparisons, too, will help to put the Italian case in perspective. In half the time and among a population little more than one-third of Italy's, left-wing and state violence in Peru produced 25,000 deaths and 22,000 attacks on property; and in Sri Lanka, over an even shorter period, ethnic and political strife caused between 70,000 and 90,000 deaths and the physical displacement of more than 10 per cent of the population.

These crude contrasts can tell us little directly about the social and political perceptions of violence in the different cases. But they do suggest a rather different degree of saturation of everyday life by violence. The chances of dangerous encounters, and the urgency of the need to choose openly to support, tolerate or oppose violence, vary greatly. Even allowing for territorial and temporal variations in the concentration of attacks, 'living with violence' must have been different in Peru, where 25,000 insurgents were active among a population of 20 million, than it was in Italy, with no more than a few hundred people directly responsible for clandestine violence active at any one time and widely dispersed among 57 million people. These contrasts can be linked to two further differences. First, the greater or lesser density of violence is likely to have consequences for the force and stability of the meanings that violence carries. In Northern Ireland, for example, the concentration of violence on a miniaturized terrain supports the highly personalized theme of 'victimhood' in a way that the dispersed, mostly experience-distant, violence in Italy could not. The Northern Irish conflict has produced a much more stable and elaborate set of conventions governing the meaning of violence than could ever be established in Italy. A second difference concerns the relative importance of particular channels of communication. The discourse community of participants, sympathizers and audiences in Italy was linked by ties that were relatively weak, indirect and impersonal.[10]

Crucial to the early successes of BR was its organisation on military lines – there was a strategic directorate, an executive committee variously in charge of logistics and mass propaganda nationwide (occasioning some cynical comment from elsewhere that Italian terrorism was becoming too bureaucratic). Field activities were the work of seven 'columns' in different areas of Italy known as 'poles', each with a delegated leader and with some operational autonomy. Actual 'missions' were assigned to subordinate 'brigades' coordinated by the column commanders. Targets were selected from a 'hit list' of some 1,100 individuals and properties on account of symbolic value and vulnerability. Prior reconnaissance and evidence from a network of informers would decide the tactics to be used, whether it would be abduction, ambush, raid, fire bomb or assassination. Robberies would bring in funds. As counter-terrorist identification and arrest increased so the proportion of regulars grew less. The BR headquarters constantly put out communiqués and strategic resolutions. In its early stages the BR owed a good deal to carefully maintained international connections. Training camps for Italian activists were offered by Angola, Cuba and Czechoslovakia. Automatic weapons were sent from the Soviet Union. France, Libya and Bulgaria offered finance and liaison personnel.

THE MORO AFFAIR

Italy's terrorists made world headlines on 16 March 1977 when a BR hit squad snatched out of Rome's traffic Aldo Moro, former Prime Minister, Foreign Minister and prominent Christian Democrat. His five-man bodyguard were all gunned down. Moro was bundled away to be imprisoned and interrogated by his captors as Public

Enemy No. 1. This abduction coincided with the arrest in Turin of Renato Curci, one of the BR leaders. Curci and others were to be put on trial, caged in a court guarded by no fewer than 8,000 armed police. 'We believed', Curci shouted, 'it was necessary to kill today in order to live tomorrow'. Moro was kept in solitary confinement in Rome. He wrote numerous letters to family and friends seeking their mediation with the terrorists. The Pope and United Nations Secretary-General Kurt Waldheim did their best to intercede, but unavailingly. At length, after 55 days, Moro was tried by a BR 'People's Court', executed, and his body dumped in a Rome side-street near the Christian Democrat headquarters.

This daring incident was, in fact, counter-productive in more than one respect. The Italian public were more cynical than sad, shaking their heads at so much political chicanery. The savage kidnapping alienated many members of the wider revolutionary movement. Moreover, there was now increasing disenchantment with these ruthless tactics among imprisoned terrorists – the 'soft' penitents who had earned some remission, the 'hard' dedicated prisoners on life-sentence, and those who were wavering in their loyalties.

Moss is one of the commentators on the Moro affair who sees the whole tragic event as posing questions. Was the abduction planned to make a clear political point or was it the outcome of some who leaned more to symbolic violence? Were the connections between intention, action and consequence carefully thought out in advance? Was the government's response to the kidnapping anything like as well-informed and well-managed as Moro's importance deserved? The conclusions of Moss are speculative:

The controversy over the 'real authorship' of Moro's letters from his 'people's prison' exhaustively rehearsed the interpretive difficulties of reading documents emanating from clandestine sources. The intentions of the BR remained uncertain: the document explaining the meaning of the attack was only distributed one year after the kidnapping and had been authored, not by those directly responsible, but by the intelligentsia [the directors of BR]. Notoriously, the 'official' BR version of the attack failed to fix its meaning [. . .] Those uncertainties were coupled with ambiguities about the primary intentions of the Red Brigades' opponents: to secure Moro's release or to use the ritual to display their own identities. These interpretive conflicts lasted throughout the 1980s, aired extensively during the sequence of trials and resurfacing unpredictably in wider party-political disputes. The prolonged interpretive sequel to the kidnapping has shown clearly their escape from determination by reference either to the intentions of the protagonists or the consequences of the events. Finally, whatever impact it may have had on its opponents, the kidnapping ritual revealed very clearly the divisions of various kinds within the community of armed struggle: between the *autonomi*, who refused the BR invitation to show support by increasing their attacks; between the BR apparatchiks, leading to the first public scission from the group, followed shortly by its definitive breakup into hostile factions; and between the BR apparatchiks and the intelligentsia, who had been in clandestine conflict for one year already.

Awareness of these multiple confusions of intention, identity and time prompted some activists to start calling publicly for an end to armed struggle in 1979.[11]

The Moro attack, indeed the whole approach and subsequent handling of it by the BR, has been the subject of much comment. There is some agreement that in 1977 the BR was already losing ground and doing it in a confused way.

THE STATE'S RESPONSE TO TERRORISM

There is more than a touch of irony in the way in which the Italian state responded to terrorism during the years that Furlong has described as 'first phase'. What better way could there be for a weak government hamstrung by discord and compromise than to announce a concerted drive to remove a social and political cancer? However, it was never to be the strident voice of an authoritative regime. Somehow, Rome must assuage the cynicism and fatalism of the electorate at large. Furlong has scrutinised the early response of government. A slow-to-act government coined the term 'strategy of tensions' to assure the public that their security would be safe in Rome's hands, provided a DC majority received firm support for its long-term strategies if not its competence in crisis management:

It took the Italian political classes at least five years to alert themselves seriously to the problem of terrorism, in the sense that their initial reactions to it were immobilist, using the events for short-term political gains and leaving their sources untouched. Initially, successive governments appeared disposed to use terrorism to reinforce the position of the DC and to a lesser extent of the minor lay parties as bulwarks of democracy. The term 'the strategy of tension' was coined to refer to the apparent coincidence of increases in terrorist activity with critical political events such as elections or the formation of new governments. The use of the phrase particularly on the left was intended to imply that terrorism was in fact being directed in a strategic manner to favour the short-term aims of the government parties, as if somewhere a 'mastermind', probably an established politician, was in control. Though a lot of evidence has come to light on the close relationship between the security services and the right-wing terrorist groups, there is no evidence to indicate that there is or was a 'mastermind' of terrorism, inside or outside the DC. There were undoubtedly neo-fascist sympathisers occupying senior positions in the security services, and some left-wing terrorist groups appear to have sympathisers at a lower level in the police and civil service. The links with the security services probably helped the right-wing groups sustain a certain level of activity, and the secret intelligence services appear to have known in advance of some of their major operations, in particular of the attempted occupation of the Ministry of the Interior in 1970 and the similar operation in August 1974. But it is not necessary to find a 'mastermind' to explain the apparent strategy of tension, for the operations of terrorists must surely be most effective when political awareness is already heightened, and it would be surprising if terrorists did not attempt to plan their activity to take account of this. To say that successive governments used terrorism reflects not 'strategy of tension' conspiracy theories but the rather less contentious observation that governments did not react vigorously against terrorism in this period and that leading politicians (of the DC in particular) took the opportunity to attack communists and socialists and to affirm their own centrality to the political system.[12] [. . .]

To talk of 'crisis management' in this period would be something of a misnomer, since the state was faced on the whole with a steady escalation of violence that required not short-term 'management' but long-term strategy. Crises of relatively lengthy duration occasioned by terrorist activity did not occur while the neo-fascist strategy predominated. In practice, as I have indicated, little was done to halt the increase in frequency and seriousness of terrorist incidents.[13]

During the 1970s and into the 1980s the failure of the Italian state to respond adequately to terrorism had a double-edged significance: it strengthened the image of a force dedicated to reform-through-violence and it eroded public confidence in the competence of a democratic government. Furlong, writing in 1981, as terrorists battled, evaluates the formidable 'professionalism' of the BR, its sharp-edged profile in media and political circles and the desperate ineffectualness of government response. He sees modern Italy both as fostering terrorism and as learning to live with it. Furlong detects ad hoc government manipulation of organised political violence (both left and right wing) by politicians intent on drawing together their own divisive tendencies, needing to strike recognisably strong attitudes to dispel public cynicism. Thus, terrorism menaces not only public security but also élitist political groups:

The responses of the state to political terrorism in Italy provide an instructive example of how the modern industrialised state may both foster terrorism and learn to survive with it. The inefficiency of the administration, of the police and of the judicial system make it unlikely that in the immediate future political terrorism can be significantly weakened by a strategy dependent on administrative efficiency in the carrying out of policy directives from elected politicians. At the same time, though some agreement has been reached over short-term measures, it is not clear that elected politicians are united either over the appropriate strategy to be followed against terrorism or over the administrative reforms that would be a necessary precondition of any long-term approach to the problem.

I have argued that the major failings in the response to terrorism have been the deliberate manipulation of organised political violence to satisfy short-term goals – goals that have been predominantly electoral but that have also been concerned with the formation of alliances within and between the parties – and, more broadly, the continued underestimation by politicians and senior civil servants of the capacity of clandestine groups to strike politically significant targets and of their intention to do so. This applies both to left-wing and to right-wing terrorism. These failings are intricately connected. The Italian state has been attempting to 'ride the tiger'. The continued support given to General Dalla Chiesa by all the major parliamentary parties is perhaps an acknowledgement of their own incapacity to produce consistent policy direction, but it is also very much a traditional solution for this political system to give a non-elected figure large amounts of free rein and to pay little attention to the less satisfactory aspects of his approach.

I have attempted in this short case study to understand political terrorism within a fragmented yet highly developed political system. If the response of the state has been less than adequate, it may be argued that the inadequacy results from the disparity between a dynamic and open political culture, based on a radical constitution and populist traditions, and the stultifying immobilism of the governmental system. The dangers for the political system are not, as may be elsewhere, that civil liberties will be snuffed out at the behest of an oppressive and authoritarian political culture but that in the face of the inefficiency and indecisiveness of the formal institutions individual actors may operate outside formal controls. The continued tendency of sectors of state administration to seek and indeed to achieve autonomy from political control is to some extent a function of the survival within the state of residues from the fascist dictatorship and from the Liberal state that preceded it. The personnel and institutions that carry these residues constitute a would-be alternative élite to the unchanging political élite of the postwar republic, just as do the terrorist groups on the left. The growth of terrorism and the responses of the state may thus both be related to the unbalanced economic development and incomplete political development of the postwar period.[14]

Moss argues that the BR and other terrorist groups view intended actions through the 'frames' of politics and violence. Actions are legitimated when frames converge; separating frames points to violence as an end in itself without achieving credible political gains. Thus, terrorist zeal might diminish, not necessarily because of the state's counter-terrorism but almost in spite of it. Terrorists were offered the chance to recant. Restrained counter-terrorism indicated the belief that a less strident response might prevent opponents proclaiming a unified, highly symbolic identity. The description of 'terrorist' was to be deflated in significance, the term 'terrorism' less explicitly condemned. Moss argues in these terms:

The increasing scale and scope of the rites of violence forced opponents and participants to clarify their commitments publicly. Opposition to violence on the Left grew, making it much more difficult for the users of violence to combine armed struggle with grassroots politics. They could no longer claim that their attacks were simply supplements to existing conflicts and spontaneous violence: the frames for violence and politics grew further apart.[15]

On particular occasions the political parties were called on to display a more focused rejection of the rites of violence. In kidnapping cases, for example, the government was invited to recognize the kidnappers as direct political antagonists and, by negotiating for the release of the victim, accept the reality of the passage between the two frames. Negotiations also carried the clear message that activities in the two frames of politics and violence were symbolically and instrumentally linked.

In sum, the obstacles which the nature of the Italian political system and the substantive disagreements of its major parties placed in the way of an agreed macro-level interpretation of violence helped to prevent the translation of highly varied local meanings into a plausible narrative of a unified assault on the Italian state. It frustrated any opportunity for the users of violence to seize on a clear set of meanings to reinforce their own understandings of what they were doing and might achieve. Moreover, the low-key, particularized defense of the state also served to undermine the Red Brigades' identification of the monolithic state as the primary antagonist for armed struggle – an identification required for assailants to be able to claim 'disarticulating' results for their actions.[16]

Italy's terrorists, rather like those in Algeria and Lebanon, in time became locked within a spiral of violence, a vortex of their own making. However rational terrorist pronouncements appeared at the beginning of their campaigning, a descent through hit-and-miss targeting to indiscriminate attacks was viewed in general as 'mindless' and 'non-negotiable' activity, obsessed with unattractive symbolism, and destructive in the main. Almost inevitably, the BR began to lose its effectiveness and credibility with the advent of the 1980s, culminating at about 1986 with a process of systematic failure which would not have surprised Furlong, writing in 1981:

The terrorists chose clandestinity and 'hit and run' tactics in Italy as an instrument of political activity, and developed around their choice a considerable volume of strategic theorising aimed at justifying *a posteriori* a choice made for quite other reasons. The world they appear to move in is inhabited by symbols, not by people. Within the terrorist groups there is, as in other exclusive homogeneous institutions, a large element of cognitive dissonance. As their violence is unsuccessful, they are drawn not to a reconsideration of their initial choice but to an exacerbation of the violence. In this sense, the system 'forces' them; granted their initial choice against other more conventional forms of political activity, the failure of their strategy leads them further into violence, and further into exclusivity and isolation.

One of the reasons for their lack of success and for the inevitable spiral of violence in which they find themselves is that the instruments they have chosen are simply not sufficient for the task. I would not argue complacently that terrorism is necessarily unsuccessful because it is 'pathological' or 'irrational'; but it does seem to me that where it is successful it is because whatever the long-term strategic aims of the terrorists, between them and their goal there is a series of negotiable demands or intermediate goals which may under certain circumstances be met by the opponent with less harm than is threatened directly by terrorist action. In some cases one of the intermediate goals most useful to terrorists and most readily obtainable is the publicity given to them and their action. But to take on the authority of the state with hit and run terrorism or with bomb attacks against civilians is to overestimate the effectiveness of the symbol, and in such cases publicity is of little value. There is little the Italian state can give the terrorists other than its own dissolution; the liberation of prisoners demanded by the BR during the Sossi and Moro kidnappings was invested with such symbolic significance that to have granted it would have been to give the BR the legitimacy of the title of 'guerrilla fighters' that they are seeking. They have succeeded in criminalising dissent, in rendering large sectors of the left, including some members of the PCI, vulnerable to the suspicion of being 'pro-terrorist'. Their actions have certainly made the task of government by consensus more difficult, and they have amply demonstrated the vulnerability of politically significant individuals to terrorist attack. But the fragmentation of the Italian state and the dispersion of authority within it make symbolic attacks against it by clandestine terrorists a particularly inefficient form of warfare.[17]

Donatella della Porta (1995) has studied at length the emergence of left-wing terrorism in Italy:

Clandestine organizations were founded by individuals who were tied to one another by a common militance in protest organizations. These organizations were not distinctive as far as interests, ideologies, or tactics were concerned. Their shared characteristic was, instead, the presence of semi-legal structures [. . .] In the case of armed formations solidarity networks were mainly composed of individuals who had previously used violent forms of political action.

Groups using illegal strategies arose when interests were not effectively mediated by the institutional system, when the political culture predisposed them to violence, and when social movements used violent tactics. By experimenting with different strategies, some organizations found that the adoption of more and more violent tactics attracted recruits. To counter state repression, clandestinity offered the advantage of minimizing some costs, such as the risk of arrest, even at the price of minimizing the benefits available in the short run.

Furthermore, with regard to the evolution of the Italian terrorist groups, the same condition of clandestinity brought about a series of vicious circles in which each attempt to face problems at a certain level produced new difficulties at the next. The centralization and structuration of the organizational model met the task of protecting the militants and involving them deeper and deeper inside the organization. Its consequence was, nevertheless, their further isolation from the outside world and, with it, the loss of channels for information and recruitment. Also, an increasingly compartmentalized structure was aimed at protecting the group and strengthening personal involvement. One of its effects was, however, to fuel personal rivalries, producing new splits.

Under pressure from the police, contacts with the external world were reduced to demands for logistical support. The tactics terrorist organizations adopted for getting financial resources were those typical of common criminality, exposed them to increased risks of armed fights with police, and damaged the image of the organizations before the public. The urgency of finding money and arms for the survival of the growing number of militants forced into clandestinity brought about a dangerous dependence on secret services and organized crime. To deny the defeats, the clandestine groups developed cryptic ideologies of highly symbolic value for insiders but with no meaning for the external world.

Underground organizations are also highly isolated from external reality, making it extremely difficult for their militants to perceive defeat. By reducing the possibilities of communicating with the external world, the terrorist organization becomes, in fact, the only source of information. This facilitates the internalization by the militants of the organization's ideology. Justification for the use of violence is therefore found in a highly abstract and simplified image of the world, where the victims are presented as small wheels of a mechanism, a small elite of 'freedom fighters'. [. . .]

In Italy, this kind of dynamic delayed the process of quitting the underground organizations but could not, however, prevent it. After frequently lengthy processes of individual and collective reflections, almost all the militants of the left-wing terrorist groups decided to abandon their commitment to violent political action. The abandonment of this commitment, as well as the reintegration of those who had quit, was facilitated by particular laws that allowed former members to maintain a collective identity and solidarity bonds among one another outside the terrorist organization. These widespread 'exits' from the terrorist groups indicate that the cycle of political violence in Italy is over. The remaining small nuclei, only sporadically active underground, represent a different, far less dangerous phenomenon.[18]

What della Porta has to say about Italian terrorism in particular would surely also apply to facets of terrorism elsewhere.

Rather as in contemporary Germany there are episodes of government warning as to a 'high risk' of potential terrorist attacks and consequently a 'state of alert'. Italians in government and public are particularly exercised about political unrest in Algeria, Libya and Egypt in 2010 and 2011. There is a current anxiety as to the intentions of Islamist youth, whether resident or immigrant. More worrying than the imminence of direct attack is the possibility that a network of small cells recruits, trains and deploys those who may turn into malevolent attackers of public order. Perhaps here and there in the larger cities there is already established a 'logistical base' was one press conjecture in February 2011.

Security control is considerably tighter and more sophisticated than in the old Red Brigade era. Quite disconcerting though is that that virulent, powerful group looks like being reconstituted. Their 'strategy of tensions' mode of operating, to alarm the public, say, at the time of election or governmental reshuffle, may now be pitched through terrorism diversity, through the new menaces of 'eco-terrorism', 'cyber-terrorism' or 'techno-terrorism'.

Government lawyers in Rome appear in the public eye no more effective than they do in Berlin. L'Osservatore Romano asked in December 2010 whether it was at all helpful not to define terrorism specifically. An individual whose ordinary type of crime was 'aggravated' towards 'subversion of democratic order' could be charged in such terms and penalised. Should not the law be more direct and tougher against the modern epidemic of terrorist violence?[19]

South Africa

THIS CASE STUDY DIFFERS from others in several respects. First, what took place in South Africa would be regarded by many as an example of state-sponsored terrorism where violence and torture were used at times by government forces to deal with domestic freedom fighters. Second, this chapter swings a spotlight on to a question frequently debated by those who vigorously protested against apartheid – namely, since there seems to be no alternative must there be resort to violence with an inevitable transition to armed struggle? Third, there is an account of an ambitious social experiment, as terrorism against oppression subsides, when a government attempts to establish truth and to unify a nation torn by conflict. The truth about terrorism is to be disclosed publicly as a prelude to reflection, amnesty, reparation and rehabilitation.

THE NATURE OF APARTHEID

The backdrop to the dramatic debate about the employment of violence was the racialist regime imposed by successive South African governments. It was in South Africa that racial segregation was translated into an ideological creed known since the 1940s as apartheid – separateness.

The origins of apartheid and its later development have been described, among others, by David Whittaker (1999), who surveys the early principles and the divide-and-rule practice and concludes by citing fresh views on the nature and extent of apartheid:

The forced separation of black and white in South Africa originated mainly as a protective response among Dutch settlers at the Cape in the 1650s who faced and feared the surrounding Bantu natives. British soldiers and farmers 150 years later displaced the Dutch (then termed 'Boers') who trekked northwards to found independent republics. The growth of industrialisation and the tapping of vast mineral resources after 1900 made South Africa dependent upon large numbers of black male workers migrating to white cities from 'reserves' where their families were left to sparse subsistence farming. Segregation of white and black was seen as defending and preserving white culture, residence and the social order, as well as operating a 'colour bar' to protect 'lower-class' whites from competition in the job market. Nelson Mandela has spoken of apartheid as 'a new term but an old idea [. . .] a monolithic system that was diabolical in its detail, inescapable in its reach and overwhelming in its power'. A creed it was, too, in that the Dutch Reformed Church regularly provided the ideologues with theological justification for white supremacy.

Apartheid was organised by parcelling out the country into white areas and African reserves. Six million white *Herrenvolk* went on to occupy 87 per cent of the land, enjoying high living standards and every amenity yet, as a 'vulture culture', growing ever more apprehensive about their future. Around the white settlements loomed a disconsolate mass of 30 million black Bantu. Originators of apartheid had an ingenious solution to the problem of finding cheap labour for factories and goldmines. Workers were bussed in from shacks in teeming 'townships' located downwind from the big cities. After 1962, country people were relegated to eight 'Bantustans' – up-country 'homeland reserves' – to develop in their own way, or so the theory went. The notion of separate development was, of course, apartheid at a remove and it was a spurious idea, for without fertile land, investment and infrastructure, no appreciable development is possible. These facilities were never made available. There were also 4 million Indians or mixed-race 'Coloured' people assigned to particular living places and occupations.

The divide-and-rule strategy of apartheid was deliberately employed to reduce black solidarity. In the reserves, government policies took advantage of long-standing tribal parochialism and feuding among Xhosa and Zulu clans. Elsewhere, the urban migrant was soon introduced to divisive perceptions of status common to white society: namely, persons who were skilled, semi-skilled, unskilled or servants. In the struggle for survival, as the Black Freedom Movement was to find, it was everyone for himself and for nobody else under the yoke. It was to take many years and much feverish political management before a black response to white overlordship shaped itself into united civil disobedience campaigns. In the 1950s the apartheid regime at last found itself engaged in conflict, as latent discontent sparked off a general strike against the Treason Trials of 1956. A fractured community was faced with draconian white laws. All Africans over the age of 16 were compelled to carry a Native Pass issued by the government for showing to any employer, policeman or civil official. Failure to produce this pass meant a fine, even detention for up to ninety days. No travel was possible without a permit. The signs 'WHITES ONLY' or 'AFRICANS ONLY' emblazoned on park benches, or at the entrance to a hotel, swimming pool, hospital, dance hall or beach, betokened the strict exclusion of the inferior race under the 1953 Separate Amenities Act. The Group Areas Act of 1950 confined Africans and Indians to specific residential areas in towns. Any trespass into white urban areas would lead to forced relocation or even imprisonment. Overall, in the white perception there was the fear of *svart gevaar*, a black danger which would always infiltrate both the white material culture and the confidence of *baasskap*, that inalienable supremacy. Exclusion through 200 legal statutes had the dual function of guaranteeing the security of white mastery and the preordained servitude of the rest. An ironical consequence of this position was the emergence of a group of middle-class Bantu professionals and intellectuals. They were lawyers, teachers, doctors, journalists and clergy – people able to recruit supporters not only for the African National Congress (ANC) but for a 'resistance front' of other political and cultural groups. They were joined by a growing band of sympathetic whites and Indians in the universities and the media. Meanwhile, the mass of the population, certainly by the 1970s, began to stir from lethargy into liberationist zeal.

Apartheid as a set of principles was never quite watertight. There were compelling reasons why apartheid could never be 'total' in spite of shrill racialist clamour and repressive legislation. White Afrikaner farmers and businessmen needed ample supplies of black labour, provided they were rigorously controlled in residence and movement. Many liberals felt they had a Christian mission to promote the 'differential development' and self-determination of blacks who had been herded away in tribal chiefdoms. As the South African economy grew ever more powerful, so apartheid policies had to address the problems of urbanisation magnetising an inflow of many thousands of black job-seekers and the consequent economic and social malaise of the reserves. 'Black power' in numbers and forcefulness was to force apartheid, that protective system for white interests, on to the defensive, revealing it as an expression of weakness rather than strength. From weakness sprang a dilemma: without a privileged position whites could not survive; without safeguarding racial separation privilege was not maintainable. For white leaders such as Hertzog, Malan and Verwoerd, apartheid was a survival mechanism, a life-raft supporting power, unity and the growth of group identity. Theirs was a backs-to-the-wall position, a fruitless posture given the dependence of the minority on the servile complacency of the majority.

Recent South African scholarship has published fresh views on the nature of apartheid:

- Ideological disunity was always more obvious than solidarity. 'Hardliners' and 'softliners' seldom agreed about the complexities of defusing potential class conflict, maintaining white supremacy, and steering between the counter-productive areas of all-out dominance and assimilation (through racial mixture or 'miscegenation').
- Apartheid was probably never a long-term Master Plan. Its principles were often hastily devised in an *ad hoc* manner to meet economic and social changes. Party leaders, industrial magnates, farmers, financiers frequently resorted to provisional and often contradictory styles of situation management.
- Already by 1930 conservative as well as liberal elements in South Africa were aware of the impossibility of ordering separate development of white and black 'to a large extent on lines of their own'. Calls for ethnic mobilisation might express nationalistic urges in rival white and black camps but the eventual emergence of a multi-racial South Africa was hardly in doubt. Equally certain was the prospect of conflict.

• Racist intolerance often had less to do with skin colour prejudice and more to do with feelings of vulnerability, fear and loss of group identity, particularly among a peripheralised white working class.[1]

APARTHEID INTERNATIONALLY CONDEMNED

At his presidential inauguration on 10 May 1994, Nelson Mandela declared that never again would his country 'suffer the indignity of being the skunk of the world'. The era of world contempt and forced isolation was now at an end. Whittaker takes up the story:

National governments, the UN, and a host of non-governmental organisations voiced a swelling protest from generalised, disapproving rhetoric just after the end of the Second World War to more specific and earnest campaigning in the 1960s. In 1952, India and states newly enfranchised from imperialism, such as Ethiopia, Iraq and Liberia, had asked the UN's General Assembly to consider urgently the question of 'Race conflict in South Africa resulting from the policies of apartheid'. Discrimination on so great a scale was a negation of the UN and its Charter and could easily lead to international conflict. South Africa resisted the allegation stating that the policies complained of were a domestic matter. This contemptuous response failed to deflect UN members from pressing home increasingly strong condemnation over the next twenty years. Attempts at persuasion and negotiation by UN Secretary-Generals and their representatives got nowhere. To help advance freedom in South Africa, many African and Arab states were prepared to supply whatever they could afford in the way of material and military aid.

By 1976 a majority in the General Assembly was explicitly supporting 'armed struggle' in South Africa as a way of defeating apartheid. Moral pressure was spearheaded by the Anti-Apartheid Movement in Britain, which recruited almost 40,000 vigorous campaigners at one point during its time of activity, 1959–94. There were similar action groups in the USA, in Scandinavia and in Holland. From time to time the US Congress expressed outrage and went on to pass legislation restricting South African trade. Indirect pressure eventually took the form of consumers and dock worker unions in Europe and the USA boycotting South African goods, and in 1977 led to mandatory embargoes on the shipment of arms, ammunition and military vehicles to Cape Town. During the following fifteen years the UN pressed, never too effectively, for the application of mandatory sanctions against South Africa and for disinvestment by trading partners, although there were certain governments, such as those of the USA, UK and France, who preferred to retain their links under the guise of 'constructive engagement', in the belief that penalising a delinquent state would lead to a siege mentality and render it impervious to dialogue and negotiation.

In 1974 the UN called for the total exclusion of South Africa from all international organisations and conferences held under the auspices of the UN, so long as apartheid was practised and in 1978 the UN established an International Anti-Apartheid Year. There was now in many lands quite uncompromising support for the 'liberation' struggles of the South Africans. The Security Council, for instance, in October 1977, had demanded the cessation of violent repression and torture, the release of detainees, the abrogation of bans on freedom groups and news media, the ending of the inferior and marginalising Bantustan system and, conclusively, a recourse to democratic elections and the establishment of black majority rule. The apartheid scenario was now one of explicit conflict. Month by month and year by year the UN and an array of 400 liberal non-governmental organisations issued condemnation of apartheid and calls for action. Sadly and quite predictably, tightening the screw from outside only led to fiercer repression and opposition. Even so, no other fight for basic freedoms has ever gained such wide political support and concrete assistance from other nations, perhaps 130 of them.[2]

THE GROWTH OF AFRICAN PROTEST

Uncertainty within South Africa and international pressure from outside shook the country's confidence and brought tension to an unendurable pitch, as Whittaker (1995 and 1999) relates, stressing the excesses of government action, the prominence of youth protest, and the dilemmas facing an international community over the extent to which their condemnation should move towards support for an armed struggle within South Africa:

Inevitably, the government sought to screw down dissent and opposition by recourse to a state of emergency in 36 areas, to the use of the armed police posse, detention and censorship. The original ANC claim that a struggle for liberation could be peaceful was no longer credible. South Africa's military budget, increased twelve times between 1960 and 1980, indicated mobilisation for civil war. Three great protests had severed the nation and angered the world: Sharpeville in 1960, Soweto in 1976, and the national strikes of 1984. It was obvious that the flailing efforts to silence the oppressed only made the voices of protest more audible.

A highly visible aspect of the liberation struggle against apartheid was the participation of young people in South Africa. One in two detainees was 18 or younger. The so-called 'children' were the most deprived and the most assertive (as they are in reports from the Palestinian conflict). There was great poignancy in 1985 when the UN proclaimed the year International Youth Year and from South Africa came the cry, 'Nothing demonstrates the utter bankruptcy of apartheid as the revolt of our youth. Never on our knees! Victory is certain!' This was a poignant message from Nelson Mandela, smuggled out of Robben Island Prison in 1980.

After forty years of a consistent stand the UN found itself faced with the issue of supporting violence as a legitimate vehicle of protest against apartheid. If the opposition persistently resorted to violent tactics as the contest burst out in virulence, what moral position should the outside world adopt? What, for instance, were the ultimate implications of the Rev. Allan Boesak's statement before the UN Special Committee on Apartheid in January 1988 when this South African freedom campaigner declared: 'Apartheid is so wrong, so indefensible, so intrinsically evil that it cannot be modernised, streamlined or reformed; it can only be irrevocably eradicated'? The UN's lawyers had found that a legally permissible right to use violence arises only in extreme situations as the final response to systematic violation. Furthermore, means used to resist violation of rights of individuals or of peoples should be 'proportionate' to the gravity of that violation. But is the right to violent combat legitimate only if it is accorded to a responsible group? Is it disproportionate to allow any individual guerrilla the option of violent tactics, perhaps irresponsibly?

With some impatience another question was being asked in South Africa: if our active resistance becomes violent can the international community really sit on its hands and take refuge in the non-violent liberalism of the Charter while our persecuted community and its oppressors are exploding? The General Assembly, after all, had challenged Pretoria in establishing the 'inalienable right' of the anti-apartheid wing to use all available means 'including armed struggle'. The ANC lost no time in blessing the militaristic efforts of its armed guerrilla force, *Umkhonto we Sizwe*, the Spear of the Nation – and it felt justified on hearing such last-ditch statements as that of President P. W. Botha in 1986, 'If we respect minority rights, we won't have black majority rule.'[3]

Black opposition to white apartheid in South Africa has moved through a number of stages. The first decade after the Second World War was one of 'soft' conflict and resentful alienation. Slowly the ANC began to build structured means of resistance through action committees, an illicit press and legal representation for detainees and the evicted. Student Power and Youth Power sharpened the intensity of conflict. They filled the prisons too. Three out of four detainees were aged between 18 and 25.

It was in March 1960 that police brutality in Sharpeville, when sixty-nine unarmed protestors were gunned down inescapably, brought 'hard' conflict in its train. There was now a polarisation of forces – a white solidarity, preventive with law and rifle, and a black solidarity movement making a stand for Black Consciousness.

> Mandela and others were taken off to years of penal servitude, their associates in the courtroom clenching fists invoking 'the anvil of united mass action and the hammer of armed struggle'. The accused used their trials as platforms for declaring beliefs rather than as any test of the law. They defended themselves in a moral sense, instead of resorting to fine forensic points. Growing protest gave way reluctantly to military training and the deployment of armed 'freedom fighters'. From its inception in 1912 the ANC had regarded non-violence as an indisputable core principle. It was best for the oppressed to pursue the unavoidable conflict in ways that saved lives, not threw them away. Guerrilla warriors, termed the Spear of the Nation, would seek to achieve liberation as far as possible without bloodshed and civil war.[4]

Black protest at the excesses of apartheid has been studied by Richard Gibson (1972), who traces the transition from early reliance on non-violent protest by the African National Congress (founded in 1912), through a period of faith in the 1940s and 1950s in the pacific principles of Mahatma Gandhi, allied to more interest in framing an activist strategy, and then to an ultimate phase after 1962 when resistance turns violent and initiates armed struggle:

The lengthy history of the ANC can conveniently be divided into four major periods. First, its founding as an élitist social movement of limited membership, enjoying mixed fortunes. Second, after a brief decline and near eclipse by the All-African

Convention, the revival of the organisation by its Youth League, which was committed to a more nationalistic, activist programme and its transformation into a mass movement. Third, the failure of the passive resistance campaign and the split of the ANC, with the most active nationalists leaving to form the Pan Africanist Congress. Fourth, its banning by the white minority regime, followed by the transfer of its leadership abroad and the belated adoption of the principle of armed struggle as the sole effective means of creating a democratic, multiracial state in South Africa.[5]

Gandhian tactics were equally out of place in South Africa, whose history is one continuous record of white brutality against black. The Afrikaner Nationalists might indeed be bigoted, racist fanatics, but, unlike their African adversaries, they had a remarkably clear vision of the goals they sought and had no scruples about the means they would use to reach them. Multiracialism as a concept, offering guarantees to the minority against arbitrary and discriminatory rule by an African majority, could only have been justified if there had been – as there was not – a substantial number of Europeans and Indians who were prepared to close ranks with the oppressed majority. As it was, the paltry numbers of European, Coloured, and Indian allies that came forward under the Congress Alliance blunted the driving force of African nationalism, the only ideology likely – as the subsequent history of the PAC [Pan-African Congress] demonstrates – to appeal to the broad masses of the black proletariat. In addition, while non-violence might have been acceptable in the short term as a tactic, nothing in the record of African struggle against European encroachment indicated that it could have any deep, long-term appeal to the African people, who passed their daily lives in conditions of often extreme social violence and brutality, harassed by white bosses and anti-social black thugs, as well as the ever-vigilant and violent South African police. Only a political programme of counter-violence on a massive scale, decided upon years earlier by an African organisation, might have mobilised the masses and permitted them to force an early clash with the regime before its repressive apparatus had been installed.[6]

The end of 1962 marked the beginning of violence, a sort of preparation for the major uprising. Groups of Africans, in the past generally docile and non-violent, even when not law-abiding, in their dealings with Europeans, mercilessly struck down individual whites in a number of localities [. . .] oppressed masses finding catharsis in the killing of their enemies [. . .] It seemed that the South African powder keg was at last exploding.[7]

The transition from non-violent protest to violent confrontation took place as part of the liberation movement that began tentatively throughout colonial Africa and then surged as a wave all through the post-colonial Africa that emerged after the Second World War. This is a process noted by A. de Braganca and I. M. Wallerstein (1982), who go on to see the advent of the 1960s as the time when massing for peace was to give way to mobilising for war. They cite the dramatic way in which the peaceful preferences of Gandhi's approach now succumbed – because all else failed – to an anxious dependence on violent assertiveness. They quote both Gandhi and Nelson Mandela as recognising the limits of non-violence:

All the national liberation movements in Portuguese and southern Africa started off by seeking to achieve change peacefully, by the pure route of dialogue and persuasion.

All without exception found after a while that this route was foreclosed to them by those who held power.

The violence of conquest was repeated in the violence of suppression of protest. Each movement paid its price, found its adherents massacred in the course of a public demonstration or a strike [. . .] Each concluded that the only road to national liberation open to them was the road of armed struggle.

It was not that they rejected dialogue. Rather they found regretfully that it was only via armed struggle that one day a real dialogue of coloniser and colonised would be possible, a dialogue rendered possible by the equalising impact of military combat.

While each movement ended at the same point, each came to it via a different logic and thus each felt it necessary to explain publicly the particular route it has taken.

The decision was particularly hard for the three countries that had a contact with the British parliamentary tradition – South Africa, Namibia and Zimbabwe. It was not that Africans were ever allowed to play a meaningful role in the local parliaments. It was rather that the values and the style of parliamentary struggle were persuasive in the society. Thus the ANC in South Africa had to overcome a long commitment to non-violence. How and why they did so is clear from the successive statements of Chief Luthuli in 1952 and 1964, Nelson Mandela in 1962, and Oliver Tambo in 1968. Furthermore they had to reconcile their views with the ideas and influence of Mahatma Gandhi who developed his theme of *satyagraha* not in India but in South Africa.[8]

Where the choice is set [wrote Gandhi in 1938] between cowardice and violence I would advise violence. I praise and extol the serene courage of dying without killing. Yet I desire that those who have not this courage should rather cultivate the art of killing and being killed, than basely avoid the danger. This is because he who runs away commits mental violence; he has not the courage of facing death by killing. I would a thousand times prefer violence than the emasculation of a whole race. I prefer to use arms in defence of honour rather than remain the vile witness of dishonour. (Mahatma Gandhi, Declaration on question of the use of violence in defence of rights, *The Guardian*, 16 December 1938.)[9]

THE DEBATE OVER THE USE OF VIOLENCE

This debate, mainly among members of the ANC, was to be long, strident and comprehensive in its range of issues. Its course has been charted by one of its leading participants, Nelson Mandela, in his autobiography (1994). Mandela outlines the shift from a passive mode in the 1940s, featuring civil disobedience with a Programme of Action dangerously on the edge of the law, to a much more active mode. Debate focuses on the uselessness, indeed impossibility, of non-cooperation, non-violence and mass-defiance; however well-planned and executed, it would earn the relentless crackdown of the Establishment. Even the doyen of the non-violent movement, Chief Luthuli (a Nobel Peace Prize winner), is seen eventually to come round to Mandela's way of thinking that black liberation must espouse violent methods. Mandela then goes on to show how, in the debate, the more conservative and the more radical

present their arguments with candour and with fear that they will soon be branded
as irresponsible terrorists. A consensus is reached that a new path must now be
planned – that of 'organised violence'. Mandela describes how he, though never a
soldier, is given the task of forming a resistance army, as an alternative to guerrilla
warfare. Leaflets describing the role of the new army were to be widely distributed
and Mandela and his fellow-liberators are now convinced that their policy is right:

The Programme of Action approved at the annual conference [ANC, 1949] called
for the pursuit of political rights through the use of boycotts, strikes, civil disobedience
and non-cooperation. In addition, it called for a national day of work stoppage in
protest against the racist and reactionary policies of the government. This was a
departure from the days of decorous protest, and many of the old stalwarts of the
ANC were to fade away in this new era of greater militancy. Youth League members
had now graduated to the senior organization. We had now guided the ANC to a
more radical and revolutionary path.[10]

Mass action was perilous in South Africa, where it was a criminal offence for
an African to strike, and where the rights of free speech and movement were
unmercifully curtailed. By striking, an African worker stood to lose not only his job
but his entire livelihood and his right to stay in the area in which he was living.[11]

We also discussed whether the campaign should follow the Gandhian principles
of non-violence or what the Mahatma called *satyagraha*, a non-violence that seeks to
conquer through conversion. Some argued for non-violence on purely ethical grounds,
saying it was morally superior to any other method.

Others said that we should approach this issue not from the point of view of
principles but of tactics, and that we should employ the method demanded by the
conditions. If a particular method or tactic enabled us to defeat the enemy, then it
should be used. In this case, the state was far more powerful than we, and any attempts
at violence by us would be devastatingly crushed. This made non-violence a practical
necessity rather than an option. This was my view, and I saw non-violence on the
Gandhian model not as an inviolable principle but as a tactic to be used as the situation
demanded.

The joint planning council agreed upon an open-ended programme of non-
cooperation and non-violence. Two stages of defiance were proposed. In the first
stage, a small number of well-trained volunteers would break selected laws in a
handful of urban areas. They would enter proscribed areas without permits, use
Whites Only facilities such as toilets, Whites Only railway compartments, waiting
rooms and post office entrances. They would deliberately remain in town after
curfew. Each batch of defiers would have a leader who would inform the police in
advance of the act of disobedience so that the arrests could take place with a minimum
of disturbance. The second stage was envisioned as mass defiance, accompanied by
strikes and industrial actions across the country.[12]

I said the government was now scared of the might of the African people. As I
condemned the government for its ruthlessness and lawlessness, I overstepped the
line: I said that the time for passive resistance had ended, that non-violence was a
useless strategy and could never overturn a white minority regime bent on retaining
its power at any cost. At the end of the day, I said, violence was the only weapon

that would destroy apartheid and we must be prepared, in the near future, to use that weapon.

I had begun to analyse the struggle in different terms. The ambition of the ANC was to wage a mass struggle, to engage the workers and peasants of South Africa in a campaign so large and powerful that it might overcome the *status quo* of white oppression. But the Nationalist government was making any legal expression of dissent or protest impossible. I saw that it would ruthlessly suppress any legitimate protest on the part of the African majority. A police state did not seem far off.[13]

In discussing the ANC's policy of non-violence, he [Chief Luthuli] emphasized that there was a difference between non-violence and pacifism. Pacifists refused to defend themselves even when violently attacked, but that was not necessarily the case with those who espoused non-violence. Sometimes men and nations, even when non-violent, had to defend themselves when they were attacked.[14]

The debate on the use of violence had been going on among us since early 1960. I had first discussed the armed struggle as far back as 1952 with Walter Sisulu. Now, I again conferred with him and we agreed that the organization had to set out on a new course. The Communist Party had secretly reconstituted itself underground and was now considering forming its own military wing. We decided that I should raise the issue of the armed struggle within the Working Committee [ANC], and I did so in a meeting in June of 1961.

I had barely commenced my proposal when Moses Kotane, the secretary of the Communist Party and one of the most powerful figures in the ANC Executive, staged a counter-assault, accusing me of not having thought out the proposal carefully enough. He said that I had been outmanoeuvred and paralysed by the government's actions, and now in desperation I was resorting to revolutionary language. 'There is still room,' he stressed, 'for the old methods if we are imaginative and determined enough. If we embark on the course Mandela is suggesting, we will be exposing innocent people to massacres by the enemy.'

I was candid and explained why I believed we had no choice but to turn to violence. I used an old African expression: '*Sebatana ha se bokwe ka diatla*' ('The attacks of the wild beast cannot be averted with only bare hands'). Moses was a long-time communist, and I told him that his opposition was like the Communist Party in Cuba under Batista. The party had insisted that the appropriate conditions had not yet arrived, and waited because they were simply following the textbook definitions of Lenin and Stalin. Castro did not wait, he acted – and he triumphed. If you wait for textbook conditions, they will never occur. I told Moses point blank that his mind was stuck in the old mould of the ANC being a legal organization. People were already forming military units on their own, and the only organization that had the muscle to lead them was the ANC. We had always maintained that the people were ahead of us, and now they were.[15]

The Executive meeting in Durban, like all ANC meetings at the time, was held in secret and at night in order to avoid the police. I suspected I would encounter difficulties because Chief Luthuli was to be in attendance and I knew of his moral commitment to non-violence. I was also wary because of the timing: I was raising the issue of violence so soon after the Treason Trial, where we had contended that for the ANC non-violence was an inviolate principle, not a tactic to be changed as conditions warranted. I myself believed precisely the opposite; that non-violence was a tactic that should be abandoned when it no longer worked.

At the meeting I argued that the state had given us no alternative to violence. I said it was wrong and immoral to subject our people to armed attacks by the state without offering them some kind of alternative. I mentioned again that people on their own had taken up arms. Violence would begin whether we initiated it or not. Would it not be better to guide this violence ourselves, according to principles where we saved lives by attacking symbols of oppression, and not people? If we did not take the lead now, I said, we would soon be latecomers and followers to a movement we did not control.

The chief initially resisted my arguments. For him, non-violence was not simply a tactic. But we worked on him the whole night; and I think that in his heart he realised we were right. He ultimately agreed that a military campaign was inevitable. The National Executive formally endorsed the preliminary decision of the Working Committee.

The chief and others suggested that we should treat this new resolution as if the ANC had not discussed it. He did not want to jeopardize the legality of our unbanned allies. His idea [Luthuli's] was that a military movement should be a separate and independent organ, linked to the ANC and under the overall control of the ANC, but fundamentally autonomous. There would be two separate streams of the struggle. We readily accepted the chief's suggestion. The chief and others warned against this new phase becoming an excuse for neglecting the essential tasks of organization and the traditional methods of struggle. That, too, would be self-defeating because the armed struggle, at least in the beginning, would not be the centrepiece of the movement.

The following night a meeting of the joint Executive was scheduled in Durban. This would include the Indian Congress, the Coloured People's Congress, the South African Congress of Trade Unions and the Congress of Democrats. Although these other groups customarily accepted ANC decisions, I knew that some of my Indian colleagues would strenuously oppose the move towards violence.

The meeting had an inauspicious beginning. Chief Luthuli, who was presiding, announced that even though the ANC had endorsed a decision on violence, 'it is a matter of such gravity, I would like my colleagues here tonight to consider the issue afresh'. It was apparent that the chief was not fully reconciled to our new course.

We began our session at 8 p.m., and it was tumultuous. I made the identical arguments that I had been making all along, but many people expressed reservations.

We argued the entire night, and in the early hours of the morning I began to feel we were making progress. Many of the Indian leaders were now speaking in a sorrowful tone about the end of non-violence. The entire debate went back to square one. But towards dawn, there was a resolution. The Congresses authorized me to go ahead and form a new military organization, separate from the ANC. The policy of the ANC would still be that of non-violence. I was authorized to join with whomever I wanted or needed to create this organization and would not be subject to the direct control of the mother organization.

This was a fateful step. For fifty years, the ANC had treated non-violence as a core principle, beyond question or debate. Henceforth, the ANC would be a different kind of organization. We were embarking on a new and more dangerous path, a path of organized violence, the results of which we did not and could not know.[16]

I, who had never been a soldier, who had never fought in battle, who had never fired a gun at an enemy, had been given the task of starting an army. It would be a daunting task for a veteran general, much less a military novice. The name of this new organization was Umkhonto we Sizwe (The Spear of the Nation) – or MK for short. The symbol of the spear was chosen because with this simple weapon Africans had resisted the incursions of whites for centuries.

Our mandate was to wage acts of violence against the state – precisely what form those acts would take was yet to be decided. Our intention was to begin with what was least violent to individuals but most damaging to the state.

I began in the only way I knew how, by reading and talking to experts. What I wanted to find out were the fundamental principles for starting a revolution. I discovered that there was a great deal of writing on this very subject, and I made my way through the available literature on armed warfare and in particular guerrilla warfare. I wanted to know what circumstances were appropriate for a guerrilla war; how one created, trained and maintained a guerrilla force; how it should be armed; where it gets its supplies – all basic and fundamental questions.

Any and every source was of interest to me. I read the report of Blas Roca, the general secretary of the Communist Party of Cuba, about their years as an illegal organization during the Batista regime. In *Commando* by Deneys Reitz, I read of the unconventional guerrilla tactics of the Boer generals during the Anglo–Boer War. I read works by and about Che Guevara, Mao Tse-tung, Fidel Castro. In Edgar Snow's brilliant *Red Star Over China* I saw that it was Mao's determination and non-traditional thinking that had led him to victory. I read *The Revolt* by Menachem Begin and was encouraged by the fact that the Israeli leader had led a guerrilla force in a country with neither mountains nor forests, a situation similar to our own. I was eager to know more about the armed struggle of the people of Ethiopia against Mussolini, and of the guerrilla armies of Kenya, Algeria and the Cameroons.

I went into the South African past. I studied our history both before and after the white man. I probed the wars of African against African, of African against white, of white against white. I made a survey of the country's chief industrial areas, the nation's transportation system, its communication network. I accumulated detailed maps and systematically analysed the terrain of different regions of the country.[17]

In planning the direction and form that MK would take, we considered four types of violent activities: sabotage, guerrilla warfare, terrorism and open revolution. For a small and fledgling army, open revolution was inconceivable. Terrorism inevitably reflected poorly on those who used it, undermining any public support it might otherwise garner. Guerrilla warfare was a possibility, but since the ANC had been reluctant to embrace violence at all, it made sense to start with the form of violence that inflicted the least harm against individuals: sabotage.

Because it did not involve loss of life, it offered the best hope for reconciliation among the races afterwards. We did not want to start a blood-feud between white and black. Animosity between Afrikaner and Englishman was still sharp fifty years after the Anglo–Boer war; what would race relations be like between white and black if we provoked a civil war? Sabotage had the added virtue of requiring the least manpower.

Our strategy was to make selective forays against military installations, power plants, telephone lines and transportation links; targets that would not only hamper the military effectiveness of the state, but frighten National Party supporters, scare away foreign capital, and weaken the economy. This we hoped would bring the government to the bargaining table. Strict instructions were given to members of MK that we would countenance no loss of life. But if sabotage did not produce the results we wanted, we were prepared to move on to the next stage: guerrilla warfare and terrorism [. . .] thousands of leaflets with the new MK Manifesto were [to be] circulated all over the country announcing the birth of Umkhonto we Sizwe.[18]

Experience convinced us that rebellion would offer the government limitless opportunities for the indiscriminate slaughter of our people. But it was precisely because the soil of South Africa is already drenched with the blood of innocent Africans that we felt it our duty to make preparations as a long-term undertaking to use force in order to defend ourselves against force. If war were inevitable, we wanted the fight to be conducted on terms most favourable to our people. The fight which held out prospects best for us and the least risk of life to both sides was guerrilla warfare. We decided, therefore, in our preparations for the future, to make provision for the possibility of guerrilla warfare.

All whites undergo compulsory military training, but no such training was given to Africans. It was in our view essential to build up a nucleus of trained men who would be able to provide the leadership which would be required if guerrilla warfare started. We had to prepare for such a situation before it became too late to make proper preparations.[19]

THE DEFEAT OF APARTHEID

The crumbling of apartheid happened with unexpected rapidity, as Whittaker (1999) relates, and its demise brought elections and a new Government of National Unity:

In the late 1980s there were secret talks between the Pretoria government and the ANC, which explored the middle ground between white fears (and a sense of retreat) and black hopes. In February 1990 President F. W. de Klerk sounded an auspicious note, declaring in Parliament, 'Now is the time to speak out loud and clear about the dreams that unite us, because these dreams are the foundation of our new South African nation'. Thus was the urgency of reconciling conflict proclaimed, and officially so. The ANC was now loosed from its ban. Mandela was released to take his 'long walk to freedom' after thirty-seven years in jail. By degrees the demeaning restrictions of apartheid were lifted. Segregation in public places was ended. Steadily, the noxious laws that had inflamed protest were repealed. As the white National Party gradually lost ground, they could dream only of a fragile retention of some of their commercial and investment privileges. Exploited black masses shared visions handicapped by 50 per cent illiteracy and 25 per cent unemployment. Right-wing factions reviled de Klerk as a traitor as he engaged in working-party discussions for a new constitution that would smoothly but irrevocably transfer power to the majority. A time of transition would be a time of compromise when a black government had to provide structural guarantees for the white minority. At the same time, 22 million black people had to be coaxed into careful acceptance of compromise. They must be ready to be enfranchised for democratic voting. For much of the time the prospects of an end to conflict and of any lasting reconciliation were bedevilled by savage fighting between the more fanatical activists of the ANC and Zulu nationalists.

Only one way of reconciling South Africa's conflict seemed practicable and fair. Power and reconciliation were to be shared. A Government of National Unity would put an end to the isolation and rejection of both black and white. ANC leaders made much of the significance of their logo of the spear and the wheel. Freedom for the deprived had required an advancing thrust; freedom for all South Africans would need a common revolution. There would be no time for recrimination: enemies must become partners. A new united government was elected, with the ANC getting 60 per cent of total votes and the National Party 20 per cent, and it took office in Pretoria in April 1994. Nelson Mandela became the first black President with F. W. de Klerk, the former President, as a Vice-President. In a Cabinet of twenty-seven there were ten white members, six of them from the National Party. South Africa was now a nation on a new footing; no longer were most South Africans co-existing in an occupied territory.[20]

TERRORISM IN THE LIGHT OF TRUTH

The newly elected Government of National Unity decided in May 1994 to set up a Truth and Reconciliation Commission (TRC) with a charge to investigate human rights abuses under the former apartheid regime that had been sanctioned by the state or were the result of action by liberation groups. Under scrutiny would be the period 1960–94. South Africa would now have its violent past acknowledged rather than covered over. Coming to terms with terror in the past must advance means of reconciliation in the present and in the future. This mammoth exercise was scheduled to take some four years of public disclosure, a process that Whittaker (1999) has summarised:

The TRC would investigate abuses by publicly hearing testimony from victims and statements from the accused. Further steps would involve report, recommendation, arrangements for reparation and rehabilitation. The truth laid bare would be beamed to all South Africans regardless of colour [. . .] Eighteen commissioners, impartial and broadly representative of the nation, were to be chosen by President Nelson Mandela. Their unenviable task was to prise apart thirty-three years of repression and counter-violence and to do it within four years. The Final Report of the TRC had to go to the State President by 31 July 1998.

The objectives of South Africa's TRC seem clear enough. Organisational arrangements provide for public disclosure before a tribunal of commissioners who are mainly figures from professional and public fields, not lawyers. Their chairman is Archbishop Desmond Tutu. The public sessions are held in Cape Town and at various locales in the countryside. The unremitting efforts to secure reliable and at times dramatic evidence are followed closely by the media. Very little is heard in camera – this would defeat the purpose of the exercise.

Three committees were formed: Human Rights Violation; Amnesty; Reparation and Rehabilitation. Agendas were carefully thought out but aroused great debate. The first committee was restricted to considering ill-treatment, torture, abduction and murder.[21]

The final report of the TRC is now available in four comprehensive volumes. In this case study it is, of course, not possible to examine the findings in detail, but even a short résumé casts light on the web of terrorism in South Africa. The TRC began its work by asking questions of the main participants in South Africa's apartheid conflict, that is the ANC and the National Party (who had a majority in the former de Klerk Government). Answers to these questions, in written form and in countless statements by witnesses, occupy 400 pages in volume 1 of the report.

A brief inspection of the actual questions throws into relief a number of the crucial issues raised by terrorism, in this case a terrorism that was widely shared by members of the South African community. First, there are the questions directed to the ANC; second, those that went to the National Party:

Questions to the ANC

In its submission the ANC uses a definition of gross human rights violations different from that in the legislation governing the TRC: 'Actions carried out in the course of the just war of national liberation do not constitute gross violations of human rights' [. . .] What does the ANC mean by this, especially with regard to amnesty application?

[. . .] does the ANC encourage all those who committed gross human rights violations as defined by the TRC to apply for amnesty?

[. . .] The ANC quotes a pamphlet identifying justified targets (page 52) as 'the racist army, police, death squads, agents and stooges in our midst'. Can this definition possibly be used to legitimise the killing of policemen, alleged informers, community councillors, and co-opted parliamentarians? [. . .] Can the ANC elaborate what is meant by 'stooges in our midst'?

Can the ANC elaborate and substantiate efforts made to avoid such attacks on civilian targets? What steps were taken, after the incidents, to investigate them? Were ANC cadres disciplined for their involvement in such activities?

Can the ANC supply any evidence substantiating the involvement of South African security forces in the death or disappearance of MK cadres and ANC members?

Questions to the National Party

The submission [by the National Party] states that 'we defended South Africa against those who planned to seize power by violent and unconstitutional means'. How does one achieve power constitutionally if one is disenfranchised and denied many of one's most basic constitutional rights? [. . .] Can one legitimately equate the struggle against apartheid with the struggle to defend it?

In the submission of the NP it is stated: 'We never hesitated to submit reasonably substantiated allegations [concerning serious violations of human rights] to vigorous investigation'.

Is this true of all periods during which the NP was in office? [. . .] Anti-apartheid perpetrators were pursued with vigour and tenacity. Did the government make an equal commitment to investigating human rights abuse by the security forces?

How does one explain the alleged ignorance of the former State President and his predecessors of gross human rights violations committed by the security forces and others? Why were the accusations of the state's critics, the media and former agents of the state not adequately investigated?

The submission indicates that no one in a position of authority can 'know everything which takes place in the realm of his or her managerial responsibilities'. This raises the question of accountability. Who should ultimately be held responsible for gross human rights violations?

Did any resolution of the SSC [State Security Council] authorise the security forces to use the same methods as revolutionaries to counter the revolutionary threat? If so, what was contemplated hereby? If this is so, to what extent is it legitimate to blame 'revolutionary strategies adopted by the government's opponent' for blurring the traditional distinctions between combatants and non-combatants, legitimate and illegitimate targets and between acceptable and unacceptable methods of police and military action?[22]

Each of those questioned was asked to furnish the TRC with a two- to three-page statement in regard to the party's underlying ideology, values, motives and reasons for involvement in violations. 'It is important', stated the TRC, 'for these views to be boldly, and yet sensitively, articulated in order to facilitate the reconciliation process'. The mind of the terrorist in South Africa was to be scrutinised.

Apart from the main issues highlighted by TRC questioning there is in the textual accompaniment explicit reference to a whole range of terrorist methods employed by both sides – death squads, demolition and burning of property, forced eviction, torture, water and food poisoning, garotting, summary execution, 'smear' and disinformation campaigns, 'disappearances' without trace, car bombs, assassination and land-mine planting.[23]

The traumatic experience of terrorism in South Africa is unlikely to bring about either swift or easy reconciliation, as Whittaker (1999) points out:

If reconciliation is to be the desirable outcome, then objective understanding of the situation is furthered by regarding both parties as victims of apartheid. There is some thought among TRC officials that the term 'victim' is better replaced by 'survivor', implying a degree of control and perhaps recovery which the other term does not connote.[24]

Rather more carefully than the authorities in the other scenarios we have studied, the South Africans are very carefully attempting to take their 'survivors' into a unified and multi-racial, post-terrorist, 'rainbow' society. It is a breathtaking experiment.

The TRC closed its public hearings early in 2002. Two years later, the paperwork behind the scenes was concluded. Statements from apartheid victims numbered 20,000; amnesty applications totalled 7,100. The aftermath of the public unveiling of 'the truth – the road to reconciliation' has seen the publication of much comment by psychologists and sociologists under such headings as 'Remorse, Forgiveness and Rehumanisation' and 'Amnesty, Memory, Justice and Impunity'. Interested readers can have access to these sources and, indeed, to the whole workings of the TRC by visiting the website of the South African Department of Justice and Constitutional Affairs.[25]

Generally, some ten years since the TRC publicly folded in 2002 there is voiced on occasion dissatisfaction as to the lack of wide political support for the Commission's Final Report and recommendations. Why is translation into firm law so tardy? A government proclaiming a three-fold mission of reviewing the past, reforming the present, and anticipating the future must expedite programmes to deal with high crime, unequal wealth and social tensions. Not all though would agree with Archbishop Desmond Tutu's belief that South Africa is 'sitting on a powder keg' because of its failure to alleviate poverty a decade after apartheid.

Sixteen terrorism case studies
Conclusion

S OMETHING OF THE EXTENT and variety of terrorism during the last half-century has been illustrated in the 16 case studies presented in Part Two. This concluding section will be brief. There are two reasons for this. In the first place, each case study should stand by itself as a distinctive example of how terrorism, as we understand it, can arise and develop. In a number of these case studies, there are already conclusions and there is no need for duplication. One or two points about each should suffice.

Hizbullah in the Lebanon and Hamas and Fatah in Iraq demonstrate the force of political action becoming violent as an alliance of religious fundamentalists and secular radicals sets out to mobilise Islamic constituencies in addition to ousting Israeli and Western influences from the Middle East. Their doctrinaire stance leads them to venerate martyrdom and, by way of mission and campaign, the Jihad, to use bombs, guns and hostages to advance their cause. Recently, however, as democratic movements ripple across Arab lands we have had an Al-jazeera news channel commentator declare that his Arab fellows are now being so violated by their own governments that they themselves have no occasion to resort to violence elsewhere.

Another enigma is that of Libya's state-sponsoring of terrorist activities. Transformed from the desert fringe to an oil-rich Socialist community and with a charismatic leader, Libya's provocative behaviour and networking of terrorist enterprise in other lands has seen it consigned as a pariah state. Since the summer of 1999, the terrorists of Libya have entered the market place, scenting the possibility of dependable trade contracts. Sanctions against them were lifted. Their arch-terrorist leader, Colonel Quaddafi, made conciliatory approaches towards his former 'imperialist' enemies. Britain and the United States renewed diplomatic relations.

The transition from terrorist exporter to internationally acknowledged respectability was an intriguing one.

Now we have a further transformation with Libya's leader and his authoritarian clique taking on the narrow majority of the population who want a transition to democracy and will fight fiercely for it. Looking ahead, Libya's future shape is unclear at the moment.

Sri Lanka's problem with the fanaticism of the Tamil Tigers remains unsolved. A desperate vortex or internal ruthless violence is fuelled by the external support of many Tamils who fund armed resistance to a government they see as unwilling to grant the Tamil minority self-determination as a separate entity. Northern Ireland, for so long imprisoned by myth and sectarian memories feeding decades of fratricide, is now, it seems, entering an area of cautious change with political concordat between parliamentary representatives at Stormont and members of diverse activist groups, the IRA and others. It is this diversity and the fragmented nature of peace observance that renders stability and calmness difficult to gauge.

Unhappily, in the cases of Basque Spain, Peru and Colombia, we have situations of whole societies caught up in many years of frenzy. The first impulses of nationalistic fervour, liberationist zeal, proletariat discontent in towns, and the grinding poverty of peasantry, have variously set elements of society against one another and brought upon those resorting to impassioned and frustrated violence the repressive force of counter-action in the shape often of 'dirty war'. Only in the instances of Spain and Colombia has there been a prospect of edging towards settlement and perhaps a chance of reconciliation. Germany and Italy reveal, in differing ways, a transition from protest demonstration to sporadic then planned violence, and in these two countries a draining away of public support for activity regarded as mindless and nihilistic. Interestingly, in Germany, the terrorist aim of attacking what they saw as a bourgeois (Neo-Nazi) authority counter-productively engendered in most Germans a feeling that they had to defend a young post-Nazi and liberal New Germany.

Finally, in the case of South Africa, terrorism in the early days came under intense scrutiny. If the 'victims' of monolithic apartheid were to emerge as 'survivors', then massing for peace might have to become mobilisation for war. Organised violence might then be the only feasible option. Terror would have its place. In the end, sabotage and other means of 'guided violence' helped to bring about the dissolution of apartheid and the creation of a peaceful and nominally united 'rainbow nation'. After the welter of division, the new South Africa hoisted into place a process of Truth and Reconciliation to look squarely at the historic incidence of discrimination and terrorist violence, and to seek to make amends for it.

This Reader, in its fourth edition, has made a special point of the 'unholy alliance' of al-Qaida, its leader, Osama bin Laden, and Afghanistan's fundamentalist regime, the Taliban. World attention remains focused on the horror of America's 11 September 2001 attacks, and on US attempts to recruit a counter-terrorist coalition to deal with what has been represented as a global threat. Afghanistan, a hornet's nest, is being pulverised in response but the Taliban there and al-Qaida in many other places remain a formidable menace. It is now urgent for the world community to think out means of dealing productively with terrorist activities and to scan carefully dissident aims, motivating circumstances and methods.

There is a second reason for the brevity of these conclusions. It was pointed out earlier that 16 case studies ought to stand separately from one another. In telling us about terrorism and its practitioners they do so in contrasted fashion, although there are some common characteristics. It is not difficult to theorise about cause and effect across a range of examples. This is frequently done yet it is simplistic and leads to invalid, unreliable judgements. In Part One, attempts to define terrorism and analyse motivation were thought problematic.

M. R. L. Smith (1995) identifies some distorted interpretations of terrorism common in print. There is often stress on non-state political actors and superficial comparison of diverse scenarios. Smith sees such procedures as weak explanatory tools. The Editor of this Reader agrees, quoting some of Smith's points:

It is possible to identify a number of problem areas with the contemporary study of terrorism. In the first instance, there has been a tendency to focus attention on non-state political actors while ignoring other agencies of terror like governments and quasi-government organisations. This has led to the assumption that most, if not all, terrorism is practised exclusively by those without direct political power and thereby equating all forms of insurgency with terrorism. This assumption is quite common in public discourse and over the years has helped foster the notion of terrorism as a pejorative term denoting criminality, psychopathology and an ethical void where the ability to distinguish between right and wrong has been lost. Such thinking can result in commentators merely making moral condemnations of those political groups with whom they happen to disagree. [. . .]

The distorted focus on non-state actors has reduced a lot of terrorist studies to a series of typologies and historical catalogues which try to identify the alleged incidence of terrorism around the world. Not only does this make the subject fairly dull, above all, it decontextualises low level conflicts by trying to connect an assortment of diverse political groups merely on the basis of their *modus operandi*. If one thinks about it for a moment, the proposition seems intellectually quite dubious. No serious historian would contend that World War Two and the Arab–Israel Six Day War in 1967 are analogous [. . .] merely because the combatants at various stages happened to use tanks. At best this would be a rather crass observation. At worst, a thoroughly misleading and bogus linkage. Yet linking the unlinkable is exactly what terrorist studies has sometimes tried to do. There is no reason why the violence of the Red Army Faction in West Germany during the 1970s, ostensibly the product of 1960s student radicalism and a frustrated post-war generation, should be associated with Irish nationalist violence the roots of which go back centuries. Even so, one will find all sorts of studies which try to link these and other disparate groups with each other as if they were in some way comparable. Instead of treating agents of political violence and the conflicts of which they are a part as singularly distinctive, each deserving separate treatment, the study of terrorism often draws together these varied low-level wars by trying to make theoretical generalisations primarily on the basis of tactical modality. Individual wars are thus disconnected from their historical and cultural backgrounds. Clearly this is an unsatisfactory way to analyse what are usually complex and highly divergent conflicts. The damage caused to the decent study of low intensity wars by the decontextualisation of conflicts as a result of terrorist studies methodology, seen in the superficiality of some works in the area, has been vast. So who are the experts on terrorism? Answer: there are no experts, just people who know a little about a lot of small conflicts.

For the strategic analyst who sees terrorism purely as an instrument of policy to be selected by any political actor from a range of options be they peaceful or violent, speculating on 'what gives rise to terrorism?' is like saying 'what gives rise to conventional war?' The question holds no meaning. All of the difficulties over causality, the over-concentration on tactical minutiae, counter-measures and so on, merely illustrates how the public debate on terrorism is flawed at the point of departure, namely at the definitional level. Nowhere is this best captured than in the expression which continues to take up an inordinate amount of space in terrorist studies literature: 'One man's terrorist is another man's freedom fighter.' This 'weary cliché', as Peter Sederburg says, 'suggests that all attempts to formulate the concept [of terrorism] will be hopelessly compromised by essentially arbitrary personal biases. Consequently, any analysis based upon such conceptual foundations will be inevitably distorted and vacuous'. Vacuous is certainly a word which can probably describe many of the tortured dissertations which have tried to resolve this alleged conundrum. Whatever significance the aphorism may have had once has now been mangled out of existence by those who have attached far more intellectual weight to the phrase than it really deserved.

Without wishing to rehearse the debate in detail, the notion of one man's terrorist is another man's freedom fighter is, to a strategic theorist at any rate, a false dichotomy. You can be both. For example, few would dispute that in its fight for independence from France between the mid-1950s and the early 1960s the Algerian *Front de Liberation Nationale* (FLN) could be justifiably described as freedom fighters. At the same time, the FLN carried out operations, most notably in the capital Algiers, which were clearly intended to terrorise the French settler population. The point is that one part of the terrorist–freedom fighter equation is a description of policy (terrorist/terrorism) while the other is a moral judgement on the nature of a belligerent (freedom fighter). They are two entirely separate intellectual issues. Why try to link them? It is illogical. [. . .]

[. . .] The persistence of the old saw 'one man's terrorist is another man's freedom fighter', and the time wasted trying to force this false linkage, illustrates both the weakness of terrorist studies as an explanatory tool and the tyranny of simplistic slogans when they become a substitute for thought.[1]

Also, in this edition, there is an account of '7/7' – the fearsome bombing of London's transport in July 2005. Readers' attention is drawn to the conclusions and recommendations in several official reports compiled and published after the incident.

There remain a good number of unresolved conjectures and queries about the bombers' intentions and the process of the official counter-terrorist response.

Many of the points that M. R. L. Smith makes are worth bearing in mind when looking through the discussion of legal and ethical issues in Part Three.

PART THREE

Prevention and control of terrorism

THE PREVENTION OF TERRORISM must reach beyond physical control measures to take account of ethical and legal considerations. Part III suggests pointers for readers' reflection, further enquiry and discussion.

Terrorism
Some ethical issues

THIS CHAPTER WILL DEAL WITH ETHICAL CONSIDERATIONS, and the following chapter will take into account legal matters. There is, of course, much common ground between these two fields.

Ethical issues are outlined here chiefly according to three presentations: that of Albert Bandura (1998) and his theories of 'moral disengagement'; that of Haig Khatchadourian (1998) with a 'moral evaluation' of terrorism; and that of Jonathan Moreno (2003), editing a wide-ranging account of bioethics.

TERRORISM AS A CRIME; TERRORISM AS WARFARE

Before looking at ethical issues raised by the three writers, it is useful as a starting point to check the definition of terrorism. Basically, one asks, is terrorism indictable as crime or warfare? A decision on this goes some way towards clarifying evaluation. Amid a host of definitions there is a straightforward statement by Brian Jenkins (1986):

Civilised nations have through law identified modes of conduct that are criminal. Homicide, kidnapping, threats to life, and the willful destruction of property appear in the criminal codes of every country. True, some of the prohibitions may legally be violated in times of war – the law against killing, for example, may be violated by those we call 'lawful combatants'. Terrorists claim to be soldiers at war, who are therefore privileged to break ordinary laws. But even in war there are rules outlawing the use of certain weapons and tactics.

The rules of war grant civilian combatants who are not associated with 'valid' targets at least theoretical immunity from deliberate attack. They prohibit taking hostages. They prohibit violence against those held captive. They define belligerents. They define neutral territory. These rules are sometimes violated – and those responsible for the violations become war criminals. But violations in no way diminish the validity of the rules.

Some international lawyers see the laws of war as possible solution to the dilemma of definition. They suggest that rather than trying to negotiate new treaties on terrorism that are not likely to be ratified or enforced, nations should apply the laws of war, to which almost all have agreed. Terrorists, they say, should be dealt with as soldiers who commit atrocities. Nearly all countries have agreed to try or extradite soldiers who commit atrocities in international armed conflicts. Why should persons not explicitly granted soldiers' status be given greater leeway to commit violence? Under the laws-of-war approach, terrorism would comprise all acts committed in peacetime that, if committed during war, would constitute war crimes.

Terrorism thus can be objectively defined by the quality of the act, but not by the identity of the perpetrators or the nature of their cause. All terrorist acts are crimes, many of which would also be war crimes or 'grave breaches' of the rules of war if we accepted the terrorists' assertion that they are waging war. All terrorist acts involve violence or the threat of violence, sometimes coupled with explicit demands. The violence is usually directed against noncombatants. The purposes are political. The actions are often carried out in a way that will achieve maximum publicity. The perpetrators are usually members of an organized group. Their organizations are by necessity clandestine, but unlike other criminals, terrorists often claim credit for their acts. And finally – the hallmark of terrorism – the acts are intended to produce psychological effects beyond the immediate physical damage.

While these criteria do not eliminate all ambiguity, they enable us to draw some limits and answer some questions. Terrorism differs from ordinary crime in its political purpose and in its primary objective. Neither the ordinary bank robber nor the man who shot President Ronald Reagan is a terrorist. Likewise, not all politically motivated violence is terrorism. The Minuteman of the American Revolution and the rebel in Central America both have political motives, but they are not automatically terrorists. Terrorism is not synonymous with guerrilla war or any other kind of war, and it is not reserved exclusively for those trying to overthrow governments.

International terrorism can be defined as incidents that have clear international consequences: incidents in which terrorists go abroad to strike their targets, stay at home but select victims because of their connections to a foreign state (for example, diplomats or the executives of foreign corporations), or attack international lines of commerce (airliners). It excludes the considerable amount of terrorist violence carried out by terrorists operating within their own country against their own nationals and in many countries by governments against their own citizens.

This definition of international terrorism admittedly reflects the particular concern of the United States and the handful of other governments frequently targeted by terrorists abroad. The issue is not the general problem of political violence or terrorism or its causes – these are domestic matters. The unit of measure is the spillover of this violence into the international domain. The terrorists would argue that the established rules of diplomacy and war were contrived by a small group of primarily western nations for their own advantage and that they deprive groups without recognized governments, territory, or armies from exercising their 'right' to resort to violence. The above definition of international terrorism is also criticized as being an artificial distinction that encompasses only a narrow slice of the total volume of political violence.

Lack of agreement on definition is further complicated by differing concepts of conflict. Many Third World governments, particularly those in Africa and Asia, may not cooperate with American and European efforts to identify and combat international terrorism, not because these governments approve of terrorist tactics, but because they see the antiterrorist efforts as part of a broader campaign aimed at outlawing the irregular methods of warfare that were developed in the Third World during the civil war in China and the anticolonial struggles in Asia and Africa. Not a few of the Third World's insurgent chiefs – today's leaders – were once called terrorists themselves. Their governments, particularly the ones that lack the tools of modern conventional war, therefore deliberately exclude from their definition of terrorism 'wars of liberation', guerrilla warfare, other means of struggle that they themselves once employed or which are now being employed on behalf of causes they support.[1]

TERRORISM AND 'MORAL DISENGAGEMENT'

Albert Bandura (1998), an eminent US social psychologist, argues that terrorists commonly employ a form of 'cognitive reconstrual' (reconstruction) and 'moral disengagement', transforming normally socialised individuals into dedicated and skilled combatants. Terrorists are social 'challengers' who morally justify their activities. There is an odd paradox here. Terrorists see themselves as 'engaging' in a campaign or crusade or in a lone task; observers see them deliberately 'disengaging' from conventional, humane, civilised values. Bandura puts the general implications of his thinking in terms that may strike some people as rather mechanistic:

People do not ordinarily engage in reprehensible conduct until they have justified to themselves the morality of their actions. What is culpable can be made honorable through cognitive reconstrual. In this process, destructive conduct is made personally and socially acceptable by portraying it in the service of moral purposes. People then act on a moral imperative. Radical shifts in destructive behaviour through moral justification are most strikingly revealed in military conduct.

People who have been socialized to deplore killing as morally condemnable can be transformed rapidly into skilled combatants, who may feel little compunction and even a sense of pride in taking human life. Moral reconstrual of killing is dramatically illustrated by the case of Sergeant York, one of the phenomenal fighters in the history of modern warfare. Because of his deep religious convictions, Sergeant York registered as a conscientious objector, but his numerous appeals were denied. At camp, his battalion commander quoted chapter and verse from the Bible to persuade him that under appropriate conditions it was Christian to fight and kill. A marathon mountainside prayer finally convinced him that he could serve both God and country by becoming a dedicated fighter.

The conversion of socialized people into dedicated combatants is not achieved by altering their personality structures, aggressive drives, or moral standards. Rather, it is accomplished by cognitively restructuring the moral value of killing, so that the killing can be done free from self-censuring restraints. Through moral sanction of violent means, people see themselves as fighting ruthless oppressors who have an unquenchable appetite for conquest, protecting their cherished values and way of life, preserving world peace, saving humanity from subjugation to an evil ideology, and honoring their country's international commitments. The task of making violence morally defensible is facilitated when nonviolent options are judged to have been ineffective and utilitarian justifications portray the suffering caused by violent counterattacks as greatly outweighed by the human suffering inflicted by the foe.

Over the years, much reprehensible and destructive conduct has been perpetrated by ordinary, decent people in the name of religious principles, righteous ideologies, and nationalistic imperatives. Throughout history, countless people have suffered at the hands of self-righteous crusaders bent on stamping out what they consider evil. Elsewhere, Rapoport and Alexander have documented the lengthy blood-stained history of holy terror wrought by religious justifications. Acting on moral or ideological imperatives reflects a conscious offense mechanism, not an unconscious defense mechanism.

Although moral cognitive restructuring can easily be used to support self-serving and destructive purposes, it can also serve militant action aimed at changing inhumane social conditions. By appealing to morality, social reformers are able to use coercive, and even violent, tactics to force social change (presumably, 'engaging' rather than 'disengaging'). Vigorous disputes arise over the morality of aggressive action directed against institutional practices. Power holders often resist, by forcible means if necessary, making needed social changes that jeopardize their own self-interest. Such tactics provoke social activism. Challengers consider their militant actions to be morally justifiable because they serve to eradicate harmful social practices. Power holders condemn violent means as unjustified and unnecessary because nonviolent means exist to effect social change. They tend to view resorts to violence as efforts to coerce changes that lack popular support. Finally, they may argue that terrorist acts are condemnable because they violate civilized standards of conduct. Anarchy would flourish in a climate in which individuals considered violent tactics acceptable whenever they disliked particular social practices or policies.

Challengers refute such moral arguments by appealing to what they regard as a higher level of morality, derived from communal concerns. They see their constituencies as comprising all people, both at home and abroad, who are victimized either directly or indirectly by injurious social practices. Challengers argue that, when many people benefit from a system that is deleterious to disfavored segments of the society, the harmful social practices secure widespread public support. From the challengers' perspective, they are acting under a moral imperative to stop the maltreatment of people who have no way of modifying injurious social policies, either because they are outside the system that victimizes them, or because they lack the social power to effect changes from within by peaceable means. They regard militant action as the only recourse available to them.

Clearly, adversaries can easily marshal moral reasons for the use of aggressive actions for social control or for social change. Different people view violent acts in different ways. In conflicts of power, one person's violence is another person's selfless benevolence. It is often proclaimed that one group's criminal terroristic activity is another group's liberation movement fought by heroic freedom fighters. This is why moral appeals against violence usually fall on deaf ears. Adversaries sanctify their own militant actions but condemn those of their antagonists as barbarity masquerading behind a mask of outrageous moral reasoning.

For Bandura, justifications spiral away as outrage calls for punitive response and as institutional repression hardens the resolve of the violent. Utilitarian principles come to the fore on all sides, narrowing the scope for options and reducing the room for compromise:

So far, the discussion has centered on how terrorists invoke moral principles to justify human atrocities. Moral justification is also brought into play in selecting counter-terrorist measures. This poses more troublesome problems for democratic societies than for totalitarian ones. Totalitarian regimes have fewer constraints against using institutional power to control media coverage of terrorist events, to restrict individual rights, to sacrifice individuals for the benefit of the state rather than to make concessions to terrorists, and to combat threats with lethal means. Terrorists can wield greater power over nations that place high value on human life and are thereby constrained in the ways they can act.

Hostage taking has become a common terrorist strategy for wielding control over governments. If nations make the release of hostages a dominant national concern, they place themselves in a highly manipulable position. Tightly concealed captivity thwarts rescue action. Heightened national attention, along with an inability to free hostages independently, conveys a sense of weakness and invests terrorists with considerable importance and coercive power to extract concessions. Over-reactions in which nations render themselves hostage to a small band of terrorists inspire and invite further terrorist acts. In contrast, hostage taking is stripped of functional value if it is treated as a criminal act that gains terrorists neither any coercive concessionary power nor much media attention.

Democratic societies face the dilemma of how to morally justify counter-measures that will stop terrorists' atrocities without violating the societies' own fundamental principles and standards of civilized conduct. A set of critical conditions under which violent counterattacks are morally justified can be spelled out. It is generally considered legitimate to resort to violent defense in response to grave threats that inflict extensive human suffering or endanger the very survival of the society. But the criterion of 'grave threat', while fine in principle, is slippery in specific application. Like most human judgments, gauging the gravity of threats involves some subjectivity. Moreover, violence is often used as a weapon against threats of lesser magnitude on the grounds that, if left unchecked, they will escalate in severity to the point at which they will eventually exact a high toll in loss of liberties and in suffering. Gauging potential gravity involves even greater subjectivity and fallibility of judgment than does assessment of present danger. Construal of gravity prescribes choice of options, but choice of violent options also often shapes construal of gravity. Thus, projected grave dangers to the society are commonly involved to morally justify violent means that are used to squelch limited present threats.

It is hard to find any inherent moral rightness in violent acts that are designed to kill assailants or to deter them from future assaults but that inevitably risk the lives of some innocent people as well. Because of many uncertain factors, the toll that counter-terrorist assaults take on innocent life is neither easily controllable nor accurately calculable in advance. To sacrifice innocent lives in the process of punishing terrorists raises fundamental moral problems. Democratic societies that happen to kill some innocent people in the process of counter-terrorist actions find themselves in the vexing predicament of violating the values of their society in defense of those values. Therefore, the use of violent counter-measures is typically justified on utilitarian grounds – that is, in terms of the benefits to humanity and the social order that curbing terrorist attacks will bring. On the assumption that fighting terror with terror will achieve a deterrent effect, it is argued that retaliatory assaults will reduce the total amount of human suffering. As Carmichael [1982] notes, utilitarian justifications place few constraints on violent countermeasures because, in the utilitarian calculus, sacrificing the lives of some innocent persons can be greatly outweighed by the halt to repeated massacres and the perpetual terrorizing of entire populations.[2]

The views presented above represent Bandura's *tour d'horizon* at the outset. He goes on to list a number of what might be termed behavioural compulsives that modify the mental 'reconstrual' of terrorists and their consequent adjustive behaviour.

First, there is 'euphemistic language':

[. . .] a device for masking reprehensible activities or even conferring a respectable status on them. Through convoluted verbiage, destructive conduct is made benign and people who engage in it are relieved of a sense of personal agency.

Laboratory studies reveal the disinhibitory power of euphemistic language. Adults behave much more aggressively when given opportunities to assault a person when assaultive acts are given a sanitized athletic label than when they are called aggression. In an insightful analysis of the language of nonresponsibility, Gambino [1973] identifies the different varieties of euphemisms.

One form, palliative expressions, is widely used to make the reprehensible respectable. Through the power of hygienic words, even killing a human being loses much of its repugnancy. Soldiers 'waste' people rather than kill them, intelligence operatives 'terminate (them) with extreme prejudice'. When mercenaries speak of 'fulfilling a contract', murder is transformed by admirable words into the honorable discharge of duty. Terrorists label themselves 'freedom fighters'. Bombing attacks become 'clean, surgical strikes', invoking imagery of the restorative handicrafts of the operating room, and the civilians they kill are linguistically converted to 'collateral damage'.

[. . .] The agentless passive form serves as a linguistic device for creating the appearance that culpable acts are the work of nameless forces, rather than people. It is as though people are moved mechanically but are not really the agents of their own acts.[3]

Second, there is 'advantageous comparison':

Whenever events occur or are presented contiguously, the first one colors how the second one is perceived and judged. By exploiting the contrast principle, moral judgments of conduct can be influenced by the expedient structuring of what it is compared against. Self-deplored acts can be made to appear righteous by contrasting them with flagrant inhumanities. The more outrageous the comparison practices, the more likely it is that one's own destructive conduct will appear trifling or even benevolent. Thus, terrorists minimize their slayings as the only defensive weapon they have to curb the widespread cruelties inflicted on their people. In the eyes of their supporters, risky attacks directed at the apparatus of oppression are acts of selflessness and martyrdom. People who are objects of terrorist attacks, in turn, characterize their retaliatory violence as trifling, or even laudable, by comparing them with carnage and terror perpetrated by terrorists.[4]

Third, responsibility can be 'displaced':

People behave in injurious ways they normally repudiate if a legitimate authority accepts responsibility for the consequences of their conduct. Under conditions of displaced responsibility, people view their actions as springing from the dictates of authorities rather than from their own volition. Because they are not the actual agents of their actions, they are spared self-prohibiting reactions. In terrorism that is sponsored by states or governments in exile, functionaries view themselves as patriots fulfilling nationalistic duties rather than as free-lancing criminals. Displacement of responsibility not only weakens restraints over one's own detrimental actions but also diminishes social concern over the well-being of people mistreated by others.[5]

Fourth, particularly in Islamic societies and communities, clerics sometimes preach moral justification for what others regard as heinous acts:

Kramer [has] described [see this Reader, Chapter 9, note 12] the great lengths to which Shi'ite clerics go to produce moral justifications for violent acts that seem to breach Islamic law, such as suicidal bombings and hostage taking. These efforts are designed not only to persuade the clerics themselves of the morality of the terrorists' actions but to preserve the integrity of the perpetrating group in the eyes of other nations. The religious code permits neither suicide nor the terrorizing of innocent people. On the one hand, the clerics justify such acts by invoking situational imperatives and utilitarian reasons, namely, that tyrannical circumstances drive oppressed people to resort to unconventional means in order to rout aggressors who wield massive destructive power. On the other hand, they reconstrue terrorist acts as conventional means in which dying in a suicidal bombing for a moral cause is no different from dying at the hands of an enemy soldier. Hostages simply get relabeled as spies. When the linguistic solution defies credibility, personal moral responsibility is disengaged by construing terrorist acts as dictated by the foe's tyranny. Because of the shaky moral logic and disputable reconstruals, clerics sanction terrorism by indiscretion, vindicate successful ventures retrospectively, and disclaim endorsing terroristic operations beforehand.[6]

Fifth, responsibility can be 'diffused':

The deterrent power of self-sanctions is weakened when responsibility for culpable behavior is diffused, thereby obscuring the link between conduct and its consequences.

Responsibility can be diffused in several ways, for example, by the division of labor. Most enterprises require the services of many people, each performing fragmentary jobs that seem harmless in themselves.

The fractional contribution is easily isolated from the eventual function, especially when participants exercise little personal judgment in carrying out a subfunction that is related by remote, complex links to the end result.

After activities become routinized into programmed subfunctions, attention shifts from the import of what one is doing to the details of one's fractional job.

Group decision making is another common bureaucratic practice that enables otherwise considerate people to behave inhumanely, because no single person feels responsible for policies arrived at collectively. When everyone is responsible, no one is really responsible. Social organizations go to great lengths to devise sophisticated mechanisms for obscuring responsibility for decisions that will adversely affect others.

Collective action is still another diffusion expedient for weakening self-restraints. Any harm done by a group can always be ascribed, in large part, to the behavior of other members. People therefore act more harshly when responsibility is obfuscated by a collective instrumentality than when they hold themselves personally accountable for what they do.[7]

Sixth, Bandura sees 'moral disengagement' as reducing 'self-censure':

When moral disengagement is promoted by diffused and displaced responsibility, functionaries carry out the orders of superiors and often perform only a small sub-function of the enterprise. Such arrangements enable people to think of themselves merely as subordinate instruments, rather than as agents, of the entire enterprise. If they regard themselves as minor cogs in the intricate social machinery, they have little reason to believe otherwise concerning their initiatory power. This is not to say that disengagement of self-censure operates flawlessly.[8]

Altogether, in this suggested behaviour schema 'reconstrual' and 'reconstructuring' are held to be paramount instigators of consequential behaviour and moral posture:

Cognitive restructuring of behavior through moral justifications and palliative characterizations is the most effective psychological mechanism for promoting destructive conduct. This is because moral restructuring not only eliminates self-deterrents but engages self-approval in the service of destructive exploits. What was once morally condemnable becomes a source of self-valuation. After destructive means become invested with high moral purpose, functionaries work hard to become proficient at them and take pride in their destructive accomplishments.[9]

A final point about the Bandura theories of 'moral disengagement' is the question of duration. Martha Crenshaw (1998), has this in mind as something deserving further research when she asks:

Another phenomenon that deserves study is brutalization as a result of participation in violence. With the passage of time does terrorism become more violent because moral restraints are eroded? Is a loss of moral inhibition more likely in certain groups or with certain types of persons? Are such persons then exploited by leaders? Alternatively, some members of terrorist organizations may become disgusted with excessive cruelty and abandon the group. Under what circumstances does moral disapproval lead to exit from the group? Are IRA apologies for 'accidental' victims, for example, directed at the public or at IRA members?[10]

TERRORISM AND MORAL EVALUATION

Another set of moral perspectives, different from those of Bandura and rather narrower, has been used by Haig Khatchadourian (1998). A very detailed scheme for the 'moral evaluation of terrorism', it is fourfold, using criteria such as just war principles, fundamental human rights, utilitarian principles, and the morality of counter-terrorist measures.[11]

The appeal to just war principles is set out as follows:

The appeal to just war theory in the moral evaluation of terrorism can be justified as follows. As a kind of violence, terrorism shares a number of important characteristics with war. Since terrorist acts are intended to realize certain immediate, intermediate, and longrange or ultimate goals for the terrorists and/or those on whose behalf they commit these acts, the principles of right intention and just cause are clearly applicable to them. Since some or all of those they harm – the immediate victims and the victimized – may be either innocent or noninnocent, and since some are deliberately targeted while others are accidentally or unintentionally harmed, the principle of innocent immunity also applies to them. Further, terrorist acts, like war, raise the question of the proportionality or disproportionality of the harm inflicted to the actual or probable benefits for their initiators and those on whose behalf the violence is done; hence the 'military' and/or political principles of proportionality also apply. Similarly, the principles of necessity, last resort, and chance of success are applicable to terrorist acts, just as they apply to war and to other kinds of uses of force or violence.[12]

Next, fundamental human rights must clearly be violated by terrorists when their destructive actions compromise a person's basic rights to physical and mental security and such associated rights as those of equal treatment, individual freedom and opportunity. Khatchadourian is at pains to stress that all types and forms of terrorism 'seriously violate the human right of their immediate victims and the victimized as moral persons'. The author, it seems, has little time for what might be regarded as careful 'moral disengagement' (Bandura style), where some terrorists might consider their responsibility for an offence as 'displaced' or 'diffused'.

The classic criterion of utilitarianism relates to the overall outcome of an action that, fundamentally, is held to promote the greatest happiness and security of the greatest number of people. Khatchadourian finds it most unlikely that acts of predatory or retaliatory terrorism can ever be ethically sound, except that for the acknowledged 'freedom fighter' successful attainments in rebellion or revolution against oppression may be regarded as morally justified.

Lastly, Khatchadourian's focus on ethical aspects of terrorism considers at some length institutional response. For him there is a distinction between 'antiterrorism', when strategies and measures are primarily judicial, and 'counter terrorism', where measures emphasise 'the tactical force options for prevention, pre-emption or retaliation against terrorist acts'. Inevitably, antiterrorist policies and measures where they are applied overzealously are liable to violate seriously the legal and human rights of suspects and their dependants. Counter terrorism, involving force and the invasion of personal privacy and freedom, is even more likely, he feels, to lead to potential and actual abuse. Indeed:

[. . .] not all possible methods or strategies designed to protect a country's established political, economic and/or social order are necessarily moral [. . .] appeals to national self-protection cannot be morally used as a blanket justification for the eradication of suspected terrorists.[13]

TERRORISM AND BIOETHICS

Ethical issues 'written large', are today highlighted as 'bioethics'. The ethical issues are 'large' in that they relate to crisis and catastrophe following major bomb incidents and also to those bioterrorist attacks that would be devastating in onset, duration and aftermath. They are large, too, in that national and local authorities have had to devise mammoth emergency plans to cope with community consequences of terrorist attacks. At the same time, authorities have had to pay regard to the moral implications of restorative programmes. Equally, there will be keen scrutiny on the part of detached observers and surviving victims.

Jonathan Moreno (2003) has edited a very readable collection of expert opinion, owing much to earlier theory and practice in public health and social work.[14] Questions such as these are prominently framed:

[. . .] whether emergency health professionals have a duty to face danger; the meaning of fairness in allocating health resources; and implications for ethics of links forged among medicine, public health, law enforcement and private industry in emergency assessment, response and preparation. In addition, how best do we resolve tension between the ideals of self-determination, voluntarism, privacy, and justice and the demands of sometimes secretive and nearly always hierarchical institutions. What constitutes just decision-making processes and is neutrality an appropriate ideal of professional practice as opposed, say, to taking stands on moral and political matters?[15]

Few of the Moreno contributors mince words: 'One of the first potential casualties of catastrophic circumstances is civil liberties.' There are further questions:

Is it true that we must trade our human rights for safety to fight terrorism effectively? Must we, for example, dispense with the core value of modern bioethics – autonomy – in the face of a bioethical attack? I think the answer to both of these questions is no, and that trading human rights for safety will leave us with neither. Far from having to compromise human rights and bioethical principles in the time of terror, honoring these principles is our best defense against future terrorist attacks.[16]

There is certainly in disaster relief planning 'an ethical interplay between inherent rights of individuals and communal interests'. Put in challenging terms, the crux of the matter rests on 'the extent to which individual rights should yield to safeguard the health and needs of persons in the community'.[17] (These are significant issues in the light, say, of terrorist happenings such as 9/11 in New York and 7/7 in London and the recent supposed aircraft bombing plot in Britain in August 2006, when authority response was widely thought to have elements that were sweepingly coercive and indiscriminate.)

Moreno urges his readers, confronted by threats and crises, to respond ethically and build a consensus around appropriate policies and procedures. Moreover, he states, 'the threshold requirement is for clear, understandable and candid discussion of the risks, objectives, problems, options, and underlying values at stake'.[18] Indeed, the ethics of catastrophe loom large in scope and raise innumerable problems. They certainly underpin legislative policies and programmes, as the next chapter, 'Terrorism and the law', will discuss.

US pronouncements on terrorism are increasingly stressing an ethical component as an energiser of collective counter-action. A rhetoric of impending peril was noted in the State of the Union Address that President George W. Bush delivered on Capitol Hill in January 2002. The sponsors of terrorism – Iraq, Iran and North Korea – formerly castigated as 'rogue states', and later (by President Clinton) as 'states of concern', were now part of an 'axis of evil'. People declared 'bad', with weapons that were 'bad', were basically the same as terrorists. America would not wait on events where Evil threatened the Good and dangers gathered. Later, in April 2002, the President insisted that an ethical choice was inescapable: 'Since September 11 I've delivered this message. Everyone must choose. You're either with the civilised world or you're with the terrorists.'[19]

Understandably, a United States still traumatised by the atrocity of 9/11 searches ethical positions for moral justifications of counter-action. The President's Manichean presentation of 'Evil' has led to great debate among politicians, philosophers and newspaper letter writers. One can discern unease (Bandura, as quoted earlier, would certainly be a critic) that ethical considerations can be manipulated. Moral justifications can be stated as moral imperatives. The 'hard-liners' may prefer soldiering to preaching and translate a moral imperative into a militaristic imperative on the lines of Get There and Get At Them.

Terrorism and the law

S POTLIGHTING TERRORISM as a challenge for which ordered responses are needed invigorates debate in the public arena and in places where lawyers meet. Three issues particularly claim time in legal discussions: first, the ethical implications of statute law in interpretation; second, the international dimension that domestic laws on terrorism inevitably acquire; and, third, relationships between lawyer and politician. As the last chapter pointed out, there are ethical points bearing on indictment, proscription, detention and the vaguely defined area of 'security assistance'. It will never be easy for a judiciary to take into appropriate account what Brian Jenkins (1986, see p. 323, Chapter 21, note 1, in this volume) termed 'the quality of a terrorist act', as well as the identity of perpetrators and the cause of their action. Then, what appears right to do in Britain will be put up against what is being done elsewhere in Europe and in the United States. As for lawyer and politician, the match or mismatch between what happens in courts and that which the executive prefers is certainly recognised. Rosalyn Higgins, President of the International Court of Justice, admits that realism will help bridge any destructive divide: 'A refusal to acknowledge political and social factors cannot keep law "neutral" for even such a refusal is not without political and social consequences. There is no avoiding the essential relationship between law and politics.'[1]

Or can there be another line of approach (perhaps also 'realistic' in a sense that might be unacceptable to some)? Lord Woolf, Lord Chief Justice, speaking in Oxford in 2003 about terrorism legislation and human rights, suggested that courts practise 'the doctrine of deference or respect ... This requires the United Kingdom courts to recognise that there are situations where the national legislature or executive are better placed to make difficult choices between competing considerations than the national courts.'[2]

In many parts of the world, there is now a great deal of counter-terrorist legislation, recently crafted and often hastily so. Recent terrorist outrages in the United Kingdom, the United States and Asia must still be in the minds of lawmakers in many countries. There has been a great flurry of newly minted legislative proposals put on drawing-boards and subjected to intense and prolonged debate, in parliaments, in the media, and on the streets. An account of terrorism as legislatures deal with it against a background of disputation and anxiety must be as far as possible non-partisan. Most of the law-making is so involved that in an account it is only really possible to consider a fraction of it. Here, in the case of the United Kingdom, the seminal Acts of 2006, 2005, 2001, 2000 and 1996 will be considered. There will also be an outline of some developments in US and European legislation.

UNITED KINGDOM: THE PREVENTION OF TERRORISM ACT 2006

Two weeks after the London bombing of July 2005, the British Government's intentions became very clear. With 'vigilance' as the keyword, the way forward must be for all political parties to be invited to reach consensus as to the shaping of provisions for the statute book. Under discussion in the Cabinet Office was the outlining of a number of new crimes to feature in a new Bill to be presented to parliament without delay. 'Acts preparatory to terrorism', if identified, should facilitate the arrest of suspects. Then, 'organising or attending terrorist training sessions either in Britain or overseas' would be a penal offence. Generally, 'indirect incitement to commit terrorist acts' would bring about scrutiny and prompt arrest. It would be illegal, for instance, to publish any statement that 'glorifies, exalts or celebrates' the commission, preparation or instigation (whether in the past, in the future, or generally) of acts of terrorism. The making of devices and materials or their possession, threat, misuse and consequent public damage would be a grievous charge. Further, these offences were to be made subject to 'extraterritorial jurisdiction' so that they could be tried in UK courts even if committed abroad. Criminalising in advance such malevolent impulses, so it was affirmed, would have prevented or surely reduced the scale of London's bomb horror. 'Let no one be in any doubt,' the Prime Minister, Tony Blair, declared at an early press conference, 'the rules of the game are changing.'

As for 'the rules of the game' changing, this statement brought at the outset a good deal of criticism both in parliament and outside. Were not the 'rules' the centuries-old assurances of justice and fairness expressed in law and in the conventional rights to freedom of conscience, expression and association? Yes, the hideous targeting of the innocent in London and New York challenged much of what we accepted as security and independent privacy, but was our response to see hard-earned rights cast away?

Part II of the Bill was to give wider powers to the Home Secretary to proscribe groups thought to be sympathetic to terrorism even where the group had changed its name. To facilitate this, the powers of the intelligence services were to be extended. This part of the Bill led to anxiety and questioning of the Government by the Muslim Council of Britain, who considered that further and wider proscription was likely to increase tension and even lead to backlash.

Downing Street may have calculated that a public so lately traumatised would find some comfort in newspaper agreement that the Prime Minister was 'emphatically right to act'. It was 'good, preventive maintenance'. A prominent headline was 'Tell Tony He's Right!'.

The Bill had been introduced in the House of Commons on 26 October 2005. It was made law on 30 March 2006, after a Second Reading that secured it by 471 votes to 94, a sure sign that many MPs were anxious as to the illiberal consequences of hard-edged legislation. Even so, a majority applauded the Home Secretary Charles Clarke's putting the Act as an inescapable response to nihilistic threats: 'Our only answer to this threat must be to contest and then defeat it, and that is why we need this legislation.'[3]

Controversy and much unhappiness in many quarters was to follow. Who were to be the prime agents in seeing the provisions of the new Terrorism Act 2006 established and methodically and fairly implemented? How much support would there be in parliament, in the constituencies among the general public, and within certain institutions? What amount of untroubled consensus would there be in and around the courts? *The Guardian* had reported, in late July 2005, the Prime Minister's oblique reference to lawyers who might seem unready to readjust to what everyone else could see as 'a new mood': 'The independence of the judiciary is a principle of our democracy and we have to uphold it but I hope that recent events have created a situation where people understand that it is important that we do protect ourselves.'[4]

Any blocking of the envisaged new legislation could compromise our security, an ironic situation if those who should help draft legislation were seen to be unhelpful. In many liberal quarters there was dismay at erosion of rights, especially since the proposed edicts were couched in imprecise and rather ambiguous terms. There was cynicism, too, again in a *Guardian* leader, as to the motives of those who were calling for hasty and harsh legal enactment:

This is not a debate about law but about politics. After the two successive bombing attacks in London in July ministers felt they had to be seen to respond for fear of being seen to be complacent should a third attack occur. So, although there are already two hundred pieces of anti-terrorist legislation on the statute book, the government drew up its fourth terrorist bill in five years.[5]

Within weeks of the London attacks the Government was announcing a raft of measures that were put about as essential if 'suspects' were to be dealt with promptly. One possibility would be to use special pre-trial anti-terrorist courts sitting in secret, whose task would be to determine how long arrested suspects should be detained without charge. Secrecy was held to be paramount since there might be access to sensitive intelligence evidence gained from phone-taps and intercepted e-mails.

There was perhaps more controversy and real anguish occasioned by those measures in the Terrorism Act 2006 that provided for the detention of suspects. Originally the Government had put all this in an amendment to the original Bill, which would lead to those arrested on suspicion being put into detention for 90 days before they were charged. This would be a considerable increase over the existing term of a maximum of 14 days allowed under the Terrorism Act of 2001. Additionally, detainees would be reviewed every seven days by a judge sitting in camera. Fairly clearly with the London bombing in mind, the police were pressing to increase maximum detention to facilitate prompt arrest and give more time for subsequent investigation. Apart from the operational needs of security enquiry and their admitted 'frightening implications of getting it wrong', their spokesman went on to speak plainly: 'Unfortunately the proposal to increase the maximum period of pre-charge detention to three months has attracted unhelpful comparisons with internment which it is not.'[6]

No extent of wide dismay at the extension proposal would shift the Government. No compromise was to risk national security. Surveying the House of Commons benches in November 2005, Tony Blair went so far in dismissive eloquence as to detect 'a worrying gap between parts of Parliament and the reality of the terrorist threat and public opinion'. No doubt his firmness was buoyed up by press accusations of 'faint-hearted liberals' being 'soft on terrorism'. Where the Commons was certainly disinclined in the main to accede to 90 days, intensive debate strengthened opposition and the Government suffered its first major defeat. The House of Lords was resolute and also refused to entertain the proposed furtherance. They backed the 28-day maximum for detention that the Commons had accepted. Indeed, apart from an unconvincing attempt to frame a new detention stint, were we really looking sensibly and humanely at our counter-terrorist law and strategies? Lord McNally went straight to the point: 'Otherwise, every terrorist outrage will bring forth another bill, another notch on the ratchet, another turn of the screw until we find ourselves without civil liberties which we are fighting terrorism to defend.'[7]

UNITED KINGDOM: THE PREVENTION OF TERRORISM ACT 2005

With this Act there appears to be a straightforward link with detention legislation and specifically with the Law Lords' ruling of 16 December 2004 that the detention of nine foreigners in the maximum security prison of Belmarsh (under Part IV of the Act of 2001) was unlawful and incompatible with the Human Rights Act of 1998 and with the European Convention on Human Rights. The new Act had now to be framed as carefully as the Government could make it.

An innovation in this Act was to permit the Home Secretary to impose 'control orders' on people suspected of involvement in terrorist activity. Restrictions could be placed on the possession of specified articles and substances, on the use of public services, even the internet, on association or communication with certain individuals, or on the place of residence. There was a requirement to report regularly. Insofar as these provisions were to be interpreted as 'derogation', that is, opting out from human rights laws, they were to lead to major controversy within Britain. While, generally, Labour MPs endorsed the thrust of their Government's thinking, there was a substantial rebellion by their fellows and opposition in the House of Lords, together leading to the tabling of several amendments. Crucially, there was to be a 'sunset clause' providing for the Act to expire in March 2006 to allow for detailed review. Further, control orders would be subject both to judicial authorisation and to restoring the 'normal burden of proof' rather than the weaker 'balance of probabilities'.

Controversy over detention legislation, in the wider meaning of control, was to dog the progress of the Bill during the year 2005. The term 'rendition' was everywhere in press leaders and letter columns. Circumstantial evidence established it as a procedure originated by the CIA in the United States for moving terrorist suspects out to secret jails, many of them 'black sites' in eastern Europe. These 'ghost flights' transported them to countries where allegedly they might be tortured and where they would be beyond the reach of UK law. The likelihood that London gave permission for British airports to be used was a definite violation of international law and, to make things worse, few governments in Europe were ready to confirm or deny the extent of the practice. Damning evidence about rendition appears in a report issued in June 2006 by the Council of Europe's legal affairs and human rights committee. Some 14 European states must have turned something of a blind eye to the use of airspace, airports and flight plans to transport terrorist suspects. The programme could only operate with 'the intentional or grossly negligent collusion of the European partners'. The report goes on to warn that the United States:

[. . .] believing that neither conventional judicial instruments nor those established under the framework of the law of war could effectively counter the new forms of international terrorism has decided to develop new legal concepts that have left hundreds of terrorist suspects deprived of their liberty, outside US territory but under US control and denied any access to their fundamental legal rights. This legal approach is utterly alien to the European tradition and sensibility, and is clearly contrary to the European Convention of Human Rights and the Universal Declaration of Human Rights.[8]

The Act of 2005 received Royal Assent on 11 March 2005. For many it illustrates the ascendancy (if not the triumphing) of the courts and traditional good English law over questionable political manoeuvring. In some ways this Act sought to rebalance the evident hastiness of previous law-making, such as the Terrorism Act of 2000 and the ensuing emergency legislation of 2001. Interestingly, within Parliament itself, a Joint Committee on Human Rights came to a conclusion that earned it wide media coverage. Members could see little justification in legislation put through at such speed that it lacked both a sense of proportion and discrimination. Particularly, should an executive responsible for national security ever abbreviate or remove adequate legal investigation and authorisation?

UNITED KINGDOM: TERRORISM ACT 2000

This Act was designed to be broader in scope and application than previous emergency and 'temporary' legislation. The remit was stated to be: 'to make temporary provision about terrorism and to make temporary provision for Northern Ireland in regard to security, the punishment of certain offences, the preservation of peace and the maintenance of order'.

With the Northern Ireland 'troubles' very much in mind, the Act is exceedingly detailed. It begins with an elaboration of a customary definition to cover involvement in violence, serious damage, and the endangering of life. The Act goes on to cite as criminal offences the membership and support of a number of named terrorist groups (many of them in this case Irish). There is to be a right of appeal and investigation by the Proscribed Organisation Appeal Commission. Terrorist property and funds will be seized and forfeited. Most carefully outlined in that disclosure of what may be understood as terrorist intent, planning or capability is the plain duty of all citizens. Police investigative and control procedures as authorised by Parliament are listed with the rejoinder that 'a constable may arrest without a warrant a person whom he reasonably suspects to be a terrorist'. Detention of such a person was not to exceed 48 hours. Perhaps for the first time, incitement to commit a terrorist act was punishable. And overall there must be a report on the working of this Act forwarded to Parliament each year.

As the Bill emerged from the House of Commons, it encountered furious debate throughout the land. One point often asked was to do with the term 'threat'. What did this mean in practice? Used pejoratively did it always describe public intimidation? How was this most often expressed? By individuals in speech? Through circulating broadsheets? By beaming out from a public meeting sentiments that were clamorous? Did not a charge of 'threat' risk cutting across freedom of speech and expression?

Yeoman efforts to reassure the public had already been mounted in December 1999 by the then Home Secretary, Jack Straw MP. His defence of the proposed 2000 Act was robust:

Legislating in this area is difficult. By its nature, terrorism is designed to strike at the heart of our democratic values. That is all the more reason why we must ensure that we get right the balance between defending the public from acts of organised terror and ensuring that human rights are protected. [. . .]

With the new terrorism bill, we are proposing to move away from the rather piecemeal and temporary approach that characterises current anti-terrorism legislation.

For a quarter of a century, the prevention of terrorism act [PTA] – introduced by one of my more liberal predecessors, Roy Jenkins – has provided the police with extra powers to counter the terrorist threat.

In opposition, the Labour party objected to three parts of that act. The terrorism bill deals with each of them.

First, the PTA allowed ministers to exclude British citizens entering the mainland from Northern Ireland, and vice versa – a form of internal exile which was ineffective, wrong and opposed by nationalists and unionists alike. I lapsed exclusion powers in early 1998 and, under this bill, they are to be scrapped altogether.

Second, the PTA allowed ministers – not judges – to decide whether a terrorist suspect should be detained by the police for longer than 48 hours. With this bill, extensions to detention will require approval by a stipendiary magistrate (or equivalent) – and at last allow the UK to overturn its derogation from a key part of the European Convention on Human Rights.

Third, the PTA was a temporary measure to deal mainly with Irish terrorism, and took no account of the changing nature of the terrorist threat. This legislation puts that right too.

The powers available under the terrorism bill will be subject to a series of checks and balances to ensure that they are used proportionately. As well as the judicial oversight of extensions of detentions, proscribed organisations will have a right of appeal to an independent body and all future authorisations of the use of stop and search powers under the bill will have to be confirmed by me or another minister.

Opponents of the bill have cited the proposed new definition of terrorism as an affront to the individual's peaceful right to protest. It is no such thing. The bill (which defines terrorism as 'the use or threat, for the purpose of advancing a political, religious or ideological cause of action which involves serious violence against any person or property, endangers the life of any person or creates a serious risk to the health or safety of the public or a section of the public'), in fact distinguishes more clearly than ever before the situations in which anti-terrorist legislation should apply.

It increases the level of the threshold before which certain powers within the bill can be activated, by making it clear that it refers to activities which constitute 'serious violence'. Moreover, the definition itself does not create any new criminal offence. Rather it is primarily the trigger for the use of the powers in the bill. Terrorists committing serious acts of violence will continue to be charged with the usual such offences, from murder to causing explosions.

The legislation is not intended to deal with alleged offences properly dealt with under the existing criminal law. Neither will it in any way curb individuals' democratic rights to protest peacefully. The difference between 'serious violence' and 'violence' will not be meaningless in a court of law, as some have suggested. Our courts are well used and perfectly able to apply the word 'serious' in the context of specific circumstances, and do so, for instance, when considering aggravating features in criminal cases. So this will make a difference.

At the same time the new bill widens the scope of the legislation, extending it to include the threats posed by terrorists both domestically and internationally. It must be right for the law to deal on the same basis with all groups or individuals intent on causing death and injury here in Britain to further a cause. This is particularly necessary as the nature of the terrorist threat changes. [. . .]

This bill strengthens the powers to meet an ever-changing, ever-present threat, yet is properly regulated by a series of safeguards. Every terrorist attack represents a violation of our democratic values, and as such our response must be sufficiently robust to challenge and defeat these vile activities at all times. I think we have got the balance right.[9]

There was no shortage of criticism as a response to Mr Straw's defence. One such critic, John Wadham, director of the civil rights group, Liberty, was in no doubt that if the new bill became law in 2000 then all who protested were liable to be branded as criminals. Would any individual be presumed guilty even before charges were laid, he wondered?

Where can you be sentenced to 10 years in prison for speaking at a meeting? The answer, I am afraid, is this country and the proposal is contained in clause 11(3)(b) of the terrorism bill which has its second reading in the House of Commons today. The bill gives the government the power to 'proscribe' organisations. Membership of a proscribed organisation would not be the only offence created. [. . .]

While the only organisations currently proscribed are those associated with Northern Ireland, the bill gives the secretary of state the power to add to these. If direct action organisations are being targeted as potential 'terrorists', then proscription is the next logical step.

The prevention of terrorism act is currently restricted to those suspected of involvement in international terrorism or terrorism connected with Northern Ireland. The government wants some of these special provisions to apply to any kind of 'terrorism'. [. . .]

The anti-terrorism laws have led to some of the worst human rights abuses in this country over the past 25 years, contributed to miscarriages of justice and have led to the unnecessary detention of thousands of innocent people, most of them Irish. Only a tiny percentage of those detained have ever been charged and almost without exception they could have been detained under ordinary criminal laws.

This bill will create a duty to report people to the police in certain circumstances. If, during the course of your work, you find information about, or become suspicious of, someone who you suspect may be using money or property to contribute to the causes of terrorism, you must report them. Failure to do so will make you liable to a five-year prison sentence. [. . .]

The offence of 'incitement' may be committed by mere words and there will be clashes with the right to freedom of expression. Investigation of such offences will often be brought about by political forces such as overseas governments complaining about the tactics of pressure groups and government opponents based in this country.

When these same offences were introduced in 1994, Lord Williams of Mostyn QC, the Labour home affairs spokesman in the House of Lords and now the attorney general, described the offences as 'alarming'; said that the offences were 'far too harsh and draconian' and would bring the law into disrepute; and that they would 'bring us into serious conflict with the European convention on human rights'.

The lord chief justice in the divisional court on March 30 this year decided that these same provisions in a 'blatant and obvious way undermined the presumption of innocence'.

The home secretary believes that this bill complies with the European convention on human rights. We would have to disagree. It risks infringing the rights to a fair trial, to freedom from unlawful detention, to freedom of speech and freedom of association. Yet the powers in the police and criminal evidence act are more than sufficient to deal with the criminal activities described under the bill.

Draconian anti-terrorist laws should be abolished and not extended: such laws have a far greater impact on human rights than they ever will on crime.[10]

UNITED KINGDOM: ANTI-TERRORISM, CRIME AND SECURITY ACT 2001 (AN AMENDING ACT)

Undoubtedly the mayhem of 9 November 2001 in the United States impelled the UK Government 'to make further provision about terrorism and security' within a month. Quite explicitly this is emergency legislation amending and amplifying the Act of 2000. The detail is there again and with a harder edge. Restraint orders to do with movement, association and fund-raising are tightened. The withholding of information, that is, non-disclosure, it should be noted, based on 'knowledge or suspicion' will be a serious offence. There is more acknowledgement, now, of the need to phase in new measures on the basis of stronger collaboration with European security agencies. A clear linking up of the three parameters in this Act, that is, anti-terrorism, crime and security, is obvious. Aviation security, stop-and-search procedures, the power to remove disguises from suspects, seizure and retention of communications data, biological and chemical weaponry, and illegal weapons training, are all prominent in amendment clauses. Perhaps for the first time, 'derogation' was mentioned, permitting the United Kingdom to opt out of human rights conventions when summary extradition is intended. This issue was to be put into larger focus in 2005 and 2006 concerning 'rendition', as we have seen.

Indeed, over derogation there was a flood of criticism from all quarters. Helena Kennedy QC, a member of the Bar Association's International Task Force on Terrorism, deplored governmental intent:

> The fact that our Prime Minister and Home Secretary have both indicated that they may have to consider a derogation from Article 51 of the Convention on the Rights of Refugees and a derogation from the European Convention on Human Rights is scandalous [. . .] the government has capitulated to an agenda set by the right [. . .].[11]

No other European country sought to introduce such changes in law for: 'Derogation is permitted only in time of war or other public emergency threatening the life of the nation and even then only to a minor extent and consistently with other international obligations.'[12]

The emergency tenor of the 2001 Act gave rise to much concern as to its appropriateness. Clive Walker (1996) had pointed out its failings quite bluntly some years previously. It would lack coherence and comprehensiveness if its mainsprings were 'chance events, outrage, or the legacy of past rancour'. Later, in 1996, Walker affirmed that the leading principle in all good legislation must be recognition of 'the limiting principles of constitutionalism and democratic accountability'.[13] About the same time, the view of David Schiff (1997) seems to have gained wide acceptance:

> counter-terrorism, in adopting abnormal rules that are distinct from the normal rules of, say, the criminal process, created organizational needs to recognise or harmonize these exceptional norms with normal, constitutionally posited rules. Without such recognition and law, counter-terrorism measures are destructive of the constitution, that is, the public law framework of the legislative exercise of authority.[14]

Nor was the judiciary silent as to the emplacement of far-reaching law. Lord Woolf, Lord Chief Justice, went to the BBC in December 2001 to broadcast his worry:

I feel that it's very important that we don't have the sort of limitations which are involved in the legislation in place for any longer than is absolutely necessary [. . .] The legislation was harmful to Britain's reputation as one of the leading countries for upholding the rule of law and sent 'damaging signals' [. . .] Are these the responses we feel appropriate for the new situation (like 9/11) with which we are faced?[15]

He intimated that a robust judiciary could and should face government to argue the necessity of what it sought to do at every stage.

UNITED KINGDOM: PREVENTION OF TERRORISM (ADDITIONAL POWERS) ACT 1996

As we have already noted, the mid-1990s saw the emergence of anti-terrorism legislation termed 'amending' and 'additional'. The 1996 Act has been described as 'rushed through Parliament in a single day'. There was to be no delay in introducing new powers to stop and search pedestrians. Reasonable grounds for suspecting a person to be guilty of an offence [to do with terrorism] were held to justify the exercise of expedient police action in order to determine whether they were or had been involved 'in the commission, preparation or instigation of acts of terrorism'. Many lawyers took exception to such a categorical clause. A requirement of 'reasonable belief' should replace mere 'opinion'. Otherwise, in relation to stop-and-search powers, the only possible legal challenge appeared to be on the grounds that the examining officer was not acting in good faith. Nor should anyone be considered at once 'guilty' if, somehow, he did not know about a restriction or prohibition. As for the special powers conferred by the Act of 1996, Kiron Reid (1996) has given a warning:

the use of special powers may be described as excessive in two senses: excessive in the sense that special powers are invoked when 'normal' powers would suffice to deal with a particular aspect of the emergency; and excessive in the sense that special powers are applied to 'normal' situations which are not part of the emergency.[16]

There is every reason to believe that similar arguments to those above are reverberating still in Britain, in the United States, and within Europe. To these other places we shall now turn.

UNITED STATES OF AMERICA: COUNTER-TERRORISM AND THE LAW

President George W. Bush, told on the evening of 11 September 2001 what terrorists had done to New York and Washington, exclaimed, 'I don't care what the international lawyers say, we are going to kick some ass'. Less emotive and more practicable steps for the United States to take have been described by David Whittaker (2007):

President Bush, after the September outrage, spoke of his country as 'at war' with terrorism and promised legislation to fight something going far beyond conventional criminality. In his view anyone who in any way finances, harbours or defends terrorists is himself a terrorist, in other words, there is no distinction between terrorists and their friends and supporters [. . .] Something similar in intention to the British anti-terrorism legislation was hastily constructed by the United States administration towards the end of December 2001 [. . .] [A new Act, the Patriot Act, was introduced as a Bill in October 2001]. There were many provisions for enhancing domestic security and curbing international terrorist attacks. New investigative procedures would allow the FBI and other federal security bodies to put wiretaps onto suspects, and permit unspecified and undefined interception of website browsing and e-mail activities, again, by suspects, all this without involving the opinion and authorisation of a judge. Search warrants could be used and searches carried out without prior warning to anyone. Any group 'seeking to influence the policy of a government by intimidation or coercion would be liable to proscription. There would be a prompt and most thorough clamping down on money laundering or any suspected deviation of funding towards terrorism'. The House of Representatives passed these provisions through by an overwhelming majority though not without an appreciable amount of political gamesmanship and lobbying by civil rights groups. In the Senate it was different and the debate proceeded at a snail's pace, to the deep concern of the White House. There were impassioned complaints from Senators aghast at 'closing down our open society' and at 'the snooping appetites which trump privacy [. . .]'.[17]

America's Attorney-General, John Ashcroft, went on to lash out at an all-night Senate sitting. 'Your tactics', he said, 'only aid terrorists; [they] give ammunition to America's enemies and pause to America's friends [. . .].' Counter-terrorist moves remained tough but the rights of the rest of the community were now more plainly respected. Investigation and disclosure were now repackaged to allow for prior notification and judicial review. Nevertheless, anxieties were not dispelled. The American Civil Liberties Union definitely did not drop their guard. Throughout 2003 they maintained a rigorous campaign to offset Ashcroft's criticism, which they considered 'fundamentally alters the Constitutional protections that allow us to be safe and free'.

US legislators work at a number of levels. The US federal system allocates a relatively high level of local autonomy to each of the 50 states. While each state has its own unique legal system, the judicial branch of government up to the US Supreme Court is the ultimate arbiter. All international treaties must be ratified by Congress, but duly ratified treaties are equal to enacted federal statutes. The US Constitution and the Bill of Rights guarantee a host of inalienable rights, including human rights.

A measure of the US Government's concern about protest over the new Patriot Act was that the Senate was asked to update the Act in July 2005 and once more in December 2005 in order to moderate a number of the requirements that liberal quarters found objectionable. Renewal of the Act was complete on 2 March 2006, when a substantial majority approved it, and the President signed it a week later.

'Does the reshaped Act do what is needed?. Congress, the courts and the public all had to be assured. Looking back to 2005, the extent of protest against the first Patriot Act was astounding. Then, no less than eight states and 396 cities had passed resolutions deploring the Act's attack on civil liberties. Polls of public opinion showed 50 per cent of Americans approving Patriot and 50 per cent against it. (There was the usual indication of many respondents being unaware of the content of the Act they were voting on.) Government had to have compromise in mind and so had to accentuate extra safeguards without hampering the use of counter-terrorism tools. Those issues that had raised most dissent – access to business records and personal correspondence, the use of wiretaps, and even revelation of library borrowings – were now subject to investigators' liability to challenge together with any suspect's right to consult an attorney.

Still important were the main sections in the Act to do with enhancing domestic security, surveillance procedures, improved intelligence arrangements, and providing for the victims of attacks. In June 2005, the House of Representatives was able to force some amendment of 'roving' surveillance and of 'sneak and peek' search warrants. Many on Capitol Hill were now ready to agree that a modified law now offered more protection against unlawful intrusions by law enforcement than did the earlier Patriot scheme. 'Making America Safer' was always the cardinal principle. Alongside the legislative scenario is always the very real day-to-day planning of preventive strategy, authorised by law. Every state administration must now fashion a 'catastrophic emergency plan' and there is now every sign that the details and practicability of these strategies fill the minds of legislators. Once more, 'Getting it Right' is the crux both of preparedness and freedom.

There were others in Washington for whom 'Getting it Right' meant 'Getting it Legal and Right'. America's Supreme Court at last in June 2006 was to stand up to the White House when the court rolled back the sweeping powers appropriated by the Bush administration in the war on terror. Henceforth, the Administration must comply with Geneva Conventions in regard to war crime trials, torture, the treatment of Guantanamo detainees, the CIA programme of rendition, and any reliance on military tribunals.

EUROPE: COUNTER-TERRORISM AND THE LAW

It was to be a hard task to encourage 25 nations to pool their law-making in regard to terrorism. Quite plainly there are differences, centuries old, in legal definitions, in court practice, in styles of judgement, and in procedures for evidence-gathering, testifying, charging, detention, appeal and sentencing. Establishing a 'Highest Common Factor', that of prevention–protection, continues to be put forward in elegant rhetoric at a pan-institutional level in the European Parliament and the European Commission. There is much talk of the sharing of values, traditions and solidarity.

In contrast, day-to-day working towards legal standardisation continues to be slow and complex. There was a promising start in November 2001 (the month of the American attack) when Brussels rushed through new proposals for a Europe-wide definition of terrorism. At the time, only the United Kingdom, France, Spain and Portugal had a specified legal definition. A consensual one was due for implementation two years later. The document put meaning in clear terms with a list of indictable offences regarded as terrorism if they were: 'intentionally committed by individuals or groups against one or more countries, their institutions or people, intimidating them, aimed at seriously altering or destroying their political, economic or social structure'. Within such a context as that, specific terrorist crimes would include murder, the taking of hostages, clear and repeated incitement to violence, the release of toxic or explosive substances, the seizure of premises, and interference with public services. States should apply similar sentencing of those who were convicted.

In March 2004 another attack, this time in Madrid, brought lawyers into conference. As was to be expected, operational cooperation was to come first, with the devising of safeguards for governments and their peoples a reluctant by-product. Rather than bringing into effect new legislation, the main task was to comb through the array of what was already available and to make sure that its implementation was appropriate and effective. A start was made using databases to list likely terrorist groups, to locate their methods and whereabouts, and to freeze assets.

In March 2005, Madrid once more was the venue for a summit meeting for leading political heads and advisers, in an attempt to forge consensus on how member states might work together. Legal progress was vital, since terrorists could move simply from one country to another where legislation appeared less stringent. Would a General Convention against Terrorism, detailed and straight to the point, weld issues together? Already in Brussels a centre for threat analysis was to provide warnings of imminent danger, but it was necessary to forestall action and to deal with its originators. After all, terrorism within a state was both an internal matter and an international problem. It would not do to have such an uneven scenario that political violence in one country was not taken seriously or was even condoned elsewhere. Pragmatically, it was decided several days after 9/11 that a European Action Plan operational programme would be linked into a set of objectives feasible in the streets and appropriate criteria for court action. The '4P Programme' laid down four objectives:

> Prevention of activities to be construed as terrorist.
> Protection of citizens and infrastructure by reducing vulnerabilities.
> Pursuit of miscreants across borders and bringing them to justice.
> Preparation of relief measures to cope with the consequences of terrorism.

Nine months later, in December 2005, European Justice Ministers met in Brussels to sort out a web of procedures and structures. They had done some preparatory work in Newcastle in the autumn. For some weeks a working party of eight international jurists had concentrated on the legal validity of what was combed through by the Ministers. Crucial to arraigning terrorists were two things: a European Arrest

Warrant and improved extradition procedures. That way, in any member state, the arrested would be brought before a judge within 48 hours. Something like a European version of Habeas Corpus was put in place. Common penalties could be levied. If extradition was considered necessary, there were now uniform ways of seeing to it.

In October 2005, the UK Foreign and Commonwealth Office published a study of counter-terrorism legislation in a number of European countries, together with that of Australia, Canada and the United States. Illustrative rather than exhaustive, the report considered the key elements of legislation and practice. The hope is stated that such enquiry could be the start of a consultative process that could be developed and augmented in the future. A brief reading of the 40 pages of this report yields interesting comparisons.[18]

France, for instance, places great reliance on a special section of the Paris Court where a special corps of magistrates expertly investigates the feasibility of sending arrested suspects forward for trial. Paris takes very seriously the obligations of terrorism-related treaties and human rights conventions. The last two decades have seen the introduction particularly of tighter control of conspiracy and terrorist financing.

Germany has relied for some time on existing laws to cover terrorist activity. There has certainly been public wariness remembering the 1960s and 1970s, when their country had been assailed by terrorist cells and the Bonn Government had used blunt legislative instruments to incapacitate all manner of radical movements, many of them entirely peaceful. Control must not degenerate once more into inhuman repression. Even so, in January 2002 the Bundestag introduced a Law on Fighting Terrorism – not a single piece of legislation but rather an omnibus package of amendments to pre-existing statutes:

The Law on Fighting Terrorism came into force on 1 January 2002. It is not a single piece of legislation, but rather the title given to an omnibus package of amendments to pre-existing statutes. These include:

- Increased investigative powers for the police, intelligence and security services, including greater access to personal, financial and immigration data, broader investigative powers and expanded powers to monitor resident extremists;
- Tougher visa and border control regulations to prevent extremists travelling into Germany, including introduction of bio-metric data for passports and visas;
- Increased vetting of those in security-sensitive occupations;
- Greater protection for critical infrastructure.[19]

Greece, rather like France, has inaugurated a special body, a Judicial Council, headed by a Special Prosecutor and backed by a designated branch of the Greek police. There are now 22 types of terrorist offence in the penal code.[20]

Spain has taken time to recover from the bomb chaos that struck Madrid's railway stations in March 2004. After that attack, and apart from anger and sorrow, there was a good deal of speculation in newspapers as to whether the new Socialist Government was not being too harsh in all directions with its 'iron fist'. Although the guerrilla attacks of the independence faction ETA have eased, there is a marked concern about conspiracy. Counter-terrorist legislation now relates to an 'aggravated' form of crime, 'which subverts constitutional order and effects serious disturbance of public order'. Spanish legislation quite clearly cites a number of indictable offences judged to constitute terrorism and it lays down penalties to be exacted:

Where an offence is committed that has a terrorist purpose then this will be considered an aggravating feature by the court when it imposes a sentence. However, there are some specific penalties in the Criminal Code that relate to terrorism, including:

- promoting or directing armed gangs of terrorist organisations: eight to fourteen years imprisonment;
- membership of an armed gang or terrorist organisation: six to twelve years imprisonment;
- terrorist murder: twenty to thirty years;
- the effective maximum prison sentence for a person convicted of two or more terrorist offences is now 40 years.[21]

Sweden now has an Act on Criminal Responsibility for Terrorist Offences, made law in 2003. Mindful that all Swedish legislation must be in conformity with the European Covenant on Human Rights, the law itself is sharply defined. It states:

The 2003 Act on Criminal Responsibility for Terrorist Offences states that a list of offences under Swedish law including murder, manslaughter, gross assault, kidnapping, the spreading of poison or contagious substances amount to a terrorist offence where the act in question might seriously damage a state or an intergovernmental organisation and the intent of the act is to:

- seriously intimidate a population or a group of population;
- unduly compel a public authority or an intergovernmental organisation to perform an act or abstain from acting;
- seriously destabilise or destroy fundamental political, constitutional, economic or social structures in a state or in an intergovernmental organisation.

If it is not possible to prove special intent, regular criminal law in the Penal Code is applicable. Any attempt, preparation or conspiracy to commit a terrorist offence or failure to disclose such an offence is also deemed an offence under this Act.[22]

It looks as though much of the European counter-terrorist legislation is not so much evolving as *revolving* around clouded ways of understanding and implementation. At the root of this are the problems of definition. Rosalyn Higgins, President of the International Court of Justice, stands resolute on this point, as Whittaker describes:

[She] points to the absence of an agreed definition of terrorism as a hindrance to counter-terrorism practice. If terrorism is so varied and so case-specific it will be almost impossible to get the firm legal grounding that will make most counter-action legitimate and publicly acceptable. All too obviously, for Higgins, the term 'terrorism' has no legal significance. It is not an umbrella concept. Rather, it is a form of shorthand referring to a number of problems with shared elements and which are strongly condemned by civilised societies. There is certainly the stuff of debate here about a 'term of convenience', as this lawyer puts it.[23]

Kennedy has talked of definition as a major obstacle to moving on a common front:

Can terrorism be defined? Different legislation in different jurisdictions has attempted the task but finding an acceptable definition is very difficult. Until there is an internationally recognised and sufficiently restrictive definition, it will be hard to have confidence that struggles for self-determination and other political activities will not be wrapped up in accusations of 'terrorism'.[24]

Undoubtedly, varying definitions, as well as a plethora of constitutional and legislative differences, beset not only European attempts to collaborate and standardise but also the Herculean effort of the United Nations where the General Assembly and its committees strive inch by inch to even up the consequences of conventions, treaties and enabling laws. Their legislative work is on a scale suited to global advance and adherence; legislators in Europe are much more concerned to define and refine what is more like case law to deal with offences and their perpetrators. Kennedy has this in mind:

So how do we proceed if we are not going to give in to terrorism? Any legal modifications should be tested against the concept of proportionality. Do the new laws reflect pressing social need? Are the reasons necessary and sufficient? Could alternative methods be used which are less abusive of civil liberties and require fewer departures from the ordinary legal arrangements? Is the deleterious effect proportionate to the value to the security forces?[25]

In some respects, we are all back to the original question about terrorism: 'Before we can deal with it in law, what is it?'

POSTSCRIPT

Recent UK anti-terrorist legislation is considered in great detail in Clive Walker's *The Anti-terrorist Legislation* (OUP/Blackstone's Guide, 2nd edition, 2009). Latest statutes are the Justice and Security (Northern Ireland) Act 2007 and the Counter-terrorist Act 2008.

Walker comments upon themes this legislation appears to reflect. First, the growing profusion, scope, complexity of law making. Second, because 'jihadist terrorism' involves indiscriminate, substantial, suicidal attacks UK response shifts further towards anticipatory moves and early executive intervention.[26] Third, there is more debate over 'balance' first, about security policies heightening risks to liberty and human rights, second, apropos the legitimate responsibilities and limitations of courts and Parliament.[27] Fourth, defining 'terrorism' presents difficulties. Walker asserts controversially that 'powerful politics have long sought to exercise hegemonic control over the ascription of legitimacy in emergencies'.[28] The 'terrorism' label, so he thinks, becomes 'an opportunistic and pejorative ascription rather than a simple description of a tactic'.[29] Do these debateable points cloud our reliance on conventional denominators – purpose, target, method? Whether these are hypothetical or plainly evident?

United Kingdom: Justice and Security (Northern Ireland) Act 2007

The security situation in Northern Ireland is much improved over three years despite the existence of some paramilitary splinter groups. The Provisional IRA formally ended its armed campaign in July 2005. The Act endeavours to ease the tightness of earlier legislative controls. There is progressive dismantling of a number of army vigilance procedures and resort to 'stop and search' tactics. There is stronger emphasis on jury trials rather than the non-jury trials (Diplock Trials) used during the peak of the 'Troubles'. The Act fairly clearly acknowledges the value of accountability and constitutional correctness in ways that some of its forerunners lacked.

Counter-terrorism Act 2008

This is now a comprehensive code covering 'security administration' executive measures and application and criminal justice procedures. A particular concern in this Act takes account of the increasing diversity of what is considered 'terrorism' and of the need of working out preventive strategies and legitimate methods. A special section deals with legal and financial measures aimed to combat terrorist financing and money laundering.[30] The Treasury is given powers of watch-and-indict control over any persons or groups involved. This Act further legalises powers to gather and share information conducive to countering terrorism, and to the use of data and questioning of suspects. A number of existing prosecution and punishment routines are clarified and amended.[31]

Europe: Counter-terrorism and the Law

Germany in mid-May 2011 presents an interesting situation. The present anti-terrorist legislation expires on 12 January 2012 and this has prompted Chancellor Angela Merkel to press the Bundestag for an extensive review and renewal. Her centre-right coalition is not unanimously in favour of continued mining of citizens' personal data for intelligence storage. The Justice Minister, indeed, considered some powers in the Law on Fighting Terrorism (2002) to be more draconian than present security needs warranted. This view was countered by the Federal Criminal Police in pointing out that 79 per cent of Germans when polled support strong anti-terrorist laws in principle.

In Spain and in Italy criticism continues to be voiced that legal definitions in contemporary statutes are so broad and vague that both protest demonstrations and actual violent dissidents may be accused of 'subversive purpose against the democratic order'. There is also unease in some quarters about governmental collaboration with the United States over databases reduces individual privacy. Are Security Branch powers sufficiently defined? In any case Spaniards are well aware of the special dangers that Basque separatism has presented.[32]

United States: Counter-terrorism and the Law

US senators and public are doing their best to bring about legislation that is appropriate, concise, fair, humane, comprehensive, protective of inalienable rights, sensitive about surveillance, personal interference and interception, prosecution and conviction. These are at least the hallmarks of American Justice according to pronouncements from the Department of Homeland Security. A large series of minor statutes emanates from the Administration in Washington and from the capitals of various states to relate to marine and air transport, to pre-empt civil disorders, to prohibit biological and chemical weapons, to assist in disaster relief, to provide for the gathering and analysis of intelligence data. When new legislation is called for and drafted there is heard on Capitol Hill the assertion that it is needed, of course, 'in view of the post 9/11 experience and normative justifications for judicial and executive review'.

A last thought might be this. Are we not all of us impaled on an intellectual hook if we find it so difficult to define what we understand by 'terrorism'? Very many international lawyers seem to be of this mind.

Counter-terrorism

Programmes and strategies

A GREAT DEAL OF WORK goes into the framing of strategies to counter terrorism and into the design and implementation of action plans. The published description is endless. It is not easy to know where to begin in this Reader with making a selection for further presentation. The most logical decision was to choose and reproduce, regardless of original date, those arguments which appear particularly ordered and clearly expressed in the hope that this provides food for reflection and debate.

For M. R. L. Smith (1995) there is an important question of standpoint: does too much dwelling on control and prevention of political violence cloud a necessary attempt to analyse and understand the causes of terrorism?

The consequence of the rather narrow concentration on the supposed tactics of terrorism, gives rise to a second area of concern which is the extent to which research has dwelt on the control and prevention of political violence. To a degree this is understandable. For many people who live in environments afflicted by terrorism, howsoever defined, their sole experience of the problem is likely to be of its disruptive effects on everyday life. The immediate inclination is likely to want to be rid of the problem – not to engage in some contorted hypothetical discourse on the subject. Nevertheless, at an academic level, too much concentration on counter-responses to sub-state terrorism can make research narrowly policy prescriptive. The violent symptoms of political conflict certainly do have to be controlled by the responsible authorities charged with upholding the public good. While not denying the right of scholars or anyone else to have their say on how to tackle such matters, academics do have to tread carefully if they start to advocate detailed policy and if they are to remain true to their vocation. Part of the problem has been that much of the literature on terrorism published over the years has betrayed an over-emphasis on, and sometimes even an obsessive concern for, tactical counter-measures which leaves the analyst poorly placed to undertake the more considered long-term diagnosis of the crisis. Undue stress on counter-terrorist techniques can also lead to an equally obsessive search for a general theory of the causes of terrorism and political violence: the thinking being that if one discovers the 'causes of terrorism' then one will be that much more able to devise policies to eliminate the problem. Since all conflicts have very diverse origins, one is not going to obtain a very meaningful theory, only ones which are so nebulous, like 'human nature is the cause of violence' that they explain everything yet nothing at the same time.[1]

Notwithstanding caution such as this the non-academic community of governments, police forces and armed services devise policies and operate programmes to pinpoint any originators of violence, to deter them from committing outrages, and to deal as best they can with a traumatised public.

COUNTER-TERRORISM PROGRAMMES

An example of clearly laid out practice in counter-terrorism is to be found in a broadsheet published in 1998 by the Terrorism Research Center in the United States in association with the Department of Defense. It is a statement of principles and an outline of practice couched in a style soberly reminiscent of an army manual. It discusses objective, unified effort, control legitimacy, the need for perseverance and restraint, and security, and ends with notes about US counter-terrorism policy:

Objective

The general objective of combatting terrorism programs is neutralizing terrorist groups. As in most stability and support operations, neutralization in this context means rendering the source of threat benign, not necessarily killing the terrorists. In antiterrorism, the objective can be further refined as preventing attacks and minimizing the effects if one should occur. It includes any action to weaken the terrorist organization and its political power and to make potential targets more difficult to attack. Counterterrorism includes spoiling action, deterrence, and response.

Unity of effort

As in all stability and support operations, interagency action is required to combat terrorism. Unity of effort requires ways to integrate the actions of various responsible agencies of the US and foreign governments. Intelligence is particularly important and sensitive. [. . .]

Unfortunately, it is easier to prescribe unity of effort than to achieve it. In circumstances where multiple police and intelligence agencies have vague and overlapping charters and jurisdictions, friction is bound to occur. As in other aspects of stability and support operations, the solution lies in negotiation and consensus-building. Fortunately, experience has proved that cooperation at the local unit or installation level is relatively easy to obtain.

Legitimacy

Legitimacy is not usually a problem in combatting terrorism since the right of self-defense is universally recognized and, as indicated above, terrorist acts are crimes in peace, conflict, or war. Security forces might bring their legitimacy into question by failing to distinguish between those perpetrating, aiding, or abetting terrorism and others who might sympathize with their cause but do not engage in violent acts [. . .] An overreaction that results in the avoidable deaths of hostages while security forces are attempting to neutralize terrorists, for example, raises questions of judgement as well as the legitimacy of the undertaking.

Patience and perseverance

Patience and perseverance are the hallmarks of successful programs to combat terrorism. In any country or region, there are few terrorists relative to the population. Identifying and capturing them is difficult and entails tedious police and intelligence work. It is filled with frustration [. . .] Perhaps the most irritating aspect of defence against terrorism is that success is hard to identify. For example, if there is no incident, it may be because the defensive measures are effective. On the other hand, it is equally likely that the terrorists never intended to attack in the first place. Rarely will success be measurable, but defensive efforts must continue.

Restraint

Restraint is necessary to both objective and legitimacy in the context of combatting terrorism. Premature action against individuals, for example, can be counter-productive if it interferes with developing intelligence in depth that might neutralize an entire terrorist group. Similarly, overreaction, such as imposing severe populace and resource control measures, can undermine legitimacy and unnecessarily irritate the civilian populace.

Security

Security is the most obvious requirement in combatting terrorism. Terrorists rely on surprise and the victim's confusion at the time of an incident. Antiterrorism involves physical security, operational security [. . .] and the practice of personal protective measures by all personnel. [. . .]

In combatting terrorism, intelligence is extraordinarily important. The essential elements of information [. . .] differ somewhat from those normally found in traditional combat situations. In addition to the terrorists' strength, skills, equipment, logistic capabilities, leader profiles, source of supply, and tactics, more specific information is needed. This includes the groups' goals, affiliations, indication of their willingness to kill or die for their cause, and significant events in their history, such as the death of martyrs or some symbolic event [. . .] Unless terrorists' specific interests are known, predicting the likely target is pure chance.

US policy for combatting terrorism

Until the 1980s, the US government, like most other Western governments, considered terrorism to be primarily a police matter. The seizure of the US embassy in Teheran and subsequent car and truck bomb attacks on our facilities in Lebanon forced us to reevaluate that position. Current US policy regarding terrorism encompasses acts against Americans at home and abroad.

The United States considers all terrorist acts criminal and intolerable and condemns them without regard for their motivation. The United States will support all lawful measures to prevent terrorism and bring perpetrators to justice. We will not make any concessions to terrorist blackmail because to do so will merely invite more terrorist actions. (No concessions does not mean no negotiations.)

The Department of Defense has identified five threat levels to standardize reporting. They are based on terrorists' existence, capability, intentions, history, targeting, and the security environment. The five levels are described below:

- Critical, which means that a terrorist group has entered the country or is able to do so. It has the capability to attack and is engaged in target selection. Its history and intentions may or may not be known.
- High indicates that a terrorist group exists which has the capability, history, and intention to attack.
- Medium describes the same conditions as high except that intentions are unknown.
- Low is a situation in which terrorist groups exist and have a capability to attack. Their history may or may not be known.
- Negligible describes a situation in which the existence or capability of terrorist groups may or may not be present.[2]

Another rather earlier example of a counter-terrorism programme is that suggested by a research criminologist, Grant Wardlaw (1982):

The following options might be suggested as parts of an anti-terrorist campaign.

1   Attempt to find long-term solutions to the underlying causes of terrorism. This approach involves a decision to acknowledge that there are remediable inequities in society which may provide objective causes of terrorism. Such an approach probably is the most significant because of the widespread policy changes with extensive effects on other aspects of the social milieu which might be occasioned by it.
2   Increase the size and powers of the security forces (for example, increase manpower, search and entry powers, power to detain without trial, etc.). This would involve major policy decisions about the nature of policing our society, civil rights, etc.

3   Introduce capital punishment for terrorist activities. Such a move involves policy decisions about the role of capital punishment, whether terrorists are to be treated as a separate class of offenders (as opposed to reintroducing capital punishment generally), which types of terrorist acts are to be made capital offences.

4   Enact legislation limiting rights of assembly and increasing controls over the members of society by way of identification cards, registration of residence and extensive use of computerised files. This has implications for the type of society we have, police powers, civil rights, etc.

5   Establish a 'third force' or special military units to cope with terrorist attacks. The decision to employ new types of force involves policy decisions about how early to commit military forces, the role of police in anti-terrorist operations, and civil–military relations.

6   Announce a policy of 'no negotiations' with terrorists. Such a policy implies a wide range of decisions about such issues as the value of individual life, the authority and prestige of the state, and how far in reality such a policy would be pursued (for example, would the government refuse to negotiate in the face of a credible nuclear threat?).

7   Increase physical and procedural security. Such an increase revolves around related issues of the economics of such measures, powers given to security officers (particularly those employed by private security organisations), and civil rights.

8   Introduce internment without trial or special legal procedures designed to limit intimidation of witnesses (such as the so-called Diplock courts in Northern Ireland). The introduction of measures outside of the normal legal process requires major policy decisions about the legal system, civil rights, and the political consequences of such changes.

9   Place legal limits on the ability of the media to report terrorist acts. This may involve suggestions as to the timing, duration, or content of news reports. Such restrictions involve some of the most controversial policy decisions about freedom of the press, free speech, and the nature of government.

10   Introduce special anti-terrorist legislation which may mandate a combination of the above or other measures. Such legislation implies that a decision has been taken that terrorists cannot be dealt with by normal legal processes and leads to consequential policy changes in the law, police powers, civil rights, and governmental intrusion into everyday life.

11   Make it illegal for individuals or private organisations to pay ransom to terrorists or to take out ransom insurance and place a legal duty on people to report hostage takings to the police. Such measures involve decisions about the rights of individuals to take whatever action they consider necessary to safeguard the lives of those for whom they are responsible when a conflict exists with what the authorities see as undesirable consequences for society in general.

12   Promote and become a signatory to international treaties providing for extradition or trial of captured terrorists, suspension of air services to countries providing safe havens for hijackers, etc. This involves decisions about the effectiveness of international measures, the definition of terrorism and whether or not to allow 'political exception' clauses.

13   Research and develop alternatives to hostage negotiations. This implies a recognition that hostage taking is likely to decrease in frequency or take on new forms as negotiation techniques appear more successful. Consequently important policy decisions would have to be made about research directions and issues such as attitudes towards more aggressive incident resolution techniques.

14   Suggest that terrorist groups be encouraged to adhere to the norms articulated by the customary laws of war, the Geneva Conventions, and the Nuremberg Principles (a suggestion which has been characterised as 'patently valueless, representing the *reductio ad absurdum* of legalistic naïveté'). To support such a suggestion would require a policy decision to recognise terrorist groups as political entities and to accord them special prisoner-of-war status if captured.

15   Develop and deploy highly intrusive technologies as pre-emptive moves (for example, technologies for monitoring and surveillance). Such deployment requires major policy decisions about civil rights, police powers, and the nature of society.[3]

The foregoing list illustrates the complexity of the decisions that face authorities in the field of counter-terrorist policy.

PROGRAMMES, PRINCIPLES, PATHWAYS

Democratic societies generally find definitive action against political violence problematic. This is understandable on account of the public's customary high regard for private opinion and action and their prompt censure of anything they believe is authoritarian intervention. Security services find it hard to initiate what is seen as 'irregular' police work, to carry out surveillance, and to resort to planted 'informers'. Walter Laqueur (1999) sees much modern counter-terrorism as hampered by bureaucracy and inconsistent collaboration among states:

Counter-terrorism naturally goes hand in hand with terrorism, but over the ages it has become less successful for a variety of reasons. Modern technology in this area has made enormous progress; for example, it can trace the movements of even small units and single tanks over a wide area day and night. But it cannot keep track of the movements of single individuals in a town carrying miniaturised bombs. The only effective weapon against terrorism in the modern era has been the infiltration of their ranks and the use of informers. Police in the last century had a much freer hand against terrorism than today's police: they placed their agents in all major and most minor terrorist movements, and paid them from special funds to which only they had access. It is probably no exaggeration to state that most of the terrorist journals at the time were paid for by secret police funds. If a police informer in the course of his duty had to carry out a terrorist act, no questions would be asked, nor would he be put to trial or lose his pension rights.

Present-day police forces in democratic societies have little freedom of manoeuvre. Too many people are involved in decisions and operations, and bureaucratic formalities have to be observed. Payments to informers have to be signed and countersigned; the interception of communications between terrorist suspects has to be approved by the judiciary; and a skilful lawyer has a good chance to get his client, the terrorist, off the hook even if he was apprehended *in flagranti*. Because of these factors the successful infiltration of terrorist groups is almost impossible.

Counter-terrorism's success in democratic societies is mainly the result of advanced computer technology and the cooperation of a population that provides important leads. On the other hand, cooperation in the international arena has been less than perfect. Governments have been afraid of extraditing terrorists for fear of retaliation and for other reasons, or they have released convicted foreign terrorists from prison after a token stay. Also, governments have invoked 'higher interests of state' – France and Greece are examples – as reasons for not dealing with terrorists harshly. In a few cases, terrorists who have lost their usefulness or lacked influential protectors have been extradited. But by and large, counter-efforts against terrorists by democratic states have been only partly effective in recent times.[4]

Problems in sustaining an adequate counter-terrorism strategy, in a democracy where authority is 'coming down hard' on terrorists, lead to much unease, anxiety and questioning. The practice of a state employing exemplary violence both to punish violent dissidence and to discourage its further spread is seen by many as 'reactive terrorism', even though it is less intimidating than that practised by authoritarian states. At the very least, this is often regarded as a 'trade-off' between normal democratic values and rights and an insistence on heightened 'security'. Paul Wilkinson, in the second edition of his aptly titled *Terrorism versus Democracy: The Liberal State Response* (2006), considers problems such as these at length.[5]

While for Wilkinson there are no simple solutions to the experience of terrorism, there are to be found a number of 'pathways' – alternatives, political in nature – which may be used to strengthen democracy and reduce violence. For example, a terrorist group in a struggle for colonial independence may eventually conclude that their goals for complete autonomy are achieved and so give up the armed battle, especially if an imperial administration imaginatively and positively opens up a genuine concessionary pathway. Something of this nature occurred in French Algeria and in British Kenya and Cyprus. In other places, terrorists have been indicted and numbers reduced under the strict application of a criminal code. The pathway here is that of the rule of law, with its provisions of defence representation and appeal. Both Germany and Italy dealt with their 'red brigades' in this way in the 1960s and 1970s.

Stern military counter-action does not necessarily block all pacific routes. While the stern measures adopted by governments in Algeria, Argentina and Colombia resulted in some known terrorists fleeing into exile, to remain a potential threat, the very draconian methods used led to much popular agitation for a reformed control policy, offering some possibilities of conflict resolution. This is a pathway dangerous to tread, but not an impossible one. Two alternative routes strike Wilkinson as worth exploring if a government stands close to its democratic credentials. Terrorist struggles may weaken where activists see their campaign as failing. Military control is gripping hard. The public is not supportive and probably increasingly hostile to the minority. In Northern Ireland, the IRA, and, in Spain, the Basque ETA, were wheedled into taking first steps along a pathway of arms decommissioning and serious settlement negotiations. Peaceful ways of dealing with grievance and conflict were hammered out.

What, though, of laying bare a pathway for individual 'disengagement'? (This was the term used by John Horgan apropos motivation – see Chapter 2, above.) Wilkinson sees this as an indispensable tactic in counter-terrorism work:

It follows that an essential part of the democratic effort must be to provide effective pathways out of terrorism for the individual. By so doing we will be constantly aiming to minimise the threat of residual or irreconcilable terrorism which may otherwise slowly regroup and regain sufficient support and strength to launch fresh campaigns of violence. In this constant moral and psychological battle of attrition, democratic authorities must constantly seek more imaginative and effective ways of enabling individual members of terrorist organisations to make a complete break with their comrades and leaders who, for their part, strive to keep their members under an iron grip.[6]

Detachment of the individual terrorist is a formidable undertaking. There is the tremendous bonding pressure that applies to each member, the individual's fear of ruthless group discipline, and the almost unmanageable climb out to rehabilitation in normal society. Food for thought is one of Wilkinson's later statements:

[. . .] terrorists know that the security forces in a liberal democracy are forced to operate at mid levels of coerciveness. Judicial restraints and civil control and accountability, all of which are essential safeguards in a democracy, prevent the security forces from deploying their full strength and firepower. These constraints are inevitable and desirable, but they do mean that the task of countering terrorism in a democracy, under the constant scrutiny of the free media, becomes an enormously complex and demanding task.[7]

A point that might be made at this juncture is to refer to the concern, even anxiety, of those who fear the erosion of basic human rights and legislative safeguards in the cause of fighting terrorism. There is certainly on every hand doubt about the proper treatment of many who are detained awaiting charge and trial. One instance, in September 2006, is found in US press reports of Republican Senators arguing that the tough new terror laws being sought by the Administration specifically in the case of detainees would weaken the force of Geneva Human Rights Conventions and raise questions about the moral bases of the legislation. The President's reluctance to accept this was evident in his declaration that it was, 'vital that our folk on the frontline have the tools that are necessary to protect the American people'. The President found the Convention 'vague' despite a Supreme Court ruling that military tribunals at the Guantanamo Detention Center violated both US law and a section of the Geneva Convention.

COUNTERING STATE-SPONSORED TERRORISM

There is a long history of terrorists finding support in a patron state that has an interest in furthering dramatic political change elsewhere. Today, Iran, Iraq, Cuba, North Korea, Syria and Sudan are all considered 'rogue states' in facilitating and harbouring terrorist elements. Since the second half of the twentieth century there has been a considerable increase in this sponsorship. Other states have attempted some form of counter-action using, for example, diplomatic pressures, negotiation, third-party mediation, and even economic sanctions and blockades. They have done this either unilaterally or in association, say, with those who have ratified the conventions and declarations of the United Nations or the European Union. Fighting state-sponsored terrorism is a problematic and frustrating concern and discussion of it deserves prominence in this section of Part Three.

Boaz Ganor (1998) has comprehensively surveyed the issues that arise in dealing with state-sponsored terrorism. He begins by pointing to the contemporary wide incidence of this type of involvement, outlining the main characteristics, namely ideological support, financial support, military support, operational support, direction of terrorist attacks, and direct state involvement in terrorist attacks. Ganor goes on to consider strategies of counter-terrorism that endeavour to treat sponsoring states as capable of rational decision. Such states are likely to respond constructively to a range of deterrent options employed against them by contemplating the ratio of cost to benefit. Ganor takes the familiar point of national conflict of interest where security and politico-economic interests seem incompatible. There is a brief discussion of the utilitarian approaches of 'critical dialogue' and 'buying silence'. Finally, given that offending states are apt to look around for loopholes in any unified counter-action, Ganor makes a case for some sort of international institution to fight terrorism, although the United Nations is not highly mentioned in this regard. His conclusion defines an agenda for internationally coordinated counter-terrorism:

Instead of the 'weapon of the weak' – minority groups, liberation movements, and revolutionary organizations – terrorism has become a tool of states and even of superpowers. In some cases, states established 'puppet' terrorist organizations, whose purpose was to act on behalf of the sponsoring state, to further the interests of the state, and to represent its positions in domestic or regional fronts. In other cases, states sponsored or supported existing organizations, thereby creating mutually profitable connections.

The patron state provided its beneficiary terrorist organization with political support, financial assistance, and the sponsorship necessary to maintain and expand the struggle until the attainment of its objectives had been achieved. The patron used the beneficiary to perpetrate acts of terrorism as a means of spreading the former's ideology throughout the world, or in other cases, the patron ultimately expected that the beneficiary would assume control over the state in which it resided or impart its ideology to broad sections of the general public. [. . .]

The high costs of modern warfare, the Cold War, and concern about non-conventional escalation, as well as the danger of defeat and the unwillingness to appear as the aggressor, have turned terrorism into an efficient, convenient, and generally discrete weapon for attaining state interests in the international realm.

Ideological support

The basic level of state support for terrorism is 'ideological support'. Terrorist organizations, as noted, are a convenient instrument for spreading ideological doctrines, particularly revolutionary ones. States such as the Soviet Union and Iran, which set themselves the operative-strategic aim of spreading their revolutionary ideology (Communism in the former case and Islamic fundamentalism in the latter) found suitable allies in terrorist organizations.

In some cases, however, terrorist organizations were founded by extreme radical activists, who were inspired to found their group by a state which supported terrorism or who had accepted the ideological sponsorship of a state sponsor in an effort to attain material assistance, after having already founded their organization. In such cases, the terrorist organization is provided with political, ideological or religious indoctrination via agents of the supporting state or is trained by institutions of the sponsoring state. (In this context one should mention communist terrorist organizations, such as the 'Popular Front for the Liberation of Palestine', which enjoyed support from the Soviet Union, and organizations with an Islamic fundamentalist outlook, such as Hizballah, with close ideological and religious ties to Iran.)

Financial support

A higher level of state support for a terrorist organization is 'financial support'. In order to continue operations and develop further, a terrorist organization requires large sums of money, which are sometimes unavailable through its own independent resources. In such cases, terrorist organizations rely on the generous support of sponsoring states. Today Iran is one of the main contributors to terrorist organizations. [. . .]

Military support

A higher level of aid involves 'military support'. Within this framework, the state supplies the terrorist organization with a broad range of weapons, provides military training, organizes courses for activists, and so on. Iran also falls in this category. [. . .]

Operational support

The next level of aid is 'operational support'. It entails the direct provision of state assistance in the perpetration of specific attacks. Operational support takes various forms: false documents, special weapons, safe havens, etc. Iranian embassies throughout the world, for instance, play a crucial role in this context. [. . .]

Initiating terrorist attacks

The next level of state involvement in terrorism is 'initiating and directing terrorist attacks'. In this category, the state no longer limits itself to providing aid indirectly to terrorist organizations. Instead, it gives specific instructions concerning attacks, it initiates terrorist activities, and it sets their aims. [. . .]

Direct involvement in terrorist attacks

The highest level of state involvement in terrorism is 'perpetrating direct attacks by government agencies'. In these cases, the state carries out terrorist attacks in order to further its interests, using agencies from its own intelligence services and security forces, or through people directly responsible to them. [. . .]

Rationality of states involvement in terrorism

Having established the various features of state sponsorship of international terrorism, we are faced with determining the possibility of preventing states interested in assisting terrorist organizations or in perpetrating terrorist acts on their own. Before turning to this issue, however, we must determine the extent to which one can view the decision to engage in terrorist activities as a rational act.

The most widely accepted strategy for coping with terrorism in general, and with states involved in terrorism in particular, is deterrence. However, if the state's decision to sponsor terrorism does not follow from rational considerations, deterrent activities against it will be meaningless. Indeed, a policy of retribution against irrational states might be ineffective, and could even lead to further escalation. [. . .]

Most states engaged in terrorism choose to do so. They take into account the price they will be required to pay for their activity, in exchange for the benefits gained by the attainment of their policy goals. Usually, these states adhere to rational cost-benefit analyses. Indeed, most countries which sponsor terrorism are not democratic, and their decision-making processes are limited to the consideration of a single ruler. The variables entering the cost and benefits equation in such cases might seem irrational to Western sensibilities, as they seemingly assign exaggerated and disproportionate weight to ideology, religion, and emotions. But even the lone decision maker tests the extent to which his activity will ultimately promote his goals, as he himself has defined them, and whether countermeasures adopted against his country, if and when its involvement in terrorism is disclosed, will endanger his and his country's basic interests.

For every country, there is a limit to the amount it is willing to pay for its continued involvement in terrorism. The price scale varies from country to country, as does each one's 'breaking point'. Hence, in order for deterrence to be successful, countries contending with terrorism must raise the costs of terrorism involvement to the point where the costs outweigh the benefits, and they must do so according to the specific characteristics of the individual state sponsors.

What is the range of activities available in the deterrence of states sponsoring terrorist activities? What is the 'price scale' that the international community can endorse in an attempt to alter the costs and benefits analysis of those states which are involved in terrorism?

The 'price scale'

[There is a] rising scale of prices of international [deterrent] efforts, each one conveying a more stringent sanction than the previous one, beginning with a warning to cease terrorism sponsorship, to international condemnation and cultural boycott (including banning the sponsor from international events, removing it from international cultural or educational programmes, and the expulsion of its citizens who live, work, or study in other countries). The next stage is a diplomatic boycott, including the removal of terrorism sponsors from international institutions, the suspension of its membership in UN institutions, removal from the UN General Assembly and even a cessation of bilateral relations (no country has ever been expelled from the UN). At the next stage (or parallel to the previous one) is an economic boycott. Such a measure could include restricting the state's ability to purchase military or dual-use equipment (in a military conflict or in its involvement in terrorism), preventing exports to it and purchases from it, freezing and confiscating its assets throughout the world, and the construction of a blockade, by air, land and sea. In addition, a secondary boycott could be imposed on countries and companies which insist on maintaining commercial ties with the sponsor. The next phase is the legal stage. Here, the sponsoring state's political and military leaders are defined as 'war criminals' or charged with 'crimes against humanity', with international show trials set to punish them (even if not in their presence). The highest stage of punishment and deterrence against a state sponsoring terrorism is the offensive stage – international coordinated military actions against the terrorist organization's facilities in the sponsoring country and the sponsor's military installations.

Conflicts of interests

The struggle against states involved in terrorism reflects many conflicts of interests in the international arena – between states and superpowers, alliances and leagues of states, groups, and organizations. At times, however, the counter terrorism effort creates conflicts of interests within a state, between its security and economic interests. Thus far, economic interests have had the upper hand, whereas security interests, expressed in the will for a more effective struggle against states engaging in terrorism, have been relegated second-class status.

An analysis of the international measures adopted against countries involved in terrorism reveals that most states are unwilling to sacrifice their economic interests for the cessation of terrorism. The most prominent example of such a tendency can be found in the attitude of European states (headed by Germany, France and Italy) towards Iran, the world's leading terrorism sponsor. Contrary to the American approach, which is intended to restrict Iranian activities and to force it to abandon terrorism by further damaging Iran's precarious economy with additional sanctions, the countries of Europe have relied on a varied set of practical arguments to justify their extensive economic and commercial ties with Iran.

The 'critical dialogue' – a utilitarian argument

Countries maintaining extensive economic links with states involved in terrorism choose to justify their policy in utilitarian-international terms rather than in economic ones. Their claim is that imposing sanctions on such states will not lead them to restrict their sponsorship of terrorism. Indeed they claim that the opposite will result, and such policies will corner them into even more extreme, violent tactics and a further escalation of international terrorism. According to such an outlook, the preferred policy is one of 'critical dialogue' – keeping channels open with states sponsoring terrorism by maintaining economic and cultural links with them. Such 'open channels' can be used as a means to voice criticism of terrorism policies and to influence terrorism sponsors against the continuation of their sponsorship.

At the Paris summit of the industrialized countries (G-7), in August 1996, which dealt with international terrorism, the Europeans blocked an American attempt to impose sanctions on four terrorism sponsoring states – Iran, Libya, Iraq and Sudan. The European participants claimed that isolating countries such as Iran has no moderating influence whatsoever on terrorism, but rather the opposite. In support of their 'critical dialogue' approach, they claimed they can make ingenious use of the 'carrot and stick' approach, thereby preserving the effectiveness of their own actions against terrorism sponsors.

Buying silence – the security argument

As previously mentioned, critics of the use of sanctions often claim that imposing sanctions on states engaged in terrorism closes channels of communication and may lead to escalation. This claim is compatible with another conciliatory strategy towards terrorists, mainly that which supports a 'dialogue' with terrorist organizations in an attempt to influence their policies. Such a policy is in effect 'buying silence'. In such cases, a terrorist organization (or sponsor) agrees to refrain from carrying out attacks within the borders of a certain country, in exchange for a commitment by that country to turn a blind eye to terrorist activities of the organization or the ideological influence or support of the sponsor. In so doing, the country conceals the responsibility of the organization or its sponsor, and can even prevent the extradition of terrorists caught in that country or lead to the release of terrorists without, or shortly after a trial.

Such a strategy is opportunist at best. It promotes particularistic interests while jeopardizing the safety of the entire international community and of other sovereign states. It also hampers all chances of effective international cooperation in the struggle against terrorism; it defeats the international effort to coerce terrorism sponsors to refrain from further involvement in the use of terror. [. . .]

Breakdown of international unity

International struggle against states which are involved in terrorism should not be limited to the imposition of economic sanctions. Rather, it should cover a full range of diplomatic, legal, economic, and offensive actions. Ultimately, such measures will raise the costs of involvement in terrorism, and therefore reduce the terrorism-related activities of sponsoring states.

States sponsoring terrorism will resort to any means to find loopholes in international boycotts and will seek out countries ready to maintain cultural, diplomatic, and economic ties, either openly or surreptitiously. In return, they will be ready to pay a high price and grant economic and other benefits to anyone prepared to cooperate with them. Alternatively, these states may threaten to harm foreign investments or assets within their territories or execute massive acts of terrorism or even an all-out war. [. . .]

The late Prime Minister of Israel, Yitzhak Rabin, also addressed this issue:

> The response to international terrorism must also be international. Nations must find ways of cooperating against the terrorist network [. . .] I propose that this type of cooperation be institutionalized and made concrete. Countries that choose to coordinate their activities against international terrorism should create a special international organization for this purpose. Obviously, this organization cannot be created within the framework of the United Nations. It can come into being only if the United States, the most powerful country in the free world, will take the initiative and call for its establishment [. . .] This organization should coordinate four main functions: first, intelligence gathering and counter-intelligence; second, protection of facilities and transportation routes [. . .] third, military operations in cases of emergency [. . .] fourth, and most difficult, political action against states that initiate and promote terror. Countries that initiate terrorism must be made to understand that they will face an organized, united front of states, a union ready to take measures that an attacked country would not be able to undertake alone. The existence of such an agency might help serve as a deterrent, and possibly an effective means of sanctions and punishment.

An international agenda for the struggle against states involved in terrorism

In conclusion, developing an effective international strategy against states which are engaged in terrorism requires the international community to adopt the following steps:

- To reach an international agreement regarding an exhaustive definition of terrorism.
- To endorse a means of classifying countries according to the features and the level of their sponsorship of terrorism.
- To publish an updated list of countries' involvement in terrorism according to their level of involvement.
- To acknowledge the necessity and the duty to punish countries because of their involvement in terrorism.
- To define a clear 'price scale' to be paid by countries engaged in terrorism.
- To adjust the 'price scale' to the various types of state sponsorship of terrorism, aiming to change their balance of interests.
- To impose a secondary boycott on states and companies that continue to maintain economic and other ties, whether open or covert, with states on which a boycott was imposed because of their involvement in terrorism.

- To establish a permanent international mechanism to combat terrorism, one of whose aims will be to ensure that punitive steps are taken against states engaged in terrorism and to warn against any infringement of these measures.

Only the careful fulfillment of all these steps can ensure effective action against terrorism sponsors. Otherwise, it will be impossible to alter the cost-benefit calculus, to reduce their involvement, or limit the scope of their attacks or their damaging effects.[8]

COUNTER-TERRORISM AND INTERNATIONAL INSTITUTIONS

Ganor's point in 1998 as to the desirability of international institutions taking on a role in counter-terrorism can be taken further with a note about what the United Nations is doing globally and what the European Union is doing regionally. The United Nations has neither the constitutional authority nor the resources to discharge an executive function. Primarily, this is up to governments alone or in association. What the United Nations can do and does do is to mobilise resolve among its 185 member states to combat terrorism by framing resolutions, conventions and declarations and then to persuade states to ratify these enabling instruments. Much is being done, too, to promote research into the causes of terrorism, and to convene workshops in co-ordinating intelligence exchange, in setting up an advisory service, and in devising training opportunities for field workers. It is the last-named who have been brought into mediation work in the Middle East and in South-East Asia, especially in crises over hostage release and the hijacking of aircraft. In Colombia, Panama, Thailand and Cambodia, teams of experts and relief workers have been drafted into areas where a growing terrorist enterprise – drug-related narco-terrorism – has devastated entire communities.

Only very slowly are the legal components of international counter-terrorism assuming shape in 13 global or regional treaties. Progress is hampered, first, by the reluctance of many states jealous about their sovereignty to give overall priority to humane considerations rather than political ones, and, second, by the fact that international law provisions, however definite, still require translation into domestic laws before offenders in those countries can be prosecuted. A statement from the United Nations in 1996 lists a number of aspects of international terrorism where coordinated counter-action has yet to be realised:

Most of the international legal instruments pertaining to international terrorism were introduced after significant international incidents had already taken place. International terrorism is in many instances associated with drug trafficking, the arms trade, smuggling or money laundering, and acts by groups with extremist persuasions. A number of subjects are not covered by existing international treaties. These include terrorist bombings, terrorist fundraising, traffic in arms, money laundering, exchange of information concerning persons or organizations suspected of terrorist-linked activities, the disruption of global communications networks, the use of weapons of mass destruction, falsification of travel documents, and technical cooperation in training for counter-terrorism. Preventing the use of weapons of mass destruction by terrorists and the use of modern information technology for terrorist purposes, such as disrupting a communications network by altering data or disseminating on a wide scale extremist ideologies inciting persons to commit terrorist acts, also requires to be addressed.[9]

Critics of the United Nations generally dismiss its power as 'all talk'. Yet, talk must precede consensual action. The UN General Assembly on 8 September 2006, as was expected, adopted a Resolution condemning terrorism in all its manifestations. This time, though, 185 member states had worked out a common strategic approach to fight terrorism and they put this into the terms of a Plan of Action. The Plan is to elaborate operationally the aims of '5Ds', namely to *dissuade* disaffected groups from choosing terrorism as a tactic to achieve goals, to *deny* terrorists the means to carry on their violence, to *deter* states from supporting terrorist groups and methods, to *develop* states' capacities to prevent terrorism, and to *defend* human rights using conference and regional monitoring groups.

Spelled out in the programme as basic to fulfilment are these priorities: to address conditions conducive to the spread of terrorism, and to combat it through enhanced international collaboration in intelligence work, security systems, building of databases, inter-agency coordination for assistance in operations and victim support. There is to be a watching brief on the possible terrorist use of biological and nuclear materials. Other priorities relate to means of codifying, implementing and ensuring obligations in the field of human rights protection and the rule of law.[10]

European states have also worked together to draft the beginnings of a legislative approach to controlling terrorism. In 1982 Grant Wardlaw listed many provisions in a European convention which appeared to offer firm grounds for states to act together: but would there be sufficient common will?

The second existing major anti-terrorist Convention is the Council of Europe's 1977 European Convention on the Suppression of Terrorism. This may on paper be seen as an advance on previous Conventions in that it strips many offences of the protection afforded by the classic 'political exception clause' (that is a clause which exempts from the criminal category those acts which are politically motivated). Article 1 of the Convention declares the following offences to be outside the purview of a political exception clause:

1   Offences within the scope of the 1970 Hague Convention for the Unlawful Seizure of Aircraft.
2   Offences within the scope of the 1971 Montreal Convention for the Suppression of Unlawful Acts Against the Safety of Civil Aviation.
3   Serious offences involving an attack against the life, physical integrity, or liberty of internationally protected persons, including diplomatic agents.
4   Offences involving kidnapping, hostage taking or serious unlawful detention.

5   Offences involving the use of bombs, grenades, rockets, automatic weapons, or letter or parcel bombs where people's lives are endangered.
6   Attempts to commit any of the above offences, or being an accomplice to such offences or attempts to commit them.

Article 2 stipulates that other particularly serious acts involving innocent persons may also be regarded as non-political. Much of the Convention deals with provisions for extradition and Article 7 states that refusal to extradite under the terms of the Convention requires the detaining State to initiate prosecution of the offender. On the face of it, the European Convention seems a worthwhile contribution to international attempts (or, in this case, regional) to combat terrorism. However, as with other cases, it is flawed by the fact that not all members of the Council of Europe have ratified it and that it contains no enforcement provisions for breaches by signatories. Thus, there is no guarantee that it will be adhered to in the cruel test of a crisis [. . .] In general, it can be expected that many, if not all, nations will put national self-interest before international treaty obligations in a crisis. This is the fatal flaw in international regulatory attempts.[11]

A later Council of Europe Convention on Terrorism (2005) has moved further to regularise surveillance, trial and extradition procedures, cleverly taking account of jealously guarded sovereignty among members.[12]

    More recently, Antonio Vercher (1992) has compiled an international comparative legal analysis of counter-terrorism moves in Europe. A good deal of progress has been made – on paper. Summit meetings, workshops, conferences, reports and inter-governmental liaison have all given the topics on cross-border terrorism many hours of earnest discussion. Numerous agendas and documents from the European Parliament in Brussels and from the European Court in Strasbourg have envisaged the facilities and rulings of a 'homogeneous judicial area'. European states, members of the European Union, have preferred a much less unified approach – that of political cooperation and police liaison. (Interpol is constrained by its narrow founding terms of reference and by a dearth of resources in mounting and sustaining any monitoring of terrorist intent.) Vercher does not doubt that much more is possible to realise a unified counter-terrorism strategy in Europe: provided that examination of feasibility does not confine itself to what he terms 'legal–technical' points. There is need of wider horizons:

It is not sufficient only to examine the legal–technical feasibility of a unified anti-terrorist system in Europe. Various other questions must be addressed simultaneously. These are concerned with the investigation of the root causes of terrorism and the protection of the fundamental rights of individuals within the EEC. Such questions are partially outside the purely legal scope of this thesis, but their importance cannot be underestimated since they are as much a guarantee of a long-standing and definite solution to the terrorist problem as the legal–technical measures themselves.
    The legal measures which are part of an anti-terrorist system are intended to deal directly with the violence and social disruption provoked by terrorism. This does not mean that in themselves they will solve the causes of that violence and

disruption. In fact, an investigation of the root causes of terrorism in any particular part of Europe may suggest the adoption of different measures, more social and political than legal.[13]

The European Union's 25 member states are now administering a very detailed Plan of Action against Terrorism, as we have noted. There is to be close collaboration between police and judicial authorities. Economic and financial controls will be tightened to deal with suspect financing and weapons trading. Emergency prepared-ness against bio-terrorist threats will reinforce warning systems and pool expertise and antidote stockpiles. Security at airports and seaports is now much more rigorous. Talks are taking place with such as Iran, Pakistan, the new Afghanistan government and the Palestinian Authority about political, economic and social measures to reduce resort to political violence.[14]

COUNTER-TERRORISM AND MASS-DESTRUCTION DEVICES

The face of terrorism and the demands on counter-action are changing fast in many ways. The potential for nuclear terrorism has been widely discussed in recent years along with the possible use of chemical, biological and computerised devices ('cyber-terrorism'). A good deal of the theory and practice of counter-terrorism becomes out of date month by month, as Bruce Hoffman (1999) believes:

Meanwhile, the face of terrorism is changing in other ways. New adversaries, new motivations and new rationales have emerged in recent years to challenge at least some of the conventional wisdom on both terrorists and terrorism. More critically, perhaps, many of our old preconceptions – as well as government policies – date from the emergence of terrorism as a global security problem more than a quarter of a century ago. They originated, and took hold, during the Cold War, when radical left-wing terrorist groups then active throughout the world were widely regarded as posing the most serious threat to Western security. Even such modifications or 'fine-tuning' as have been undertaken since that time are arguably no less dated by now, having been implemented a decade ago in response to the series of suicide bombings against American diplomatic and military targets in the Middle East that at the time had underscored the rising threat of state-sponsored terrorism.

In no area, perhaps, is the potential irrelevance of much of this thinking clearer, or the critical lacuna more apparent, than with regard to the potential use by terrorists of weapons of mass destruction (WMD): that is, nuclear, chemical or biological weapons. Most of the handful of publications that have authoritatively addressed this issue are themselves now seriously dated, having been conceived and written in some instances nearly two decades ago when very different situations, circumstances and international dynamics existed. Indeed, much of the research on potential uses of WMD during the Cold War understandably concentrated on nuclear confrontation involving almost exclusively the two superpowers and their allies. Potential terrorist use of such devices was either addressed within the Cold War/

superpowers framework or else dismissed, given the prevailing patterns of substate violence and the aims and objectives of violent non-state groups active at the time.

Today, the threat of a general war – nuclear and/or conventional – between the superpowers of the Cold War era and their respective alliances has faded. But it has been replaced by new security challenges of a potentially far more amorphous, less quantifiable and perhaps even more ominous character, that may also be far more difficult to meet [. . .] the increasing salience of religious motives for terrorist activity has already contributed to the increasing lethality of international terrorism. Moreover, many of the constraints (both self-imposed and technical) which previously inhibited terrorist use of WMD are eroding. The particular characteristics, justifications and mindsets of religious and quasi-religious – as compared with secular – terrorists suggest that religious terrorists will be among the most likely of the potential categories of non-state perpetrators to use WMD.[15]

Is it possible that a terrorist group could produce a nuclear device? A democratic state needing to counter-act such an eventuality would face agonising choices in the view of Laqueur:

Democracies that have faced a terrorist challenge have tended toward under-reaction, because the identity of the perpetrator may not have been clear, or because restraint and a response commensurate with the damage caused and the number of victims suffered was called for. But the reaction to the use of a weapon of mass destruction might be the opposite, one of overreaction. In such a case there is bound to be overwhelming pressure to retaliate on a bigger scale, both as an act of revenge and to forestall future attacks.

Despite the reasons one can marshal against the use of nuclear bombs by terrorists acting as substitutes for foreign countries, one can still think of a variety of scenarios in which this could happen, whether because a country with a nuclear capacity has descended into chaos, or a government has temporarily lost control, or any other circumstance in which those in power have ceased to act rationally.

What if a domestic terrorist group should produce one or more nuclear devices without any foreign help at all? It is difficult to think at the present time of an effective defence to prevent an attack in this case. Given the amount of fissionable material that is available, the voluminous literature on nuclear weaponry, and military and state budgets in which hundreds of millions of dollars is a paltry sum, the chance that a terrorist group will come into possession of a nuclear device is significant.[16]

Laqueur at the same time has speculatively surveyed what he terms the 'terrorism of the future', in which sophisticated lethal devices pose problems both for the would-be terrorist and for those called to counter-act.

There are many questions regarding the effective use of chemical and biological weapons. Chemical substances and biological organisms have to be more than highly toxic; they also need the right atmospheric conditions. Success depends on a variety of factors, including the direction and strength of the wind, the temperature, and other climatic factors. A massive dispersal may have a very limited effect, or it may create enormous damage.

Recent research in biotechnology has made the construction of fusion toxins possible, and bacteria and viruses can now be made more dangerous and resistant to antibiotics through genetic modification. But at the same time, biotechnology makes it possible to manufacture antisera and vaccines to protect a civilian population.[17]

The possibilities of 'mega terrorism', where a nuclear or biological weapon attack causes mass casualties and calamitous destruction of infrastructure, are very much in the minds of governments and regional authorities. Three scenarios, at least, have been envisaged: one, the use of radioactive materials in an attack on a power plant or similar public utility (perhaps delivered via conventional explosives to force entry); two, the release on a proliferating scale of toxic or infectious agents; and, three, cyber-terrorism, where illegitimate computer 'hackers' cripple communications, transport systems and power supplies. There are multiple considerations for civic and health planners devising 'states of readiness'.[18]

THE DYNAMIC OF TERRORISM AND THE NEED OF RESPONSE

However sophisticated the means employed, the essence of political violence is that it is dynamic and constantly evolving. Counter-terrorism, to have any success at all, must keep in pace. Again, it is Hoffman sensing the urgency of mounting intelligible and intelligent strategies to contain something that can drain life out of ordered living:

At the same time, perhaps the most sobering realisation that arises from addressing the phenomenon of terrorism is that the threat and the problems that fuel it can never be eradicated completely. Their complexity, diversity and often idiosyncratic characteristics mean that there is no magic bullet, no single solution to be found and applied *pari passu*. This conclusion, however, reinforces the need for creative solutions if not to solve, then at least to ameliorate both the underlying causes and the violent manifestations. Only in this way will the international community be able prudently, effectively and productively to marshal its resources where and against whom they will have the greatest positive effect.

In sum, the emergence of this new breed of terrorist adversary means that nothing less than a sea-change in our thinking about terrorism and the policies required to counter it will be required. Too often in the past we have lulled ourselves into believing that terrorism was among the least serious or complex of security issues. We cannot afford to go on making this mistake.[19]

Since 11 September 2001, Britain and the United States, in liaison, have put in hand a number of practical approaches to counter-terrorism. New measures include the recruiting and training of special police/military units to pre-empt and prevent threatened attacks if these are reported by intelligence sources. There is to be increased security and checks in 'sensitive zones' and the use of intrusive surveillance technology. Searches and inspection of computer traffic and office files may be authorised subject to legal advice. (There was much public debate on both sides of the Atlantic as to the permissiveness of such scrutiny.) A range of sanctions and punishments is now in hand for those indicted for terrorism promotion or assistance with it. Now there will be moves against any state identified as involved in terrorism by means of diplomatic and economic boycotts, the freezing of assets and trade, scrutiny and control of air and sea linkages, and even possible military action.

The last chapter referred to terrorism and legal considerations. Again, Britain and the United States have had new counter-terrorism legislation designed, debated and finally given statutory authority. In both countries parliamentary and public debate became anguished over possible threats to individual liberties, despite the exigencies of recent atrocities. Governments finally won the day. Now there is an association of anti-terrorism and crime prevention, in that criminal law is to be amended and extended to defeat international terrorism.

In Britain, on 14 December 2001, there came into force the Anti-Terrorism, Crime and Security Act, superseding an Act of 1999 and itself the forerunner of much later legislation. The new Act was a comprehensive attempt to plug loopholes and create a rigorous system of protection and deterrence. In the United States, new legislation has been enacted, also since December 2001, under the rubric of 'Uniting and Strengthening America'. Courts in both countries will have similar powers in regard to the regularisation of police powers to search, arrest, examine and, if necessary, convict. Suspect financial transactions can be frozen, and cash and even property may be seized and forfeited. Information about acts of terrorism must be divulged: non-disclosure will be a punishable offence. What is termed 'communications data' may be intercepted, scanned and held in the interests of 'safeguarding national security', and the 'providers' of these communication services can be asked to volunteer to keep records of their clients' use of channels. (Once more, there has been unease and protest at the prospect of the authorities trawling through confidential e-mails and internet browsing.)

WE ARE IN THIS TOGETHER

President George W. Bush has spoken of his 'unyielding anger' and of the need for unity to conduct a 'war' against terrorism. US diplomats flew everywhere in the autumn of 2001, after the disaster of 9/11, to talk, induce and cajole governments into joining a coalition. Whittaker records this enterprise with some doubt:

There was a ready agreement to join from most countries and, to Washington's delight, even from somewhat dubious ones, namely, Sudan, Oman, Saudi Arabia, Iran, Syria, Egypt and Indonesia [. . .] A candid observer might have wondered whether states such as these, so recently tarnished by terrorist activity, would ever stand 'shoulder to shoulder' (as the President hoped) with a frequently-despised

United States. The coalition turned out to be stronger on rhetoric than on physical mobilisation. Not only British opinion disliked the idea of giving the Americans a 'blank cheque' with the expected payment of a part in a military adventure. It so happened that Washington decided, for the present and for military reasons, to limit military response to an assault on the terrorist nest in Afghanistan. The hawks had given way to the doves.[20]

Elsewhere, in Europe, the terrorist threat has transformed many political relationships. Russia, so long suspicious of American intentions, was prompt in declaring support for coordinated action against terrorism. There followed, in May 2002, an unprecedented convergence of political will when Russia joined 19 members of NATO in a new Nato-Russia Council (NRC) as an equal. Counter-terrorist policies were prominently on the agenda. As one wag from the White House put it: 'Revolutionary terrorism has spawned a revolution in counter-terrorism'.

Being together may suggest a united front against a cohesive entity that is relatively easy to identify and locate. As has been pointed out earlier, terrorism is not like that, in that it is so disparate that talk of a 'war against terror' is not helpful and, indeed, is misplaced. A final thought here in this Reader might be that of US philosopher, Haig Khatchadourian (born an Israeli), quoting a fellow academic, Abraham Edel: 'Terrorism is an emerging concept rather than one endowed with an established essence, and what will emerge will be a quasitechnical usage on which will hang a variety of legal and moral consequences.'[21]

Notes

1 Definition of terrorism

1   Terrorism Research Center, United States. Available at www.terrorism.com/terrorism/basics.html. Printout of pp. 11–12 (listing definitions).
2   Hoffman, Bruce (2006), *Inside Terrorism*, 2nd edn, New York: Columbia Press, pp. 1–3. The text in this Reader chapter owes much to Hoffman's thorough discussion on pp. 1–44.
3   Hoffman, p. 17.
4   Hoffman, pp. 20–3.
5   Hoffman, pp. 26, 28.
6   Hoffman, pp. 35–8, 40–1.
7   Rapoport, David C. and Wilkinson, Paul (2005), 'Analysing terrorism and counter-terrorism', *Terrorism and Political Violence*, pp. 17, 83–4, vol. 17, no. 3.
8   Wilkinson, Paul (2006), *Terrorism versus Democracy: The Liberal State Response*, 2nd edn, London: Routledge, p. 2.
9   Wilkinson, p. 4.
10 Horgan, John (2005), *The Psychology of Terrorism*, London: Routledge; Tore Bjorgo (ed.) (2005), *Root Causes of Terrorism*, London: Routledge; A. P. Schmid and R. D. Crelinsten (eds) (1993), *Western Responses to Terrorism*, London: Frank Cass.
11 Horgan, p. 20.
12 Horgan, p. 80.
13 Horgan, p. 81.
14 Bjorgo, p. 262.

2 Motivation for terrorism

1   Bjorgo, Tore (ed.) (2005), *Root Causes of Terrorism*, London: Routledge.
2   Horgan, John (2005), *The Psychology of Terrorism*, London: Routledge – questions considered in detail on pp. 80–106.

3   Horgan, pp. 83–4.
4   Horgan, p. 83.
5   Horgan, p. 85.
6   Horgan, p. 105.
7   Horgan, John (2005); Bruce Hoffman (2006), *Inside Terrorism*, revised edn, New York: Columbia University Press; Walter Laqueur (1999), *The New Terrorism*, Oxford: Oxford University Press; A. P. Schmid and A. J. Jongman (eds) (1988), *Political Terrorism*, Amsterdam: North Holland Publishing Company.
8   Horgan, p. 105.
9   Reprinted from US Army's Command and General Staff College, Fort Leavenworth, Kansas, by Terrorism Research Center. Extract from printout of 31 December 1998, pp. 1–5.
10   Post, Jerrold M. (1998), 'Terrorist psycho-logic: terrorist behavior as a product of psychological forces', in Walter Reich (ed.), *Origins of Terrorism*, Baltimore, MD: Johns Hopkins University Press, pp. 25–38.
11   Laqueur, Walter (2004), *No End to War: Terrorism in the Twenty-first Century*, London: Continuum, p. 71.
12   Laqueur, p. 79.
13   Laqueur, p. 92.
14   Hoffman, Bruce (2006), *Inside Terrorism*, New York: Columbia University Press, pp. 131–3.

3   Terrorism's worldwide occurrence

1   Laqueur, Walter (1999), *The New Terrorism*, Oxford: Oxford University Press, pp. 22–30.
2   Laqueur, pp. 31–2.
3   Hoffman, Bruce (2006), *Inside Terrorism*, New York: Columbia Press, pp. 17–18.
4   Hoffman, pp. 267–8.
5   Hoffman, p. 269.
6   Hoffman, pp. 271–2.
7   Laqueur, Walter (2004), *No End to War: Terrorism in the Twenty-first Century*, London: Continuum, pp. 209–10.
8   Whittaker, David J. (2006), *Terrorism: Understanding the Global Threat*, London: Pearson Education, pp. 53–4.
9   Crenshaw, Martha (1995), *Terrorism in Context*, University Park, PA: Pennsylvania State University Press, p. 24.
10   Terrorism Research Center, United States. Available at www.terrorism.com/terrorism/basics.html. Printout of p. 6.
11   International Policy Institute for Counter-terrorism, Herzliya, Israel. Available at www.ict.org.il/inter/org.cfm. Printout of pp. 1–2, accessed 9 December 1999 and October 2006.

4   Jihad: mission and campaigning

1   Brachman, Jarret M. (2009) *Global Jihadism Theory and Practice*, London and New York: Routledge, pp. 4–5. See also Whittaker, David J. (2006) *Terrorism: Understanding the Global Threat*, London: Pearson, pp. 101–15.
2   A most useful discussion also is in Cook, David (2005) *Understanding Jihad*, Berkeley, CA: University of California Press.
3   Bracham, p. 5.
4   Bracham, p. 10.

5   Williams, Paul L. (2002), *Al-Qaeda: Brotherhood of Terror*, London: Alpha, Pearson Education, p. 76.
6   Williams, pp. 76–7.
7   Williams, pp. 79–80.
8   Whittaker, David J. (2002), *Terrorism: Understanding the Global Threat*, London: Pearson Education, pp. 99–101.
9   Whittaker, pp. 101–2.
10   Whittaker, pp. 103–4.
11   Wilkinson, Paul L. (2001), *Terrorism and Political Violence*, vol. 13, Winter 2001, no. 4, p. vii.
12   Bodansky, Yossef (2001), *Bin Laden: The Man Who Declared War on America* (2nd edn), Roseville, CA: Prima Publishing, pp. 1–2.
13   Bodansky, pp. 2–3.
14   Bodansky, pp. 4–5.
15   Bodansky, p. 10.
16   Bodansky, pp. 19–20.
17   Bodansky, pp. 43–4.
18   Bodansky, p. 91.
19   Hoffman, Bruce (2006), *Inside Terrorism*, New York: Columbia Press, p. 295.
20   Whittaker, David J. (2006), *Terrorism: Understanding the Global Threat*, London: Pearson Education, p. 108.
21   *The Guardian*, 3 July 2006.
22   Booth, Ken and Dunne, Tim (2002), *Worlds in Collision*, London: Palgrave Macmillan, pp. 297–8.

5   United States: Ground Zero

1   Cox, M. (2002) 'American power before and after 11 September', *International Affairs*, vol. 78, no. 2, pp. 261–71.
2   Cf Internet US Ground Zero advice to NATO states 9/11/2001.
3   Cf Hoffmann, B. (2002) 'Rethinking terrorism and counter-terrorism since September 11', *Studies in Conflict and Terrorism*, vol. 25, pp. 303–16.
4   Whittaker, David J. (2009) *Counter-terrorism and Human Rights*, London: Pearson, Longman, pp. 71–6.
5   Maniscalo, P. M. and Christen, H. T. (2002) *Understanding Terrorism and Managing the Consequences*, passim. See also Geltzer, J. H. (2010) *US Counter-terrorism and Al-Qaeda*, London: Routledge (pp. 77–82) for discussion of the terrorists' 'grand strategy'.
6   Cf Internet *United States: 9/11 Commission* for the Report, Findings, and recommendations in detail, passim.
7   Heymann, Philip B. (2003) *Terrorism, Freedom and Security*, London: MIT Press, and Cambridge, MA, passim.
8   Heymann, p. 168
9   Strawson, John (ed.) (2002) *Law After Ground Zero*, London: Glasshouse Press, and Portland, OR, pp. 139–40.
10   Strawson, p. 163
11   Strawson, p. 145. See also Geltzer, J. H. *US Counter-terrorism and Al-Qaeda*, London: Routledge, pp. 32–40.
12   Strawson, p. 145.
13   Wilkinson, Paul, Editorial in *Terrorism and Political Violence*, vol .13, Winter 2001, no. 4, p X. See also Wilkinson, Paul and Ranstorp, Magnus (2008) *Terrorism and*

Human Rights for a useful report on UN action in response to post-9/11 US attitudes to human rights safeguards.

6   Britain: London as target

1   Whittaker, David J. (2006), *Terrorism: Understanding the Global Threat*, London: Pearson Education, pp. 34–5.
2   *Report of the Official Account of the Bombings in London on 7 July 2005* (2006), ordered by the House of Commons, 11 May 2006, London: HMSO, *passim*.
3   Whittaker, pp. 35–7.
4   *Report of the Official Account of the Bombings in London on 7 July 2005*, pp. 26–7.
5   Whittaker, pp. 37–8.
6   Intelligence and Security Committee (2006), *Parliamentary Report into the London Terrorist Attacks on 7 July 2005*, London: HMSO, p. 4.
7   *Government Response to the Intelligence and Security Committee's Report into London Terrorist Attacks on 7 July 2005* (2006), London: HMSO, pp. 2–4.
8   *Government Response*, p. 4.
9   *Government Response*, p. 7.
10 Black, Crispin (2005), *7/7: The London Bombs. What Went Wrong?*, London: Gibson Square, *passim*.
11 *Hansard,* 13 September 2005, London: HMSO.
12 *Government Response*, p. 2.
13 Parliamentary Report on the London terrorist attack on 7 July 2005/ Intelligence and Security Committee (2006) London: HMSO.
14 *Government Response*, p. 3.
15 Black, p. 90.
16 Black, p. 8.

7   Israel

1   UN statistics give Israel's population 1922–45 increasing by 500% – a rough demographical estimate. See note 6 below.
2   See citations under Arab terrorists in Laquer, W. (2000) *A History of Terrorism*, London: New Brunswick.
3   Searching the Internet for Fatah and Hamas is particularly useful.
4   Khatchadourian, Haig (1998) *The Morality of Terrorism*, New York: Peter Lang, pp. 138–40, 141–5.
5   Quotations here are from Gunning, Jeroen (2009) *Hamas in Politics*, London: Hurst, pp. 197–8.
6   Cf Gunning, Jeroen p. 218 ff, and also searching Internet sites for Stockholm International Peace Research Institute (SIPRI) and the UN Office for Humanitarian Affairs.
7   Crenshaw, Martha (1995) *Terrorism in Context*, Pennsylvania, USA: Pennsylvania Press. Chapter 12 by Ian S. Lustick is invaluable (pp. 514–52). See also Whittaker, David (1999) *Conflict and Reconciliation in the Contemporary World* and Whittaker, David (2004) *Terrorists and Terrorism*. Both books are London: Routledge.

8   Libya

1   Laqueur, Walter (1999), *The New Terrorism*, Oxford: Oxford University Press, pp. 168–72.
2   Habib, Henri Pierre (1975), *Politics and Government of Revolutionary Libya*, Ottawa: Le Cercle du Livre de France, pp. 13–15.

3   Blundy, David and Lycett, Andrew (1987), *Quaddafi and the Libyan Revolution*, Boston, MA: Little, Brown and Co., p. 44.
4   Blundy and Lycett, p. 64.
5   Blundy and Lycett, p. 68.
6   Habib, p. 121.
7   Habib, p. 122.
8   Habib, p. 124.
9   Habib, p. 127.
10 Habib, p. 151.
11 Ibrahaim, Ahmed (1983), *Revolutionary Organization, Revolutionary Committees: The Instruments of Popular Revolution*, Tripoli: Socialist Peoples Libyan Arab Jamahiriya (General Publications), p. 89ff.
12 Ibrahaim, p. 121.
13 Haley, P. Edward (1984), *Qaddafi and the United States since 1969*, New York: Praeger Special Studies, p. 35.
14 Haley, pp. 37–8.
15 Haley, p. 39.
16 Haley, pp. 49–50.
17 Haley, pp. 51–2.
18 Haley, p. 54.
19 Haley, pp. 231–2.
20 Haley, p. 224.
21 Blundy and Lycett, pp. 74–5.
22 Blundy and Lycett, p. 212.
23 Falk, Richard (1986), 'Rethinking counterterrorism', in E. P. Thompson and Mary Kaldor (eds.), *Mad Dogs: The US Raids on Libya*, London: Pluto, p. 139.
24 Hoffman, Bruce (1998), *Inside Terrorism*, London: Indigo, pp. 191–2.
25 Quoted in *The Guardian*, 27 September 1999.
26 See www.bbc.co.uk, 25 March 2006, for an account of the visit and the Blair statement.
27 See www.telegraph.co.uk, 16 May 2006, for a fuller account of this historic renewal.
28 Kaplan, Eben (2007) *How Libya Got Off the List*, US Council of Foreign Relations. Brief but thoughtful.

9   Lebanon I

1   Lebanese website www.almashriq.hiof.no in July 2006 had this statement under the rubric, 'Hizbullah: views and concepts (Statement of Purpose)'. They add that it was originally broadcast on Al Manar TV, Beirut, 20 June 2006, a television station referred to as a facility of 'Islamic resistance'.
2   Picard, Elizabeth (1997), 'The Lebanese Shi'a and political violence in Lebanon', in Apter, David E. (ed.), *The Legitimization of Violence*, New York: New York University Press, p. 190.
3   Picard, pp. 193–4.
4   Picard, p. 197.
5   Picard, p. 199.
6   Picard, pp. 206–8.
7   Palmer Harik, Judith (2004), *Hezbollah: The Changing Face of Terrorism*, London: Tauris, I. B., pp. 2–3.
8   Harik, pp. 3–4.
9   Khalil, A. A. (1991), 'Ideology and practice of Hizballah in Lebanon: Islamization of Leninist organization and principles', *Middle Eastern Studies*, vol. 27, no. 3, pp. 390–9.
10 Harik, pp. 71–2.
11 Khalil, pp. 398–9.

12   Kramer, Martin (1998), 'The moral logic of Hizballah', in Walter Reich (ed.), *Origins of Terrorism*, Baltimore, MD: Johns Hopkins University Press, pp. 132–3.
13   Kramer, pp. 136–7.
14   Ranstorp, Magnus (1997), *Hizb'allah in Lebanon: The Politics of the Western Hostage Crisis*, London: Macmillan, pp. 60–1.
15   Ranstorp, pp. 108–9.
16   Ranstorp, pp. 134–5.
17   Ranstorp, pp. 135–6.
18   Ranstorp, pp. 192–4.
19   Kramer, pp. 156–7.
20   Saad-Ghorayeb, Amal (2002), *Hizbu'llah Politics and Religion*, London: Pluto Press, pp. 145–7.
21   Saad-Ghorayeb, pp. 98–9.
22   Saad-Ghorayeb, p. 160.
23   Kramer, p. 132.

10   Lebanon II

1   www.almashriq.hiof.no in July 2006, quoting from A. R. Norton (1987), *Amal and the Shia: Struggle for the Soul of Lebanon*, Austin, TX: University of Texas. This website commended Norton's view of Hizbullah's move 'from radicalism to pragmatism'.
2   Murphy, Richard W. (1996), 'The costs of war: an American perspective', in Hollis, Rosemary and Shehadi, Nadim (1996), *Lebanon on Hold: Implications for Middle East Peace*, London: Royal Institute of International Affairs, p. 9.
3   Seale, Patrick (1996), 'The address is Syria', in Hollis and Shehadi, p. 21.
4   Agha, Hussein (1996), 'The Syrian–Iranian axis in Lebanon', in Hollis and Shehadi, pp. 27–8.
5   Hussein, p. 29.
6   Sobelman, Daniel (2003), *New Rules of the Game: Israel and Hizbollah after the Withdrawal from Lebanon*, Tel Aviv: Jaffee Center for Strategic Studies, pp. 48–9.
7   Sobelman, p. 49.
8   Sobelman, p. 84.
9   Sobelman, pp. 85–6.
10   Sobelman, p. 89.
11   Sobelman, p. 102.
12   Sobelman, p. 103.
13   Malik, Habib C. (2000), *Between Damascus and Jerusalem: Lebanon and Middle East Peace*, Washington, DC: The Washington Institute for Near East Policy, p. 93.
14   Chartouni-Dubarry, May (1996), 'Hizballah: from militia to political party', in Hollis and Shehadi, p. 59.

11   Sri Lanka

1   Laqueur, Walter (1999), *The New Terrorism*, Oxford: Oxford University Press, pp. 191–6.
2   Whittaker, David J. (2004), *Terrorists and Terrorism in the Contemporary World*, London: Routledge, pp. 38–41.
3   Whittaker, pp. 41–2.
4   Cf. Whittaker, David J. (ed.) (2003), *The Terrorism Reader*, London: Routledge, p. 91; and Whittaker (2004), p. 41.
5   *The Times*, 23 October 1997.

6   Kapferer, Bruce (1997), 'Remythologizing discourses: state and insurrectionary violence in Sri Lanka', in David Apter (ed.), *The Legitimization of Violence*, New York: New York University Press, p. 174.
7   Kapferer, pp. 178–9.
8   Kapferer, p. 175.
9   Joshi, Manoj (1996), 'On the razor's edge: the Liberation Tigers of Tamil Elam [*sic*]', *Studies in Conflict and Terrorism*, vol. 19, pp. 19–42.
10   Kapferer, p. 163.
11   Kapferer, p. 183.
12   Kapferer, pp. 182–3.
13   Joshi, p. 27.
14   Laqueur, pp. 230–1.
15   Laqueur, pp. 100–1.
16   Joshi, pp. 25–6.
17   'Sri Lanka Outlook', Summer 1997, reprint of article, *Indian Express*, 27 May 1997.

12   Spain

1   Shabad, Goldie and Ramo, F. J. L. (1995), 'Political violence in a democratic state: Basque terrorism in Spain', in Martha Crenshaw (ed.), *Terrorism in Context*, University Park, PA: Pennsylvania State University Press, pp. 411–13.
2   Shabad and Ramo, pp. 415–17.
3   Shabad and Ramo, pp. 418–19.
4   Shabad and Ramo, p. 422.
5   Shabad and Ramo, p. 423.
6   Shabad and Ramo, pp. 427–8.
7   Shabad and Ramo, p. 436.
8   Wieviorka, Michel (1997), 'ETA and Basque political violence', in David Apter (ed.), *The Legitimization of Violence*, New York: New York University Press, p. 300.
9   Wieviorka, p. 294.
10   Shabad and Ramo, pp. 444–5.
11   Zirakzadeh, Cyrus E. (1991), *A Rebellious People: Basques, Protests and Politics*, Reno, NV: University of Nevada Press, p. 204.
12   Shabad and Ramo, pp. 441–3.
13   Trevino, Jose A. (1982), 'Spain's internal security: the Basque autonomous police force', in Y. Alexander and K. A. Myers (eds), *Terrorism in Europe*, London: Croom Helm, p. 142.
14   Shabad and Ramo, p. 465.
15   Shabad and Ramo, pp. 466–9.

13   Northern Ireland

1   Whittaker, David J. (1999), *Conflict and Reconciliation*, London: Routledge, pp. 80–3.
2   Whittaker, pp. 83–4.
3   Whittaker, pp. 84–7.
4   Arthur, Paul (1997), '"Reading" violence', in David Apter (ed.), *The Legitimization of Violence*, New York: New York University Press, p. 234.
5   Arthur, pp. 238–9.
6   Arthur, pp. 240–1.
7   Arthur, p. 241.

8   Arthur, pp. 242–3.
9   Arthur, pp. 254–5.
10 Arthur, pp. 255–6.
11 Kearney, Richard (1997), *Postnationalist Ireland*, London: Routledge, p. 109.
12 Townshend, Charles (1995), 'The culture of paramilitarism in Ireland', in Martha
    Crenshaw (ed.), *Terrorism in Context*, University Park, PA: Pennsylvania State
    University Press, pp. 330–1.
13 Townshend, p. 324.
14 Townshend, p. 317.
15 Townshend, p. 317.
16 Townshend, pp. 336–7.
17 Arthur, pp. 270–2.
18 Kearney, pp. 110–12.
19 Kearney, p. 121.
20 Arthur, p. 235.
21 Townshend, pp. 339–40.
22 Whittaker, pp. 89–90.
23 See Northern Ireland website, www.nio.gov.uk/agreement.htm.
24 Quoted in Mitchell Report to British and Irish Governments, January 1996. For text
    reference, see the above website.
25 Hattersley, Roy, *The Guardian*, 1 August 2005.
26 Horgan, John (ed.) (2006) *The Psychology of Terrorism*, London: Routledge,
    p. 143.
27 O'Brien, Conor Cruise (1988) *Passion and Cunning and Other Essays*, London:
    Weidenfeld and Nicholson, passim.
28 Wilkinson, Paul (ed.) (2007) *Terrorism versus Democracy The Liberal State Response*,
    London: Routledge, p. 68.
29 Wilkinson, p. 200.

14 Algeria

1   United Nations General Assembly (July–August 1998), Report of the Panel Appointed
    by the Secretary-General to Gather Information on the Situation in Algeria [. . .]
    (Report of Eminent Persons Panel). Extracts from website printout (published April
    1999), pp. 1–7. Available at www.un.org/NewLinks/dpi2007/contents.htm.
2   Stone, Martin (1997), *The Establishment of Algeria*, London: Hurst & Co, pp. 1–3.
3   Stone, pp. 37, 42.
4   Stone, pp. 177–8.
5   Stone, pp. 180–1.
6   Stone, pp. 185–6.
7   Stone, pp. 189–96.
8   United Nations, Report of Eminent Persons Panel (see Note 1).
9   United Nations, Report of Eminent Persons Panel, p. 20.
10 See US Department of State, 28 April 2004, www.icar.org.uk.

15 Peru

1   Palmer, David Scott (1995), 'The revolutionary terrorism of Peru's Shining Path', in
    Martha Crenshaw (ed.), *Terrorism in Context*, University Park, PA: Pennsylvania State
    University Press.
2   Palmer, Scott, pp. 251–3.
3   Palmer, Scott, pp. 254–5.

4   Palmer, Scott, p. 257.
5   Palmer, Scott, pp. 260–1.
6   Palmer, Scott, pp. 262–3.
7   Palmer, Scott, pp. 265–6.
8   Palmer, Scott, pp. 267–8.
9   McClintock, Cynthia (1984), 'Why peasants rebel: the case of Peru's Sendero Luminoso', *World Politics*, October, pp. 81–2.
10   Palmer, Scott, p. 270.
11   Palmer, Scott, pp. 270–8.
12   Palmer, Scott, p. 285.
13   Palmer, Scott, p. 280.
14   Izaguirre, Carlos R. (1996), 'Shining path in the twenty-first century: actors in search of a new script', *NACLA Report on the Americas*, vol. XXX, no. 1, July/August, pp. 37–8.
15   Izaguirre, p. 38.
16   Palmer, Scott, pp. 301–2.
17   Izaguirre, p. 38.
18   Palmer, Scott, p. 305.
19   *The Guardian,* 31 December 2005.
20   See also Strong, S. (1993) 'Shining path: a case study in ideological terrorism', Conflict Studies 260, London RISCT. Tarazone-Sevillano, G. (1990) 'Sendero Luminoso and the Threat of Narco-Terrorism', *Washington Papers no. 144*, New York: Praegor.

16   Colombia

1   Pearce, Jenny (1990), *Colombia: Inside the Labyrinth*, London: Latin American Bureau, pp. 4–5.
2   Pearce, pp. 64–5.
3   Pearce, p. 69.
4   Pearce, pp. 76–9.
5   Oquist, Paul (1980), *Violence, Conflict and Politics in Colombia*, London: New York Academic Press, pp. 1–6.
6   Oquist, p. 153.
7   Oquist, p. 133.
8   Oquist, pp. 134–5.
9   Oquist, p. 135.
10   Oquist, p. 138.
11   Oquist, p. 139.
12   Oquist, pp. 143–4, 145–6, 147.
13   Oquist, p. 150.
14   Pearce, pp. 52–4, 55–6, 56–7.
15   Pearce, pp. 61–2.
16   Pearce, pp. 165–6.
17   Pearce, pp. 167–8. The quotation is from *L'Humanité*, 3 June 1966.
18   Pearce, pp. 168–9. See the useful references to the relationship between the guerrillas and the drug cartels in Walter Laqueur (1999), *The New Terrorism*, Oxford: Oxford University Press, pp. 27, 188–91, 212–14.
19   Pearce, pp. 171–2, 173.
20   Pearce, p. 207.
21   Pearce, p. 231.
22   Pearce, pp. 278–9.
23   Pearce, p. 284, quoting from William Ramirez Tobón (1988), Un Campesinado Illicito in *Analísis Política*, no. 5, 1998, pp.54–62.

24   Pearce, pp. 286–7.
25   Pearce, p. 287.
26   Cf note 18. Other references Lee, R. W. (1989) 'Narco-terrorism – the Colombian case', *Terrorism* vol. 12, no. 6, pp. 435–7; Ehrenfeld, R (1990) *Narco Terrorism*, New York: Basic Books; Steinitz, M. S. (1987) 'Insurgents, terrorists and the drug trade' in Laquer, W. (ed.) *The Terrorism Reader*, New York: Meridian, pp. 327–36.

17   Germany

1   Cook, Schura (1982), 'Germany, from protest to terrorism', in Y. Alexander and K. A. Myers, *Terrorism in Europe*, London: Croom Helm, p. 165.
2   Cook, p. 161.
3   Cook, p. 170.
4   Merkl, Peter H. (1995), 'West German left-wing terrorism', in Martha Crenshaw (ed.), *Terrorism in Context*, University Park, PA: Pennsylvania State University Press, pp. 176–8.
5   Pridham, Geoffrey (1981), 'Terrorism and the state in West Germany during the 1970s: a threat to stability or a case of political over-reaction?', in Juliet Lodge (ed.), *Terrorism: A Challenge to the State*, Oxford: Martin Robertson, p. 18.
6   Pridham, pp. 16–17.
7   Pridham, pp. 20–2.
8   Pridham, pp. 22–5.
9   Pridham, pp. 27–8.
10   Pridham, pp. 28–9.
11   Merkl, pp. 202–5.
12   Wright, Joanne (1990), *Terrorist Propaganda: The Red Army Faction and the Provisional IRA 1968–86*, New York: St Martins Press.
13   Becker, Jillian (1989), *Hitler's Children*, London: Pickwick, pp. ix–x.
14   Wright, p. 116.
15   Pridham, pp. 41, 44.
16   Wright, p. xiii.
17   Wright, pp. 226–9.
18   Wright, p. 168.
19   Pridham, p. 52.
20   Pridham, p. 52.
21   Kellen, Konrad (1998), 'Ideology and rebellion: terrorism in West Germany', in Walter Reich (ed.), *Origins of Terrorism*, Baltimore, MD: Johns Hopkins University Press, pp. 54–5.
22   Becker, p. 250, quoting Norman Cohn (1970), *The Pursuit of the Millennium*, London: Paladin.
23   Kellen, p. 58.
24   Readers can follow reports and some controversy searching the Internet for 'Germany: terrorism and terrorists' and 'Germany: anti-terrorist legislation'.

18   Italy

1   Jamieson, Alison (1989), *The Heart Attacked*, London: Marion Boyars, p. 9.
2   Salvioni, Danila and Stephanson, Anders (1985), 'Reflections on the Red Brigades', *Orbis,* Forum, Fall, p. 491.
3   Furlong, Paul (1981), 'Political terrorism in Italy: responses, reaction and immobilism', in Juliet Lodge (ed.), *Terrorism: A Challenge to the State*, Oxford: Martin Robertson, pp. 61–2.

4   Furlong, p. 63.
5   Apter, D. E. (1997), 'Political violence in analytical perspective', in D. E. Apter (ed.), *The Legitimization of Violence*, New York: New York University Press, p. 19.
6   Furlong, pp. 69–71.
7   Furlong, pp. 74–8.
8   Moss, David (1997), 'Politics, violence, writing: the rituals of "armed struggle" in Italy', in Apter (ed.), *The Legitimization of Violence*, p. 85.
9   Moss, pp. 92–3.
10 Moss, p. 83.
11 Moss, pp. 105–6.
12 Furlong, p. 77.
13 Furlong, p. 80.
14 Furlong, pp. 85–6.
15 Moss, pp. 103–4.
16 Moss, pp. 114–15.
17 Furlong, pp. 88–9.
18 Della Porta, Donatella (1995), 'Left-wing terrorism in Italy', in Martha Crenshaw (ed.), *Terrorism in Context,* University Park, PA: Pennsylvania State University Press, pp. 156–9.
19 Rather as with the preceding chapter readers can easily track reports of Italian terrorist events and government counter-terrorism by searching the Internet.

19   South Africa

1   Whittaker, David J. (1999), *Conflict and Reconciliation*, London: Routledge, pp. 21–4.
2   Whittaker, pp. 24–5.
3   Whittaker, David J. (1995), *United Nations in Action*, London: University College London Press, p. 168.
4   Whittaker (1999), pp. 25–6.
5   Gibson, Richard (1972), *African Liberation Movements: Contemporary Struggle against White Minority Rule,* London: Oxford University Press for Race Relations Institute, p. 38.
6   Gibson, p. 64.
7   Gibson, p. 92.
8   de Braganca, A. and Wallerstein, I. M. (1982), *The African Liberation Reader*, vol. 2, London: Zed Press, p. 33.
9   De Braganca and Wallerstein, p. 43.
10 Mandela, Nelson (1994), *Long Walk to Freedom*, London: Abacus, p. 132.
11 Mandela, p. 135.
12 Mandela, pp. 146–7.
13 Mandela, pp. 181–2.
14 Mandela, p. 277.
15 Mandela, pp. 320–1.
16 Mandela, pp. 321–4.
17 Mandela, pp. 325–6.
18 Mandela, pp. 336–8.
19 Mandela, p. 434.
20 Whittaker (1999), pp. 27–8.
21 Whittaker (1999), p. 30.
22 Detail as to questioning process obtained from South Africa's Truth and Reconciliation (TRC) website, October 1999, www.truth.org.za/submit/q-anc.htm, and from printout extracts, pp. 1–9.

23   Further TRC detail may be obtained by searching the website given in note 22.
24   Whittaker (1999), p. 33.
25   See www.doj.gov.za.

20 Sixteen terrorism case studies: conclusion

1   Smith, M. R. L. (1995), 'Holding fire', in Alan O'Day (ed.), *Terrorism's Laboratory: The Case of Northern Ireland*, Aldershot: Dartmouth.

21 Terrorism: some ethical issues

1   Jenkins, Brian (1986), 'Defence against terrorism', *Political Science Quarterly*, vol. 101, no. 5, pp. 779–81.
2   Bandura, Albert (1998), 'Mechanisms of moral disengagement', in Walter Reich (ed.), *Origins of Terrorism*, Baltimore, MD: Johns Hopkins University Press, pp. 163–7.
3   Bandura, p. 170.
4   Bandura, p. 171.
5   Bandura, p. 173.
6   Bandura, p. 174.
7   Bandura, p. 176.
8   Bandura, p. 190.
9   Bandura, p. 172.
10   Crenshaw, Martha (1998), 'Questions, research and knowledge,' in Reich (ed.), p. 255.
11   Khatchadourian, Haig (1998), *The Morality of Terrorism*, New York: Peter Lang.
12   Khatchadourian, p. 40.
13   Khatchadourian, p. 129.
14   Moreno, Jonathan (ed.) (2003), *In the Wake of Terror: Medicine and Morality in a Time of Crisis*, Cambridge, MA: MIT Press.
15   Moreno, p. 112.
16   Moreno, p. 36.
17   Moreno, p. 19.
18   Moreno, p. x.
19   The President's White House statement of 4 April 2002 may be read on the website www.al-bab.com.

22 Terrorism and the law

1   Higgins, Rosalyn (1995), *Problems and Process. International Law and How We Use It*, London: Clarendon Press.
2   Lord Woolf (2003), Speaking on 'The impact of human rights' at a conference in Adelphi House, Oxford, 6 March 2003.
3   *Hansard*, House of Commons debate, 26 October 2005.
4   Prime Minister Tony Blair, Downing Street Press Conference, 27 July 2005.
5   *The Guardian*, 5 November 2005.
6   Robinson, C. G., Chief Constable, Greater Manchester, at meeting of Police Federation, 12 November 2005 (*The Guardian* report).
7   *Hansard*, House of Lords debate, 21 November 2005.
8   Council of Europe Legal Affairs and Human Rights Committee, 7 June 2006.
9   The views of Jack Straw MP, *The Guardian*, 14 December 1999.
10   The views, in contrast, of John Wadham, *The Guardian*, 14 December 1999.
11   Kennedy, Helena (2005), *Just Law* (reprint), London: Vintage Press, pp. 198–9.

12   Kennedy, p. 39.

13   Walker, Clive (1996), 'Anti-terrorism laws for the future', *New Law Journal,* pp. 586–8.

14   Schiff, David (1997), in Rosalyn Higgins and Maurice Flory (eds), 'Managing terrorism the British way', *Terrorism and International Law,* London: Routledge, p. 126.

15   Lord Woolf, Interview at BBC, London, 17 December 2001. See www.news.bbc.co.uk.

16   Reid, Kiron (1996), 'Prevention of Terrorism (Additional Powers) Act 1996', *Web Journal of Current Legal Issues,* London: Blackstone Press, p. 12.

17   Whittaker, David J. (2006), *Terrorism: Understanding the Global Threat,* 2nd edn, London: Pearson Education, pp. 193–4.

18   Foreign and Commonwealth Office (FCO), London (2005), *Counter-terrorist Legislation and Practice: A Survey of Selected Countries,* Research Paper, London: HMSO, paras 124–5. (Also on www.fco.gov.uk and www.homeoffice.gov.uk.) See also information on www.en.wikipedia.org/anti-terrorismlegislation.

19   FCO, Research Paper, (2005), para 18, citing 'omnibus package'.

20   FCO, Research Paper, (2005), para 39.

21   FCO, Research Paper, (2005), para 97.

22   FCO, Research Paper, (2005), para 110.

23   Whittaker, p. 197, quoting Rosalyn Higgins and Maurice Flory (eds) (1997), *Terrorism and International Law,* London: Routledge, pp. 27–8.

24   Kennedy, p. 45.

25   Kennedy, p. 51.

26   Walker 1.10 to 1.17 and generally to 1.97.

27   Walker 1.49 to 1.59.

28   Walker 1.18. See further 1.18 to 1.42.

29   Walker, Chapter 9 passim and Appendix 5.

30   Walker deals mainly with financial matters against terrorist activity in the EU.

31   Walker 1.93–1.96, 3.75–3.82, Appendix 6.

32   European counter-terrorism law is best surveyed using internet references to particular European states and their law-making which is slow-moving and often controversial.

23   Counter-terrorism: programmes and strategies

1   Smith, M. R. L. (1995), 'Holding fire', in Alan O'Day (ed.), *Terrorism's Laboratory: The Case of Northern Ireland,* Aldershot: Dartmouth, p. 23.

2   Terrorism Research Center, United States. Available at www.terrorism.com/terrorism/ basics.html. Printout of 31 December 1998, pp. 7–9.

3   Wardlaw, Grant (1982), *Political Theory, Tactics and Counter-measures,* Cambridge: Cambridge University Press.

4   Laqueur, Walter (1999), *The New Terrorism,* Oxford: Oxford University Press, pp. 45–6.

5   Wilkinson, Paul (2006), *Terrorism versus Democracy: The Liberal State Response,* London: Routledge, p. 199.

6   Wilkinson, p. 199.

7   Wilkinson, p. 205.

8   Ganor, Boaz (1998), 'Countering state-sponsored terrorism'. Full text of article dated 25 April 1998, in printout of 12 January 1999, available from International Policy Institute for Counter-terrorism, Herzliya, Israel at www.ict.org.il/interter/org.cfm, pp. 1–19.

9   United Nations (1996), *UN Chronicle,* no. 3, p. 31.

10   UN Plan of Action (September 2006). Available on UN website, www.un.org/terrorism strategy. See also Chapter 22 in this Reader.

11   Wardlaw, p. 114.

12   Whittaker, David J. (2006), *Terrorism: Understanding the Global Threat*, London: Pearson Education, p. 216.

13   Vercher, Antonio (1992), *Terrorism in Europe: An International Comparative Legal Analysis*, Oxford: Clarendon Press, p. 369.

14   Whittaker, pp. 213–16.

15   Hoffman, Bruce (1999), *Inside Terrorism*, London: Indigo, pp. 196–7.

16   Laqueur, pp. 256–7.

17   Laqueur, pp. 259–60. Cf. his discussion in Laqueur (2004), *No End to War: Terrorism in the Twenty-first Century*, London: Continuum, pp. 226–31.

18   Moreno, J. D. (2003), *In the Wake of Terror: Medicine and Morality in a Time of Crisis*, London: MIT Press. See the ongoing discussion here of 'mega terrorism' in Chapters 2 and 4.

19   Hoffman, pp. 211–12.

20   Whittaker, p. 221. Cf. Chapter 10.

21   Khatchadourian, Haig (1998), *The Morality of Terrorism*, New York: Peter Lang, p. 9.

Guide to further reading

There are two reasons why this guide lists fewer books than might be expected. First, most people who consult this Reader on terrorism will be able to search for relevant literature and, to some extent, select it, via computer terminals and internet facilities in today's libraries and through the on-line catalogue AMAZON (www.amazon.co.uk).

Second, in the 16 case studies in Part Two of this book there are ample references that need no repetition in this guide. A number of additional references are listed. It is worth looking at the extensive bibliographies in Walter Laqueur (1999), *The New Terrorism*; Laqueur (2004), *No End to War: Terrorism in the Twenty-first Century*; and Laqueur (2002) *A History of Terrorism*. Further, the Routledge book catalogue on www.routledge.com/strategicstudies has an up-to-date list of a wide variety of books on terrorism.

Most of the other references are fairly general recent texts useful for readers of Part One (chiefly about definition and motivation) and of Part Three (counter-terrorism). The author has found these sources invaluable. An introductory text bringing in some of the issues discussed in this Reader is David J. Whittaker (2004), *Terrorists and Terrorism in the Contemporary World*.

PART ONE

Bjorgo, T. (1995), *Terror from the Extreme Right*, London: Cassell.
Bremer, L. P. (1989), *Terrorism: Its Evolving Nature*, Washington, DC: Bureau of Public Affairs.
Clutterbuck, Richard (1973), *Protest and the Urban Guerrilla*, London: Cassell.
Clutterbuck, Richard (1994), *Terrorism in an Unstable World*, New York: Routledge.
Crederberg, P. C. (1989), *Terrorism: Myths, Illusions, Rhetoric and Reality*, Oxford: Prentice Hall.

Gaines, Ann (1998), *Terrorism*, Philadelphia, PA: Chelsea House.

Hobsbawm, Eric (1995), *Age of Extremes*, London: Michael Joseph. See particularly Chapter 15.

Kushner, H. H. (1998), *The Future of Terrorism: Violence in the New Millennium*, Thousand Oaks, CA: Sage Publications.

Kushner, H. H. (1998), *Terrorism in America: A Structured Approach to Understanding the Terrorist Threat*, Springfield, IL: C. C. Thomas.

Laqueur, Walter (1986), 'Reflections on terrorism', *Foreign Affairs*, Fall, pp. 86–100.

Laqueur, Walter (1996), 'Postmodern terrorism: new rules for an old game' in *Foreign Affairs*, Sept/Oct.

Long, D. E. (1990), *The Anatomy of Terrorism*, New York: Free Press.

Moxon-Browne, E., Alexander, Y. and O'Day, A. (1994), *European Terrorism*, International Library of Terrorism No. 3, New York and Toronto: G. K. Hall.

Nash, J. R. (1998), *Terrorists in the Twentieth Century: A Narrative Encyclopaedia*, New York: M. Evans & Co.

O'Kane, R. H. T. (1991), *The Revolutionary Reign of Terror: The Role of Violence in Political Change*, Aldershot: Elgar.

Rapoport, D. C. (1998), *Inside Terrorist Organizations*, New York: Columbia University Press.

Schmid, A. (1983), *Political Terrorism*, New Brunswick, NJ: Transaction Books.

Shubik, Martin (1998), *Terrorism, Technology and the Socio-economics of Death*, New Haven, CT: Cowles Foundation, Yale.

Stohl, M. (ed.) (1979), *The Politics of Terrorism: A Reader in Theory and Practice*, New York: Marcel Dekker.

Wilkinson, Paul (1974), *Political Terrorism*, London: Macmillan.

Wilkinson, Paul (1977), *Terrorism and the Liberal State*, London: Macmillan.

PART TWO

Alexander, Y. and Myers, K. A. (1982), *Terrorism in Europe*, London: Croom Helm.

8   Libya

Harris, L. C. (1986), *Libya: Qaddafi's Revolution and the Modern State*, London: Westview.

9   Lebanon I

Jaber, Hala (1977), *Hezbollah: Born with a Vengeance*, New York: Columbia University Press.

11   Sri Lanka

Schwartz, Walter (1998), *The Tamils of Sri Lanka*, London: Minority Rights Group.

Spencer, J. (ed.) (1990), *History in Sri Lanka: The Roots of Conflict*, London: Routledge.

12   Spain

Medhurst, Ken (1982), 'Basques and Basque nationalists', in C. H. Williams (ed.), *National Separatism*, Cardiff: University of Wales Press.

Sullivan, John (1988), *ETA and Basque Nationalism: The Fight for Euskadi 1890–1986*, London: Routledge.

13   Northern Ireland

Bruce, Steve (1992), *The Red Hand: Protestant Paramilitaries in Northern Ireland*, Oxford: Oxford University Press.
Coogan, T. Pat (1995), *The Troubles*, London: Hutchinson.
O'Brien, Brenda (1999), *The Long War: The IRA and Sinn Féin*, Dublin: The O'Brien Press.
O'Day, A. and Alexander, Y. (1994), *Dimensions of Irish Terrorism*, Aldershot: Dartmouth.
Smith, M. I. R. (1994), *Fighting for Ireland? The Military Structure of the Irish Republican Movement*, London: Routledge.

14   Algeria

Abucar, M. A. (1996), *The Post-colonial Society: The Algerian Struggle for Economic, Social and Political Change 1965–90*, New York: Peter Long Publishing Co.
Jackson, H. F. (1977), *The FLN in Algeria: Party Development in a Revolutionary Society*, London: Greenwood Press.
Stone, Martin (1997), *The Agony of Algeria*, London: Hurst & Co.

17   Germany

Aust, Stefan (1987), *The Baader-Meinhof Group*, London: Bodley Head.

18   Italy

Cantanzaro, R. (1991), *The Red Brigade and Left-wing Terrorism in Italy*, London: Pinter.
Pisano, V. S. (1981), *The Dynamics of Subversion and Violence in Contemporary Italy*, Stanford, CA: Hoover Press.

19   South Africa

Beinart, William and Dubow, Saul (eds) (1995), *Segregation and Apartheid in Twentieth Century South Africa*, London: Routledge.

PART THREE

Bassiouni, M. C. (ed.) (1988), *Legal Response to International Terrorism*, The Hague: M. Nijhoff.
Blakesley, C. L. (1992), *Terrorism, Drugs, International Law and the Protection of Human Liberty: A Comparative Study*, Ardsley-on-Hudson: Transnational Books.
Duffy, Helen (2005), *The 'War on Terror' and the Framework of International Law*, London: Cambridge University Press.
Evans, A. E. and Murphy, J. F. (1978), *Legal Aspects of International Terrorism*, Lexington, MA: D. C. Heath.
Hyunwook, H. H. (1993), *Terrorism and Political Violence: Limits and Possibilities of Legal Control*, New York: Oceana Publications.
Jenkins. B. M. (1997), *The Potential for Nuclear Terrorism*, Santa Maria, CA: Rand.
Rockmore, Tom and Margolis, Joseph (2003) *The Philosophical Challenge of September 11*, New Haven, CT: Southern Connecticut State University Press.

Schmid, A. P. and Crelinstein, R. D. (eds) (1993), *Western Responses to Terrorism*, London: Cassell.
United Nations General Assembly (1973), Report of the Ad Hoc Committee on International Terrorism, XXVIII, A/9028, Supplement 28, 1973.

OTHER SOURCES OF FURTHER INFORMATION

From time to time articles of relevant interest appear in:

Foreign Affairs, International Affairs, International Relations, International Studies, Millennium Review of International Studies (not just the year 2000!), *Political Science Quarterly, Studies in Conflict and Terrorism, Terrorism and Political Violence, The World Today, Third World Quarterly.*

USEFUL ADDRESSES

UK Islamic Mission, 202 North Gower Street, London NW1 2LY.
United Nations Department of Public Information, Public Enquiries Unit, UN Plaza, New York NV 10017, United States.
United Nations Information Centre, Millbank Tower (21st floor), 21–24 Millbank, London SW1P 4QH.

Apart from printed material readily obtainable from the above, these international websites will yield a great deal of information:

United Nations
    www.un.org
Terrorism Research Center
    www.terrorism.com
International Policy Institute for Counter-terrorism
    www.ict.org.il
The Center for Defense and International Security Studies
    www.cdiss.org/hometemp.htm
Jane's Information Group
    www.janes.com
US State Department Office of Counter-Terrorism
    www.state.gov/www/global/terrorism/index.html

Index

Afghanistan: 26, 38, 47–51, 53–4, 57–9, 63, 289, 341
Agha, Hussein: 126
Algeria: 6, 21, 29, 33, 49–50,107, 145
Algeria case study: 187–200
al-Qaeda: 37, 47, 59, 63–4, 76, 289
apartheid: 271–287
Apter, D. E.: 171, 256–7
Arafat, Yassir: 6, 81–3, 90
Argentina: 11, 19, 30, 37, 174, 330; see also Montoneros II
Arthur, Paul: 170–4, 178–9

Baader-Meinhof group: 31–2, 174, 234–259; see also Red Army Faction
Bandura, Albert: 297
Basques: 6, 7, 20, 34, 289, 331; see also Spain and ETA case studies
Becker, Jillian: 245–6, 251
Bin Laden see Osama Bin Laden
Bjorgo, Tore: 12–13, 15
Black, Crispin: 74–7
Blair, Tony: 308
Blundy, David and Lycett, Andrew: 94, 101–2
Bodansky, Yossef: 52–5
Braganca A. de and Wallerstein, I.M.: 277–8
Brandt, Willy: 239
Brigate Rosse: 31; see also Red Brigade
Bush, President George: 107, 305, 331, 344, 351–6

Castro, Fidel: 134, 282
Chad: 90–1
Chile: 37
Clinton, President Bill: 50, 83, 103, 119
Colombia: 11, 26, 289
Colombia case study: 216–33
Cook, Schura: 235–6
Council of Europe: European Convention on the Suppression of Terrorism, 1977 339–421
counter-terrorism: 56, 168–70, 181–5, 196–200, 211–5, 228–33, 249–52, 265–70, 322–45; and ethical issues: 297–305; and international bodies: 338–421; legal considerations: 296–7, 306–323; see also International Policy Institute for Counterterrorism; terrorism, prevention and control
Crenshaw, Martha: 4, 11–12, 14–15, 17, 22, 24, 32, 57, 302
Cuba: 102, 226, 335
Cyprus: 6

Della Porta, Donatella: 263–70
drug trade: 136, 210, 219, 229

Egypt: 28–9, 49, 53, 55, 81–2, 93, 98
ELN (Ejercito de Liberacion Nacional) see Colombia case-study
ETA (Euskadi ta Askalasuna): 6, 20, 33–4, 151–64, 331

European Union: 200, 317–321; *see also* Council of Europe

Falk, Richard: 102
FARC (Fuerzas Armadas Revolucianarias de Colombia): 216–233; *see also* Colombia case study
FLN (Front de Liberation Nationale) *see* Algeria case study
France: 20, 91, 101–6, 109, 117, 175, 190, 200, 318, 335
'freedom fighters': 6–9, 95–6, 106, 151, 176, 269, 276, 291
Furlong, Paul: 254–60, 265–8

Gandhi, Mahatma: 30, 276–7
Gandhi, Rajiv: 135
Ganor Boaz: 332–8
Germany: 20, 31, 55, 57, 90, 200, 213, 270, 289–319, 322–335; *see also* Baader-Meinhof group; Red Army Faction
Germany case study: 234–252
Gibson, Richard: 276–7
Government Response to the Intelligence and Security Committee's Report into London Terrorist Attacks: 13–5
Greece: 91, 319
Guardian, The: 308, 354n19, 357n5
guerilla warfare: 7, 82, 229–30, 282–3
Guevara, Che: 134, 240
Gunning, Jeroen: 85–6

Habib, Henri Pierre: 92–3
Haley, P. Edmund: 98–101
Hamas: 27, 82–5, 288
Hansard: 349n11, 357n3, 357n7
Harik, Judith Palmer: 110–111
Hattersley, Roy: 183
Higgins, Rosalyn: 306, 320
Hizbullah (Hizb'allah): 27, 106, 110–123, 124–132, 174, 194, 233, 288
Hoffman, Bruce: 4–5, 16, 25, 36, 56, 103, 341–3
Horgan, John: 11–12, 15–6, 114, 331
hostages: 39, 116–9

India: 49, 55, 135, 146–7; *see also* Gandhi, Mahatma and Rajiv; Sri Lanka case study
International Criminal Court: 306

International Policy Institute for Counterterrorism: 40–3
IRA (Irish Republican Army): 10, 22, 23–4, 303
Iran: 34, 38–43, 84, 102, 109, 110, 116, 117–124, 127, 335, 338, 341
Iraq: 26, 29, 34, 43, 49, 50, 60, 102, 288, 338
Islam: 7, 26, 38, 47–59, 60, 74, 106–23, 301; *see also* Algeria, Lebanon I and II, Libya case studies
Israel: 6, 26, 40, 79–87, 106–10, 111, 115, 126–9, 288, 290; *see also* Palestinians, PLO, Israel case study
Italy: 26–31, 57, 91, 200, 213, 289, 335; *see also* Red Brigade
Italy case study: 253–70
Izaguirre, Carlos: 211–2, 214

Jamieson, Alison: 253–4
Japan: 32, 171
Jenkins, Brian: 3, 7, 295, 306
Johnson, Paul: 4
Jordan: 29, 33, 35, 39, 81–2
Joshi, Manoj: 142, 145, 146–7

Kapferer, Bruce: 141–4
Kellen, Konrad: 9, 251, 252
Kennedy, Helena: 314, 321
Kenya: 6, 26, 50
Khalil, A. A.: 113–5
Khatchadourian, Haig: 303–4, 345
Kramer, Martin: 115–6, 301

Lacquer, Walter: 3, 16, 25–7, 29–34, 36–7, 89–92, 133–7, 145–6, 227, 329–30, 342
Lebanon: 26, 28, 29, 82, 288
Lebanon I case study: 106–23
Lebanon II case study: 124–32
Libya: 28, 35, 43, 82, 258, 336; *see also* Quaddafi, Muammar
Libya case study: 88–105

McClintock, Cynthia: 206–8
Malik, Habib: 130–1
Mandela, Nelson: 105, 272–87; *see also* South Africa case study
martyrdom *see* Sri Lanka, Northern Ireland, Lebanon I and II case studies
Merkl, P. H.: 236–7, 244

Mitchell, George: 182–3
Moreno, Jonathan: 304–5, 343
Moro, Aldo: 262–4
Moss, David: 260–4, 267
Murphy, Richard: 125
myth: 107, 141–2, 165, 174–5

NATO: 57–9, 62
North Korea: 102, 305
Northern Ireland: 11, 33–4, 37, 163,
    262, 322, 331; see also IRA
Northern Ireland case study: 165–186

Oquist, Paul: 219–22
Osama Bin Laden: 49–59, 63, 89, 289

Pakistan: 26, 38, 49, 55, 58, 71, 75, 89
Palestine: 7, 29, 33, 80–1, 90, 128, 341;
    see also Israel; Palestinians; PLO
Palestinians: 15, 20, 33, 49, 80–7, 109,
    113, 121, 145
Parliamentary Report into the London
    Terrorist Attacks (ISC): 73–5
Pearce, Jenny: 217–8, 223–31
Peru: 11, 37, 289
Peru case study: 201–15
Picard, Elizabeth: 107–9
PLO (Palestine Liberation Organisation):
    6, 33; see also Israel; Palestinians
Post, Jerrold: 21–25
Pridham, Geoffrey: 237–44, 247, 249–50

Quadaffi, Muammar: 86–105, 288;
    see also Libya case study

Ranstorp, Magnus: 116
Red Army Faction (Rote Arme Faktion,
    RAF): 23, 234–53, 290
Red Brigade (Brigate Rossi, BR): 31–2
Reich, Walter: 3, 4
Reid, Kiron: 315
Report of the Official Account of the
    Bombing in London: 70–3
Russia: 17, 26, 82, 84; see also Soviet
    Union

Saad-Ghorayeb, Amal: 120–2
Salvioni, Danila and Stephanson, Anders:
    254
Saudi Arabia: 26, 38, 50, 54–5, 101, 132
Schiff, David: 214
Schmid, Alex P.: 12, 16, 24

Shultz, Richard
Scott Palmer, David: 201–6, 208–10, 213
Seale, Patrick: 125–6
Sederbeg, Peter: 4
Shabad, Goldie and Ramo, F. J. L.:
    150–5, 157–9, 160–3
Shining Path (Sendero Luminoso): 7;
    see also Peru case study
Smith, M. R. L.: 290–1, 324
Sobelman, David: 127–30
Somalia: 55
South Africa: 136, 183, 192, 289; see also
    South Africa case study
Soviet Union: 99, 100, 333
Spain: 15, 37, 69, 73, 200, 289, 318–20,
    331; case study 150–64
Sri Lanka: 26, 38, 163, 262, 289; case
    study 133–149
Stone, Martin: 189–96
Straw, Jack: 312
Sudan: 38, 49–50, 92, 102, 109, 336
suicide missions: 15, 25–7, 105, 139,
    145–6
Sweden: 320
Syria: 28, 29, 34, 43, 81, 83, 98, 102,
    110, 111, 115, 118, 124–6, 332

Taliban: 47, 57–9, 66, 269
Tamil Tigers: 10, 27, 37, 164, 174, 289;
    see also Sri Lanka case study
terrorism: contemporary: 28–43; and
    crime: 9–10, 196, 268–70, 306–23;
    definition of: 3–13, 295–7; and
    economic factors: 3–15, 93, 152–3,
    167–8, 201–5, 209–10, 218–9,
    225–7; ethical issues: 295–305; group
    psychodynamics: 9–10, 15–16, 19–25,
    101, 105, 178–9, 201–5, 222, 235–6,
    267–73; and ideology: 3, 9–10, 30–2,
    55–57, 63–75, 111–116, 145–6,
    155–8, 170–4, 239–43, 246–9,
    254–62, 271–8; legal considerations:
    306–23; militarism: 8, 137–8, 144–5,
    168–70, 179–80; organisational
    aspects: 9, 35–7, 54–6, 175, 191–4,
    205–10, 212–3, 225–7, 242–3;
    prevention and control: 15, 293–345;
    religion inspired: 3, 29, 47–59, 63–8,
    111–4, 136–7, 165–9, 179, 191–3,
    254; revolutionary aspects: 3, 5–6, 19,
    28–33, 138–40, 155–7, 170–4,
    179–80, 201–6, 211, 222–3; and

separatism: 6–7, 15–16, 21–7, 170–80, 185–6; and social factors: 20–1, 108, 157–8, 162, 173–4, 184–5, 217–22, 243–5, 290; state sponsored: 6, 37–8, 97–101, 114–6, 118–23, 297, 316; strategic aspects: 21–3, 205, 208–10, 247–9, 266–70, 275–8; typology: 40–2

Terrorism Research Center (USA): 17–21, 325–7; *see also* counterterrorism

Terrorist(s): aggression: 5, 9–10, 12, 21–5; fanaticism: 47–59, 84–7, 135–7, 219–224; goals: 5–6, 9, 17–20, 23–5, 32–6, 76–80, 179–81, 205–6, 222–8; motivation: 4, 14–27, 48–9, 54–5, 70–1, 81–3, 89–91, 97–100, 107–11, 114–6, 133–7, 155–7, 170–3, 217–9, 233–5, 254–6, 275–8; terrorist avoidance of name: 201–2; terrorist self-perception: 7–9, 18–25, 138–40, 234–5, 297–302; terrorist targeting: 8–9, 17–19, 32–3, 157–8, 178–80, 194–6, 240–3, 257–62

Townshend, Charles: 175–6, 179–80

Trevino, Jose: 159

Tupamoros: 19, 30

United Kingdom: definition of terrorism: 3, 4; and terrorism: 26, 49, 55, 57, 66–7, 69–78, 91, 103–4, 117, 291, 307–15, 321–3, 327, 343; *see also* Northern Ireland case study

United Nations: 11, 84, 91–2, 103–5, 106, 188–9, 196–8, 262, 274, 310, 331, 335, 338–9

United States: definition of terrorism: 3–4, 19; and terrorism: 18, 47, 49–59, 60–8, 91, 98–105, 115, 117–8, 131, 233, 289, 296, 305, 307, 310, 315–7, 335, 343; *see also* Terrorism Research Center

Uruguay: 19–31; *see also* Tupamoros

Vercher, Antonio: 340–1

Wadham, John: 313

Walker, Clive: 314, 321–2

Wardlaw, Grant: 127–9, 339

Weapons of Mass Destruction: 341–3

Whittaker, David J.: 38, 50–2, 57, 70–1, 138–40, 165–70, 180–1, 271–6, 316, 344–5

Wieviorka, Michel: 156–7

Wilkinson, Paul: 11, 52, 67, 184–5, 331

Williams, Paul: 49–50

Woolf, Lord: 306, 315

Wright, Joanne: 245–9

Zirakzadeh, Cyrus: 157–8